AN
INTRODUCTION TO A
HISTORY OF WOODCUT

AN INTRODUCTION TO A
HISTORY OF WOODCUT

WITH A DETAILED SURVEY OF WORK DONE IN

THE FIFTEENTH CENTURY

BY

ARTHUR M. HIND

KEEPER OF PRINTS AND DRAWINGS IN THE BRITISH MUSEUM

WITH FRONTISPIECE AND 483 ILLUSTRATIONS IN THE TEXT

IN TWO VOLUMES

VOL. II
BOOK-ILLUSTRATION
AND CONTEMPORARY SINGLE CUTS

BOSTON AND NEW YORK
HOUGHTON MIFFLIN COMPANY
1935

PRINTED IN GREAT BRITAIN
BY R. & R. CLARK, LIMITED, EDINBURGH

CONTENTS

Bibliographies come at the end of each chapter or section, while references to special books are given in the footnotes. Additions and Corrections to Vols. I. and II. are given in Vol. I. at p. 265, and space is left for further notes

VOL. I

CHAPTER I

2002

VOL. II

CHAPTER V

CHAPTER VII

BOOK-ILLUSTRATION AND CONTEMPORARY SINGLE CUTS IN THE
NETHERLANDS

CHAPTER VIII

BOOK-ILLUSTRATION AND CONTEMPORARY SINGLE CUTS IN FRANCE
AND FRENCH SWITZERLAND

REFERENCES TO THE LOCALITY OF BOOKS

In respect to German books reference is seldom given to locality as these are recorded in Schreiber's *Manuel*. The locality of books of other countries is only given if there is no copy in the British Museum, and then only to one or more of the most easily available copies.

THE DATING OF BOOKS

Variety in the styles of calendar in the xv century presents difficulties, as the year began at various dates in relation to the present style beginning 1st January, i.e.

(*a*) 25th March, preceding (the Pisan style in Italy).

(*b*) 1st September, preceding (the Byzantine style).

(*c*) 25th December, preceding (common in Germany and Austria; occasional in France).

(*d*) 1st January (infrequent, but occasional at Paris).

(*e*) 1st March, succeeding (the Venetian style in Italy).

(*f*) 25th March, succeeding (the Florentine style in Italy; the usual style in England).

(*g*) Easter Day, succeeding (the usual style in the Netherlands and France).

The styles (*a*) and (*b*) hardly touch the books described.

In style (*c*) the dates from 25th to 31st December might be quoted as (say) 1492/91, the second figure denoting the year in the present style. This mode, however, would affect only a small number of books, and has not, I think, been followed in bibliographies.

In styles (*e*), (*f*) and (*g*) the dates from 1st January to the 31st February, the 24th March, or Easter-Eve, might be quoted as 1491/92. This has been done to a large extent in the description of Netherlandish, French and English books.

It is evident how easily error may arise without detailed investigation of each case, and I plead this excuse in advance. The question is unimportant in our study except in occasional questions of priority in design.

The form 1491–92 implies an issue at dates in both years.

The most convenient reference book for matters of calendar style is A. Cappelli, *Cronologia, Cronografia, e Calendario Perpetuo*, 2nd edition, Milan (Hoepli) 1930, but it cannot, of course, be used for final reference in detail.

THE most frequent abbreviations used in Volume II. are:

S.   for W. L. Schreiber, *Manuel de l'Amateur de la Gravure sur Bois et sur Métal au xve Siècle* (Vol. V., Parts 1 and 2), and in the case of single cuts, for W. L. Schreiber, *Handbuch des Holz- und Metallschnittes des xv Jahrhunderts.*

H.   for L. Hain, *Repertorium Bibliographicum.*

C.   for W. A. Copinger, Supplements to Hain.

GW.   for *Gesamtkatalog der Wiegendrucke.*

E.   for Prince d'Essling, *Livres à Figures Vénitiens.*

PK.   for Paul Kristeller, *Early Florentine Woodcuts*, and *Die Lombardische Graphik.*

CA.   for Campbell, *Annales de la Typographie Néerlandaise.*

CN.   for Martin Conway (Lord Conway), *Woodcutters of the Netherlands.*

STC.   for A. W. Pollard and G. R. Redgrave, *Short-Title Catalogue of Books printed in England, 1475-1640.*

n.d.   for no date quoted in colophon.

n.p.   no place of printing noted.

n.pr.   no printer named.

Other references, if not given in footnotes, will be readily solved by consultation of the bibliography at the end of each chapter.

CHAPTER V

BOOK-ILLUSTRATION AND CONTEMPORARY SINGLE CUTS IN GERMANY, AUSTRIA AND GERMAN SWITZERLAND

In the preceding chapter I discussed at some length the obscure question as to whether the block-book might properly be regarded as the 'precursor' or 'prefigurement' of printing from movable type, in the sense intended by the writer in the Cologne Chronicle. The present chapter, dealing with book-illustration in Germany, Austria and German Switzerland during the xv century, only demands the shortest reference to a question of almost equal obscurity, i.e. the exact date and authorship of the introduction of printing from movable type, for it is a matter which has an extensive literature of its own.[1] It will suffice here to say that the discovery must have taken place within a few years of 1450, that JOHANN GUTENBERG (who was working at Strassburg about 1436–44, and at Mainz between 1448 and his death about 1468, except for a short stay at Bamberg in 1457 and 1458) was among the prime movers, if not the actual or sole originator of the new art. The fact that this new art was for some time regarded as secret, and that the earliest printed sheets and books were not signed with the printer's name, preserves the obscurity. A *Calendar* assigned to the year 1448 (preserved in a unique copy at Wiesbaden), various editions of the Grammar (*De Octo Partibus Orationis*) of Aelius Donatus, several Papal Indulgences of the years 1454 and 1455, the 42-line Latin Bible (about 1455),[2] and the 36-line Latin Bible (about 1458) are the chief works hitherto ascribed to Gutenberg, though the 42-line Bible and the 30-line Indulgence are now more generally attributed to JOHANN FUST and PETER SCHOEFFER.[3] The

---

[1] See p. 208, footnote 2.   [2] Popularly called the Mazarin Bible, as it was Cardinal Mazarin's copy (Collection Mazarine in the Bibliothèque Nationale) to which attention was first drawn.

[3] Johann Fust was originally a goldsmith: he obtained judgment in 1455 against Gutenberg, for the repayment of loans advanced in 1450 and 1452 in connection with printing. Peter Schoeffer, who was a witness in this lawsuit, married Fust's daughter, and was in partnership with his father-in-law until the latter's death in 1467. Fust was evidently the capitalist of the firm, but as a trained goldsmith he may have collaborated with Schoeffer on the technical side as well. But it is noteworthy that verses appended to the colophon of the *Institutiones* of Justinianus (printed by Schoeffer in 1468) while praising both the Johns (i.e. Gutenberg and Fust) for their skill in engraving (*in arte sculpendi*), claim that Schoeffer had surpassed them both in the same field. For early Mainz books see Seymour de Ricci, Gutenberg Gesellschaft, 1911.

type used in the 36-line Bible, and the other works attributed to Gutenberg, came later into the hands of ALBRECHT PFISTER of Bamberg,[1] to whom Gutenberg, when pressed by his creditors, may have sold his stock.

The earliest book, which gives the names of its printers in addition to its date or place, is the *Latin Psalter* issued by Fust and Schoeffer at Mainz in 1457. It is, moreover, the earliest book printed from movable type in which woodcut of any importance occurs. The woodcuts are merely initial letters and not subject illustrations, but such decorative designs always form an important part of the woodcutter's craft, and these early examples are of considerable beauty.

I say 'woodcut', though these initial letters were more probably printed, or stamped, from metal,[2] but the form was no doubt first cut in wood and a mould taken from this to make the metal cast. Throughout the history of woodcut and wood-engraving initial letters, borders and other pieces of decoration have been printed somewhat promiscuously either from the original wood blocks, or from casts,[3] and the very need for constant repetition of initials would incline the printer to preserve the wood, and from time to time to renew his casts. In some examples the appearance of the print may indicate the material to a practised printer, but as in many cases we must be in doubt, it is reasonable to include such casts in a survey of woodcut as if they were woodcuts, just as we have included the relief-cuts in metal. Some of the initials may of course be relief-cuts in metal, but in general casting would probably be the more expeditious method.

The simpler initials in the 1457 *Psalter* are merely stamped or printed in a single colour (generally in red),[4] but the really noteworthy initials are those stamped or printed in two colours. They occur again in the same printers' *Latin Psalter* of 1459, and generally in blue and red, the most remarkable being the large initial B occurring on the first page of both editions. Indentation of the vellum is very clearly marked in the British Museum copy of the 1459 *Psalter*, particularly at the foot of the decorative portion, where the block has been wiped and the stamping is blind to leave

---

[1] See p. 193, for metal-cuts printed with this type.

[2] See G. Mori, *Was hat Gutenberg erfunden? Ein Ruckblick auf die Frühtechnik des Schriftgusses*, Gutenberg Gesellschaft, Mainz 1921 (Beiträge zum 19ten Jahresbericht, 1919–20). Cf. p. 183.

[3] See Index of Subjects (*casts*). The general practice of the Kelmscott Press in the XIX century was to print the decorative pictures from electrotypes, and the subject cuts from the original wood.

[4] Indentation seems to indicate stamping in most cases, but occasionally a letter may be found which looks as if done by stencil (e.g. 1459 *Psalter*, B.M.L., a large I on p. 116).

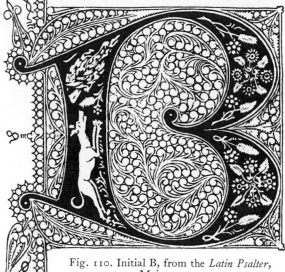

Fig. 110. Initial B, from the *Latin Psalter,* Mainz 1457.

place for a second and smaller initial. The printers use the blue or the red promiscuously either for the letter itself or the decorative ground.

Similar bichrome initials, in which the decorative portion often borrows suggestion from the Lily of the Valley (*Maiblume*), occur in Duranti's *Rationale*, printed by Fust and Schoeffer, 1459, and in the *Canon of the Mass*, printed by Fust and Schoeffer about the same date (Proctor 68, Oxford), but thereafter they are only found in later reprints of the *Psalter*.

There is an example in a leaf from Schoeffer's reprint of 1490 in the British Museum (IB. 259), and the worn condition of such later initials proves that they were done from stamps or blocks and not by the aid of stencils as has been sometimes suggested. The only part of such initials to which the stencil might have been applied with success is the flat surface of the letter itself (like the single-colour initials), not the background of delicate line.

It should be noted that the ornamental part sometimes overlaps the text, which shows that they have been printed separately, and were probably stamped on in the rubricator's shop after the printing of the book. A small letter to guide the rubricator is often visible beneath the initial.

The 42-line *Bible* shows exactly the same kind of bichrome initial, not stamped but done by the hand of the rubricator, a fact which in itself lends some support to the attribution of this work to Fust and Schoeffer. For it is noteworthy that the books generally assigned to Gutenberg, e.g. the 36-line *Bible* and Balbus, *Catholicon* (1460), have no initials either drawn or printed in this style. Apart from the simpler red initials, the more important initials are fully illuminated in the British Museum copies of these works, and certainly show a different illuminator from Fust and Schoeffer's craftsman.

For rather more than a decade after the remarkable essays of the years 1457 to 1459, Fust and Schoeffer and other printers kept to monochrome initials, whether stamped or printed, or drawn by the rubricator with the brush, direct or with the aid of stencil. Then, about 1470, monochrome initials, designed in a style entirely suited to the woodcutter's craft, came into fashion, largely through the influence of the printers of Augsburg and Ulm. To these we shall revert later.

Examples of the same style of bichrome initials as originally used by Fust and Schoeffer, drawn by hand, and often in more than two colours, are occasionally found in the books of other printers. They are sometimes seen in books printed by JOHANN MENTELIN of Strassburg, done by a somewhat coarse hand, e.g. in his *Latin Bible* (about 1460–61), British Museum, King's Library copy. Three examples outside Germany may be noted, i.e. an initial Q in the Grenville Library copy of the *Dyalogus Creaturarum* (Gouda, 3rd June 1480) in the British Museum, initials in a copy of J. de Turrecremata, *Expositio in Psalmos* (about 1482, attributed by Haebler to Paulus Hurus, Saragossa),[1] and another initial Q in a copy of Jean Trechsel's Latin edition of Thomas à Kempis, *Imitation of Christ* (Lyon 1489), in the library of St. Geneviève, Paris.[2]

BAMBERG

The first subject illustrations in printed books are those which were issued from the press of ALBRECHT PFISTER of Bamberg, who, as already noted, had taken over some of Gutenberg's type.[3] Pfister printed in all nine editions of five books, all of extreme rarity, and eight (or at least seven) of these were richly illustrated with woodcuts,[4] as follows:

(1) Johannes von Saaz, *Der Ackermann aus Böhmen*,[5] 1st edition, about 1460, H. 74. The only copy known, at Wolfenbüttel, is without woodcuts, but it probably had the same as the second edition.

2nd edition, about 1463, H. 73. With five full-page cuts (about $8\frac{1}{2} \times 5\frac{5}{8}$ inches). The Wolfenbüttel copy reproduced by the Insel Verlag, Leipzig 1919 (ed. Alois Bernt). Other copies at Paris and Berlin (Print Room). Fig. 111.

(2) Ulrich Boner, *Der Edelstein* (Fables in German). Two editions:

---

[1] See E. P. Goldschmidt, Catalogue viii. No. 96.

[2] Reproduced in A. Claudin, *Histoire de l'imprimerie en France*, vol. iv., 1914, p. 55.

[3] See also p. 193, for a series of metal-cuts printed with the same type.

[4] See Albert Schramm, *Der Bilderschmuck der Frühdrucke*, i., Albrecht Pfister, Leipzig 1922. Pfister's one book without illustrations is Jacobus de Theramo, *Belial*.

[5] See G. Zedler, Gutenberg Gesellschaft, 16 and 17 Jahresbericht.

Dated edition, 1461, with 101 cuts, H. 3578. The earliest dated book in the German language, Wolfenbüttel.[1]

Undated edition, probably about 1464, with 103 cuts, C. 1203. Berlin (Staatsbibl.).[2]

The cuts of the Fables are oblongs about 3×4 inches; and at the side of each is placed a small upright cut, about 3×1 inches, of a man pointing to the illustration. There is only one 'indicator' cut repeated throughout the first edition, while the second edition has three varieties. The Fable cuts are from the same blocks in each edition. There are illustrated MSS. of Boner's Fables at Munich and Heidelberg (cf. p. 306).

(3) *Vier Historien* (i.e. of Joseph, Daniel, Esther and Judith), 1462, H. 8749. Paris, Manchester. 52 oblong subjects (several being repeated), about $3\frac{1}{8} \times 5\frac{3}{8}$ inches. The carelessness of the printer is shown by the printing of one of the cuts (the *Death of Jacob* on f. 12) upside down, and the illuminator, not unnaturally, omitted to colour this illustration.

(4) *Biblia Pauperum*. Three editions:

 (*a*) German (1462). H. 3176. Wolfenbüttel. Paris. Manchester.
 (*b*) Latin (1463). H. 3177. Munich (Staatsbibl.). Manchester.
 (*c*) German (1464). Pell. 2387. Paris.

On each page there are four cuts: in the upper row, a New Testament subject (about $2\frac{1}{2}$ inches square) flanked by two small blocks with two busts of prophets (oblongs, about $\frac{7}{8} \times 1\frac{5}{8}$ inches); below, two subjects from the Old Testament on one oblong block (about $2\frac{1}{2} \times 5\frac{5}{8}$ inches). In editions (*a*) and (*b*) there are 34 pages of this arrangement; in the second German edition additional cuts appear.

The cuts are largely pure outline, with only a slight use of shading in short parallel strokes. Practically all the copies known are coloured by hand, and the style of the cuts shows that this was the printer's intention, and most copies were probably coloured in his shop. Pfister, with several of the other early printers,[3] may have been his own cutter, but there is no direct

---

[1] Reproduced from the Wolfenbüttel copy by Schramm, with the three additional 'indicator' figures from the undated edition.

[2] Reproduced by P. Kristeller, Graphische Gesellschaft (I. Ausserordentl. Veröffentlichung), Berlin 1908.

[3] Lienhart Ysenhut, who printed at Basle from 1489 to 1507, is recorded in documents as *Briefdrucker, Heiligendrucker, Maler, Briefmaler, Heiligenmaler* and *Kartenmacher*.

evidence in his case. In style of design and cutting the prototype is certainly to be seen in the Heidelberg *Biblia Pauperum* block-book, but there is more

Fig. 111. Death on Horseback, from *Der Ackermann aus Böhmen*, Bamberg, about 1463.

angularity in the line, and the fingers are shorter, more nearly as in the *Septimia Poenalis* block-book. The design and cutting are crude, but as illustrations the blocks are not wanting in spirit.

After these essays of Pfister between 1460 and 1464, there is an interval of some six years before any other woodcut illustrations appeared in Germany. The woodcutters were still engaged, apart from their single cuts, in making block-books, and there was evidently guild jealousy between the cutters and those parvenus, the printers of books in movable type. The printers had doubtless attempted at first to make their initials and other cuts in their own workshops, and the professional woodcutters were perhaps slow to realise the opportunity that was opening to them in the new rival to their block-books.

The guild jealousy is clearly shown in the experience of Günther Zainer, the printer, on his arrival at Augsburg in 1468, to which we have already alluded.[1] An attempt was first made to hinder the stranger from obtaining citizen's rights and the privilege to print, though these were actually granted on the intervention of the Abbot of St. Ulrich and St. Afra. But at first he was not allowed to decorate his books with initials or other woodcuts, and only obtained this right subsequently, on the express condition that he should only use the woodcutters of the guilds. This points very directly to the probability that either Zainer himself or one of his assistants had intended to cut the blocks.

The early printers would in general have had more than enough to do in perfecting the new craft of printing from movable type, without giving thought to the art of illustration. But even so, it is a natural inference from the Zainer episode to regard guild regulations[2] and jealousies as among the reasons for the interval of some half-dozen years that elapsed between the last of Pfister's woodcuts and the resumption of woodcut illustration, which occurred at Augsburg about 1471.

There are few known artists among the illustrators of xv-century books, and it is only here and there that critics have attempted to group the cuts under anonymous personalities with convenient titles, such as the MASTER OF THE AMSTERDAM CABINET (or the MASTER OF THE HAUSBUCH as he is also called).[3] Such groupings, which have only been consistently carried out in Conway's *Woodcutters of the Netherlands*, are too uncertain and conjectural, and the soundest and most convenient method of describing the anonymous woodcuts of the xv century is still that of classification under the various printers. The woodcutters probably kept for the most part to one town and to special printers, so the division corresponds, at least partially, with grouping according to artist or style.

[1] See pp. 91 and 211.

[2] It must always be remembered that each town had its own regulations.

[3] See below, p. 346.

The appearance of woodcuts by the same hand in various towns need not of course imply a change of habitation in the woodcutter. Wood blocks passed fairly frequently from one printer to another, not only within the country of origin, but sometimes from one country to another. Thus the original blocks illustrating Breydenbach's *Travels* (Mainz 1486) were afterwards printed at Lyon (1489–90), at Speier (1490, lacking one little cut of the *Holy Sepulchre*, which was probably lost in transit) and at Saragossa (1498).[1]

Before continuing further description of German woodcut illustrations according to the method proposed, that of towns and printers, I would add a few general remarks about the beginning of book-illustration.

Occasionally series of woodcuts are found pasted in manuscripts, in spaces left on purpose for the prints, in a way that foreshadows ordinary book-illustration. One of the best examples of this is the *Gulden Püchlein von unser lieben frawen Maria*, dated 1450, preserved in the Graphische Sammlung, Munich.[2] The manuscript contains seventy small cuts, which appear to be copies of a better set, of which examples are known in several collections (e.g. Berlin and Nuremberg, and others once at Maihingen, mostly coming from Swabian convents, at Inzigkofen and Elchingen). An inscription on the back of a drawing of St. Agnes that it was by a 'sister', and the correspondence of a border used in the *Gulden Püchlein* with one that appears on the title of a Codex known to have been written in the Carthusian convent of St. Catherine at Nuremberg in 1451, renders it probable that the book was written and made up with the cuts, collected perhaps from various sources, and coloured in the same convent.

In the above example the prints were pasted in, but another manuscript,

---

[1] See A. W. Pollard, *The Transference of Woodcuts in the XV and XVI Centuries*, Bibliographica, ii., 1896, 343. Numerous examples are cited in Conway's *Woodcutters of the Netherlands*. There are various examples of German dotted prints issued later in France and Spain (see p. 194); the blocks of Grüninger's *Virgil* (Strassburg 1502) were printed by Sacon at Lyon in 1517; those of Rodericus Zamorensis, *Spiegel des menschlichen Lebens*, first printed by Günther Zainer at Augsburg about 1475–76, were issued later by N. Philippi and M. Reinhard at Lyon in 1482, and by Hurus at Saragossa in 1491; those of Boccaccio's *Les Cas et Ruynes des nobles hommes et femmes*, Paris (J. Dupré) 1483/84, appeared later at London in Pynson's *Fall of Princes*, 1494; and a block from Couteau and Menard's *Danse Macabre* (Paris 1492) was used later by Quentell at Cologne (see p. 362).

[2] See Otto Weigmann, *Holzschnitte aus dem Gulden Püchlein von 1450 in der Graphischen Sammlung zu München*, Berlin (Graphische Gesellschaft, xxiv.) 1918. Dr. Erwin Rosenthal has recently recognised that a later series of blocks of the same subjects appeared in Ludwig Moser, *Bereitung zum hl. Sacrament*, Basle, M. Furter, about 1493 (S.4811, C.4368).

a *Dominican Prayer Book*, preserved in the Department of Prints and Drawings at the British Museum (Dodgson, A. 142), and written at Nuremberg before 1461, shows the cuts printed on the vellum page of the manuscript. This example is coloured in the miniaturist's style in body-colour and gold, and one of the illustrations is purely a miniature without woodcut outline, so that the book is a very good instance of how woodcut was first used to save the illuminator the initial labour of making or copying the main elements of his design.

The *Delbecq-Schreiber Passion*[1] is another example of a series of cuts mounted in a manuscript book of devotion (though only preserved in fragmentary form), but this is already nearer the end of the century.

Very few drawings have been recognised as studies for the anonymous xv-century woodcuts. One of the rare examples, a study for the textile print of the *Virgin, Child and St. Anne*, has been noted in an earlier chapter.[2]

But there are a certain number of drawings done somewhat in the style of woodcuts which may possibly be by the hand of a designer or cutter of wood blocks. Such are the drawings in the manuscript *Livre de Genesis* in the British Museum (Add. MS. 39657, from the Curzon Collection), done with the pen in thick outline, with slight parallel shading, and tinted. From its dialect the manuscript is probably Northern French; and from its costume, about 1450, though the pen-work suggests the latter part of the xv century. It has some relation in style to the Netherlandish *Biblia Pauperum*, and in particular to a draughtsman illustrated on plate xix of Paul Durrieu's *Miniature flamande*. In their crude but vivid handling both may be examples of early popular art.[3]

Two drawings in the British Museum, placed for comparison with the early woodcuts, show a style deceptively near to woodcut in character, and apparently contemporary with the style they reflect, i.e. the *Infant Christ in the midst of Flowers* and the *Virgin and Child in a Glory, with Angels* (C. Dodgson, i. pp. 61 and 78). The same deceptive character is seen in the *Angel appearing to Joachim* originally described by Schreiber as a woodcut, but noted as a drawing in his second edition (S. 624).

[1] See p. 582.

[2] See p. 67, footnote 6. Cf. also p. 93, footnote 2. See also Helmut Lehmann-Haupt, *Schwäbische Federzeichnungen: Studien zur Buchillustration Augsburgs im xv Jahrhundert*, Berlin and Leipzig 1929.

[3] They should be compared with the 'Meister des Wavrin', e.g. in the illustrations to the MS. History of Thebes of 1469 in the Dyson Perrins Collection (see F. Winkler, *Vlämische Buchmalerei*, p. 69).

Other good examples of drawings in the woodcutter's style occur in a copy of Gregorius IX., *Novae Compilationes Decretalium Libri V*, Basle (M. Wenssler) 1478, quoted as No. 71 in J. Rosenthal's Catalogue 80, of 1924 (with reproduction). They fill the spaces which had evidently been intended for woodcut illustration.

An early Italian example of a book with spaces left for woodcuts which were never made is Nicolaus de Lyra, *Postilla super Bibliam*, Rome (Sweynheym and Pannartz) 1471–72. A copy is cited in a catalogue of *L'Art Ancien S.A.* (Lugano 1924), No. 2956, in which a series of pen drawings are added in these spaces, in the style of a weak follower of Mantegna. The drawings were possibly commissioned by an owner of the book in North Italy, but it is noteworthy that the maps in the Ptolemy's *Geographia* printed at Rome by Arnold Buckinck in 1478 are engraved in the style of the Ferrarese 'Tarocchi Cards', so that a North Italian artist might have been working for the Roman printers.

In the same way nearly every copy of the French *Valerius Maximus* of about 1476 has the empty spaces at the head of each book filled with miniatures.[1] French woodcut in the xv century is in general rather more nearly related to the style of the illuminators of manuscripts than the woodcut illustrations of other countries, and it is possible that in 1476 the French printer may have originally intended his book to be illustrated with drawings and not with woodcuts.[2]

It is probable that early woodcut book-illustrations are based on miniatures in MSS. more often than we know. Examples in which definite relationships have been established are the *Cologne Bible* of about 1478–79, the Bruges *Ovid* of 1484, and St. Augustine, *Civitas Dei*, Abbeville 1486–87.

It was evidently the aim of the printers in the first two decades of their practice to imitate a manuscript page in type, coloured initials and illustrations. Just as the type economised in scribes, so the outline woodcut saved the illuminator much labour, and the labour of filling in simply outlined spaces with colour could be given to poorer craftsmen than would be re-

---

[1] *Le Livre de Valerius Maximus translaté de latin en françois par Simon de Hesdin*, n.p., n.d., n.pr. (Paris, certainly not later than 1477), Claudin, i. p. 199. Two copies with illuminations are in the Bibliothèque Nationale, another in the Bibl. S. Geneviève, Paris, and a fourth was described in the Fairfax Murray Catalogue (H. W. Davies, 1910, No. 557).

[2] For the relation of the woodcutter to the illuminator see André Blum, *Des rapports des miniaturistes françaises du XVe siècle avec les premiers artistes-graveurs*, Revue de l'Art Chrétien, 1911, p. 357; and R. Kautzsch, *Einleitende Erörterungen zu einer Geschichte der deutschen Handschriften-Illustration im späteren Mittelalter*, Strassburg 1894 (pp. 60-63, 73, 74, 76-80); and *Die Holzschnitte der Kölner Bibel von 1479*, Strassburg 1896, p. 67, note 27, etc.

quired for both drawing and painting a subject throughout. The printer in fact was working in these early years for a public who could not afford the manuscript. Within a short time, however, both type and illustration achieved individual character apart from the scribe and illuminator. From about 1470 woodcut developed its own schemes of shading in line to deal with modelling and tone, and colour gradually became less essential, and by the end of the century had become superfluous.

A German example, in which the illustrations are sometimes printed from wood blocks and sometimes purely painted, is Sensenschmidt's *Missale Benedictinum,* Bamberg 1481 (S. 4676, H.11267). In one of two copies in the British Museum the *Christ on the Cross* (f.144 b) is a painting, and the pictorial initial T (f.145 a) a coloured woodcut; in the other the *Christ on the Cross* is a coloured cut, and the T a painting.[1]

Fig. 112. Printer's mark of Günther Zainer.

---

[1] The *Christ on the Cross between the Virgin and St. John* is the regular illustration in all missals, occurring at the *Canon of the Mass*, and often described as the *Canon* cut. Missals and breviaries, being the service-books of the Church (the former the office of the Mass, the latter the abridged daily service, excluding the Eucharist) and in constant use, have for the most part been worn out and destroyed, and of most editions only a few (and sometimes only a single copy) are known, often in cathedral or local libraries. In several of the earliest printed Missals single cuts are found pasted in on fly-leaf or in the binding (e.g. a metal-cut of the *Crucifixion*, S.2338, in the binding of the Oxford copy of a *Canon of the Mass*, printed by Schoeffer, Mainz, *c.*1460, Proctor 68). The earliest German Missals with the *Canon* cut printed in the text are those of Bernhard Richel, Basle, 20th January 1480–81 (*Missale Basiliense*, S.4670, H.11266), of Sensenschmidt, Bamberg 1481, of Schoeffer, Mainz 1483 (*Missale Wratislaviense*, S.4777, H.11333) and Koberger, Nuremberg 1484 (*Missale Strigoniense*, S.4763, H.11429, Budapest). From 1485 Erhard Ratdolt of Augsburg was the most prolific printer of liturgical books (see p.299). Other subjects most commonly found in their illustration are the *Virgin and Child between Saints*, the *Bishops* or their *coats-of-arms*, the *Agnus Dei*, and an initial T figured with *Abraham's Sacrifice*. See W. L. Schreiber, *Christus am Kreuz. Kanonbilder der im Deutschland gedruckten Messbücher des XV Jahrhunderts*, Strassburg 1910. See also in relation to Venice, p. 501, and France, p. 628. The standard catalogue of Missals is W. H. J. Weale, *Bibliographia Liturgica. Catalogus Missalium*, London 1886 (ed. H. Bohatta, 1928).

Several printers later in the century had recourse to various means of economising in their woodcut material, but not without detriment to the appearance of the book. BELLAERT of Haarlem and GRÜNINGER of Strassburg were notable sinners in this respect, applying the same blocks to various situations and often combining several blocks in one subject (e.g. in Jacobus de Theramo, *Der sonderen Troest* (*Belial*), Haarlem 1484, and in Grüninger's *Terence* 1496, *Horace* 1498,[1] and *Virgil* 1502).

Similarly DINCKMUT in his edition of *Seelenwurzgarten*, Ulm 1483 (S. 5229, C. 5345), constantly repeats the same cut, one block, representing the tortures of the damned, being used thirty-seven times.

Fig. 113. Jacob's Ladder, from the *Speculum Humanae Salvationis*, Augsburg 1477.

Moreover, one design, or series of designs, would frequently serve several printers. Copies were constantly being made, with or without leave, for copyright hardly existed, and the same printer would often have to replace worn cuts by new blocks in successive editions.

It is not always an easy task to distinguish copy from original. Immediately recognisable as from different blocks are subjects which appear in reverse directions, for the copyist who does not take the trouble to reverse his drawing from the original print, will make a block that will print the subject reversed. If there is uncertainty as to which is the original of two cuts in reverse to each other, a clue may sometimes be given by details

[1] See C. Dodgson, i. p. 232, D. 32.

wrongly expressed (e.g. a sword held in the left hand). But such details are not always decisive, as even the original cutter may be careless of such reversals of the natural order of things in his prints.

Occasionally copies (or later versions of the same originals) may be found better in quality than earlier cuts, so that quality is not invariably the test of an original. The most interesting copies are those like the cuts in the French edition of Francesco Colonna's *Hypnerotomachia Poliphili* (Paris 1554), which reflect the original series in an entirely new idiom.

The bichrome printed initials of Mainz and the woodcut illustrations of Pfister at Bamberg have already been discussed as isolated phenomena which stand rather apart from the main body of German woodcut decoration and illustration of the xv century. In continuing our survey of the chief woodcut illustrations of the period, we shall pursue a course based on chronology, only in so far as we start with *Augsburg* where appeared the earliest illustrated books after Pfister's at Bamberg. Then we shall pursue a course that follows geographical lines, passing from Augsburg to *Ulm*, leaving aside Munich, the present centre of Bavaria, as no illustration of importance appeared there during the xv century. Then we shall find a few works to mention in the neighbouring towns of *Urach*, *Reutlingen* and *Esslingen* before turning south-east to *Basle*, which only developed as an important centre in the last decade of the century. Thence, after a glance at work in other parts of German Switzerland, we shall journey down the Rhine to *Strassburg*, where the most individual work was produced between 1490 and 1500.

From Strassburg proceeding north to the Palatinate, with *Speier* and *Heidelberg* as its centres, and to the Archbishopric of *Mainz*, where illustrations appeared of comparable interest to those of Augsburg and Ulm, though only after about 1480.

Cologne, our next centre, exhibits closer relations to Netherlandish work, and the same may be said of *Lübeck*, both of which towns are notable for their illustrated Bibles of about 1478–79 and 1494 respectively. From Lübeck we turn south again, and after turning aside for some moments to the Cistercian Convent at *Zinna*, to *Leipzig* and to *Würzburg*, we reach *Nuremberg*, the most vital centre of German graphic art in the last decade of the xv century.

Thence via *Passau* and the Danube we may cross the border, and note the few and rare productions of Austria and Bohemia at *Vienna*, *Brünn* and *Prague*.

Alongside book-illustration we shall intercalate, according to known or conjectured locality, some notes on the single cuts of the period. This treatment is the more justified through the fact that, in the second half of the century, book-illustration offers a standard in the development of the art, and the designer and cutter of the single cuts undoubtedly progressed to some extent along lines indicated by the character of book-illustration and the demands of the printers.

I would here mention only one cut, or rather fragment, which I am unable to place in any group, i.e. an *Angel*, apparently from a subject of the *Crucifixion* (S. 1825 x, Oxford). The fragment alone measures about $11\frac{1}{2} \times 8$ inches, so that the whole subject must have been very large. The angel is holding the end of a cloth, and Schreiber refers to it as part of a subject of *Angels holding the Veronica Napkin*, but the aureoles below (of Christ and St. John?) support the title which has been suggested by Mr. Dodgson. It has a fine breadth of style, and from the character of its work probably dates about 1475.

AUGSBURG [1]

We have already spoken of the Augsburg printer GÜNTHER ZAINER,[2] and the difficulties he encountered from the guilds in regard to extra-mural woodcutters. These difficulties settled, he issued a remarkable series of illustrated books from about 1471 (three years after his first printed book) until his death in 1478. The great qualities of his work and of that of several of the other printers of Augsburg and Ulm were first fully recognised by William Morris.[3]

The Abbot Melchior of SS. Ulrich and Afra, who had helped Zainer in his encounter with the guilds, established a press at his monastery in 1472, and obtained a succession of Augsburg printers to direct and instruct his monks. That Günther Zainer was among those so invited is proved by a MS. note in the Fairfax Murray copy [4] of the *Speculum Humanae Salvationis* (S. 5273, H. 14929), showing that it was printed at the monastery with his type in 1473. Baemler and Sorg also printed at the monastery in the same, and succeeding years, with their own types.

The *Speculum* may be taken as typical of the greater part of Zainer's

---

[1] See Hellmut Lehmann-Haupt, *Schwäbische Federzeichnungen. Studien zur Buchillustration Augsburgs im xv Jahrhundert*, Berlin and Leipzig 1929.

[2] Schramm, *Bilderschmuck der Frühdrucke*, ii. *Günther Zainer in Augsburg*, Leipzig 1920.

[3] William Morris, *On the Artistic Qualities of the Woodcut Books of Ulm and Augsburg in the xv Century*, Bibliographica, I., 1895, 437.

[4] Now in the Pierpont Morgan Library, New York.

woodcut illustration, besides presenting one of the finest examples of balance between type and the illustration on the page.

His Gothic type is strong and simple, and the cuts have the requisite strength of line and simplicity of treatment to preserve this balance. The figures are characteristically squat, with large heads on short bodies; the simple outline design is only slightly helped out with some parallel shading, a scheme which the illuminator was still expected to complete with his colour (so that uncoloured copies are rare); the drawing is angular and of little subtlety, but not lacking in expression or vigour.

Like the majority of Augsburg illustrations the cuts of the *Speculum* are enclosed in double border-lines, and are the width of the page of type. In larger books with two columns the smaller cuts are, as a rule, similarly limited by the breadth of a column of type.

Zainer's *Speculum* must have appeared about the same date as the Netherlandish block-book, with its far shorter version of the text, and there is no direct relation between the designs of the two works. The main idea of the *Speculum Humanae Salvationis* (*Spiegel Menschlicher Behältnis*) was the same as that of the *Biblia Pauperum*, i.e. a harmony between incidents of the Old and New Testaments, and of the German type-printed versions some were fairly independent (like Günther Zainer's), and others more directly influenced in design by the *Biblia Pauperum*.[1]

Günther Zainer and his kinsman Johann Zainer (both originally from Reutlingen) had worked in the 'sixties at Strassburg; both are recorded as

Fig. 114. Initial B, from *Plenarium*, Augsburg 1473.

of the Guild of the Painters and Goldsmiths, to which the printers of Strassburg belonged, and it is probable that they learnt their craft, and practised as writers and illuminators, in Mentelin's printing-house. It is also probable from the incidents of his early years at Augsburg that Günther Zainer may have had some part in the designing of initials, if not of other cuts in his books; but we can do no more than indicate the likelihood of such participation in the illustrative side of their publications by Günther and other early printers, for there are no clues to definite attributions. The Augsburg and Ulm printers were particularly happy in their designs of initials decorated with lily of the valley (*Maiblumen*), of which an example is reproduced in fig. 114.

---

[1] See under the printers B. Richel of Basle (p. 325), and Peter Drach of Speier (p. 346).

Among other books printed by Günther Zainer, with blocks by the same designer as the *Speculum*, or in very similar style, may be noted:[1]

> Jacobus de Voragine, *Leben der Heiligen*, 1471, 1472.
>> S.4298, H.9968.
>> Later Augsburg editions: Baemler, 1475 and later; Sorg, 1478.
>> Schreiber has noted that in the *Winterteil* (1471) the blocks are printed separately[2] as the text occasionally strays over the border of the cuts. This seems to imply that the blocks were thicker than the depth of the type. This difference was soon adjusted to the economy of book-illustration, and the *Sommerteil* (1472) shows no such anomaly.
>
> Jacobus de Theramo, *Belial*, 1472.
>> S.4279, C.5805.
>> Later Augsburg editions: Baemler, 1473; Sorg, 1479, 1481.
>
> Ingold, *Das goldene Spiel*, 1472.
>> S.4259, H.9187.
>
> *Plenarium*, 1473.
>> S.4945, C.2316.
>> Later Augsburg editions: Baemler, 1474; Sorg, 1478.
>
> J. M. Tuberinus, *Geschichte und Legende von dem seligen Kind Simon*, n.d. (about 1475–76).
>> S.5258, H.15658.
>
> *Schwabenspiegel* (*Spiegel kaiserlicher und gemeiner Landrechte*), n.d. (about 1475–76).
>> S.4465, H.9868, and S.4466, H.9869.
>
> Johannes Damascenus, *Josaphat und Barlaam*, n.d. (about 1477).
>> S.4346, H.5915.
>> Later Augsburg edition: Sorg, n.d.
>
> Jacobus de Cessolis, *Schachzabelbuch*, 1477. S.4273, H.4895.

Apart from its smaller cuts the *Plenarium* has an important full-page frontispiece with a representation of *Christ blessing* (fig. 115).[3] It is the

---

[1] Many series of designs for popular books were repeated by one printer after another, sometimes from the same blocks, sometimes from copies. I have aimed at referring to books in their first issues, sometimes appending later editions, without specifying whether the illustrations in these later editions are reprints or copies. Details and dates in Muther can only be accepted after careful checking.   [2] Cf. p. 411.

[3] The passages from the Epistles and Gospels read in the Mass form the chief contents of a *Plenarium*. For further details see Paul Drews, *Realencyklopädie für protestantische Theologie und Kirche*, 3ᵉ Aufl., xv. p. 486.

Fig. 115. Christ blessing, from *Plenarium*, Augsburg 1473.

Fig. 116. Initial U, from the German Bible,
Augsburg (G. Zainer), about 1475–76.

earliest issue of a compilation of which numerous editions, with illustrations of the Life of Christ, were published throughout Germany (though chiefly at Augsburg and Strassburg) during the xv century. Similar series of cuts appeared in editions of Guillermus, *Postilla super Epistolas et Evangelia.*[1]

Günther Zainer's large folio *German Bible* demands some notice, as it is one of the three earliest illustrated Bibles printed in Germany, and was probably printed in 1475 or 1476 (S. 3456, H. 3133). The two others of near date are those of PFLANZMANN of Augsburg (S. 3455, H. 3131), and of SENSENSCHMIDT and FRISNER of Nuremberg[2] (S. 3457, H. 3132).

Pflanzmann's Bible has been often conjecturally dated about 1470 (e.g. by Muther), and regarded in consequence as the earliest German illustrated Bible. But the only dated books printed by Pflanzmann belong to the year 1475, so that a date about 1475 or 1476 is the most probable, and it is difficult to decide whether Pflanzmann or Günther Zainer has the priority. Sensenschmidt's Bible was also conjecturally dated about 1472 by Muther, but as it was printed by Sensenschmidt and Frisner (whose partnership occurred between 1474 and 1476), it cannot be before 1474, and is more likely to have appeared about 1476.

In Zainer's and Sensenschmidt's Bibles, the illustrations are chiefly contained in the pictorial capitals, the designs correspond fairly closely, and it is almost certain that Sensenschmidt's blocks, though the more accomplished in cutting, were the later works and based on Zainer's originals.

Pflanzmann's cuts are single column upright blocks, generally occurring at the beginning of each book; those for the prophets are several times repeated, while the New Testament is sparsely illustrated. In cutting,

---

[1] E.g. at Lyon (see p. 604) and Salamanca (see p. 754).

[2] For the general subject of early German Bibles see Richard Muther, *Die ältesten deutschen Bilder-Bibeln*, Munich 1883 (conjectured dates erroneous); Albert Schramm, *Die illustrierten Bibel der Incunabelzeit*, Leipzig 1922.

Fig. 117. Initial U, from the German Bible, Nuremberg (Sensenschmidt and Frisner), about 1476.

they are similar in character to Zainer's blocks (angular design, and slight parallel shading), and one degree poorer in quality. In design, they are for the most part independent, though occasional correspondences occur, which may be the repetition of typical renderings. The two designs of the *Days of Creation* in Pflanzmann similarly have their counterpart in the *Rudimentum Noviciorum*, Lübeck (Lucas Brandis) 1475.

Two other illustrated German Bibles, those of Cologne (about 1478–79) and of Lübeck (1494), both of far more artistic importance than the three just mentioned, will be described later.

Artistically the most attractive of Günther Zainer's books is the undated Rodericus Zamorensis, *Spiegel des menschlichen Lebens* (S. 5102, H. 13948), which was probably issued about 1475–76. The MS., a translation by Heinrich Steinhöwel of the *Speculum Vitae Humanae* preserved in the Munich Library, is dated 1474, and in the *Habsburg Genealogy*, which stands at the head of the printed volume, an event of 1475 is included.[1]

Unlike other illustrations published at Augsburg, the woodcuts are nearly related to Ulm work,

Fig. 118. From the German Bible, Augsburg (Pflanzmann), about 1476.

and the fact that Steinhöwel lived at Ulm and edited various books published in that town (of which more later) renders it probable that

[1] I.e. unless the 1475 given for the Baptism of Maximilian (*b.* 1459, later Emperor) is a misprint.

the blocks were done by an Ulm artist in touch with Steinhöwel, and sent
to Günther Zainer for printing.

There were undoubtedly two designers engaged on these illustrations.[1]
Some thirteen or fourteen blocks (i.e. ff. 1 a, 3 a, 8 a, 9 a, 48 b, 50 a, 53 a,
63 b, 65 b, 66 b, 69 a, 83 a, 99 b, 135 b) are somewhat more grotesque
in their convention than the rest, with a tendency to parallel lines of drapery,
and very definitely lined features, and somewhat related in style to work
published at Mainz and Speier, e.g. the frontispiece to Schoeffer's *Gart der*

Fig. 119. The Singing Lesson, from *Spiegel des menschlichen Lebens*, Augsburg, about 1475–76.

Gesuntheit (Mainz 1485) and the subject cuts in Breydenbach's *Peregrinationes* (Mainz 1486).[2] The illustration of the *Singing Lesson*, f. 83 (fig. 119),
is a good example of this group.

The remaining small cuts are by a more genial, though not more gifted,
illustrator; inclining to a less angular style, and to slightly fuller use of
parallel shading. The illustration of a *Wedding*, f. 29 (fig. 120), is characteristic of this latter group.

Both groups show taller figures with smaller heads than those of Günther

[1] See Erwin Rosenthal, *Die Anfänge der Holzschnittillustration in Ulm*, Halle 1912.

[2] Cf. pp. 352-356. He is more grotesque and formal, and less functional in line and shading,
than the designer of the *Spiegel menschlicher Behältnis*, printed by Drach at Speier.

Zainer's *Speculum*, and there is far greater harmony and sense of silhouette in the design.

The full-page woodcut at the beginning of the book illustrating the *Genealogy of the House of Habsburg* is an exceedingly skilful piece of work, by which a somewhat monotonous material is welded into a most successful decorative design. Most of the cuts appeared later in editions issued by Baemler, Augsburg 1479 (S. 5103, H. 13949), by N. Philippi and M. Reinhard at Lyon 1482 (*Le Miroir de la Vie Humaine*), and by Hurus at Saragossa 1491 (*Spejo dela Vida Humana*).

Fig. 120. A Wedding, from the *Spiegel des menschlichen Lebens*, Augsburg, about 1475–76.

Like Günther Zainer, JOHANN BAEMLER [1] was known as a scribe for some years before he worked as a printer, his name appearing as *Schreiber* in Augsburg records as early as 1453. Moreover, his name in copies of Eggestein's second *German Bible*, Strassburg 1466 (H. 3037), preserved at Wolfenbüttel, and of Mentelin's Augustinus, *De Arte Predicandi*, Strassburg, about 1466 (H. 1956), in the John Rylands Library, Manchester, are among the rare records identifying rubricator's work. On this evidence he seems to have learnt his printing, like the Zainers, at Strassburg. Two miniature paintings are also known bearing his signature (B. Quaritch,

[1] See A. Schramm, *Bilderschmuck der Frühdrucke*, iii. *Johann Baemler in Augsburg*, Leipzig 1921.

General Catalogue, London 1887, vi. 35777). His activity as a printer in Augsburg extended from 1474 to 1495.

A considerable number of his books contain cuts printed from blocks already used by Günther Zainer, or from copies of Zainer's illustrations. The list of his more important illustrated works here given is chiefly of those of which he was the original publisher:

Eusebius, *Historie vom grossen Alexander* (translated by J. Hartlieb), 1473.
> S. 3132, H. 785.
> Later Augsburg editions: Sorg, 1478, 1480, 1483; Strassburg, M. Schott, 1488 and 1493.
> This and many other books of Baemler contain cuts designed in the same style as G. Zainer's *Speculum*, but generally less well cut.
> The interesting *Portrait Bust* is generally regarded as reproducing Eusebius, but a copy in *Apollonius von Tyrus* (German, by Steinhöwel), Augsburg, Dinckmut, 1495, is labelled *Alexander*.

Gregorius I, *Dialogi* (German), 1473 (printed in the Monastery of SS. Ulrich and Afra).
> S. 4119, H. 7970.

Guido de Colonna, *Historie von Troia*, about 1474.
> S. 4131, H. 5514.
> Several of the battle-scenes repeated from Eusebius, *Alexander*.
> Later Augsburg editions: G. Zainer, about 1476 and 1477; Sorg, 1479 and 1482; Schoensperger, 1488.
> Strassburg: M. Schott, 1489; B. Kistler, 1499.

Jean d'Arras, *Melusina*, 1474 (and 1480).
> S. 4626, H. 11064; S. 4630, C. 3974.
> Later Augsburg edition: Sorg, n.d. (about 1485).
> Another edition, n.d., n.p. (S. 4627, H. 11063), is now attributed to B. Richel, Basle, about 1476. The illustrations suggested by Baemler's edition, but fairly independent.
> Strassburg: Knoblochtzer, n.d., about 1478 (S. 4629, H. 11061); J. Prüss, n.d., about 1481 (S. 4631) (both the latter based on Richel's Basle edition).

Von den sieben Todsünden und von den sieben Tugenden, 1474.
> S. 5354, H. 15535.
> Later editions 1479 and 1482.

Konrad von Megenburg, *Buch der Natur*, 1475.

 S. 3778, H. 4041.

 Later editions, 1478, 1481.

 Numerous later editions by other printers: e.g. Augsburg, Sorg, n.d.; Schoensperger, 1499.

 This is one of Baemler's most individual works, a book on the Essence of Natural Things, human, animal, vegetable, mineral, etc., with twelve full-page cuts, of which one is here reproduced.

Johann Baemler, *Chronica von allen Kaisern und Königen*, 1476.

 S. 3754, H. 9792.

 Generally, but erroneously, known as Königshofen's Chronicle.

Geschichte des Königs Apollonius von Tyrus, 1476.

 S. 3341, H. 1295.

 Later editions: Sorg, 1479, 1480; Dinckmut, 1495. *Buch der Kunst dadurch der weltliche Mensch mag geistlich werden*, 1477.

 S. 3647, H. 4036.

 Later editions, Baemler, 1478 and 1491, and in 1497 by Schoensperger under the title *Ein löblich Büchlin der Gmachelschafft zwischen Gott und der Seele*.

Robertus de Sancto Remigio, *Historie wie die Turken die christlichen Kirchen angefochten*, 1482.

 S. 5391, H. 8753.

 The earliest illustrated book on the Crusades. Some of the cuts repeated from the *Historie von Troia*.

Calendar in German (in book form), 1483.

 S. 4417, H. 9736.

 This may be noted as one of the most interesting of Baemler's illustrated Calendars.

ANTON SORG,[1] who is recorded as *Briefmaler* and *Kartenmaler* soon after the middle of the xv century, became the most prolific of the Augsburg printers, issuing over a hundred illustrated books between 1475 and 1493. Among a great variety of subject, they include the first editions of many romances of considerable literary interest, though their illustration is below the average of Günther Zainer and Baemler in quality of cutting. He frequently followed Günther Zainer and Baemler with later editions of their books, e.g. in his *Spiegel Menschlicher Behältnis* of 1476, with cuts based on Günther Zainer's *Speculum*, while in his *Aesop* of about 1480 he reprinted

---

[1] A. Schramm, *Bilderschmuck der Frühdrucke*, iv. *Anton Sorg in Augsburg*, Leipzig 1921.

the cuts originally issued by Johann Zainer at Ulm. His most richly illustrated book is Ulrich von Reichenthal, *Concilium zu Constanz*, 1483 (S. 5095,

Fig. 121. Studies of Trees, from Konrad von Megenburg, *Buch der Natur*, Augsburg 1475.

H. 5610),[1] but its subject and portrait cuts are of much less value than
its wealth of heraldic illustration.

The little cuts in Cyrillus, *Buch der natürlichen Weisheit* (translation of the
Speculum Sapientiae), 1490 (S. 3650, H. 4047), a popular book of fables,
are more generally attractive, though crudely enough cut. The frontispiece
(eight figures representing virtues and vices) is cut in an angular style,

[1] Facsimile, ed. E. Voulliéme, Muller & Co., Potsdam.

with strong outline, similar in character of composition to the company of philosophers which appears as frontispiece to the *Gart der Gesuntheit* Mainz (Schoeffer) 1485, and *Hortus Sanitatis*, Mainz (Meydenbach), 1491, and resembling the latter in style of work as well. The following illustrated books printed by Sorg also deserve mention:

Die neue Ehe (von der Kindheit und von dem Leiden Jesu Christi), 1476.
    S. 3723, H. 4057.
    Several of the blocks based on line-engravings, e.g. on IA of Zwolle.
Hans Schiltberger, *Reisebuch*, n.d. (about 1476).
    S. 5208, H. 6674.
    Schiltberger was a prisoner in Turkey, 1395–1417.
    The book is often found together with the two following works:
Historie von Herzog Ernst von Bayern, n.d. (about 1476).
    S. 3908, H. 6672.
Historie von St. Brandon, n.d. (about 1476).
    S. 3533, H. 3718.
Historie von Herzog Leuppold und seinem Sohn Wilhelm von Oesterreich, 1481.
    S. 4492, H. 11041.
Seelentrost, 1478.
    S. 5225, H. 14582.
    Full-page cuts illustrating the Ten Commandments.
Otto van Passau, *Die verundzwanzig Alten* (or *Der guldin Tron*), n.d. (about 1479) and 1480.
    S. 4877 and 4878, H. 12128.
    Later editions, Strassburg, J. Prüss, about 1482; M. Schott, 1483.
Passion, various editions from 1480.
    S. 3739, H. 12441, etc.
Mandeville, *Reise nach Jerusalem*, 1481.
    S. 4798, H. 10647.
Hans Tucher, *Reise in das gelobte Land*, 1486.
    H. 15667.
    The Portrait representing Tucher is copied from the portrait of Marco Polo in the latter's *Reisebeschreibung*, Nuremberg (Creussner) 1477, showing how little actual truth of representation mattered, as the same features serve for both.
    Cf. edition by Knoblochtzer, Strassburg, 1484 (see below, p. 337).

Fig. 123. Initial B, from the Psalter,
Augsburg (Ratdolt) 1494.

other works printed at Augsburg. Several of these unsigned cuts dating between 1499 and 1502 are now commonly regarded as the work of HANS BURGKMAIR the elder (*b.* 1473), and one has been attributed to him dating as early as 1491.[1]

The *Virgin and Child with SS. Corbinian and Sigismund* (Schottenloher, p. 46), in the *Freising Missal* of 1502, is one of these, and certainly by the same designer is the *Virgin and Child between SS. Conrad and Pelagius*,[2] dated in one state 1499 (S. 2022, Schottenloher, pp. 62 and 63), used in the *Constance Breviary*, 1499 (S. 3595, H. 3830), and the *Constance Missal*, 1505. In the 1499 impression St. Pelagius has cap and beard; in the impression reproduced by Schottenloher from the 1505 Missal, the Saint's head is re-cut, beardless and without cap. Schreiber describes these states in the reverse order.

I would also mention here that a few single woodcuts have recently been attributed to another great Augsburg painter, HANS HOLBEIN the elder, e.g. an *Annunciation*, among the blocks of the Derschau Collection at Berlin, which Friedländer dates about 1500,[3] and a *Virgin of Pity* at Basle.[4]

Among the chief editions of Ratdolt's liturgical books issued in the xv century may be noted:

Augsburg Obsequiale, 1487.
 S. 4861, H. 11925.
 Ratdolt's first Augsburg book. Containing a cut representing Ratdolt's patron, *Bishop Friedrich von Hohenzollern*, printed in black and two or three colours, the first example, apart from Schoeffer's

---

[1] I.e. the *Virgin and Child in a Glory of Flames* (Freising Breviary, 1491; Freising Obsequiale, 1493). See Hans Rupé, *Beiträge zum Werke H. Burgkmairs des Älteren*. Dissertation, Freiburg im Breisgau 1912 ; Hans Rupé, *H. Burgkmair I. as an illustrator of books*. Print Collector's Quarterly, x (1923) 167.

[2] Dörnhöffer, *Beiträge zur Kunstgeschichte F. Wickhoff gewidmet*, Vienna 1903, p. 116. Dodgson, who formerly attributed this cut to J. Breu (Pr. Jahrbuch, 1900, p. 207), now accepts as Burgkmair.

[3] M. J. Friedländer, Zeitschrift für bildende Kunst, N.F. xxxiii., 1922, 101.

[4] H. Rupé, Münchner Jahrbuch, N.F. iii., 1926, 1. Rupé dates this about 1500; Dodgson inclines to place it about ten years later.

Fig. 124. The Virgin and Child, with St. Hermagoras and St. Fortunatus, from *Aquileia Missal,*
Augsburg (Ratdolt) 1494.

(H. 11210), usually known under its later title *Mirabilia Romae*, and a broadside *Zeichen der falschen Gulden*,[1] with a woodcut representing ten coins (S. 4176, *Einbl.*, Kommission für den GW., 1914, No. 1566).

A single sheet *Confession Table* in the British Museum dated 1481 (S. 1855) is signed *hanns schawr*, and the cut as well as printing might be his work, and an undated *Virgin with the Rosary* at Nuremberg (S. 1128),[2] which contains a reference to Pope Sixtus IV (regn. 1471–84), also bears his name. Very near in style to the *Confession Table* is a sheet dated 1482 representing the *Ten Ages of Man*, in the British Museum (S. 1881).

HANS RÜST (RIST) is another Augsburg craftsman (recorded as a *Karten-macher* in various Augsburg documents between 1477 and 1497) who was responsible for a strong but crudely cut representation of *Death* (Munich, S. 1885), and for a woodcut *Map of the World*, to which we shall recur later.[3]

ULM

Ulm had been famous in the late XIV and early XV century as the chief centre for the making and distribution of playing-cards throughout Europe,[4] and its record in the early years of woodcut illustration was as brilliant as that of any other town in Germany. But nearly all its early printers fell on evil days, and were hampered in their publishing by business difficulties, in many cases possibly due to the losses inherent in the frequent visitations of the plague (particularly in the years 1473, 1474, 1483 to 1485, and 1494). Augsburg was a richer commercial centre, and its larger colony of printers would have had more chance of pulling through these years of devastation.

But in the two decades from 1470 to 1490 Ulm possessed illustrators more gifted than any of the same period at Augsburg.[5] That two members of the same family, Günther and Johann Zainer, were printing in Augsburg and Ulm respectively must have to some extent encouraged closer relations, as has been surmised in one instance already noted in

---

[1] See C. Haebler, '*Falsche-Gulden*' *Blätter*, Zeitschrift für Bücherfreunde xi (1907) 219.

[2] S. 1129 is another version of the same subject, bearing an indistinct coat-of-arms (Ulm ?) and dated 1485. [3] See p. 315. [4] See p. 84.

[5] See Erwin Rosenthal, *Die Anfänge der Holzschnittillustration in Ulm*, Dissertation, Halle 1912; Monatshefte für Kunstwissenschaft, 1913, p. 185; Ernst Weil, *Der Ulmer Holzschnitt im XV^{ten} Jahrhundert*, Berlin 1923; Erwin Rosenthal, *Zur Ulmer Formschneidekunst im XV Jahrhundert* (Beiträge zur Forschung: Studien aus dem Antiquariat J. Rosenthal), Munich 1930; W. Cohn, *Untersuchungen zur Geschichte des deutsch. Einblattholzschnitts*, Strassburg 1934, p. 22.

which Ulm designs were published in an Augsburg book (Rodericus Zamorensis, *Spiegel des menschlichen Lebens*).

JOHANN ZAINER,[1] who, like Günther, had learnt his craft at Strassburg, must have settled at Ulm about 1472, for his first book (Steinhöwel, *Büchlein der Ordnung der Pestilenz*) was dated 11th January 1473 (S. 5312, H. 15058).[2] Its only woodcut decoration is a half-border and capitals (U with *Martyrdom of St. Sebastian* on the first page, the other capitals being in plain outline without pictures). We have already referred to Heinrich Steinhöwel as the author of the translation from Rodericus Zamorensis, *Spiegel des menschlichen Lebens*, published at Augsburg about 1475–76. Besides being medical officer to the town of Ulm and the writer of various medical books, he was one of the most distinguished humanists of the day. He had travelled in Italy and other parts of Europe, and did much to introduce foreign literature to general readers in Germany by his translations. He was probably as much interested as his printer, Johann Zainer, in directing his illustration.

The first of Johann Zainer's fully illustrated works was Boccaccio, *De Claris Mulieribus*, issued in two Latin editions with some eighty cuts, 1473 (H. 3329 and variant), and in two undated editions with about four cuts less in Steinhöwel's German version (S. 3506, 3507, H. 3333, 3334). To the same year also belongs Petrarch, *Historia Griseldis*[3] (S. 4914, C. 4715), with its ten illustrations in similar style, published as a sort of epilogue to the Boccaccio.

The first page is decorated with a beautiful and entertaining half-border, including the capital letter S (fig. 126). The other illustrations are oblongs about $3 \times 4\frac{1}{4}$ inches in size, full of life and humour, but restrained in action. The figures are longer, smaller-headed and more graceful than those in most Augsburg blocks of the same period, and the compositions are more rhythmical in character. As an example of book-production in fine type, good printing and clear cutting of blocks, the Boccaccio does not reach the same level as Günther Zainer's contemporary books, such as the *Speculum Humanae Salvationis*, but in the gentle and alluring character of its designs it easily surpasses the Augsburg work. The *Procris and Cephalus*

---

[1] See A. Schramm, *Bilderschmuck der Frühdrucke*, v., *Johann Zainer in Ulm*, Leipzig 1923; Johann Wegener, *Die Zainer in Ulm*, Strassburg 1904.

[2] See Karl Sudhoff, *Der Ulmer Stadtarzt und Schriftsteller Heinrich Steinhöwel. Mit Faksimile von Steinhöwels Büchlein der Pestilenz*, Ulm 1473 (issued with A. C. Klebs, *Die ersten gedruckten Pestschriften*, Munich 1926).

[3] Facsimile of the German ed. (C. 4715), ed. E. Voulliéme, Muller & Co., Potsdam.

Fig. 126. Initial S and half-border, from Boccaccio,
De Claris Mulieribus, Ulm (J. Zainer), 1473.

is a good example of more lively action, while the *Sappho* (fig. 127) shows the more gentle characteristics and an excellent sense of interior composition. The designs were copied a few years later in Sorg's Augsburg edition of 1479, while those of the *Historia Griseldis* were repeated at Augsburg by Sorg (n.d.) and Baemler (1482).

More powerful than the Boccaccio designs are those in Johann Zainer's Aesop, *Vita et Fabulae* (*Das Buch und Leben des hochberühmten Fabeldichters Aesop*), S. 3020, H. 330,[1] which was issued about 1476–77, to which the *Historia Sigismundae* formed a supplement (S. 4487). The original blocks of the *Aesop* were printed later at Augsburg by Günther Zainer about 1477–78 (S. 3025, H. 331),[2] by Sorg soon after 1480, and those of *Sigismunda* by Baemler in 1482 (S. 4490), and the popularity of the work is shown by the fact that the designs were borrowed in some twenty German editions within the xv century.

The book appeared both in Latin and in a German version by Heinrich Steinhöwel. Parts of Aesop had appeared before in German in such popular collections of Fables as Boner's *Edelstein* (see p. 276), and Steinhöwel and his artist no doubt referred to such series, and perhaps to Boner's MSS. such as those preserved

[1] W. Worringer, *Hauptwerke des Holzschnittes*, Munich (Piper & Co.) 1924.
[2] Facsimile ed. E. Voulliéme, Potsdam (Muller & Co.) 1922.

at Munich and Heidelberg. The illustrations to Aesop's Life were entirely original, and show the designer at his best (e.g. *Young Aesop and the Philosopher*, fig. 128). The difference in character in drawing between the *Boccaccio* and the *Aesop* cuts is more than can be explained by a few years' development: it almost certainly shows the hand of another draughtsman. He is more naturalistic in his drawing of the figure; his lines are more functional in their rendering of the varieties of form; they tend to fall in short knots and curves rather than in a continued decorative

Fig. 127. Sappho, from Boccaccio, *De Claris Mulieribus*, Augsburg 1473.

stroke, giving more articulation to the joints and more volume and modelling to face and figure. He shows, moreover, considerably more interest in his landscape backgrounds than most of his contemporary woodcut designers.

In Ulm illustration the *Aesop* master stands alone, and his nearest relation in style is found in the *Spiegel menschlicher Behältnis* printed at Speier about 1478, and in some of the cuts in the *Hortus Sanitatis* and the *Cronecken der Sassen* printed at Mainz in 1491 and 1492 respectively (see pp. 351, 352). In fact so near is the relation that it seems possible that they are the work of the same designer. And the disappearance of this very individual personality from participation in further works at Ulm adds colour to the hypothesis that he left the district. In general character, in the vigour and naturalism of their drawing, there is considerable resemblance in both the *Aesop* and the other works mentioned, to the style of the Master of the Amsterdam Cabinet (the Master of the Hausbuch), but not, I think, sufficient to justify the identification which has been suggested.[1]

One very problematic work should perhaps be quoted in this connection, i.e. Johann Lichtenberger, *Prognosticatio*, n.d., n.p., n.pr. (S. 4499, H. 10080), as the general style of its illustration suggests relationship both to the *Aesop* master and the Mainz cuts mentioned above, and even more to the *Totentanz* (S. 5372), which is now generally ascribed to Heidelberg or Mainz. The *Prognosticatio* is generally assigned to Johann Zainer, about

Fig. 128. Young Aesop and the Philosopher, from Aesop, *Vita et Fabulae*, Ulm, about 1476–77.

1488, but it is by no means certain, and its cuts were printed in 1492 by J. Meydenbach at Mainz (S. 4500, H. 10082). The *Totentanz* itself has been sometimes ascribed to Johann Zainer, Ulm, e.g. by Schreiber, and it would not be surprising if both were found to belong to the region of Heidelberg or Mainz.[2]

There are many beautiful woodcut capitals and pieces of border decoration (generally half-borders, i.e. for the top and left side of the page) in Johann Zainer's books not otherwise illustrated, especially between 1473

[1] For book-illustrations printed at Ulm, Augsburg, Esslingen, Urach, Nuremberg, Heidelberg and Speier attributed to this master see K. F. Leonhardt and H. T. Bossert, *Studien zur Hausbuchmeisterfrage*, Zeitschrift, N.F. xxiii., 1912, 132, 191, 239; W. Bühler, *Heinrich Mang der Hausbuchmeister*, Mitteil. der Gesellsch. für vervielf. Kunst, 1931, p. 1. For further bibliography in this relation see notes below in reference to books printed at Speier, Heidelberg and Mainz, p. 346.

[2] Cf. p. 345, for further notes on the *Prognosticatio*.

Fig. 129. Initial O, from Alvarus Pelagius, *De Planctu Ecclesiae*, Ulm 1474.

and 1476. Noteworthy is the half-border with the figure of a fool which appears in several books, e.g. Duranti, *Rationale*, 1473 (H. 6474), Petrus Berchorius, *Liber Bibliae Moralis*, 1474 (H. 2794), and Alvarus Pelagius, *De Planctu Ecclesiae*, 1474 (S. 4904, H. 891). After the later edition of the *Rationale* (18th March 1475, H. 6475), the half-border shows an amusing change and the figure of the fool was cut out and replaced by the figure of a student, appearing thus in Gritsch, *Quadragesimale*, of the 20th October 1475 (H. 8063). One of the most attractive of his pictorial and anthropomorphic capitals, the O from Alvarus Pelagius, *De Planctu Ecclesiae*, is reproduced in fig. 129.

The most interesting of Johann Zainer's later illustrated books is the *Geistliche Auslegung des Lebens Jesu Christi* (S. 3722, H. 2146), which was published without name of place, printer or date. Richard Muther was right in placing the book at Ulm, though his conjectural date of 1470 was certainly too early, and confusion was caused later by one of Robert Proctor's few errors in ascribing the book to the printer Schobser of Augsburg as late as 1494-95. It is now fairly established that it is in the same type of Johann Zainer's, as e.g. Peregrinus, *Sermones*, n.d., about 1485 (H. 12581),[1] with some of the same woodcut capitals which appeared in J. Nider, *Sermones*, n.d., about 1480 (H. 11802), so that a conjectural date of 1480-85 cannot be wide of the mark.

The *Geistliche Auslegung* is a poor piece of book-making, and as far as the illustrations are concerned it is made up in a somewhat haphazard manner, blocks of various sizes and in somewhat diverse state of preservation being fitted into the requisite spaces by the provision of printed rules, for border lines, outside the blocks.

There are two clear groups of cuts by different hands: (1) thirty-two cuts, whose design has sometimes been attributed to Martin Schongauer, of

[1] British Museum *Catalogue of xv-Century Printed Books*, Type 96 b (P. 7), distinct from Schobser 96 (P. 3), in having no tails to its small *f* and *s*.

which fig. 130, from sig. c. 3, verso, the *Flight into Egypt*, is a good example; (2) forty-eight outline cuts by a designer of more archaic style and less skill in drawing, of which the *Christ and Peter's Wife's Mother*, from sig. k. 4, verso (fig. 131), is one of the more interesting subjects.

In addition there are some eight other blocks by one or two other hands, one of whom has been conjecturally, but not, I think, convincingly, identified by Weil with Johannes Schnitzer de Armszheim.[1]

Fig. 130. The Flight into Egypt, from *Geistliche Auslegung des Lebens Jesu Christi*, Ulm, about 1480–85.

The group of thirty-two cuts shows a hand of some naturalistic power of drawing, influenced perhaps by the designer of the *Aesop*, and certainly inspired by the general style of Martin Schongauer (and in the *Nativity*, sig. b. 3, verso, copying one of his line-engravings, B. 4, in reverse).

The group of forty-eight cuts has been attributed by Weil to the author of the *St. Peter and St. Paul with the Veronica Napkin* signed H.B. (with crossed arrows) (Tübingen, S. 1659 a), but not, I think, with any certainty. The type at the foot of the H.B. cut is the same type as used by Zainer in the *Geistliche Auslegung*, which fixes the locality, and Schreiber has suggested the possibility that he may be the HANS BAYER recorded in Ulm documents in 1461, 1481 and 1484.[2]

As in the *Aesop*, many of the blocks have only partial borders, the silhouette of the upper part of the subject being regarded as sufficient termination to the design, though in the *Geistliche Auslegung* this is made up by the outer border lines of printers' rules.

Later in the 'eighties Johann Zainer fell into debt and was no doubt forced to sell some of his decorative material, as some of his borders and woodcut capitals appear in books printed by H. Knoblochtzer at Heidel-

[1] I.e. the *Christ carrying the Cross* at f. 114, and five other cuts. See p. 314, for Schnitzer.
[2] Weyermann, *Stuttgarter Kunstblatt*, 1830, Nos. 64-67.

berg (e.g. in the *Totentanz*, S. 5372, about 1489), by Meydenbach at Mainz, after 1491, and by Matthias Hupfuff at Strassburg, after 1498.

He went on printing at Ulm (with intervals of absence) well into the XVI century (the last record being 1523), but his later illustrated books, mostly popular books in German, are comparatively negligible from their artistic quality, and very rare outside German libraries.

One of the exceptions in quality is the little German edition of Thomas à Kempis, *Imitatio Christi* (*Wahre Nach-folgung Christi*) (S. 5346, H. 9115), which probably dates about 1487, with its attractive cut of the *Dead Christ supported by an Angel, the Virgin and St. John.*

Another example above the general average in quality are the six cuts in Ulricus Molitoris, *Tractatus von den bosen Weibern, die man nennet*

Fig. 131. Christ and Peter's Wife's Mother, from *Geistliche Auslegung des Lebens Jesu Christi*, Ulm, about 1480–85.

die Hexen, n.d., about 1490-91 (Schramm, v. 416-421), in which one begins to see some relation to the early style of Dürer. They show the same subjects which appeared in two other books on witches, printed by Michel Greyff and Johann Otmar at Reutlingen about 1489 (Ulricus Molitoris, *Von den Unholden oder Hexen,* or *De Lamiis*), and though they appear to be the later versions, are certainly by far the better drawn and cut. As examples of the cruder type (coarse and angular in cutting) may be mentioned:

Frag und Antwort Künigs Salomon und Marcolfus, 1496.
    S. 5191, C. 5248.
Saint Brandons Leben, n.d., about 1499.
    S. 3540, H. 3723.
Tondalus ain Riter (Ritter) aus Hibernia, n.d. (about 1500).
    S. 5362 (based on cuts in Schobser's edition, S. 5358, H. 15545).

We have already noted CONRAD DINCKMUT[1] as the printer of a block-book. His earliest type-printed books with illustrations belong to 1482, i.e. *Schwester Demut*, of which only a fragment is known in the Liechtenstein Collection (Schramm, vi. 6-22), and the *Ordnung der Gesundheit* (with only a single cut). In 1483 appeared a *Plenarium* with crude and angular but lively cuts (H. 6733), the *Büchlein genannt der Rosenkranz*, H. 14036 (with three attractive blocks, each containing five roundels, within flower borders, illustrating the Life of Christ), and two editions of the *Seelenwurzgarten* (S. 5229, 5230, C. 5345, H. 14584), and in 1485 the *Erklärung der zwölf Artikel* (S. 4106, H. 6668). The *Seelenwurzgarten* book, with its nineteen blocks repeated so as to offer one hundred and thirty-four illustrations, is an egregious example of an economy of illustrative material frequently practised by the printers of the time.

Dinckmut's best illustrations are contained in two books of 1486, Thomas Lirer, *Chronica von allen Königen und Kaisern* (three editions, one undated with nineteen cuts, two dated 1486 with twenty-three cuts, S. 4507-4509, H. 10116-10118),[2] and Terence, *Eunuchus* (in German). They are the work of a designer and cutter of individual style and sensitive quality, who relied on a delicate outline, with little shading. They are possibly by the same hand as the *Erklärung der zwölf Artikel*, though they show a considerably finer performance. The undated edition of Lirer in the British Museum from which the illustration is taken (fig. 132) shows the line printing more delicately than in the dated edition in the same place, and is undoubtedly the earlier. For the tendency of delicate lines on a block is to be flattened out in the printing, so that later impressions often show a broader line.

The Terence is still better in its drawing and expression than the Lirer, perhaps from the inspiration of a congenial subject. The figures are well drawn, the faces lively in expression and the setting of interest as it no doubt indicates a definite scheme of staging. His edition of Bertholdus, *Andächtig Zeitglöcklein des Lebens und Leidens Christi*, 1493, will be noted under its *editio princeps* at Basle.[3]

Conrad Dinckmut, like Johann Zainer, had his financial difficulties and debts, and these are reflected in the inferior quality of his later illustrations. Steinhöwel's German version of *Apollonius von Tyrus*, 1495 (Schramm, vi. 652-678) is an example, to which we have already alluded under Baemler

---

[1] A. Schramm, *Bilderschmuck der Frühdrucke*, vi., *Conrad Dinckmut in Ulm*, Leipzig 1923.
[2] Facsimile of ed. 12th January 1486 (H. 10117), ed. E. Voulliéme, Muller & Co., Potsdam.
[3] See p. 328.

for its portrait-bust inscribed *Alexander*. In 1499 Dinckmut left Ulm, and thereafter records cease.

LIENHART HOLLE[1] was another of the unfortunate printers of Ulm,

Fig. 132. From Thomas Lirer, *Chronica von allen Königen und Kaisern*, Ulm, about 1486.

chiefly known for two illustrated books of the year 1482 and 1483, the *Ptolemaeus* and the *Buch der Weisheit*. His edition of Ptolemaeus, *Cosmographia* of 1482 (S. 5031, H. 13539) is an epoch-making work, the earliest

[1] A. Schramm, *Bilderschmuck der Frühdrucke*, vii., *Lienhart Holle, J. Reger, J. Schaeffler, and Hans Hauser in Ulm*, Leipzig 1923.

collection of woodcut maps in Germany, and one of the earliest printed editions of Ptolemy's maps (the earlier editions being those of Bologna, 1477, and Rome, 1478, with the maps engraved on copper). The book is

Fig. 133. From Terence, *Eunuchus*, Ulm 1486.

not only interesting in the history of geography, but a really beautiful production with its fine type, woodcut borders and initial letters. The *Map of the World*, which like the rest is double folio in size, is signed *Insculptum est per Johannē Schnitzer de Armszheim*,[1] and Johannes is no

---

[1] Armsheim is situated about eighteen miles south-west of Mainz, west of the Rhine.

doubt responsible for the cutting of all the thirty-two maps. Whether Schnitzer is actually a surname, or merely an indication of his craft, cannot be answered with certainty. Various other cuts have been attributed to JOHANNES DE ARMSHEIM, e.g. Johann Zainer's *Aesop* cuts, by Douce, according to his MS. note in the Oxford copy, the illustrations of Dinckmut's *Seelenwurzgarten* (1483), and of Holle's *Buch der Weisheit der alten Weisen* (1483), and certain of the cuts in Johann Zainer's *Geistliche Auslegung des Lebens Jesu Christi*, by Weil.[1]

The wind-faces are comparable to the full-page portrait figure of Aesop, and in the treatment of the hair at least not unlike the cuts in question in the *Geistliche Auslegung*, but neither here nor in the other cases mentioned is there a sufficient basis for any dogmatic assertion of authorship.

I would interpolate in this place notes on other German woodcut maps of the period, though out of their local order.

In the first place there are three known versions of a *Map of the World*,[2] which shows an earlier stage of knowledge than is seen in Ptolemy's Maps, first introduced to Germany by Holle's edition of 1482, so that in design, and probably in cutting, they are anterior to 1482.

The best version, and perhaps the earliest, is the one signed by HANS RÜST, a craftsman recorded in Augsburg documents between 1477 and 1497, of whom we have already noted another cut (p. 304). The only impression known,[3] now in the Pierpont Morgan Collection, New York (S. 1950 a), came from the binding of a copy of Strabo, *Geographia*, Venice (Vindelinus de Spira) 1472. The two other versions, less carefully cut, are both signed *Hanns Priefmaler* (with the mark of a spur), who is undoubtedly the HANS SPÖRER of Nuremberg who printed two block-books, the *Biblia Pauperum* and *Ars Moriendi* at Nuremberg in 1471 and 1473, and worked after 1487 at Bamberg, and from 1494 until about 1504 at Erfurt. One of these, in the Stiftsbibliothek at St. Gallen, was inserted under the cover of a Latin Bible of Johann Zainer (Ulm 1480); the other, now at Würzburg,[4] was inserted in a copy of Duranti's *Rationale*, Ulm (J. Zainer) 1473. There is no further clue to the dates of these maps, but they were probably all cut within a few years of 1480.

[1] See pp. 304 and 310, and L. Baer, Monatshefte für Kunstwissenschaft, v., 1912, 447.

[2] See H. Hassinger, *Deutsche Weltkarten-Inkunabeln*, Zeitschrift der Gesellschaft für Erdkunde, Berlin 1927, Nos. 9-10.

[3] Reproduced in facsimile, 1924, by J. Rosenthal, Munich, from whom the map was purchased, and in *Einbl.* LXXI., 1929, 31.

[4] S. 1950, the inscription being read *Thomas priefmaler*.

Another map of historical and social interest is the *Pilgrims' Road to Rome from Germany* which is known in several early woodcut versions, e.g.:

(1) Printed by ERHARD ETZLAUB, Nuremberg, about 1492, with title *Das ist der Rom-weg von meylen zu meylen mit puncten verzeychnet von eyner stat zu den andern durch deutzsche lantt*.[1] British Museum, etc.

(2) A different block of the same map. Linz (reproduced, G. Gugenbauer, *Einbl.*, 28, *Linz*, 1912, pl. 25). From the large type used for Nuremberg in the centre of the map, it is probably also a Nuremberg work. S. 1951 m.

(3) Printed by JORG GLOCKENDON, Nuremberg 1510. Liechtenstein Collection. Löbau. A later edition signed *Albrecht Glockendon* 1533 is at Nuremberg (Germ. Museum). S. 1951 n.

Erhard Etzlaub may also have been responsible for drawing the *Plan of Nuremberg and its Environs*, cut by Jorg Glockendon, 1492 (S. 1951 x); Munich Library.

Lienhart Holle's second interesting work, the *Buch der Weisheit der alten Weisen*, 1483 (S. 3484, H. 4029), is one of the earliest European versions of the *Kalīla Wa-Dimna*, by Bidpai, as the author is usually called in Western form.[2] Bidpai is said to have been a wise Brahman of Kashmir, vizier of an Indian ruler of about 300 B.C., and his work a collection of fables, a sort of Mirror for Princes. The book contains a large number of full-page illustrations, about $7\frac{3}{8} \times 6$ inches, crude, but powerful and full of humour, and sometimes, as in the illustration reproduced (fig. 134), evincing real harmony of design. It was evidently a very popular work, for Holle issued several editions in 1483 and 1484.

Another edition was printed at Ulm by Dinckmut in 1485, with the same designs cut down at the sides, the new blocks being about $\frac{7}{8}$-inch narrower.

An earlier edition had been published by Conrad Fyner at Urach about

[1] See *Six Early Printed Maps*, British Museum, 1928 (pl. i.); W. Wolkenhauer, *Erhard Etzlaubs Reisekarte durch Deutschland* 1501, Nikolassee bei Berlin 1919. It appears from Wolkenhauer that other variant blocks are known, so that the sheet was evidently printed in large numbers for pilgrims to Rome.

[2] See the *Encyclopaedia of Islam* (ed. by M. T. Houtsma, T. W. Arnold, etc.), London 1913, etc. An English version, 'The Morall Philosophie of Doni', by Sir Thomas North, was published about 1570 (ed. J. Jacobs, London 1888). It is also included in Somadeva, *Ocean of Story* (tr. C. H. Tawney), London, 1924-28, vol. v., with a chart showing all the known versions and editions.

1481–82 (see p. 319), but Holle's designer was fairly independent, and considerably stronger.

In spite of the popularity of the *Buch der Weisheit*, Holle no doubt lost largely through his lavish illustration of this work and the Ptolemy, and his stock was acquired by JOHANN REGER,[1] who printed a second edition of

Fig. 134. From the *Buch der Weisheit*, Ulm 1483.

the *Cosmographia* in 1486 (S. 5032, H. 13540). The chief difference in this edition from that of 1482 is that the maps are provided with headlines, and that the borders to the text on the reverse are omitted.

Holle continued occasional printing at Ulm until 1492, but issued no other illustrated books of note. He was later at Nuremberg, but no longer worked as an independent printer.

Of Reger's original illustrated books may be mentioned the *Walfart*

[1] A. Schramm, *Bilderschmuck der Frühdrucke*, vii., Leipzig 1923.

oder bylgerung unser lieben Frawen, 1487 (S. 4586, H. 9325; Latin ed., *Itinerarius*, S. 4575, H. 9323), with title cut and eighteen full-page illus-

Fig. 135. The King entertained, from G. Caorsin, *De Casu Regis Zyzymy*, Ulm 1496.

trations (each divided into three compartments) of the life of the Virgin and Christ, and the *Schon teutsch Kalender* of 1491 (S. 4079), a miniature calendar with attractive little initials, figures of saints and Passion cuts.

Fig. 136. Initial N, from the *Buch der Weisheit*, Urach, about 1481–82.

But far more important historically and artistically are the two volumes he printed about the Knights Hospitallers (the Knights of St. John of Jerusalem, at Rhodes) written by their Vice-chancellor Gulielmus Caorsin, the *Stabilimenta militum Hierosolymitanorum* of 23rd August 1496 (S. 3669, H. 4364 a) and a volume of various tracts beginning with the *Obsidionis Rhodiae Urbis Descriptio* of 24th October 1496 (S. 3667, H. 4369). The illustrations are all full-page upright cuts, mostly compositions of numerous figures. Those of the *Stabilimenta* are powerful and well composed, but lack the vivacity of some of the others in the volume of tracts. The series of ten plates *De Casu Regis Zyzymy* (from which the reproduction, fig. 135, of *King Zyzymy entertained by the Master of the Order* is taken) are particularly vivacious in handling; one of the subjects, that of Zyzymy riding with his suite, is certainly suggested by the cut of Turkish riders in Breydenbach, *Peregrinationes* (Mainz 1486) and the designer has other qualities in common with Reuwich. The topographical cuts in the title section are also comparable in style to the views in Breydenbach.

Of towns in the neighbourhood of Ulm, a few illustrated books printed by CONRAD FYNER[1] at Esslingen and Urach, and by MICHEL GREYFF[1] at Reutlingen, should be noted.

We have already mentioned Conrad Fyner's[2] edition of the *Buch der Weisheit der alten Weisen* (Urach; n.d.; about 1481–82; S. 3483, H. 4028) as the predecessor of Holle's more remarkable edition. But Fyner's book deserves further notice for its very attractive anthropomorphic initials, full of ingenuity, yet harmonious in design, of which he used seven in this and other books (Schramm, ix. 407-13) (fig. 136), and his *I with Samson and the Lion* (e.g. in Georgius de Hungaria, *De Moribus Turcorum*, n.d., about 1480–81) is another charming example.

Fyner's earlier activity as a printer, from 1472 to 1478, was at Esslingen, and it was here in 1474 that he printed Johannes von Saaz, *Der Ackermann aus Böhmen* (Schramm, ix. 3-5; GW. 197). Beside the half-border on the first page it only contains three little outline cuts (independent of Pfister's designs), and its chief interest is its subject and its rarity, for only one

[1] A. Schramm, *Bilderschmuck der Frühdrucke*, ix., Leipzig 1926.   [2] See p. 316.

copy is known (Bamberg; reproduced by A. Schramm, *Deutscher Verein für Buchwesen*, Leipzig 1924).

Apart from the general interest of Fyner's books for their initials, occasional borders, and decorations, two works printed at Urach in 1481 should be noted, the *Plenarium* (S. 4953, C. 2322) and *Leben der Heiligen* (S. 4304, H. 9974), for numerous illustrations of considerable spirit, possibly by the same hand as his *Buch der Weisheit*. An excellent three-sided border occurs in each of these books but in different state: (1) in the *Plenarium*; (2) in the *Leben der Heiligen*, with the upper piece replaced by a new block; (3) in the *Buch der Weisheit*, with the second upper piece reduced in width.

We have already mentioned in relation to Johann Zainer[1] the two editions of a book on witches by Ulricus Molitoris printed at Reutlingen about 1489 under the titles *Von den Unholden oder Hexen* (Michel Greyff) and *De Lamiis* (Johann Otmar).[2] The illustrations in each are from the same blocks, with very little difference in condition, but the edition of Michel Greyff, entitled *Von den Unholden oder Hexen* (H. 11540), probably precedes Johann Otmar's *De Lamiis* (S. 4785, H. 11536).

I would note three other books printed by Michel Greyff at Reutlingen:

> Guillermus, *Postilla super Epistolas*, 1494 (suggested by Kesler's Basle edition of 1492).
>> S. 4150, H. 8287.
>
> Sebastian Brant, *Narrenschiff*, 1494.
>> S. 3557, H. 3738. The illustrations copied from the first Basle edition of the same year (S. 3555), and
>
> Heinz von Beschwinden, *Gedicht vom Krieg mit Schweizern und Türken*, n.d. (Schramm, ix. 629-633).
>> The two latter are chiefly remarkable for their borders, rare examples in the dotted manner (white dots on black ground), more characteristic of French books of the period.

Another work where woodcut borders are inspired by contemporary French work printed by Dupré, i.e. Bertholdus, *Andächtig Zeitglöcklein des Lebens und Leidens Christi*, n.d., will be described below under its first dated edition at Basle (see p. 328).

Greyff also issued a considerable number of single-sheet calendars with attractive woodcut decoration.

Before proceeding to Basle and its book-illustration, I would add a few

---

[1] See p. 311.   [2] A. Schramm, *Bilderschmuck der Frühdrucke*, ix., Leipzig 1926.

notes about certain single cuts of Ulm and the neighbourhood, chiefly where names attached to the prints give a definite local clue. The Ulm master, BASTION, and another of the neighbourhood, JERG HASPEL, whose work possibly falls within the first half of the century, have already been mentioned.[1]

A small group of cuts belonging to the collection preserved at Ravenna (e.g. the *Last Supper*, S. 169) has been recently assigned by Dr. Kristeller to Ulm. They show a certain relationship to the Ulm school, but I think it very possible that they may have been done by a German hand in Italy, and reserve their discussion, in consequence, for a later chapter.[2]

MICHEL (or MICHIL) is another name which occurs on other single cuts of uncertain locality, but probably produced in Upper Germany about 1450-70, i.e. on the *Christ Child with a Bird*, at Halle (S. 782); *The Man of Sorrows*, at Nuremberg (S. 877); a *Pietà* (S. 986 m; present locality unknown); *St. Bridget*, John Rylands Library, Manchester (S. 1289); and a *Political Allegory relating to the Meeting of Pope Paul II and the Emperor Frederick III* (S. 1956, Munich). The last print is a copy of a Venetian line-engraving,[3] which seems to refer to a meeting which took place between 24th December 1468 and 9th January 1469, and both original and copy probably date soon after the event. The artist may perhaps be identical with a *Formschneider* of the name of MICHEL who occurs in Ulm records in 1476, though the prints noted would appear to be somewhat earlier.

Another single cut, probably of Upper German origin about the same date, is signed *Leinhart*, i.e. a *St. Ottilia* at Graz (S. 1645 b), and Schreiber has conjectured that he may be identical with the printer Lienhart Holle. Two other prints at Graz, *Christ on the Cross* (S. 417 a), and *St. Apollonia* (S. 1235 a), are probably by the same hand.[4]

Ludwig mäler ze Ulm 68 is inscribed on a large cut with full-length figures of *St. Christopher and St. Anthony* (S. 1379, Stuttgart), and he is probably identical with the *Ludwig ze Ulm* who signed a block-book of the *Ars Moriendi* (S. ed. VII A). The 68 probably indicates the date 1468, which at least agrees with his style and with the probable date of the block-book, which was copied by Hans Spörer in 1473. He may be identical with either LUDWIG KUCH or LUDWIG FRIESS, who are recorded at Ulm about 1475. Other cuts which have been attributed to him with some probability,[5] i.e. the

---

[1] See p. 128. [2] See p. 424.

[3] A. M. Hind, *Catalogue of Early Italian Engravings in the British Museum*, p. 276, No. 7.

[4] There is a Lienhart recorded as a *Formschneider* at Ulm *c.* 1442, but this would appear to be too early.

[5] See Molsdorf, *Schrifteigentümlichkeiten auf älteren Holzschnitten*, Strassburg 1914.

Y

Good Shepherd (S. 839, Dresden);[1] *Christ on the Cross* (S. 936a, Dillingen); and *St. Sebastian* (S. 1678), of which an old impression is in the Guildhall Museum, and the original block and two modern impressions in the British Museum. On the reverse side of the *St. Sebastian* block is cut the *Sacred Monogram with the Crucifix and the Four Evangelists* (S. 1812), of which several other woodcut versions exist. It is probably copied from S. 1810 at Berlin. The *St. Sebastian* is a copy of a print at Munich dated 1472 (S. 1679).

Peter mäler ze ulme is another name recorded in a signature, on an *Agony in the Garden* (S. 192) from a *Passion* series (of which ten are preserved at Munich, S. 151, etc.). They appear to be based on an earlier series of cuts, of which a fragment exists at Vienna (Haberditzl 32). An interesting subject of the *Soldiers falling in fear before Christ* (Munich Library, S. 214), is certainly by the same hand, and others near in character are the *Agony in the Garden* (S. 189, once at Maihingen), the *Flagellation* (S. 649, Paris and Salzburg), and the *Holy Trinity* (S. 740, British Museum from St. Gallen). There are Ulm records of a *Peter* 'Kartenmaler' about 1460, and a *Peter Heckenagel* in 1481, and he might be identical with one or the other, or with both.

MICHEL SCHORPP of Ulm is responsible for two cuts of interest for their subjects, a large print of the *Kindred of Christ* signed *Michel Schorpp zu Ulm* (formerly in the Collection Friedrich August II, Dresden, S. 1779a) with inscriptions and names attached to the various members of the Holy Kindred, and a *Byzantine Madonna* signed *Michel Schorpp maler zu Ulm*, 1496 (Paris and Nuremberg, S. 1032, Lemoisne, cxxi.), supposed to have derived from a painting by St. Luke at Rome.

A series of sixteen subjects illustrating the life of *St. Catherine of Alexandria* was recently found by Mr. Campbell Dodgson at Schloss Hohen Liechtenstein (S. VIII, 1315 x).[2] They are fragmentary in condition, intended apparently for wall decoration, and originally printed on two double sheets, and the authorship seems fairly certain from the *rpp* which remains of the signature. Their style shows more angularity and less shading than the other two cuts, an indication either of an earlier period of the artist's activity (about 1470–80), or of some lost originals from which they may have been copied.

---

[1] Based on a line-engraving by the Master E.S. (Lehrs 52). There are two copies, S. 839a (Paris), S. 839b (formerly St. Gallen), and a modified version at Frankfurt (S. 839c). It should be compared with the Netherlandish *Good Shepherd* (S. 838), which is described and reproduced below (p. 594 and Fig. 347).   [2] See *Einblattdrucke*, No. 75 (1931).

In the case of an inscription with *maler* distinguishing the artist as a painter, it is natural to infer that the design is his, if not the cutting. Michel Schorpp occurs as *Maler* and *Briefmaler* in Ulm records between 1495 and 1500.

HANS HAUSER[1] is responsible for a broadside with a cut of *Death in the Jaws of Hell*, signed *Hanns hauser briefmaler zu Ulme*, the text being in one of Johann Reger's types which points to the probability of a date about 1495 (S. 1894, British Museum).

A woodcut of *Christ on the Cross appearing to a Sick Man* (S. 969, British Museum) signed *Hans husser*, is probably by the same artist, and the different spelling might be an indication of the usage of another district, the south-western region of Germany, where he might have worked before settling at Ulm.

Fig. 137. Book-plate of Hilprand Brandenburg of Bibrach. S. 2038.

The last name which can be connected with Ulm is that of HANS SCHLAFFER. His name occurs on a *Martyrdom of St. Sebastian* (S. 1682 a, Dresden), of which there is another version at Vienna (S. 1680), a *St. Veronica Napkin* at Lucerne (S. 759 a), and an *Adoration of the Magi* (S. 99, present locality unknown). The signature on the *Adoration* has been read as *Hans Schlaffer von Ulm*, and he is no doubt identical with a craftsman recorded in 1492–1500 at Nuremberg, in 1501 at Ulm, and between 1506 and 1515 at Constance.

Among the small single prints of the region of Ulm which deserves mention is the *Book-plate of Hilprand Brandenburg of Bibrach* (S. 2038), a cut of about 1475-80 and one of the earliest book-plates known (fig. 137). It has interest in relation to our history in indicating provenance from the Carthusian Convent of Buxheim, near Memmingen (to which Hildebrand gave his library), as this was also the original home of the famous *St. Christopher* woodcut of 1423.

Another interesting German book-plate of about the same period is that of *Hans Igler* with its device of a hedgehog (S. 2036), and two other examples worth noting, probably nearer the end of the century, are those of

[1] A. Schramm, *Bilderschmuck der Frühdrucke*, vii., Leipzig 1923.

Niklaus Meyer and Barbara zum Luft, of Basle (S. 2036 e Basle; reproduced Heitz, *Einbl.*, Basel i., 1908, pl. 20), and of the *Carthusian Convent of Thorberg, near Berne*, at Berne (S. 2038 n).

Another book-plate of more problematic origin is that of *Johannes Plebanus*, dated 1407, which is designed in the form of an oval seal (S. 2039). The plate occurs chiefly in incunabula of about 1470-80 in the Munich Library, and the date of the cut can hardly be earlier. Schreiber's explanation is that the date referred to some fund for the purchase of books left by Plebanus, who is known to have been living in 1405.

A certain CLAUS probably belongs to Breisach, on the Rhine, near Freiburg, as the arms of that town appear on a *Christ on the Cross between the Virgin and St. John* which bears his name (S. 947). A *Satire on the Jews* (*Die Juden-Sau*, S. 1961) occurs in several cases on the reverse of impressions of S. 947, and as its size is identical, the subject was probably cut on the back of the same block. Most of the impressions known (e.g. Basle and Augsburg) are considerably later than the date of production. Considering the interpretation of the arms, Nagler's identification with Claus Wolff Strigel of Augsburg is improbable.[1]

One of several versions of a *Crucifix with signs of the Passion* is signed *firabet ze raperswil* (S. 940 m; Zürich, Polytechnicum,[2] and Minnesota Institute of Arts, Minneapolis, from the Herschel V. Jones Collection).[3] A family of the name of Firabet (the local form for Feierabend) was known at the time in Rapperswil on Lake Zürich. Other unsigned versions of about the same date (1460–80) are known (S. 940 n, Graz; S. 941, British Museum; S. 942 a, Boerner Sale, 19th-23rd May 1924, No. 60; S. 944, Darmstadt), and another signed by Caspar (S. 943, British Museum).[4] The British Museum version (S. 941) is stronger and probably earlier than Firabet's, though its faulty inscription makes it probable that it is likewise based on an earlier version. In view of the other existing versions, Firabet is almost certainly the cutter rather than the designer.

The figure of St. John in S. 941 suggests relationship with the style of the Apocalypse block-book, so that the original work may be of Netherlandish design.

Another important woodcut signed by FIRABET OF RAPERSWIL, a *Virgin*

---

[1] Nagler, *Monogrammisten*, ii. 361; W. Bühler, Mitteil. der Gesellsch. für vervielfalt. Kunst, 1925, p. 68.

[2] S. 942 at Sigmaringen is probably a cut impression from the same block.

[3] See *Einblattdrucke*, 73, 1930.

[4] See p. 389.

in Robe decorated with Ears of Corn (*Madonna im Ährenkleid*) (S. 999 y), has recently been acquired by the Polytechnicum at Zürich.

More attention has no doubt been given to the rare signed prints of the xv century than would be justified by their comparative artistic value in relation to anonymous cuts of the period. But it must be remembered that when such names are also connected with records, they at least offer a definite basis in helping to group anonymous work.

Fig. 138. The Marriage at Cana, from the *Spiegel menschlicher Behältnis*, Basle 1476.

BASLE

In Basle[1] we find a centre definitely poorer in original work than Augsburg and Ulm, and one in which, during the xv century, outside influences were stronger than any indigenous strain. There is at first the marked influence of the schools of Augsburg and Ulm; then an occasional reflection of French modes, and during two brilliant years (1493, 1494) an appearance which is now generally thought to be that of the young Dürer on his *Wanderjahre*.

The most important book of the earliest group is the *Spiegel menschlicher Behältnis* printed by BERNHARD RICHEL, 1476 (S. 5274, H. 14936). The

[1] Werner Weisbach, *Die Baseler Buchillustration des XV*[ten] *Jahrhunderts*, Strassburg 1896; Weisbach, *Der Meister der Bergmannschen Officin und Albrecht Dürers Beziehungen zur Baseler Buchillustration*, Strassburg 1896; C. C. Bernoulli, *Basler Büchermarken*, Strassburg 1895; A. F. Johnson, *Early Basle Printing*, London 1926. For other Swiss towns see Paul Heitz, *Die Zürcher Büchermarken bis zum Anfang des XVII*[t.n] *Jahrhunderts*, Zürich 1895; Paul Heitz, *Genfer Buchdrucker- und Verleger-zeichen*, Strassburg 1908 (Geneva is treated in the French section; see p. 617).

blocks are single column uprights about $5 \times 3\frac{1}{2}$ inches, broad in outline, angular in style, with slight parallel shading.[1] They derive to some extent from Günther Zainer's *Speculum Humanae Salvationis*, but with variations

Fig. 139. From *Die sieben geistlichen Laden*, Basle 1491/92.

which show a more direct dependence on the Nether-landish editions of the *Biblia Pauperum* block-book. A later Augsburg edition printed by Peter Berger in 1489 (H. 14937) follows Richel's subjects more nearly than it does Zainer's, and is even more directly influenced by the *Biblia Pauperum*.

The Speier edition of Peter Drach (about 1478) likewise shows numerous points of contact with the *Biblia Pauperum*. It is note-worthy that these type-printed editions of the *Speculum Humanae Salvationis* show no relationship to the Nether-landish block-book of the same title.

In another book published by Richel, Jean d'Arras, *Melusina*, of about 1476 (S. 4627, H. 11063, Berlin, Munich, etc.), the subjects are again suggested by an Augsburg edition (Baemler, 1474), though they are treated with con-siderable independence, and, like the *Spiegel*, transformed from small oblongs into larger upright designs. They have something of the same crude strength as the cuts in Holle's Ulm edition of the *Buch der Weisheit* (1483).

Other examples comparable with Augsburg and Ulm work may be noted in the title cuts to St. Augustine, *De Civitate Dei*, 1489 (S. 3393, H. 2064), and Ambrosius, *Opera*, 1492 (S. 3264, H. 896), both printed by JOHANN AMERBACH.

---

[1] The majority of the original blocks were reprinted in *Le Mirouer de la Redemption*, printed by Martin Huss at Lyon, 1478.

Another work printed by Amerbach, *Die sieben geistlichen Laden*, 27th January, 1491/92 (S. 4462, Berlin Print Room; fig. 139), contains seven cuts of curious subject in which Christ is represented as a pedlar with horse and cart, showing a hermit his wares, the treasures contained in seven boxes. In their vivid style they form something of a bridge between the *Spiegel menschlicher Behältnis* of 1476 and the illustrations attributed to Dürer (see pp. 328–32). But with their straight parallel shading, they belong more to the earlier tradition than to the structural modelling and curved shading of the master of the 'Ship of Fools'.

Among miscellaneous work of poorer quality may be mentioned:

> Guillermus, *Postilla in Evangelia et Epistolas*, M. Furter, 1491.
>> S. 4146, H. 8273.
>> Crude little cuts, copied in an edition of N. Kesler, Basle 1492.
>
> Bernardinus, *Sermones de Evangelio*. N. Kesler, about 1494.
>> S. 3428, H. 2828.
>> The title cut of St. Bernardino, with an Italian town in the background, is the same subject as the larger single cut (S. 1278 a), which is possibly Italian (see p. 428).
>
> Albertus de Bonstetten, *Passio Sancti Meinradi*. M. Furter, 1496.
>> S. 4607, H. 12453.
>> Also German editions of about the same date, Copinger 3966, and E. P. Goldschmidt & Co., Catalogue ix., No. 49.
>> The cuts probably based on the block-book.
>
> Methodius, *Revelationes Divinae* (ed. S. Brant). M. Furter, 1498.
>> S. 4648, H. 11121.
>> Crude little cuts in the same style as Furter's *St. Meinrad*.

One of the most attractive printer's marks of the earlier period at Basle is that of JACOB WOLFF of Pforzheim, and the little illustrations in one of Wolff's books, Christoforus Columbus, *Epistola de insulis nuper inventis* (n.d., about 1493, H. 5491), are at least of interest from their subject.[1]

The printer LIENHART YSENHUT has already been mentioned[2] for the variety of crafts under which he figures in records, as *Maler, Briefmaler, Briefdrucker, Heiligenmaler, Heiligendrucker, Kartenmacher*. His *Walfart Marie* (S. 4587, H. 9327) is known to have been issued in 1489 (and there is a Latin edition *Itinerarium Mariae* of about the same date), and he published *Calendars* for 1498 and 1499, but otherwise there is no record

---

[1] The same cuts also occur in an edition by J. Bergmann de Olpe, Basle 1495 (Copinger 1697).
[2] See p. 91.

of the date of his books. They all contain cuts, of no great merit, and he may have been partly responsible for the cutting of the blocks. They include Franciscus de Retza, *De Generatione Christi, seu Defensorium inviolatae Castitatis Mariae* (S.4047, H. 6086), and a German *Aesop* (S. 3034) which is largely based on J. Zainer's Ulm edition.

An example which very clearly reflects the style of the French *Horae* of Jean Dupré is Bertholdus, *Andächtig Zeitglöcklein des Lebens und Leidens Christi*, printed by Johann Amerbach, 1492 (S.3448, H. 16278; see fig. 140). It is a most attractive little book with occasional subject illustrations and borders to every page, including eight different designs.

Fig. 140. From Bertholdus, *Andächtig Zeitglöcklein*, Basle 1492.

There are similar borders, some based on Amerbach's blocks, in editions printed by Dinckmut at Ulm, 1493 (S. 3452, H. 16280), and by M. Greyff at Reutlingen, n.d. (Schramm, ix. 639-683).

Similar French influences will be noted in *Horae* printed about the same time by Marcus Reinhard at Kirchheim and by his brother Johann Grüninger at Strassburg.[1]

By far the most interesting incident in book-illustration at Basle is the visit of ALBRECHT DÜRER between 1492 and 1494.[2] A woodcut of *St.*

[1] See p. 340.
[2] See Daniel Burckhardt, *Albrecht Dürers Aufenthalt in Basel*, 1492–94, Munich 1892

Jerome (Kurth 22; fig. 141) which appeared in an edition of his *Epistles*, printed at Basle by Nicolaus Kesler in 1492 (S. 4227, H. 8561; Basle, Berlin, British Museum, Oxford, etc.; the edition of 1497, S. 4228, H. 8565, contains a copy).[1] Direct evidence of Dürer's authorship is provided by the authentic signature written on the back of the block which is still preserved at Basle. In its angular style it stands so far apart from the earliest of Dürer's woodcuts after his return to Nuremberg in 1494 (e.g. *The Men's Bath*, B. 128; fig. 179), that but for the documentary evidence and the links in development provided by the other works of Basle printers to be mentioned, it might have remained permanently anonymous. It shows distinct

Fig. 141. Albrecht Dürer, St. Jerome. From St. Jerome's *Epistles*, Basle 1492.

relationship to contemporary Basle work, such as the *St. Ambrose in his Study* in Ambrosius, *Opera* (Johann Amerbach, 1492), to which we

(reproducing some of Dürer's drawings for an unpublished *Terence*); and Pr. Jahrbuch, xxviii., 1907, 168; H. Koegler, Repert. xxx., 1907, 195; and the works cited above (p. 325) by W. Weisbach; Erich Roemer, *Dürers ledige Wanderjahre*, Pr. Jahrbuch, xlvii., 1926, 118; xlviii., 1927, 77, 156 (with complete reproduction of the *Terence* drawings and cuts); J. Meder, *Dürer-Katalog*, Vienna 1932, p. 13.

[1] See R. Schrey, Mitteil. der Gesellsch. für vervielfält. Kunst, 1908, p. 40.

have referred among the cuts showing the influence of Ulm and Augsburg.

The other works at Basle attributed to Dürer are the cuts in the *Ritter vom Turn* and the *Narrenschiff (Stultifera Navis)*. The *Ritter vom Turn*,[1] printed by MICHAEL FURTER in 1493 (S. 5392, H. 5514), contains forty-

Fig. 142. Albrecht Dürer (?). From the *Ritter vom Turn*, Basle 1492.

five cuts each flanked by floral borders, the title cut of the *Knight instructing two Priests and two Writers to compile his book* being repeated, all uniform in style of design, but with a variation in quality of cutting which seems to show two hands. The larger group, including the illustration reproduced (fig. 142), is excellently cut, and the style of all the subjects, both

[1] Reproduced and described by R. Kautzsch, Strassburg 1903, and K. Pfister, Munich 1922, Kurth, *Dürer*, 36-48. There is no copy of the original edition in English libraries. The cuts in Schaur's Augsburg edition of 1495 and Furter's edition of 1513 (reprinted by J. Knoblouch, Strassburg 1519) are copies. See p. 265 for further notes.

in figure and landscape, seems the natural source from which the acknowledged works of Dürer sprang.

Sebastian Brant's *Narrenschiff*, first printed by JOHANN BERGMANN DE OLPE on the 11th February 1494 (containing considerably over a hundred cuts), was a most popular work, which passed through more than fifteen editions before the end of the century (see S. 3555 and H. 3736 and following numbers; Kurth, *Dürer*, 49-62).[1] The original series of cuts, with certain variations and additions in different issues, was reprinted in German editions by Bergmann in 1495, 1497 and 1499, and in Latin editions (*Stultifera Navis*) in 1497 (three editions) and 1498. Copies were issued by Peter Wagner at Nuremberg, by M. Greyff at Reutlingen, by J. Schoensperger at Augsburg, and by J. Grüninger at Strassburg, in the year of original publication, and Schoensperger and Grüninger issued several later editions.

Fig. 143. Albrecht Dürer (?). From Sebastian Brant, *Narrenschiff*, Basle 1494.

There is less uniformity in style throughout this series than in the *Ritter vom Turn*. Some of the blocks are markedly angular in character (fig. 143), while others (fig. 144) have the rounded manner of drawing that characterises Dürer's certainly authentic work. The landscape is throughout in Dürer's style, though the two examples reproduced show considerable difference in the method of coping with details of foliage, which is much more significantly drawn in fig. 144. Granting the prob-

[1] See Bibliography, p. 325 (Weisbach), and Hans Koegler, Gesellschaft der Bibliophilen, Weimar 1906, and F. Schultz, Gesellsch. für Elsäss. Literatur, Strassburg 1913, for facsimiles of the original edition of 1494.

ability that the design and cutting of the *Narrenschiff* series were spread over a longer period than the less numerous and more uniform designs of the *Ritter vom Turn*, I think that the development from angu-

Fig. 144. Albrecht Dürer (?). From Sebastian Brant, *Narrenschiff*, Basle 1494.

larity to more sensitive and significant methods of design might easily allow certain sections of the work, apparently divergent in style, to be by the hand of the one artist who was responsible for the *St. Jerome* and *The Men's Bath*.

There may be a proportion of designs by other hands, and if there is uncertainty in the attribution of the main body of the illustrations, it lies rather on the side of the more angular group, for the style of the remainder is entirely in harmony with the drawings preserved on the wood blocks at Basle (of which only a few were cut) for an unpublished edition of *Terence*, which can be accepted for the most part with even less hesitation as Dürer's work (see figs. 145, 146). There are 130 of these blocks, and only a small proportion cut, and these perhaps only cut experimentally at a later period (Kurth, *Dürer*, 23-35). In any case, comparison of the cuts with the drawings show how considerably the original design is coarsened in the process.[1]

---

[1] The opinion that the *Ritter vom Turn*, *Narrenschiff* and *Terence* designs are largely by Dürer is supported by Dr. Burckhardt and Erich Roemer in the works cited above. Dr. Hans Koegler, who shares the same view, has also attributed to the master certain small cuts originally intended as a series for a *Gebetbuch*, but actually only published in various other books (*Repertorium*, xxx., 1907, p. 195, and the Gutenberg Gesellschaft Jahrbuch, 1926; Kurth, *Dürer*, 63-80). The same writers also include in Dürer's work the *Canon* cut from a *Missal* printed by

A few other books published at Basle undoubtedly reflect the influence
of the same master's designs, e.g. Johannes Meder, *Quadragesimale novum
de Filio Prodigo*, printed by M. Furter, 1495 (S. 4604, H. 13628), three
books of Sebastian Brant, printed by Johann Bergmann, *In Laudem Virginis
Mariae*, about 1494 (S. 3554, H. 3733),[1] *De Origine et Conversatione
bonorum Regum*, 1495 (S. 3574, H. 3735), and *Varia Carmina*, 1498
(S. 3543, H. 3731). Brant's *Varia Carmina* were also issued by Grüninger

Fig. 145. Albrecht Dürer (?). Design for *Terence*. Drawing on the wood block.

at Strassburg in 1498, but one of the subjects (*Ad Divum Maximilianum*)
appeared in the work of 1495, and it seems probable that the Basle
designs are the originals throughout. Certainly the portrait in the Basle
edition is more convincing, as if based on a drawing from the life, than the
more conventionalised Strassburg cut.

Grüninger at Strassburg in 1493, and the much-debated illustrations to the *Revelationes Sanctae
Brigittae*, printed by Koberger at Nuremberg, 1500. A summary of this view is given in Dr. F.
Winkler's edition of Dürer in the Klassiker der Kunst series. Divergent views are held by other
critics, such as Dr. Röttinger, who once attributed the group largely to Hans Wechtlin (Vienna
Jahrbuch, xxvii., 1907, Heft 1), but now in part to Peter Vischer 1. (*Dürer's Doppelgänger*,
Strassburg 1926), and by Hans Tietze and E. Tietze-Conrat (*Der junge Dürer*, Augsburg 1928).
  [1] Two of its cuts are repeated in Jacob Wimpheling, *De conceptu Mariae*, J. Bergmann, 1494
(S. 5473, H. 16171).

Sebastian Brant was one of the most distinguished of the humanists of the day, and exerted an immense influence through his original writings and translations, which were printed by Bergmann at Basle, and Grüninger at Strassburg.[1] His interest in the illustration of his works is recorded, and he appears to have controlled his designers in detail in their interpretation of his ideas.

Before leaving Basle, I would mention a book published in the early years of the XVI century, and therefore strictly outside my province, i.e.

Fig. 146. Albrecht Dürer (?). Design for *Terence*. Woodcut.

Paulus Olearius, *De Fide Concubinarum*, first issued without date or name of place or printer. Muther (No. 380) describes this first edition under the authorship of Jacob Wimpheling, and attributes it to the printer LUDWIG HOHENWANG, who he thought might also be the designer of the illustrations, three statements which all need correcting. It appears to have been printed at Basle between 1501 (a date which occurs in the text) and 1505, when a reprint was issued by Froschauer at Augsburg. There seems no doubt that its interesting cuts are by the Basle master, who is only known by the monogram D.S., which occurs on certain of his other works.[2]

---

[1] See G. R. Redgrave, *The Illustrated Books of Sebastian Brant*, Bibliographica, ii., 1896, 47.

[2] For description and reproduction of his work see E. Bock, *Die Holzschnitte des Meisters D.S.*, Berlin 1924; cf. C. Dodgson, Pr. Jahrbuch, xxviii. (1907), 21.

Freiburg im Breisgau

Two books printed by FRIEDRICH RIEDRER at Freiburg im Breisgau deserve mention, as containing cuts now attributed to Dürer, i.e. the *Septem Horae Canonice Virginis*, about 1493 (S. 4574; Kurth, *Dürer*, 82) with a cut⁺

of the Virgin adored, by A. Bonstetten, and Riedrer's own *Spiegel der wahren Rhetorik*, 1493 (S. 5096, H. 13914; Kurth, *Dürer*, 83, 84), with an excellent title-cut and an interesting rendering of the *Fall of Icarus*.

Fig. 147. From Jean d'Arras, *Melusina*, Strassburg, about 1478.

Strassburg

The earliest book-illustrations printed at Strassburg[1] are those of the press of HEINRICH KNOB-LOCHTZER[2] between 1476 and 1484. Knoblochtzer afterwards left Strassburg, and is known to have been at Heidelberg in 1489, and may have already been there in the intermediate years.

His illustrations and the earlier Strassburg cuts in general, like those of Basle, reflect the style and often repeat the subjects of Augsburg and Ulm books, but with considerable originality of treatment. For example, his cuts to Jean d'Arras, *Melusina*, n.d., about 1478 (S. 4629, H. 11061, S. and S. 7; see fig. 147), and 1481 (S. 4632, S. and S. 18), derived originally from Baemler's Augsburg edition of 1474, though immediately from Richel's Basle edition of about 1476 (the subjects being upright in form), are treated

---

[1] See Paul Kristeller, *Die Strassburger Bücher-Illustration im XV und in Anfang des XVI Jahrhunderts*, Leipzig 1888; P. Heitz and K. A. Barack, *Elsässische Büchermarken*, Strassburg 1892.

[2] Karl Schorbach and Max Spirgatis, *H.K. in Strassburg* (1477–84), Strassburg 1888.

in bold and vivacious style, with an occasional effective use of white on black (e.g. in the fifth illustration). The cuts in his edition of Jacob de Theramo, *Belial*, 1477 and later editions (S. 4281, C. 5808, S. and S. 1, etc.) are equally broad in treatment, and almost entirely in outline. Simple rounded forms are characteristic of two large cuts in Hans Erhard Tusch, *Burgundische Historie*, 1477 (S. 5398, H. 6664, S. and S. 3), and the *Historie von Peter Hagenbach* of the same year (S. 4182, H. 8345, S. and S. 4), a battle-scene, which occurs in both, and *Religious Procession at Strassburg Minster* (possibly the earliest print of the Cathedral) from the latter book.

His Aesop, *Vita et Fabulae*, n.d. (S. 3021, S. and S. 37; see fig. 148), and his *Historia Sigismundae*, n.d. (S. 4488, C. 2885), both between about 1478–81, are based on Johann Zainer's Ulm editions, and his Pius II, *De Duobus Amantibus* (Aeneas Sylvius, *Euryalus und Lucrecia*) (S. 3017, H. 242, S. and S. 10) is equally in the Ulm manner.

Single cuts of interest may be noted in Maphaeus Vegius, *Philalethes*, n.d., about 1478–80 (S. 5416, H. 15926, S. and S. 11),

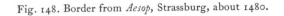

Fig. 148. Border from *Aesop*, Strassburg, about 1480.

Fig. 149. Initial D, from Jean d'Arras, *Melusina*, Strassburg, about 1478.

which is a copy (and improved rendering) of the same subject in the Nuremberg edition of Johannes Regiomontanus (of about 1474), and in Hans Tucher, *Reise zum heiligen Grabe*, 1484 (S. 5385, S. and S. 31),[1] with its pretended portrait of Tucher standing against a tapestry background. How little consideration is paid to truth of portraiture at this period is shown by the fact that Knoblochtzer's cut is copied (with no change of feature) from a supposed representation of Marco Polo, printed by Friedrich Creussner at Nuremberg in an edition of his *Travels*, 1477.

Knoblochtzer's work is distinguished by good ornament in borders, and initials. A two-sided border (of leaf, flower and bird) occurs in *Melusina* and various other books, and an excellent complete border of similar character on the front page of his *Acsop* (fig. 148). He follows Ulm and Augsburg in his *Maiblumen* initials, and copied an *Initial I with Samson and the Lion* from a block of Conrad Fyner of Urach,[2] using it in his 1483 edition of Jacobus de Theramo, *Belial* (S. 4288, C. 5813, S. and S. 15), and in Jacobus de Cessolis, *Schachzabelbuch*, 1483 (S. 4276, H. 4897, S. and S. 40).

An *Initial D with St. John the Baptist, and other Figures*[3] is in the style of Fyner's anthropomorphic initials, but it is actually copied from the engraved alphabet of the Master E.S. (Lehrs, 286). It occurs in the *Lucidarius*, n.d., n.p., n.pr. (S. and S. 17), described by Kristeller as printed by Martin Schott, but rightly assigned by Schorbach and Spirgatis, and in the British Museum Catalogue, to Knoblochtzer.

Apparently his own are the set of twelve *Calendar Initial D's with the occupations of the Months* (see fig. 149), issued complete in his *Calendar* of 1483 (H. 9734) and imitated later in a German Calendar by Johann Schaeffler at Ulm, 1498 (Schramm, vii. 360-371).

And in the broad style of his own early cutter is the large *Pictorial Initial A with Christ washing the Disciples' Feet*, which occurs in Thomas Ebendorfer de Haselbach, *Sermones*, 1478 (S. 5344, H. 8370).

The work done for Knoblochtzer is easily the most important part of the earlier Strassburg woodcut illustration, but certain other books deserve mention for one reason or another.

The numerous illustrations in Sir John Mandeville, *Itinerarius*, 1483

---

[1] Cf. edition, Augsburg, Sorg, p. 297.   [2] See p. 319.
[3] Reproduced Kristeller, *Strassburger Bücher-Illustration*, Abb. 2, and S. and S., p. 72.

(S. 4801) and 1484 (S. 4802, H. 10649), printed by JOHANN PRÜSS, crudely and angularly cut, are interesting for their subject, though based on the better cuts in an undated edition (about 1481) of Bernhard Richel of Basle (S. 4799, C. 3833). Moreover, the book is among the few in which the headlines are also cut.[1] To the same printer should also be assigned the edition of Otto von Passau, *Die vierundzwanzig Alten* (or *Der guldin Tron*), n.d. (about 1482) (S. 4879, H. 12127, Muther 6), which Muther attributed to an unrecorded 'Sebastian Pfister' of Bamberg. It contains twenty-six illustrations, made by repetition from four blocks, two of which were based on an edition printed by Sorg, at Augsburg, about 1479 and 1480 (S. 4877 and 4878, H. 12128).

Another Strassburg edition of the same work, printed by MARTIN SCHOTT in 1483 (S. 4881, C. 4541), is chiefly notable for a good three-sided border with scroll work and wild folk in the lower piece, which also occurs in the same printer's edition of Guido de Colonna, *Historie der Stadt Troia*, 1489 (S. 4138, H. 5518). Martin Schott's woodcuts in the latter book, and in his Eusebius, *Historie vom Grossen Alexander*, 1488 (S. 3138, H. 791), are largely based on Baemler's Augsburg edition.

Printed in type used by both Prüss and Grüninger (and left unassigned in the British Museum Catalogue) are the works of Joannes Gerson, 1488 (S. 4101, H. 7622). A large cut of *Gerson as Pilgrim* occurs at the beginning of each of the three volumes. It was copied in the edition of Nicolaus Kesler, Basle, 1489 (S. 4102, H. 7624), in which a single border-line immediately distinguishes it from the original. A third edition, also of 1489, which has also been regarded as a Strassburg issue, now generally assigned to Georg Stuchs at Nuremberg (S. 4103, H. 7623), contains a cut in which the same subject is treated quite independently, and is possibly one of the earliest works of Albrecht Dürer (fig. 177). Finally, an additional fourth volume of the first Strassburg edition, printed by the younger Martin Flach in 1502, contains a further independent version, which is attributed by Passavant to Wechtlin (P. iii. 334, 59).

Of other books issued by Johann Prüss, one of the richest in illustration (with over 200 cuts) is *Das Heldenbuch, oder Wolfdieterich*, of about 1483 (S. 4197, H. 8420), and one of the more interesting, though only for a single cut of *Tubal Cain*, is Hugo Reutlingensis, *Flores Musicae*, issued in 1488, and in two undated editions (about 1490 and 1492) (S. 5270, 5271, and 5271 a, H. 7174 and 7173).

A rare book of very individual character is the *Directorium Statuum, seu*

---

[1] Cf. Josephus, *De Antiquitate Judaica*, Lübeck (Lucas Brandis), n.d. (about 1475) (S. 4402, H.C. 9450).

Tribulatio Seculi printed by Johann Prüss for Peter Attendorn, about 1489 (S. 3831, H.C. 6274).[1] It contains three cuts illustrating treatises dealing with the morals of the lower clergy and university students, the two latter sections on the inebriety and prodigality of students being lectures delivered before Heidelberg students in 1489. The woodcut of a *Students' Drinking-bout* (fig. 150) certainly reproduces the sketch of an artist of considerable gifts, with a vivid touch comparable to that of the Master of the Amsterdam Cabinet, and with something of the spirit of the young Dürer, or whoever was responsible for the cuts of the *Narrenschiff* at Basle.

Of considerable originality in its decorative setting is the frontispiece to the *Evangelien und Episteln*, 1488, the only book printed at Strassburg by THOMAS ANSHELM. It also contains numerous small oblong illustrations, of less interest,

Fig. 150. A Students' Drinking Bout, from *Directorium Statuum*, Strassburg, about 1489.

which are sometimes made up from more than one block, a practice of which we shall find Grüninger constantly taking advantage.

JOHANN (REINHARD) GRÜNINGER[2] was not a maker of beautiful books; he was too devoted to such economies as the combination and repetition of various blocks in different subjects not to sacrifice harmonious design in the process, but he is of great interest in our history for the new character of woodcut which appears to have been introduced in his workshops. It con-

---

[1] For a full note on the book see E. P. Goldschmidt & Co., London, *Catalogue IX.*, No. 24.

[2] Called Grüninger from his birthplace of Grüningen. See Paul Heitz, *Zierinitialen in Drucken des Johann Grüninger*, Strassburg 1897.

sisted in a close system of parallel lines of shading, straight or curved, according to the requirements of form, which approximated more nearly than woodcut had hitherto done to the richer tonal character of line-engraving. The resemblance is more apparent than real, for cross-hatching of lines (which causes infinite labour to the cutter) occurs only little, and much less than in the style of woodcut developed by Albrecht Dürer.

Fig. 151. April, from a Roman *Horae*, Kirchheim, about 1490.

One of the earliest books he printed with any cuts of artistic value, the *Cursus beatae Mariae Virginis*, n.d. (about 1494), is in a different vein and modelled on the style of French *Horae*. Its immediate source is a German Book of Hours (*Die sieben Zeiten unser lieben Frauen*) printed by Grüninger's kinsman, MARCUS REINHARD, at Kirchheim (Alsace) in 1491, though the blocks are largely different. Reinhard himself had issued a Latin edition about

1490 (*Horae secundum usum Ecclesiae Romanae*), which again was composed for the most part of different blocks. The most attractive section of this edition of 1490, which is not repeated, is the Calendar, from which the *Month of April* is here reproduced (fig. 151). Except for the Calendar, most of the borders in this edition show a plain black ground (but not dotted as usually in French *Horae*). In the edition of 1491 most of the borders are in black line and only the *Dance of Death* on a black ground. Grüninger's edition is in black line throughout.[1]

[1] For a study of these three *Horae* (all in the British Museum) see Robert Proctor, *Marcus Reinhard and Johann Grüninger*, Bibliographical Essays, 1905, pp. 19-38. Proctor is wrong in

THEATRVM

Fig. 152. The Theatre. Frontispiece to *Terence*, Strassburg 1496.

Another book printed by Grüninger before the appearance of his more characteristic cutter, the *Missale Speciale* of 1493 (S. 4758, H. 11250), contains a *Canon* cut which is now generally accepted as by Dürer (Kurth 85).

The Latin *Terence* of 1496 (S. 5331, H. 15431; German edition, 1499, S. 5333, H. 15434) is the first important work with cuts in the new style.

Fig. 153. Illustration to *Heautontimoroumenos*, from *Terence*, Strassburg 1496.

Apart from the practice of making up his smaller illustrations from various stock pieces, the marginalia to his text militate in this and his other editions of the Roman classics against a harmonious page. There is an amusing fantasy in the frontispiece, the *Theatre of Terence* (fig. 152), and a full-page cut preceding each play, while the various characters, properties and backgrounds reappear in a variety of combinations in the smaller composite illustrations (one reproduced in fig. 153 being made up of five different blocks).[1]

The two other classical editions which followed the *Horace* of 1498 (S. 4240, H. 8898) and the *Virgil* of 1502 were produced in the same style, with the same wealth of illustration. The *Virgil*, edited by Sebastian Brant,

stating that the borders are largely the same blocks in each edition. Marcus Reinhard had printed at Lyon with N. Philippi, 1477–82, before returning to his native Alsace.

[1] There are numerous earlier examples of the practice of making up illustrations from various blocks, especially in Holland (e.g. Jacobus de Theramo, *Der sonderen Troest*, printed by Bellaert, Haarlem 1484, see p. 574).

Fig. 154. The First Eclogue, from *Virgil*, Strassburg 1502.

is the finest book of the three, and the printer did not resort to the ugly economy of composite blocks as in the two preceding works. Moreover, there is more embellishment in the nature of pictorial capitals, used in different sizes for text and marginal notes. Brant did not escape abuse from his contemporaries for the unclassical fantasy of his illustrator's works. The illustration to the apocryphal *De Copa et Hortulo* is an attractive anticipation of the style of Augsburg illustration of about 1520–30 (e.g. that of Hans Weiditz). The *C A* on the cartouche has sometimes been interpreted as the artist's initials, but it is probably only the beginning and end of COPA.

Other cuts of a similar character occur in several medical works of Hieronymus Braunschweig, printed by Grüninger, i.e. the *Chirurgia* (*Wundartzny*) of 1497 (S. 3642, H. 4017), the *Liber de Arte Distillandi* (*Distillirbuch*) of 1500 (S. 3644, H. 4021), the *Liber Pestilentialis* (*Buch der Vergift der Pestilenz*) of the same year (S. 3645, H. 4020), and Boethius, *De Consolatione Philosophiae*, 1501.

A cut of *Master and Pupils* occurs in these, and was borrowed by Johann Prüss for his edition of the *Hortus Sanitatis*, n.d., about 1497 (S. 4284, H. 8941), in which the numerous other illustrations were based on Meydenbach's Mainz edition of 1491.

Good examples of the same style occur in Grüninger's Frater Petrus, *Legenda de vita S. Catherinae*, 1500 (S. 4291, H. 12850), both in the illustration and in the delicately cut initials, and in Jacob Wimpheling, *Adolescentia*, which was printed by MARTIN FLACH in 1500 (S. 5471, H. 16190). Similar but less well cut are the illustrations in Johann Lichtenberger's *Prognosticatio*, printed by BARTHOLOMEUS KISTLER in 1497 (S. 4505, H. 10088),[1] and small examples of the same character of engraving are the cuts in the *Hortulus Animae* (the German counterpart of the French *Horae*) printed by WILHELM SCHAFFENER, in 1498 and 1500 (S. 4242, H. 8936).

HEIDELBERG

We have already mentioned Knoblochtzer's removal from Strassburg to Heidelberg, and he is now generally thought to have printed at this place about the year 1489, or within the preceding four years, the Dance of Death, entitled *Doten dantz mit figuren clage und antwort* (S. 5372).[2]

[1] Based on the Ulm blocks of about 1488 (J. Zainer) (S. 4499, H. 10080), which were used later by J. Meydenbach, Mainz 1492 (S. 4500, H. 10082).

[2] Facsimile, ed. Albert Schramm, Leipzig 1922; L. Baer, *Der Heidelberger Totentanz und die Mittelrheinische Buchillustration des XV Jahrhunderts*, Gutenberg Gesellschaft, 1925, p. 269.

This first edition, containing forty-one cuts, has woodcut initials from the stock of Johann Zainer of Ulm, and it is not surprising that the book itself has been sometimes ascribed to Zainer (e.g. by Schreiber).

Moreover in style of design it has considerable relationship to another book issued *sine nota*, but commonly assigned to Johann Zainer of Ulm, about 1488, Johann Lichtenberger's *Prognosticatio* (S. 4499, H. 10080), though the cuts in the latter are somewhat cruder and less sensitive.[1] But it is not beyond the bounds of possibility that the *Prognosticatio* itself (whose

Fig. 155. From the *Doten dantz*, Mainz, about 1492.

cuts were printed later by J. Meydenbach at Mainz in 1492, S. 4500, H. 10082) may have been printed by Knoblochtzer at Heidelberg.

A second edition of the *Doten dantz*, with forty-two illustrations (one cut being repeated), without the woodcut capitals, was issued by Jacob Meydenbach at Mainz, about 1492 (S. 5373, C. 3733; fig. 155).[2] The *Totentanz*, as already noted,[3] has a very definite resemblance in style to the cuts of the Ulm *Aesop*, and an equally close relationship to certain Mainz cuts, more particularly to the frontispiece in Meydenbach's edition of the *Hortus Sanitatis*, and to various cuts in Schoeffer's *Cronecken der Sassen*.

SPEIER[4]

The earliest of the books of this middle Rhine group to share the char-

---

[1] See p. 308.

[2] It is curious that Low German characteristics which appear in the text of the first edition, e.g. *Doit* for *Dot*, disappear in the second.   [3] See p. 308.

[4] See Albert Schramm, *Bilderschmuck der Frühdrucke*, xvi., Leipzig 1933.

acteristics which have suggested attribution of their designs to the Master of the Amsterdam Cabinet is the *Spiegel menschlicher Behältnis*, printed by PETER DRACH of Speier, about 1478 (S. 5276, H. 14935, Berlin; fig. 156).[1]

The treatment of the subjects derives more closely from Richel's Basle edition of 1476 than from Günther Zainer's *Speculum Humanae Salvationis* (Augsburg 1473), showing variations which are sometimes more nearly allied to the Netherlandish block-book of the *Biblia Pauperum*.[2]

The best of the plates are extraordinarily vivid in draughtmanship, with a rounded and sensitive line, far more expressive of form than most contemporary woodcuts, and it has already been suggested that they may be by the hand of the designer of the Ulm *Aesop*.[3]
A small proportion of the plates are more angular and

Fig. 156. The Marriage at Cana, from the *Spiegel Menschlicher Behältnis*, Speier, about 1478.

less sensitive in character, e.g. the *Baptism of Christ* (Naumann, pl. 50), which denotes a second designer, as the difference seems too much to be explained by the varying skill of cutters.

---

[1] See Hans Naumann, *Die Holzschnitte des Meisters vom Amsterdamer Kabinett zum Spiegel menschlicher Behältnis* (Speier, Drach), Strassburg 1910. I keep to the title 'Master of the Amsterdam Cabinet' as the author of the engravings of which the largest collection is at Amsterdam, rather than 'Master of the Hausbuch', as only the Planets series in the Hausbuch are generally accepted as by the engraver, the rest being by an assistant. Naumann reserves the title 'Master of the Hausbuch' to this assistant, and it seems a necessary distinction. For further literature on the attribution of cuts to the Master see W. F. Storck, Monatshefte, iii., 1910, 285; E. Flechsig, Monatshefte, iv., 1911, 95, 162; W. F. Storck, Kunstchronik, N.F. xxii., 1911, 407; K. F. Leonhardt and H. T. Bossert, Zeitschrift, N.F. xxiii., 1912, 133, 191, 239; W. Bühler, *Heinrich Mang der Hausbuchmeister*, Mitteil. der Gesellsch. für vervielf. Kunst, 1931, p. 1.

[2] Cf. pp. 326 and 230.   [3] Cf. p. 307.

A very attractive little cut by the same hand showing the *Bishop of
Speier adoring the Virgin and Child* occurs at the head of an Episcopal

Fig. 157. The Bishop of Speier adoring the Virgin and Child, from an Episcopal Proclamation,
Speier 1483.

Proclamation for Advent 1483, printed by Peter Drach of Speier (British
Museum, C.D., A 134, S. 2021; fig. 157), and on an *Ordo Hyemalis* for
1484 of the same printer (British
Museum, Proctor 2355).

Another interesting book printed
by Peter Drach in both Latin and
German editions, in and about 1493,
is Petrus de Crescentiis, *Opus Ruralium Commodorum* (S. 3788, 3789,
3790, H. 5826, 5833, 5834). Its
text and numerous cuts are a wonderful storehouse of country lore
(illustrating agricultural work, sports,
animals, plants, etc.). In style they
are nearly related to Drach's *Spiegel
menschlicher Behältnis*, and to Meydenbach's *Hortus Sanitatis* (1491), but
for the most part cruder and more
angular in design, and poorer in
quality (see fig. 158).

One of Peter Drach's later books,
the *Reformation der Stadt Worms*,
1499 (S. 5054, H. 13719), is note-

Fig. 158. From Petrus de Crescentiis, *Opus
Ruralium Commodorum*, Speier, about 1493.

worthy for the woodcut arms of Worms, designed by NICOLAUS NYFERGALT.

Of other illustrated books printed at Speier, German and Latin editions of *Tondalus der Ritter* (*De Raptu animae Tondali*), printed by JOHANN and CONRAD HIST, about 1483 (H. 15540, 15541), barely deserve mention for their crude little cuts.

MAINZ[1]

The earliest books with woodcut decoration printed at Mainz by Fust and Schoeffer have already been described.[2] Fust appears to have died from the plague on a visit to Paris about 1466, and from 1467 Schoeffer continued printing alone until the end of the century, but only issued three books of importance for their woodcuts, the *Herbarius Latinus* (1484), *Gart der Gesuntheit* (sometimes called *Herbarius zu Teutsch*) (1485), and the *Cronecken der Sassen* (1492).

Fig. 159. Mulberry, from *Herbarius Latinus*, Mainz 1484.

Except perhaps for the *Herbarius* of Lucius Apuleius, printed in Rome, and described below,[3] Schoeffer's *Herbarius Latinus* was the earliest of a series of Herbals, with text compiled from a variety of sources, very popular in the xv century, and still of great interest for their woodcut illustrations.[4] These woodcuts must in part have been based on earlier drawings in manuscripts, but a considerable number were undoubtedly newly and faithfully designed

[1] See Albert Schramm, *Bilderschmuck der Frühdrucke*, xiv. and xv., Leipzig 1931, 1932.

[2] See p. 274. For Mainz books in general see Paul Heitz, *Frankfurter und Mainzer Drucker- und Verlegerzeichen*, Strassburg 1896.   [3] See p. 402.

[4] See Dr. J. F. Payne, Bibliographical Society, vol. vi.; Arnold C. Klebs, Papers, Bibliographical Society of America, Chicago, xi., 1917, p. 75, and xii., 1918, p. 41; *Hortus Sanitatis Deutsch*, Mainz, Schoeffer, 1485: Facsimile (with text by W. L. Schreiber, on the Herbals of the xv and xvi centuries), Munich 1924.

Fig. 160. Group of Thirteen Physicians. Frontispiece to the *Gart der Gesuntheit*, Mainz 1485.

from nature, and all are cut with a charming simplicity and true decorative quality.

The first work, the quarto *Herbarius Latinus* of 1484 (S. 4203 and variants 4204 and 4205, H. 8444), contains descriptions and figures of 150 plants. The second book, of 1485, is not merely a German version of the Latin Herbal, but a far more comprehensive work in folio, in 435 chapters, with 381 illustrations (from 380 blocks), including the frontispiece (fig. 160), the *Physician with a Woman* at the beginning of Part V. (on urines), 369 plants (all different blocks from those in the 1484 *Herbarius*, and mostly in larger scale), and 9 animals (the *elephant* being repeated). Like many xv-century books, it has no title-page, but in his preface the author (Dr. Johann Wonnecken von Cube of Frankfurt) calls it *Gart der Gesuntheit*, and this is certainly a better description than the *Herbarius* of its colophon. It is not a mere herbal, but a book of medical science, which has a short section on urines, and includes the properties of a few animals as well as the more numerous plants. In spite of correspondence of title, the Latin *Hortus Sanitatis*, printed by Meydenbach, 1491, is an independent work, though of course largely derived from its greatest predecessor in the same field. Schoeffer's *Gart der Gesuntheit* is a smaller folio than Meydenbach's book, and they are also occasionally referred to respectively as the 'smaller' and the 'larger' *Hortus*.

The frontispiece to the *Gart der Gesuntheit* is a most vividly rendered *Group of Thirteen Physicians* and has all the characteristics of Erhard Reuwich's draughtsmanship, as seen in his illustrations to Breydenbach, and is almost certainly by his hand.[1] And the same may be said of the second figure subject.

A passage in the preface of the *Gart der Gesuntheit* refers to a noble personage, accompanied by a wise and skilful painter, who procured information and drawings of the rarer herbs and plants, and the route they followed on their journey makes it at least possible that the reference was to Breydenbach and Reuwich. Breydenbach's journey was completed January 1484, so there would have been ample time for Reuwich to develop his designs before the *Gart der Gesuntheit* (March 1485). There is nothing in the style of the plants to compare with the known illustrations of Reuwich, but some of the animals, e.g. *elephant* (cap. 172 and 371), *gazelle* (cap. 272) and *stag* (cap. 292), are more evidently compatible with his style.

Schreiber speaks of the *Herbarius* of Lucius Apuleius, printed at Rome by J. P. de Lignamine (H. 1322), as of about 1493 and based on the

[1] As has been suggested by L. Baer, Gutenbergfestschrift, 1925. Cf. p. 354.

Herbarius Latinus, but it is more probably contemporary or even earlier than the Mainz *Herbarius*, and perhaps the earliest of the printed herbals.[1]

The *Hortus Sanitatis*, printed by JACOB MEYDENBACH at Mainz in 1491 (S. 4247, H. 8944), is a more extensive work than Schoeffer's *Gart der Gesuntheit*, having a second part supplementary to the herbal, dealing comprehensively with beasts, birds, fishes, stones, and urines. The cuts of plants are based on Schoeffer's, and equally good but even more interesting are the new designs to the second part, numerous illustrations with figures, of which we have already spoken as probably in part by the hand of the Master of the Ulm *Aesop*, and the Speier *Spiegel menschlicher Behältnis*. Later editions of the *Hortus Sanitatis* of 1491, with newly cut designs, were issued by Johann Prüss at Strassburg, about 1497 (S. 4248, H. 8941) and about 1499 (S. 4249, H. 8942).

Fig. 161. Illustration to the Chapter on Stones, in *Hortus Sanitatis*, Mainz 1491.

Dr. Arnold Klebs's studies in the Papers of the Bibliographical Society

[1] See p. 402.

of America, with his lists of incunabula, give a clear picture of the comparative popularity of the three chief herbals during the xv century. Of the *Herbarius Latinus* (Mainz 1484) there are about eleven later editions, three printed by Veldener at Culenborg and Louvain, four by J. Petri at Passau, and others by J. and C. Hist at Speier, by Leonardus Achates and Gulielmus of Pavia at Vicenza, by Bevilaqua at Venice and Jean Bonhomme at Paris. Of the *Gart der Gesuntheit* (Mainz 1485) there are some fourteen later editions, nine printed by Schoensperger at Augsburg, two by Grüninger at Strassburg, and others by Dinckmut at Ulm, by M. Furter at Basle, and Steffen Arndes at Lübeck (the last with additions from the *Hortus Sanitatis*). Of the *Hortus Sanitatis* (Mainz 1491) there are only four later editions, three printed by J. Prüss at Strassburg, and one by Vérard at Paris, about 1500 (see p. 670). There is also a French work largely based on the *Gart der Gesuntheit*, of which the only xv-century editions known are (*a*) *Arbolayre*, probably printed by P. Metlinger, Besançon, about 1487–88, and (*b*) *Grant Herbier en françois*, printed by P. Le Caron, Paris, between 1495 and 1500 (see p. 672).

To return to Schoeffer's books, the *Cronecken der Sassen* of 1492 (S. 3531, H. 4990) contains a large number of interesting cuts, views of towns with their founders and patron saints, genealogical, heraldic and portrait illustrations and the like. Such cuts as that of *Two Men bartering* (sig. a 8, rev.) and *Otheberne* (sig. v 8, rev.) are entirely in the manner of the *Portrait of Aesop* in the Ulm *Aesop*, and can hardly be due to any other designer. Many of the other illustrations are cruder in execution than the Aesop cuts, but their vivid mode of expression seems to derive from the same source. The *Wedekind Duke of Saxony and his Duchess*, on sig. d 8, is a fine example of heraldic decoration.

Perhaps the most interesting of all the Mainz books of this period is Bernhard von Breydenbach's *Sanctae Peregrinationes* (Journey to the Holy Land), which was illustrated and printed by ERHARD REUWICH in 1486.[1] Erhard Reuwich was an artist of Utrecht, and though this is the only book in which he is noted as the printer, there is no direct evidence to support Voulliéme's suggestion that he was helped in this capacity by Schoeffer except the fact that the types used corresponded with two of the latter's founts. Breydenbach was a man of noble family, and Dean of Mainz, who according to his own account lived somewhat loosely in his youth, and undertook the pilgrimage in 1483–84 as a sort of penance. There were

---

[1] See H. W. Davies, *Bernhard von Breydenbach and his Journey to the Holy Land*, 1483–84. A Bibliography, London 1911.

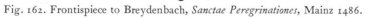

Fig. 162. Frontispiece to Breydenbach, *Sanctae Peregrinationes*, Mainz 1486.

altogether some 150 members of the pilgrimage, including Felix Fabri, who also wrote an account of the journey.[1] Apart from his journal of the pilgrimage, Breydenbach included in his work a description of Palestine, a Life of Mahomet, accounts of the sieges of Constantinople and Rhodes, and notes on the laws and manners of the inhabitants of the Holy Land.

Erhard Reuwich went as Breydenbach's official artist, and was responsible for all the 'embellishment' of the book. No other designs are recorded as his, but to judge from its style he very probably designed the frontispiece to Schoeffer's *Gart der Gesuntheit*, 1485, and possibly also the other illustrations of the same book.[2]

The style of his figures has very definite relation to the woodcuts in various Dutch books of the period, especially to those by the Delft designer, who has been identified conjecturally with the Master of the Virgo inter Virgines.[3]

The work must have been exceedingly popular, for it was issued in thirteen editions between 1486 and 1522, of which the following summary is taken from Davies:

A. *Editions with the Original Cuts*

MAINZ (REUWICH). 11th February 1486. Latin text. S. 3628, H. 3956.
MAINZ (REUWICH). June 21st 1486. German text. S. 3630, H. 3959.
MAINZ (REUWICH). 1488. Flemish text. S. 3633, H. 3963.
LYON (ORTUIN). 1489–90. French text.
SPEIER (DRACH). 1490. Latin text. S. 3629, H. 3957.
SPEIER (DRACH). About 1495. German text. S. 3632, H. 3958.
SARAGOSSA (HURUS). 1498. Spanish text (with a new cut, a view of Rome, added).

B. *Editions with Copies of the Original Cuts*

AUGSBURG (SORG). 1488. German text. Copies A. S. 3631, H. 3960.
LYON (TOPIÉ and JACOBUS OF HERRNBERG). 1488. French text. Copies B (the folding plates now engraved on copper).
SPEIER (DRACH). 1502. Latin text. Copies C.
SPEIER (DRACH). About 1505. German text. Copies C.
PARIS (N. HIGMAN for REGNAULT). 1517. French text. Copies D.
PARIS (N. HIGMAN for REGNAULT). 1522–23. French text. Copies D.

The cuts of the original edition included a frontispiece, seven folding plates of views (*Venice, Parenzo, Corfu, Modon, Candia, Rhodes* and

[1] MS. in the Stadtbibliothek, Ulm, 1st ed., 1843. See p. 84, for another work by Fabri.
[2] See p. 350. [3] See p. 572.

Fig. 163. Part of the View of Venice, from Breydenbach, *Sanctae Peregrinationes*, Mainz 1486.

Jerusalem), two cuts printed on the reverse of the *Jerusalem*, i.e. *Animals seen in the Holy Land* (including a Unicorn!), and the *Holy Sepulchre*; and the following illustrations in the text: the *Church of the Holy Sepulchre*,

Fig. 164. Mounted Turks, from Breydenbach, *Sanctae Peregrinationes*, Mainz 1486.

six plates illustrating various races (*Saracens, Jews, Greeks, Syrians, Abyssinians* and *Turks*; see fig. 164), and seven plates of Alphabets in various languages. The little cut of the *Holy Sepulchre* does not appear in the Speier edition of 1490, so it was probably lost on the journey from Lyon.

The frontispiece is one of the finest pieces of allegorical and heraldic decoration produced in Germany during the xv century. It was evidently a model for decorative work in the frontispiece to the *Nuremberg Chronicle* (1493), which also borrowed from its views of towns. The views are perhaps the earliest cuts of any importance which can definitely be regarded as based on genuine topographical studies, and the lively figure designs are equally interesting as examples of studies from nature, at a period when 'historical' illustrations were mostly imaginary fictions added to please the reader's eye.

Another illustrated book printed at Mainz has already been described in the section devoted to Dotted Prints (Turrecremata, *Meditationes*, 1479).[1]

COLOGNE

Descending the Rhine from Mainz to Cologne,[2] and coming to other

[1] See p. 194.

[2] See Paul Heitz and O. Zaretzky, *Die Kölner Büchermarken*, Strassburg 1898; E. Voulliéme, *Der Buchdruck Kölns bis zum Ende des xv^ten Jahrhunderts*, Bonn 1903; A. Schramm, *Bilderschmuck der Frühdrucke*, viii., Leipzig 1924.

towns of North Germany, one is immediately struck by the comparative dearth of fine illustrated books; in fact there are only three works of out-standing importance for their cuts, i.e. the *Cologne Bible* of about 1478–79, the Lübeck *Dance of Death* of 1489, and the *Lübeck Bible* of 1494. We shall need, however, to describe, or refer to, certain other books for various other reasons beside their artistic virtues.

Fig. 165. Noah's Ark, from *Fasciculus Temporum*, Cologne (Gotz), about 1473.

The earliest book of historical importance illus-trated with woodcuts at Cologne is Werner Role-winck, *Fasciculus Temporum*, which was issued in numer-ous editions (with many varieties of cuts) by printers at Cologne and elsewhere from 1473 or 1474 on-wards. The earliest dated editions printed at Cologne, by NICOLAUS GOTZ (S. 5105, H. 6917) and ARNOLD THER HOERNEN (S. 5106, H. 6918), belong to the year 1474. The *Fasciculus Temporum* was the first and most popular of the printed Epitomes of History, being quickly followed by the anonymous *Rudi-mentum Noviciorum* of Lübeck, 1475 (translated into French as *La Mer des Hystoires*), and at a longer interval by the much more valuable *Welt-chronik* of Hartmann Schedel, Nuremberg 1493. Apart from the circles of the genealogical tables, there are only a few unimportant diagrams and illustrations in the various editions of the *Fasciculus*, which generally include a *Noah's Ark*, a *Rainbow*, the *Tower of Babel*, the *Temple at Jerusalem*, a *Christ on the Cross*, a *Christ blessing*, and some views of towns (invariably in the Cologne editions, a *View of Cologne*).

The Gotz edition, though undated, probably precedes that of Ther Hoernen, but it has fewer cuts (five in all) and is without the subject of the *Christ blessing*. Ther Hoernen's edition may be regarded as the type followed with modifications in most of the later issues of the book in Germany and elsewhere.

Of the later editions, that of Quentell (first issue 1479, S. 5110, H. 6923) is among the best, the view of Cologne being an interesting variation on Ther Hoernen's version.

In the section on Dotted Prints we have already mentioned Nicolaus Gotz's printer's mark, which occurs in various editions of the *Fasciculus Temporum*.[1]

The earliest of Cologne printers, ULRICH ZEL, whose publications extend from 1466 to 1507, was not the first in the field with illustrated books. His earliest illustrated work was Nicolaus de Lyra, *Postilla in Universas Biblias*, n.d., about 1485 (S. 4844, H. 10368), but the cuts are even less important than those in the *Fasciculus Temporum*, being chiefly diagrams, illustrations

Fig. 166. View of Cologne, from *Fasciculus Temporum*, Cologne (Ther Hoernen) 1474.

of the Temple and its Treasure, and the like. The only other illustrated work of any note that he printed during the xv century has already been mentioned in the section on Dotted Prints (Bertholdus, *Horologium Devotionis*).[2]

The great *Cologne Bible*, printed by HEINRICH QUENTELL about 1478–79,[3] is perhaps the most epoch-making of all contemporary Bibles for the influence its woodcuts had on Bible-illustration in general for generations. It is a large folio, printed in two columns, issued in two editions: I. in *Low Saxon* dialect (S. 3465, H. 3142, GW. 4307); II. in *West Low German*, the Cologne dialect (S. 3466, H. 3141, GW. 4308). The bulk of the woodcuts are some hundred illustrations to the Old Testament, the *Creation* $7\frac{1}{2}$ inches square, the rest oblongs extending to the breadth of the

[1] See p. 195.   [2] See p. 194.
[3] R. Kautzsch, *Die Holzschnitte der Kölner Bibel von 1479*, Strassburg 1896; W. Worringer, *Die Kölner Bibel*, Munich 1923.

page, $4\frac{3}{4} \times 7\frac{1}{2}$ inches, all being within double border-line. Then four similar oblongs illustrating the four evangelists, two small column cuts of a messenger and letter repeated in the Epistles, and finally nine oblong cuts to the Apocalypse. The last eight of the Apocalypse cuts (Schramm, figs. 465-472) and the second of the Epistle cuts (Schramm, fig. 463) only appear in Edition II, and there are also a few differences in the Old Testament cuts in the two editions.

In addition to the subjects there is a four-sided border composed of three blocks, one block a for the top and left, alternatives b 1 and b 2 for the right side, and alternatives c 1 and c 2 for the lower member.

The variant blocks may be distinguished as follows: (b 1) with a jester and five other figures (Schramm, figs. 357 and 464), (b 2) with an archer, dragon and standard-bearer (Schramm, fig. 473), (c 1) the *Adoration of the Magi* (Schramm, figs. 357, 464 and 473), (c 2) nude men and woman supporting two shields.

In the British Museum copy of Edition I borders occur: (1) f 1, with a, b 2 and c 1 (see fig. 167); (2) Genesis I, with a, b 2 and c 2; (3) Proverbs I, with a, b 2 and c 2; (3) Apocalypse, with a, b 2 and c 2.

In the British Museum copy of Edition II (imperfect; only to end of Kings, with 2 leaves, including Genesis I, wanting) the only border, f 1, is composed of a, b 1 and c 1.

The dating and even the order of the two editions (neither of which bear dates) have been matters of considerable conjecture. The order given above is now generally accepted, and the *Gesamtkatalog* dates them both about 1478. The borders occur in various forms in other books printed by Quentell and the *Adoration of the Magi* appears as a separate illustration in his *Fasciculus Temporum* of 1479. Comparison of the condition of the blocks of the borders in the British Museum copies of the two editions seems to support the order given above, though I can only state that the impression in Edition I is generally clearer. On the other hand, comparison with dated editions of other works in which the border occurs proves that both Editions I and II precede 31st August 1479, as neither of them show the break in the middle of the rim of the hat of the top figure in b 1 which occurs in Astesanus, *Summa de Casibus Conscientiae*, 31st August 1479 (H. 1894, GW. 2755, Pr. 1236, B.M.L. IC. 4362). Therefore, even if some copies of either edition might have been printed later,[1] the first printings of both editions must have been made before 31st August 1479, and the date 1478–79 is therefore probable for both.

[1] Mr. Dyson Perrins's copy of Edition I has a contemporary MS. date of 1480 at the end.

Fig. 167. Page with border, from the *Cologne Bible*, about 1478–79.

The subject blocks which appeared in those editions were reprinted, with certain variations and omissions, by Koberger in his *German Bible*, Nuremberg 1483 (S. 3461, H. 3137).

The design of the woodcuts is Netherlandish in character, an influence very marked in the *Abraham and Melchisedek*, which is one of the best of the cuts in figure and expression. But it is probable that they are based on miniatures done in Cologne, where the Netherlandish influence was strong, and Kautzsch is probably right in referring to the miniatures in MS. 516 in the Berlin Library as the originals used by the designer, or if not these

Fig. 168. Jacob's Blessing, from the *Cologne Bible*, about 1478–79.

actual drawings (they are done in the pen, some being lightly tinted), at least some unidentified series of the same school. For the most part the cuts are without much subtlety of expression, heavy in outline and hard and angular in linear style.

Shading is in straight parallels and parallel series of short strokes are often used for the ground as in Netherlandish woodcuts of the period. The style is nearer to that of the weaker *Biblia Pauperum* block-books than to the majority of Netherlandish book-illustrations, which are generally treated with a lighter and more mobile touch. The resemblance sometimes noted to the style of French cuts (e.g. to that of Vérard's book-illustrations) consists more in the blunter expression of the Netherlandish modes, common to both, than in any intrinsic relationship. The borders used in Quentell's *Missale Itinerantium*, n.d. (S. 4714, C. 4140), are certainly French in inspiration, though the influence probably came through the Low Countries. Quentell must however have had relation with Paris printers, for he actually borrowed a large French block of a *Student in his Chamber*, and used it in several of his books, e.g. as a portrait of *Albertus Magnus*, in Aristotle, *De Anima, cum Commentario Alberti Magni*, n.d. (S. 3349, H. 1711, Schramm 493). The block had originally belonged to Gillet Couteau and Jean Menard and was first used in their *Danse Macabre* of 1492 (see Claudin, *Histoire de l'imprimerie en France*, ii. p. 176).[1]

Other examples near in style to the cuts of the *Cologne Bible* are a *Scene in a Court of Justice* in the *Sachsenspiegel*, printed by BARTOLOMAEUS DE UNKEL, 1480 (S. 5169, H. 14081), a *Crucifixion* in the *Missale Coloniense*, printed by CONRAD WINTERS DE HOMBORCH, 1481 (S. 4683, C. 4114), and the illustrations in Otto von Passau, *Die vier und zwanzig Alten*, printed by JOHANN KOELHOFF THE ELDER, 1492 (S. 4882, C. 4543). Still in the same tradition but rather more allied to the harder French manner, are the cuts in the *Cologne Chronicle* (*Die Cronica van der hilliger Stat van Coellen*) printed by JOHANN KOELHOFF THE YOUNGER in 1499 (S. 3753, H. 4989), which we have already quoted for its passage on the invention of printing.[2] There are over fifty woodcuts, but they are of far less importance in illustration than the *Cologne Bible*, and poorer in quality.

Blocks originally belonging to Knoblochtzer of Strassburg were reprinted by Johann Koelhoff the elder (e.g. in his Low German *Aesop*, 1489, S. 3039, C. 118), and many of the cuts used by Ludwig von Renchen go back to the same source. But a greater number of contemporary Cologne illustrations derive from the Netherlands, and Koelhoff the elder actually borrowed Antwerp blocks to illustrate his edition of the *Historia Septem Sapientum Romae*, 1490 (S. 5139, H. 8725). The blocks were originally printed by Claes Leeuw in his Flemish edition of 1488 (H. 8739, CA. 954), and later by Gerard Leeuw in 1490 (CA. 950).[3]

One other book printed by Koelhoff the elder deserves mention for its attractive floral border design (leaves and flowers on a black ground), i.e. Gerardus de Vliederhoven, *Die Vijer Vijssersten*, 1487 (S. 4095).

The last of the Cologne printers to whom reference might be made is HERMANN BUMGART, but only for the cut of the *Adoration of the Magi* in an architectural setting which he used in various books before the end of the xv century as his printer's mark.

[1] See p. 647.   [2] See p. 207.   [3] See p. 579.

Lübeck

Lübeck[1] was a far less important centre than Cologne in the printing of books, but it can boast one designer (the author of the cuts in the *Dance of Death* of 1489, and Steffen Arndes's *Bible* of 1494) of greater individuality than any of the Cologne illustrators.

One of the earliest illustrated works issued at Lübeck, the *Rudimentum Noviciorum* printed by LUCAS BRANDIS, 1475 (S. 5159, H. 4996),[2] is notable among early printed Universal Histories, following within about a year the first dated Cologne edition of Rolewinck's *Fasciculus Temporum*. This compilation, intended for the instruction of young ecclesiastics, had an even greater vogue in its French translation, under the title of *La Mer des Hystoires*, in the fine editions printed by Pierre Le Rouge in Paris, 1488-89, by Jean Dupré at Lyon, 1491,[3] and in various later issues.

The numerous cuts of the Lübeck edition include genealogical tables (in the forms of chains, the round links sometimes filled with figure subjects), maps of the world and of the Holy Land; little upright cuts of stock subjects (for repetition on various occasions) such as the storming of a city, the building of a town, and typical representations of emperor, pope, saints and philosophers; and numerous Bible subjects, including a full-page woodcut in compartments illustrating the Passion of Christ.

The designer, who generally uses shading in parallel series of short strokes, is either from the Low Countries or directly under Netherlandish influence. The cuts are of no great quality, but possess certain characteristics of vivid representation.

Certain of the decorative cuts in the *Rudimentum* had appeared earlier (it seems) in the same printer's Josephus, *De Antiquitate Judaica*, n.d. (S. 4402, H. 9450), i.e. the *Initial I with the portrait of Josephus* (fig. 169), and a three-side scroll border, with lions supporting a shield at the foot. The *Josephus* has already been noted for its woodcut headlines,[4] and is remarkable too for its large pictorial initials in which a few subjects are printed from separate blocks within different letters.

A *Psalter*, of about 1483, printed by Lucas Brandis without date (S. 5026, H. 13520), is also chiefly attractive for its initials and border decoration. Two other works of the same printer, *Die Nye Ee und dat Passional van*

---

[1] A. Tronnier, *Die Lübecker Buchillustration des XV Jahrhunderts*, Göttingen Dissertation (1904), Strassburg 1904; A. Schramm, *Bilderschmuck der Frühdrucke*, x., xi., xii., Leipzig 1927, 1928, 1929.

[2] See p. 569.   [3] See pp. 632 and 612.   [4] Cf. p. 338.

Fig. 169.
Initial I,
from
Josephus,
Lübeck,
about 1475.

Ihesus und Marien (several editions, in and about 1478 and 1482, C. 3349 and H. 4061)[1] and *Spiegel menschlicher Behältnis*, n.d., about 1483 (S. 5283, H. 14941), contain some hundreds of illustrations, but crude and angular, chiefly in outline, and far less individual than those of the *Rudimentum*.

An undated work printed by Lucas's brother, MATTHAEUS BRANDIS, Meister Stephan, *Dat Schaekspel* (S. 5318, H. 4898), contains crude but amusing cuts illustrating the various classes and occupations of mankind.

The *Revelationes Sanctae Brigittae*, printed by BARTHOLOMAEUS GHOTAN, 1492 (S. 3502, H. 3204), is a far more important work for its full-page woodcuts, designed and cut with considerable force, and interesting also for its pictorial initials.

The *Lübeck Bible*, in Low Saxon, printed by STEFFEN ARNDES in 1494 (S. 3467, H. 3143),[2] was probably less epoch-making than the *Cologne Bible* in its influence on other designers, but it certainly stands higher for the individual genius of its chief illustrator. Herein lies its real virtue, for as a book it cannot compare in beauty with the best works issued by the Zainers at Augsburg and Ulm. Most of the illustrations are oblong, covering the two columns of the text. There is a large square cut of *St. Jerome* at the beginning and a smaller one of the same saint repeated in various other places; a *Roundel of the Creation* at the beginning of Genesis; four cuts of the *Evangelists*, and one of an *Apostle handing a messenger a letter*, used at various places throughout the Epistles, these five already issued in a *Plenarium* printed by Arndes in the previous year (S. 4985, H. 6753).

Most of the large oblong cuts are in the earlier portion of the Bible, and of these the better part are at the beginning. There are certainly two designers, as Romdahl first contended: the better and more individual hand (Master A)

---

[1] Cf. p. 569.

[2] A. L. Romdahl, Zeitschrift für Bücherfreunde, 1905–06, p. 391; Hans Wahl, *Die 92 Holzschnitte der Lübecker Bibel*, Weimar 1917; M. J. Friedländer, *Die Holzschnitte der Lübecker Bibel zu den 5 Büchern Mose*, Berlin 1918; M. J. Friedländer, *Die Lübecker Bibel*, Munich 1923.

shows characteristic circular strokes and shading, a great command of
human expression and of the rendering of solid form, and the use of types
both of figure and architecture which seem to betoken knowledge of Italy
(see fig. 170); the second designer (Master B) has a more angular method,
with harder outline and straighter shading. General characteristics of
design and treatment show that he was inspired by the Master A, though
he was far more limited in power, and more Gothic in style.

Practically all the illustrations to the Pentateuch (with the possible
exception of Genesis iii., Leviticus x. and Numbers xiii., and the few cuts

Fig. 170. Jacob's Ladder, from the *Lübeck Bible*, 1494.

of other forms than oblong are designed by Master A; from the First Book
of Kings (our 1st Samuel) onwards nearly all are by the Master B, with two
exceptions from the Pentateuch which are repeated as different subjects.
Sometimes the second designer's work is powerful and spirited in design
(e.g. the *Death of Absalom*, 2nd Book of Kings, i.e. 2nd Samuel xviii.), but it
has none of the subtle qualities of the chief designer. I refer to two designers,
as I hardly think the distinction could be caused by the difference in
merit of two cutters: it is a definite difference in the character of the
drawings cut.

In general style of figure and landscape composition both derive from
the Netherlands, even if they are not by Netherlandish designers, and the

peculiar touch of the chief illustrator has much in common with the early
work of Jacob Cornelisz and Lucas van Leyden.

Fig. 171. The Burgomaster, from the
Lübeck *Dance of Death*, 1489.

This comparison was rightly suggested by Dr. Max Friedländer in his
edition of the Lübeck *Dance of Death*
(*Des Dodes Dantz*), issued by an unknown
printer in 1489 (S. 5375),[1] where cuts of
Death and members of the various classes
of mankind are certainly designed by the
same hand. The book is very rare, the
first edition being only known at Nuremberg and Linköping (Sweden), the second
Lübeck edition of 1496 (S. 5376) at
Wolfenbüttel, and xvi-century editions at
Oxford (Lübeck 1520) and Copenhagen
(in Danish, Copenhagen 1536). The text
is based on the inscriptions attached to a
series of wall-paintings of the subject in
the Marienkirche at Lübeck.

The earlier Lübeck editions bear the
colophon mark of *Three Poppies on a Shield*,
and books with this mark are generally
assigned to 'the Poppy Printer', who has
been generally identified with Matthaeus Brandis. But recent researches
by Swedish authorities tend to regard such books as by several printers
(e.g. Matthaeus Brandis, Johann Snel, and Steffen Arndes) issued under
the literary and commercial direction of HANS VAN GHETELEN. The relations of Lübeck printers with Denmark and Sweden render the study
of their publication by students of Scandinavian bibliography of great
importance.

Occasional impressions from blocks of the *Dodes Dantz* occur in other
books, e.g. *Death with a Scythe* in the *Navolghinge Jesu Christi* (*Imitatio
Christi*), Lübeck ('The Poppy Printer') 1489 (S. 5349),[2] the *Pope*, *Cardinal*
and *Bishop* in the *Speygel der Leyen*, Lübeck ('The Poppy Printer') 1496
(S. 5284), and the *Nun* in the anonymously printed *S. Birgitten Openbaringe*,
Lübeck 1496 (S. 3501, H. 3206).

[1] M. J. Friedländer, Graphische Gesellschaft, xii., Berlin 1910 (facsimile of the Nuremberg
copy).

[2] In very good impression in British Museum Library copy, before the breaks in the border
seen in the 1st ed. of *Dodes Dantz*.

Considering that the style of the chief designer of the *Lübeck Bible* (1494) is fully developed in the *Dance of Death* of 1489, I cannot agree with Schreiber's suggestion that the cuts in Ghotan's *Revelationes S. Brigittae* of 1492 (S.3502), with their much less mobile touch, are by the same hand. Schreiber also attributes to the same master the cuts in the *Life of St. Jerome*, Lübeck (Ghotan) 1484 (S.4229, H.6723), the *Heiligenleben*, issued by an anonymous printer, Lübeck 1487 (S.4322, H.9989), and the *Upsala Breviary*, Stockholm (Johannes Fabri) 1496 (S.3627).

Confusion as to other attributions has been caused by regarding the whole series as by one designer, and Romdahl was on the right track in estimating the relationship of other Lübeck cuts (apart from the *Dodes Dantz*) as nearer to the Master B rather than to the Master A. And if Goldschmidt's suggestion that the Lübeck painter BERNT NOTKE may be the designer is correct,[1] he is more probably the designer B than the other remarkable but somewhat alien personality who disappears from Lübeck after 1494 (and may perhaps have died in the course of the work, as its completion by another would suggest). The nearest of the related cuts appear to me to be the illustrations added in the second edition of Steffen Arndes' *Heiligenleben*, 1492 (S.4324, H.9991), but several other works, e.g. Ghotan's *Revelationes Sanctae Brigittae*, 1492, already mentioned, might be noted as possibly from the same workshop.

Comparison was first made by Dr. Kristeller between the *Lübeck Bible* and the *Terence*, printed by Trechsel at Lyon in 1493, and Friedländer suggested identity of authorship. There is undoubtedly kinship in general style between the better cuts of the *Lübeck Bible* and these *Terence* illustrations, though the latter are cut with all the characteristic precision of certain French woodcutters. The kinship might come from common education in some German atelier, for Trechsel's designer might have gone with Trechsel himself from Mainz to Lyon. Something peculiar to both the Lübeck Master and Trechsel's designer might have found inspiration in the lively style of the Utrecht painter who designed and printed Breydenbach's *Peregrinationes* at Mainz in 1486.

ZINNA—LEIPZIG—WÜRZBURG

Turning southwards from Lübeck in our survey, I would mention a curious book of about 1494, the only work printed at the Cistercian Convent of Zinna, i.e. Hermann Nitzschewitz, *Novum beatae Mariae Psalterium*

---

[1] A. Goldschmidt, Zeitschrift für bildende Kunst, 1901, pp. 33, 55.

(H. 11891, S. 4859). Nitzschewitz, who was chaplain to the Emperor, had appealed to Frederick III for funds for the publication, and these were granted by his son and successor Maximilian I in 1494. Thus the two full-page blocks on the first and second pages show the *Virgin and Child supported by the two Emperors, and adored by four Ecclesiastics* and the *Two Emperors adoring the Virgin and Child*, while the series of cuts illustrating the life of the Virgin and of Christ are flanked by border-pieces which again represent the two Emperors in adoration. This latter part of the book, with its subject cuts at the head and borders at the outer sides and foot of each page, shows a richness of woodcut illustration comparable with French *Horae*, though far below the best of these in quality. The most attractive decorative feature in the book is the large floral border and initial letter occurring at signatures a ii and a v. It is probable that the convent obtained the collaboration of some Leipzig printer such as CONRAD KACHELOFEN.

We then pass Leipzig itself,[1] which is only notable in xv-century book-illustration for Kachelofen's block-book calendars,[2] and Böttiger's *Auslegung der Messe* of 1495 with its dotted prints,[3] and turning aside to note the Missals and Breviaries of Würzburg and Eichstätt printed by GEORG and MICHAEL REYSER,[4] though these are chiefly remarkable for the occurrence of line-engraving[5] instead of the usual woodcut in illustration, we may come without further delay to our last important centre of German book-illustration, i.e. Nuremberg.

NUREMBERG

Woodcut work produced at Nuremberg and the not far distant towns of Nördlingen and Regensburg has already been noted in the block-books issued by Hans Spörer, Friedrich Walther and Hans Hurning, Johannes Eysenhut and the Master Lienhart, between about 1470 and 1473. And we have already described one of the earliest illustrated Nuremberg books, i.e. Sensenschmidt's *German Bible*, n.d., about 1476 (S. 3457, H. 3132), in relation to the *Bibles* of Günther Zainer and Pflanzmann of Augsburg.[6]

Reference has also been made to a cut in Maphaeus Vegius, *Philalethes*, printed by JOHANN MÜLLER about 1474, and to a supposed *Portrait of Marco Polo* in an edition of his *Travels* printed by FRIEDRICH CREUSSNER,

[1] See A. Schramm, *Bilderschmuck der Frühdrucke*, xiii., Die Drucker in Leipzig und Erfurt, 1930.   [2] See p. 262.   [3] See p. 195.
[4] See A. Schramm, *Bilderschmuck der Frühdrucke*, xvi. Leipzig 1933.
[5] See M. Lehrs, *Geschichte und Kritischer Katalog*, vi. pp. 124 and 155.
[6] See p. 290. For notes on single cuts assigned to Nuremberg see W. Cohn, *Untersuchungen zur Geschichte des deutschen Einblattholzschnitts*. Strassburg 1934, p. 37.

Nuremberg 1477 (S. 5002, H. 13245), in describing copies issued by Knoblochtzer of Strassburg.[1] And of Creussner's early books we may mention two more, Tuberinus, *De Puero Simone*, n.d., about 1476 (S. 5260, H. 15654), for its large and crude cut of the notorious *Ritual Murder of St. Simon of Trent* (S. 1967),[2] which took place in the year 1475, and the *Auslegung des Amts der Heiligen Messe*, n.d., about 1482 (S. 4643, H. 2143), for its charmingly naïve rendering of the *Visitation*, with its round and angular conventions for trees.

Three other books printed by Johann Müller may be mentioned for their initials of strapwork on a black ground based on those used by Sweynheym and Pannartz at Rome (e.g. in the *Suetonius* of 1470), i.e. Basilius, *Opusculum ad Juvenes*, n.d., about 1474 (H. 2683), Marcus Manilius, *Astronomica*, n.d. (H. 10703), and J. Müller, *Tractatus contra Cremonensia*, n.d., about 1475 (H. 13805, S. 4374). It appears probable that the German initials may be casts from the Italian blocks.[3]

Fig. 172. The Visitation, from *Auslegung des Amts*, Nuremberg, about 1482.

Of the other earlier Nuremberg printers, HANS FOLZ, a barber-surgeon, holds a somewhat special place for the variety of popular poems he wrote

---

[1] See pp. 336 and 337.

[2] The cut, which occurs as a separate print in Paris (Bouchot 125), appears in the Munich and Bamberg copies of the book.   [3] See p. 398.

and issued in the few years succeeding 1479, each illustrated with one crude cut. But books of this character, which are of great rarity outside German libraries, are of far less interest for their woodcuts than for their illustration of social history.

And a *Salzburg Missal* printed by GEORG STUCHS in 1492 (S. 4755, H., C. 11420) deserves mention for a powerful frontispiece, a full-page *Portrait of Bishop Friedrich von Schaumburg, standing behind his Coat-of-arms*.[1]

By far the most important of Nuremberg books are those issued by ANTON KOBERGER,[2] the most famous of the printers of his day. He was a man who had made himself a great position in Nuremberg; who was reputed even in 1470 (i.e. the year before his first book was issued) to have had a hundred craftsmen and twenty-four presses at work, and who more than any of his contemporaries developed extensive international relations in printing and book-selling. The records of his work and establishment which are preserved throw much valuable light on the methods of publication at the period.

The illustrations to an edition of Nicolaus de Lyra, *Postilla super Bibliam*, of 1481 (S. 4843, H. 10369), recut in smaller scale in his *Latin Bible* of 1485 (S. 3472, H. 3166), are chiefly diagrams and plans of little artistic interest. They certainly served as models for the *Latin Bibles* (*cum postillis N. de Lyra*), Venice, 1489 and 1495. And his *German Bible* of 1483 merely reprinted the blocks of the great *Cologne Bible* of about 1478–79.

His first illustrated book of individual interest was Jacobus de Voragine, *Passional* (*Leben der Heiligen*), 1488 (S. 4313, H. 9981), containing many cuts very closely resembling the style of the illustrations in Lirer's *Chronica* and Terence, *Eunuchus*, printed at Ulm in 1486.

It is difficult to believe that such a print as *St. Helena finding the Cross* (f. xxv) is not by the author of Lirer's illustrations, and the *Salome with the Head of John the Baptist* (f. xlviii; fig. 173) not the work of the Terence Master; in fact they may all be by the same designer.

The lively style that originated in this Ulm designer must have been an important factor in the development of Dürer's genius, if the early illustrations which have recently been attributed to the great painter and engraver

[1] Reproduced, Rosenthal, Catalogue 80 (1924), No. 190. The Rosenthal copy is now in the collection of Mr. Campbell Dodgson.

[2] O. von Hase, *Die Koberger, Buchhändler Familie zu Nürnberg. Eine Darstellung des deutschen Buchhandels*, Leipzig 1869; *Die Koberger, ein Darstellung des buchhändlerischen Geschäftsbetriebes in der Zeit des Überganges vom Mitlelalter zur Neuzeit*, Leipzig (2e Auflage) 1885; Albert Schramm, *Bilderschmuck der Frühdrucke*, xvii. *Die Drucker in Nürnberg*. (1) *Anton Koberger*. Leipzig 1934.

are actually his design. To these we shall return after some survey of the work of Dürer's master, Wolgemut, and that of Wolgemut's stepson, Wilhelm Pleydenwurff.

MICHEL WOLGEMUT (1434–1519)[1] is the earliest painter, whose work is recognised in this capacity, known also as a designer of book-illustrations, for Erhard Reuwich is only a name to us outside the cuts he designed for Breydenbach's *Peregrinationes* (1486). As a painter Wolgemut was the head

Fig. 173. Salome with the Head of St. John the Baptist, from the *Passional*, Nuremberg 1488.

of a flourishing workshop, but the quality of the pictures that issued from this source is so variable that no certain estimate has been formed of his individual powers.

The only direct evidence of his participation in woodcut design is contained in the colophon of Schedel's *Nuremberg Chronicle*, 1493, where both he and WILHELM PLEYDENWURFF are described as painters and the authors of the illustrations, and in the contracts for the illustrations of the work.[2] Of Wilhelm Pleydenwurff little is known; he was the son of a painter Hans Pleydenwurff, whose widow Wolgemut married in 1473; the date of his birth is unknown; the only documentary evidence is limited to the

[1] For the most valuable notices on Wolgemut as designer of woodcuts see: Valerian von Loga, *Beiträge zum Holzschnittwerk M. W.'s.* Pr. Jahrbuch, xvi., 1895, 224; C. Ephrussi, *Étude sur la Chronique de Nuremberg de H. Schedel*, Paris 1894; C. Dodgson, *Some Rare Woodcuts by W.*, Burlington Magazine, iv., 1904, 245; Franz J. Stadler, *M. W. und der Nürnberger Holzschnitt im letzten Drittel des XV Jahrhunderts*, Strassburg 1913.

[2] A. Gümbel, *Die Verträge über die Illustrierung und den Druck der Schedelschen Weltchronik*, xxv. (1902), 430.

years 1490–95, and he died before the 6th February 1495. There is no direct evidence that he collaborated with Wolgemut in the *Schatzbehalter*, though it is often assumed that he did.

Attempts have been made to distinguish the hands of Wolgemut and Pleydenwurff in the *Chronicle*, but the difficulty of unravelling Wolgemut's style as a painter from that of his workshop, the entire lack of knowledge of Pleydenwurff's painting, and the evident variety of cutters who took part in the work and no doubt modified to varying degrees the designers' styles, would vitiate any dogmatic conclusions. The large W which appears on banners in half a dozen of the *Schatzbehalter* cuts has sometimes been interpreted as Wolgemut's signature, but letters A and G similarly occur on another cut, so that the explanation is hardly probable, and, in consequence, a dangerous basis for a distinction.

The *Schatzbehalter* by Father Stefan Fridolin, issued by Koberger on the 18th November 1491 (S. 52021, H. 14507), is a folio printed in double column with ninety-six full-page illustrations from ninety-one blocks. The book according to its second title is a 'Treasury of the true Riches of Salvation', and apart from a few allegories, the cuts are entirely subjects from the Bible.

A certain proportion of the subjects are suggested by earlier prints, but there is a considerable residue of original invention, showing at the lowest estimate the virtues of lively humour and vivid expression, while an occasional subject, such as the *Annunciation*, contains elements of real beauty. The design is intensely Gothic in its angular conventions, enhanced by the curled beards and hair which are so characteristic of the Wolgemut cuts. Here and there a design lacks the characteristic verve, but on the whole the quality of both design and cutting is fairly regular throughout.

One of the subjects (No. 66, the *Virtues of Christ and The Wickedness of his Enemies symbolised by divers birds and beasts*) occurs in a separate print at Munich, with a border containing the arms of Nuremberg and the signature *Wolfgang* (S. 1216, described wrongly as a *Temptation of St. Anthony*), and it seems possible that a WOLFGANG HAMER, to whose prints we shall refer later, might have been one of Wolgemut's cutters.

A sketch-book containing over a hundred drawings, probably by Wolgemut, several being original studies for the *Schatzbehalter's* subjects, once in the possession of Rosenthal, Munich (Catalogue 90 of 1892, No. 4), was later in the collection of Professor V. Goldschmidt at Heidelberg. Von Loga noted that one of the drawings was very near a cut

Fig. 174. The Finding of Moses, from the *Schatzbehalter*, Nuremberg 1491.

of *St. Jerome* signed *Wolfgang* (S. 1530, Munich), which is further support
to the suggestion made above.

Hartmann Schedel's *Weltchronik* (commonly called the *Nuremberg Chronicle*), issued in July 1493 in the Latin edition (*Liber cronicarum ab inicio mundi*,

Fig. 175. Part of the View of Salzburg, from Schedel, *Weltchronik*, Nuremberg 1493.

S. 5203, H. 14508), and in December of the same year in a German translation by Georg Alt (*Buch der Chroniken*, S. 5205, H. 14510),[1] is a much larger
folio than the *Schatzbehalter*, and contains a far greater number of illustra-

---

[1] Later editions with new blocks copied from Koberger's were issued at Augsburg by J.
Schoensperger, in German, 1496 (S. 5206, H. 14511), in Latin, 1497 (S. 5204, H. 14509).
On the question of binding see E. P. Goldschmidt, *Gothic and Renaissance Bookbindings*, London
1928, vol. i. p. 165, No. 38.

tions. From an analysis made by Sir Sydney Cockerell,[1] it appears that the number of separate blocks (with certain unimportant exceptions) is 645; and that with repeats, the total number of illustrations comes to 1809. The contract for the illustrations to be supplied by Wolgemut and Pleydenwurff was made in December 1491, but references in the contract to blocks already cut, and the date 1490 in Wolgemut's original drawing for the title-cut in the British Museum, prove that the work was in hand some time earlier.

The cuts include numerous scriptural and other subjects, genealogical trees and portraits, maps and many views of towns.[2] There is little historical value in the portraits, and only a beginning of faithful topography in the views (though these are by far the most valuable part of the illustration). Kristeller has aptly said that the illustrations were more often finger-posts to the ordinary reader wishing to find his place in a voluminous text, than any definite attempt at actual illustration. Blocks of the greatest variety of subject and shape scattered almost haphazard, as it seems, over the large areas of type (views often extending over a complete opening), entirely stultified any attempt at making a harmonious page. Moreover, there are far fewer subjects of attractive individual invention in the *Chronicle* than in the *Schatzbehalter*, and far greater diversity of quality in the cutting. The extensive character of the project carried through within so short an interval after the *Schatzbehalter* was enough to damp the invention of far greater talents. The *Roundel with Angels* (f. 2) and the *Roundel with the Creation of the Birds* (f. 4, verso) are graceful examples among many instances of clumsy or awkward design.

We have referred to the sketch-book which contains designs of the *Schatzbehalter*, but by far the most important of Wolgemut's original drawings is his design for the frontispiece of the *Chronicle*, dated 1490, in the British Museum.[3] The pen-drawing is in a style very near in linear conventions to the woodcut; but it differs considerably in details (of shading, etc.), and is in the same direction as the print. It is natural to infer that a transfer drawing on the surface of the block must have intervened, and the question arises whether the painter himself made this final drawing for the cutter to follow in facsimile, or whether another assistant, or the cutter himself, made the drawing on the block from this original of Wolgemut.

[1] S. C. Cockerell, *Some German Woodcuts of the XV Century*, London (Kelmscott Press) 1897.
[2] V. von Loga, *Die Städteansichten in H. Schedel's 'Weltchronik'*, Pr. Jahrbuch, ix., 1888, 93, 184.
[3] See Sidney Colvin, Pr. Jahrbuch, vii., 1886, 98.

That Wolgemut having made a drawing in this detail should make another on the block seems unlikely, and the inferiority of the cut to the drawing in many painter-like characteristics rather supports this theory. But it would be dangerous to dogmatise, or to infer a general practice from this one case. In fact, as it seems to be the only important study for the *Chronicle* existing, it is more likely that as a general rule the painter made his own finished drawing on the block.

In discussing the general question of designers and cutters[1] we quoted at length from an account of the costs of another large project of book-illustration which was never published (for Peter Danhauser, *Archetypus Trimphantis Romae*), covering the years 1493–97. The first agreement in this relation occurred in July 1493, only a few days from the publication of the first edition of the *Chronicle*. Sebald Schreyer was chiefly responsible for this work, as for the *Chronicle*, so that, although the painters are not mentioned by name, it seems almost certain that they were Wolgemut and Pleydenwurff. Pleydenwurff, however, can have taken little part, as he died in January 1494. It seems almost certain that a series of allegorical cuts only known in comparatively modern impressions (e.g. at Berlin and Vienna)[2] is a small remnant of the *Archetypus*. Besides miscellaneous allegories, it includes copies after the Ferrarese 'Tarocchi' engravings, and after the *Triumphs of Petrarch* in the 1490 Venetian edition of Pietro de Plasiis Veronese (H. 12771).[3]

The actual woodcutter of the *Archetypus* blocks, SEBALD GALLENSDORFER, is mentioned, so that it is probable that he worked on the earlier books as well. It is interesting to note that he receives much larger fees than the painters. This must imply that the work of cutting so many blocks engrossed the majority of his time, while the painters undertook their designs for book-illustration very much as side-issues from their larger works.

It has sometimes been categorically stated that Wolgemut was a wood-cutter as well as a painter,[4] and considerable confusion has been caused by the vague statements of C. G. von Murr in his articles on *Formschneider-kunst* and *Versuch einer Nürnbergischen Kunstgeschichte* in his *Journal zur Kunstgeschichte* (Nuremberg 1766), and by the haphazard way in which he placed painters in his lists of *Formschneider*, without any documentary basis.

---

[1] See p. 90.   [2] Described by von Loga, Pr. Jahrbuch, xvi., 224.

[3] Which are in their turn free renderings of the Florentine Broad Manner engravings (A. M. Hind, *Early Italian Engravings in the British Museum*, B. ii. 1-6).

[4] E.g. W. von Seidlitz, in the article on Wolgemut in the *Deutsche Allgemeine Biographie*, lv. (1910), p. 118.

Fig. 176. Frontispiece to Schedel, *Weltchronik*, Nuremberg 1493.

The best available reference for Nuremberg documents on artists is Albert
Gümbel, in the *Repertorium für Kunstwissenschaft*, xxviii., xxix. and xxx.
(1905–07), and there no painter is found noted in contemporary records as
Formschneider as well. Confusion of thought goes back through statements
of Heinecken (*Nachrichten*, II Theil, 1769, p. 100), to Sandrart (*Teutsche
Akademie*, 1676, p. 216, II Theil, III Buch) and Karel van Mander (*Het
Schilderboeck*, 1604, part i. f. 204 b); but the original statement of Karel
van Mander that *meest alle Plaet-snyders oock Schilders waren*, certainly
refers to line-engravers, though two of the masters he cited designed woodcuts. Bartsch in his introduction to the work of Dürer (*Peintre Graveur*,
vol. vii.) strongly contests the statements that Dürer and painters generally
were also cutters. Since his day the battle has raged on either side of the
controversy, and the old error is by no means extinct. For the whole question
see E. Flechsig, *Dürer*, 1928, to whom I owe various references, and to my
Chapter III., pp. 90–92.

Apart from the works already mentioned, there is only a comparatively
small number of other woodcuts attributed to Wolgemut. The most attractive of these is undoubtedly the *Virgin as Queen of Heaven* (S. 5152 a),
known in two states, the first, dated 1492, on a broadside printed in
Koberger's types (Graphische Sammlung, Munich), the second in which the
cut is surrounded by a scroll border with two angels (Munich Library, in a
copy of the *Nuremberg Chronicle*, which belonged to Schedel himself). It
has much the same gracious character as the *Annunciation* in the *Schatzbehalter*.

The earliest cut attributed with any certainty is the frontispiece to
the *Reformation der Stadt Nürnberg*, printed by Koberger, 1484, S. 5051,
H. 13716 (the *Arms of the Empire and Nuremberg flanked by SS. Sebald
and Lawrence*), and one of the latest, the *St. Sebald* which occurs on a
broadside, Conrad Celtis, *Sapphic Ode to St. Sebald*, printed by Bergmann
von Olpe at Basle, about 1494–95 (S. 1673, H. 4844). Another cut used
outside Nuremberg was done for the 1493 edition of the *Würzburg Missal*
(S. 4707, H. 11312), replacing a copper engraving by A.G. in earlier
editions, appearing again in the edition of 1495 (S. 4708, H. 11313)
but replaced by another woodcut in 1497.

Kristeller mentions the cut in Isocrates, *Praecepta*, printed by Creussner,
n.d. (a *Knight beheading a Lady*), as possibly early work of Wolgemut. But
the type used seems to place the book nearer 1497, and the work, though
resembling Wolgemut in landscape and general style, seems from a certain
refinement to be rather that of a follower. And by 1489 Wolgemut was

certainly doing better work than the *Deathbed Scene* in *Versehung von Leib Seele Ehre und Gut*, printed in that year by Peter Wagner (S. 5423, H. 16019).

ALBRECHT DÜRER (1471–1528)[1] found in woodcut the most perfect medium for the expression of his genius, and is perhaps the greatest figure in the whole history of the art. But the greater part of his production falls within the XVI century, so that his work cannot be treated adequately within the limits of our study, and an estimate of his achievement is more appropriately left to a history dealing with the later period.

The early work, of which we shall give a short survey, formed the climax of the Gothic spirit, yielding, as the century waned, to the Renaissance influences which moulded the development of his later years.

Dürer entered Wolgemut's studio on the 1st December 1486, and his apprenticeship was over on the same day in 1489. Wolgemut's serious participation in designing book-illustration only began with the *Schatzbehalter*, which was issued nearly two years after Dürer had left his studio, while the *Weltchronik* takes us nearly two years later still. So that the assumption, often made, that he might have helped Wolgemut in preparing the designs of one or other of these works is not very convincing; and it is unlikely that block-cutting would have formed any part of his education. On the other hand, he may have followed his master in these early years in making occasional designs for book-illustration, if the cuts attributed to him by Dr. Kurth, which nearly all belong to the period of his apprenticeship, are actually his work, e.g. illustrations in:

Nicolaus von der Flühe, *Brüder Claus*, Nuremberg (Marx Ayrer) 1488 (S. 4839, II. 5380, K. 1-5; later edition, n.d., printed by Peter Wagner).

---

[1] H. W. Singer, *Dürer Bibliographie*, Strassburg 1903; J. Heller, Bamberg 1827; M. Thausing, *Leben*, Leipzig 1876 and 1884 (English ed., 1882); William Martin Conway (Lord Conway of Allington), *Literary Remains of Albrecht Dürer*, Cambridge 1889; D. Burckhardt, *Aufenthalt in Basel*, Munich 1892; H. Woelfflin, Munich 1905; W. Weisbach, *Der junge Dürer*, Leipzig 1906; the Dürer Society, London 1898–1911; C. Dodgson, *Catalogue of Early German and Flemish Woodcuts in the British Museum*, vol. i., 1903; M. J. Friedländer, *Albrecht Dürer: der Kupferstecher und Holzschnittzeichner*, Berlin 1919; Erich Roemer, *Dürers ledige Wanderjahre*, Pr. Jahrbuch, xlvii., 1926, 118; xlviii., 1927, 77, 156; Willi Kurth, *The Complete Woodcut Work of Albrecht Dürer*, London 1927; E. Flechsig, Berlin 1928; Hans Tietze and E. Tietze-Conrat, *Der junge Dürer, Verzeichnis der Werke bis zur venezianischen Reise 1505*, Augsburg 1928; F. Winkler, *Dürer* (Klassiker der Kunst), Stuttgart 1928; F. Stadler, *Dürers Apocalypse und ihr Umkreis*, Munich 1929; Joseph Meder, *Dürer-Katalog*, Vienna 1932 (the most detailed catalogue of Dürer's prints). For special bibliography on work done at Basle see p. 328.

Philipp Frankfurter, *Die Geschichte des Pfarrers von Kalenberg*, Nuremberg (Peter Wagner), about 1490 (S. 4410, K. 6-12).

Bertholdus, *Horologium Devotionis*, Nuremberg (Creussner, 1489) (S. 3441, H. 8934, K. 13, 14).

Ein allerheilsamste Warnung vor der falschen Lieb dieser Welt, Nuremberg (Wagner), before 1490 (S. 5455, H. 16150, K. 15-17).

Oratio Cassandre Venete, Nuremberg (Wagner), about 1489 (S. 3675, H. 4553, K. 18).

Wie der Würffel auff ist kumen, Nuremberg (M. Ayrer), 1489 (S. 5490, K. 19).

Johannes Gerson, *Opera*, Nuremberg (G. Stuchs), 1489 (S. 4103, H. 7623, K. 20; see fig. 177).[1]

Alexander Gallus, *Prima Pars Doctrinalis*, Nuremberg (Creussner) 1491 (S. 3079, H. 682, K. 21).

Dürer left Nuremberg on his *Wanderjahre* soon after Easter 1490, returning after Whitsun in 1494. He married Agnes Frey in July of the latter year, and Flechsig very reasonably suggests that his visit to Italy took place in the same autumn (i.e. after the completion of his *Wanderjahre*), and that both this Italian visit and the second of 1505 were in part due to a desire to avoid the plague by which Nuremberg was severely ravaged in those years. The actual course of Dürer's wanderings between 1490 and 1494 has been much debated, for no word from the master himself is preserved to enlighten us, apart from the period of departure and return. The one definite clue is the block of *St. Jerome* designed by Dürer for a Basle book of 1492, which we have already discussed in the section on book-illustration at Basle. We have also described other cuts done at Basle, Freiburg im Breisgau, and Strassburg, attributed to Dürer. The arguments in favour of Dürer's authorship on the side of style are very strong. The weak points are the entire lack of reference in Dürer's writings to so important a series of cuts as those of the *Narrenschiff*, and the fact that a young painter on his *Wanderjahre* could hardly be expected to undertake so extensive a commission as this implied. But in spite of these *a priori* objections, no more plausible solution has yet been found for the authorship of the Basle series. And granting that the *Terence* subjects are by Dürer, it would be difficult not to accept so kindred a design as the woodcut of *Gerson as Pilgrim* (fig. 177), with its background of town and lake in so similar a rhythm to that of *Terence writing* (fig. 145). Both the Terence and many of the earlier

[1] Cf. p. 338.

Nuremberg cuts attributed show how direct is the descent in style from the Ulm designer of Lirer's *Chronica* and Terence, *Eunuchus*, a relation which we have also noted in Koberger's *Passional* cuts of 1488. Perhaps this very family likeness in other Nuremberg cuts should induce some further hesitation in accepting all the work noted above as by Dürer.

The *St. Jerome* is somewhat isolated in a certain formal Gothic character of design, in the midst of other cuts attributed, both before and after its date of 1492. But this difference may depend to some extent on the cutter in the same way as the woodcut frontispiece to the *Nuremberg Chronicle* is so much stiffer than Wolgemut's own original drawing.

There is something peculiarly attractive about these presumed beginnings of Dürer's work. But if it were not for later developments there would be little in it to disclose any greater

Fig. 177. Albrecht Dürer (?). Title-cut to Joannes Gerson, *Opera*, Nuremberg 1489.

personality than the anonymous Master of the Amsterdam Cabinet, or even the designer of the Ulm Terence. For the world at large it would matter little if his woodcuts remained unrecognised before those signed with his well-known monogram and produced after the return from his first visit to Italy, which undoubtedly inspired him to the nobility of style that characterised all his work thereafter. His Gothic traditions were never wholly shed, but they were gradually mellowed by the influence of the great Venetian masters of composition.

In subjects like the so-called *Hercules* of about 1496 (B. 127, K. 99)[1] the

[1] The original block of B. 127 is in the British Museum, which also possesses the block of

dependence on Italian modes, especially on Mantegna, is evident, while in others such as many of the *Apocalypse* series, the Gothic character persists in company with an enhanced sense of dignity in both form and composition, which undoubtedly derived from Italian inspiration.

The complete series of fifteen large cuts of the *Apocalypse* was published with text in Koberger's type in both German and Latin editions in 1498; so that Dürer had probably begun their design considerably earlier. The titles, *Die heimlich offenbarūg iohn̄is* and *Apocalipsis cū Figuris* respectively, are cut in ornamental Gothic letters on separate blocks, and in the second Latin edition of 1511 a cut of *St. John with the Virgin and Child* (B. 60) is added beneath the title. There is only one German edition.

The text occurs on the reverse of the woodcuts, each cut on the right-hand page being faced by text on the left.[1] There are also proofs without text, generally with the 'Reichsapfel' water-mark (the imperial orb, Hausmann 24, Meder 53), the same water-mark which is most frequently found on other proofs of the large woodcuts done between about 1495 and 1500. These (unless they show indication of flaws in the blocks, not seen in the 1498 edition, but corresponding to the 1511 edition) may be regarded as

B. 117 (*Martyrdom of the Ten Thousand Christians*). Two other large original blocks are in the Metropolitan Museum, New York, i.e. B. 2 (*Samson and the Lion*) and B. 120 (*The Martyrdom of St. Catherine*). The British Museum also possesses thirty-five of the original blocks of Dürer's *Small Woodcut Passion*, i.e. all but the title-cut, and *Christ taking leave of his Mother* (B. 16 and B. 21).

[1] The following are the subjects, and a few of the distinguishing marks in text between the 1498 (I) and 1511 (II) Latin editions (first given fully by Cornill d'Orville, Naumann's *Archiv für die zeichnenden Künste*, Leipzig, ix., 1863, p. 204; cf. Meder, 163-78):

(1) Title B. 60. I, Title only; II, title cut added.
(2) The Martyrdom of St. John. B. 61. Line 1 ends: I, *beati 10*; II, *beati*.
(3) The Seven Golden Candlesticks. B. 62. Line 2 ends: I, *pphetem*; II, *pphetem do*.
(4) The Four and Twenty Elders. B. 63. Line 15 ends: I, *se*; II, *sedis*.
(5) The Riders on the Four Horses. B. 64. Line 28 ends: I, *inter*; II, *in*.
(6) Stars falling from Heaven. B. 65. Line 4 ends: I, *quatuor*; II, *quattu*.
(7) Angels restraining the Winds. B. 66. Line 24 ends: I, *septimi*; II, *septi*.
(8) The Seven Angels with Trumpets. B. 68. Line 31 ends: I, *cū*; II, *cum*.
(9) The Four Destroying Angels. B. 69. Line 12 ends: I, *fro*; II, *fron*.
(10) St. John swallowing the Book. B. 70. Line 5 ends: I, *magnu ≋*; II, *magnum*.
(11) The Dragon with Seven Heads. B. 71. Line 3 ends: I, *decē ≋*; II, *decē*.
(12) Michael and Angels fighting the Dragon. B. 72. Line 6 ends: I, *descē*; II, *descen*.
(13) The Beast with Lamb's Horns. B. 74. Line 8 ends: I, *magna ≋*; II, *magnam*.
(14) The Adoration of the Lamb. B. 67. Line 13 ends: I, *gē*; II, *gen*.
(15) The Whore of Babylon. B. 73. I, dated 1498; II, dated 1511.
(16) The Angel with the Key of the Pit. B. 75. Blank on reverse.

Fig. 178. Albrecht Dürer. The Riders on the Four Horses, from the *Apocalypse*.

before the edition of 1498. If there are intermediate impressions without the text, these would more probably be on paper with the 'bull's head' water-mark.

The *Great Passion* series of twelve woodcuts corresponding in size with the *Apocalypse* (i.e. about 15 × 11 inches) was first published complete with Latin text in 1511, but seven of the subjects were certainly done about 1497–1500, for their style is of this period, and proofs without text are on the 'Reichsapfel' paper which was most generally used at this time. These early subjects are the *Agony in the Garden* (B. 6), the *Scourging of Christ* (B. 8), *Christ shown to the People* (B. 9), *Christ bearing the Cross* (B. 10), the *Crucifixion* (B. 11), the *Lamentation* (B. 13) and the *Entombment* (B. 12). The later subjects are dated 1510, i.e. *The Last Supper* (B. 5), the *Betrayal of Christ* (B. 7), the *Descent to Hell* (B. 14) and the *Resurrection* (B. 15), while the title-cut, *Christ crowned with Thorns* (B. 4), was no doubt added about the same time for the edition of 1511. Impressions without the text are also known later than 1511, e.g. from the reprint without text of Jakob Koppmayer, Augsburg 1675 (with water-mark of the Augsburg arms, a fir-cone on a base).

Dürer issued the two series, the *Apocalypse* and the *Great Passion*, with the *Life of the Virgin* (whose production falls entirely in the XVI century), as a single book from his own printing-press in 1511. The double-column black-letter text of the *Apocalypse* (printed in the same form in the 1498 and the 1511 editions) makes a good balance to the cuts. On the other hand, the single-column Roman type text of the *Great Passion* and the *Life of the Virgin*, with its short-lined verses, is far less harmonious, presenting pages inadequate in weight to the powerful cuts they face.

In addition to the *Hercules* (B. 127, K. 99) already mentioned, the other large woodcuts of the early period, corresponding in form with the *Apocalypse* and the *Large Passion*, are the *Martyrdom of the Ten Thousand Christians* (B. 117, K. 98), the *Holy Family* (B. 102, K. 104), the *Knight and Man-at-Arms* (B. 131, K. 100), the *Men's Bath* (B. 128, K. 101; fig. 179), the *Martyrdom of St. Catherine* (B. 120, K. 102) and *Samson and the Lion* (B. 2, K. 103).

All these examples, in varying degrees, are stronger in cutting than three large and rare unsigned prints, the *Lamentation* (K. 87, British Museum and Berlin), the *Crucifixion* (K. 88, British Museum and Berlin) and the *Martyrdom of St. Sebastian* (K. 90, British Museum, etc.). The designs of the latter are certainly by Dürer, and the difference in quality is probably

Fig. 179. Albrecht Dürer. The Men's Bath.

explained by the poorer skill of a cutter, working perhaps away from the master's supervision.

The great strength of the *Apocalypse* woodcuts has inclined Friedländer[1] to the view which I have already combated in regard to Wolgemut, and would equally combat in the case of Dürer and other painters of the period who designed for woodcut, that he cut some of the blocks himself. The strength of the cut seems to me to depend entirely on the design, and on a craftsman skilful enough to cut a true facsimile. Granting a good design on the block, it is even more likely that a successful result would be achieved by the cutting of an experienced craftsman than if the painter should turn his own hand to the negative labours entailed.[2] Nor is the inference from Dürer's own words in his 'Bücher von menschlicher Proportion',[3] that the artist occasionally cut his own blocks, entirely indisputable, for his use of the words *Eiselein* and *versticht*, for the usual *Messer* and *schnitt*, would hardly fall from one accustomed to the craft of woodcutting, if indeed it does not, as Flechsig suggests, refer to sculpture in wood.

On the other hand, it is more than probable that difference of quality in the cutting of his designs depended partly on whether Dürer actually made the drawing on the surface of the block, or merely gave a design on paper for a woodcutter to transfer. In the latter eventuality, even a good cutter might have lost the subtle qualities of the original in transferring to the block; in the former case, a good craftsman would have no reason to blunt the artist's design. And in the best of Dürer's work it is fairly certain that

---

[1] *Der Holzschnitt*, Berlin 1921, pp. 56-57.

[2] Dürer has himself left a reference to his own drawing on a block in the Diary of his Netherlands journey (Antwerp, 3rd September 1520), *Item die zween herrn von Rogendorff haben mich geladen. Ich hab einmal mit ihren gessn und ich hab ihr wappen gross auf ein holz geriessen das mans schneiden mag* (J. Veth and S. Muller, *Dürers niederländische Reise*, Bd. I., *Die Urkunden*, Berlin and Utrecht 1918), a passage rendered by Conway (*Literary Remains*, p. 103): 'The two Lords of Rogendorf invited me. I dined with them once and drew their arms large on a wood-block for cutting'. The only known impression of this cut is in the German National Museum, Nuremberg.

[3] Nuremberg 1528, Bk. III., Sig. T ii; the British Museum MS. (slightly differing from the printed text) transcribed in K. Lange and F. Fuhse, *Dürers schriftliche Nachlass*, Halle 1893, p. 221, and translated in Conway, *Literary Remains*, p. 244. The MS. reads: *Daraus kummt, dass mancher etwas mit der Federn in eim Tag auf ein halben Bogen Papiers reisst oder mit sein. Eiselein etwas in ein klein Hölzlein versticht, dass würd künstlicher und besser dann eins Andern grosses Werk, daran derselb ein ganz Jahr mit höchstem Fleiss macht,* and is translated by Conway: 'For this reason a man may often draw something with his pen on a half-sheet of paper in one day or engrave it with his tool on a small block of wood, and it shall be fuller of art and better than another's great work whereon he hath spent a whole year's careful labour'.

he not only drew on the block, but supervised the cutting as well as the printing.

In addition to the large unsigned cuts of inferior cutting already mentioned, the other chief examples which come under the same category are the four unsigned blocks of the *Albertina Passion*, so called as the Albertina, Vienna, is the only collection which possesses impressions of all four. The subjects are *Christ crowned with Thorns* (K. 94), *The Scourging of Christ* (K. 95), *Christ bearing the Cross* (K. 96) and *Christ on the Cross* (K. 97). Somewhat similar in quality of line, and weaker than the signed and certainly authentic woodcuts, are the numerous illustrations to the *Revelationes S. Brigittae*, printed by Koberger, 1500 (H. 3205, K. 128-142), the two frontispieces to the *Opera Hrosvite* (edited by Conrad Celtis) (P. 277 a and b, K. 143-44), two of the twelve blocks in Conrad Celtis, *Quattuor libri Amorum* (H. 2089; P. 217 and B. 130; K. 145-146), the Celtis books printed respectively in 1501 and 1502 for the Sodalitas Celtica, at Nuremberg, and a series of small cuts used in two Nuremberg prayer-books of about 1503, one being a *Salus Animae* printed by H. HÖLZEL (K. 147-66).[1] But though some of the designs were done within the XV century the detailed discussion of their authorship must be left to the historian of the XVI century. Suffice it to say here that the designs of the two latter books are more certainly Dürer's than the St. Bridget illustrations; and that even in this case the greater distance from Dürer's more convincing draughtsmanship of the same period might have depended on the craftsman employed by the printer to cut the artist's design.

One other attractive little woodcut of the early period, which has only been recently recognised as by Dürer, is the *Head of a Man with Phrenological Notes* (K. 93) from Ludovicus de Prussia, *Trilogium Animae*, printed by Koberger in 1498 (H. 10315, at f. 77 a). As a portrait it bears very direct resemblance to Dürer's friend Willibald Pirkheimer.

I would add here note of a woodcut peculiarly interesting for its subject, and clearly influenced by Dürer's work, which appeared on the title-page of Jacobus Issickemer, *Büchlein der Zuflucht der Maria*, printed at Nuremberg by Caspar Hochfeder, 1497 (S. 4271, H. 9319; fig. 180). It represents an Altar hung with offerings to the Virgin of Alt-Oetting, in the shape of

---

[1] See C. Dodgson, *Holzschnitte zu zwei nürnbergischen Andachtsbüchern aus dem Anfange des XVI Jahrhunderts*, Graph. Gesellschaft, xi., Berlin 1909. For other views on the authorship of the group see H. Röttinger, *Hans Wechtlin*, Vienna Jahrbuch, xxvii. (1907), Heft 1.; and *Dürers Doppelgänger*, Strassburg 1926. In the last-named work Röttinger attributes to Peter Visscher I. part of the group which he had earlier ascribed to Wechtlin.

casts of human figures and limbs for which healing was sought, and a man broken on the wheel, a cripple, and three kneeling figures before the altar.

Before leaving Germany we would make some reference to certain single cuts of Nuremberg and neighbouring regions, of whose designers or cutters occasional record is preserved.

Fig. 180. From J. Issickemer, *Buchlein der Zuflucht der Maria*, Nuremberg 1497.

In the first place, there are several cuts, mostly large representations of saints, signed WOLFGANG, or WOLFGANG HAMER, e.g. the *St. Minus* (S. 1632, British Museum, Basle, and the block in the Derschau series at Berlin) and the *Kindred of Christ* (S. 1779, Munich) with the full name, and a *St. Jerome* (S. 1530, Munich) signed *Wolfgang*. We have already referred to one of Wolgemut's *Schatzbehalter* cuts occurring within a border signed *Wolfgang*, and to the similarity of a supposed Wolgemut drawing to the *St. Jerome* cut,[1] and it appears a very probable inference that Wolfgang Hamer was one of the Nuremberg cutters. His name has not been found in Nuremberg documents, but several others of the family are recorded among Nuremberg *Briefmaler* and *Kartenmaler* in the XVI century.

Various other large anonymous cuts of saints have been attributed to his hand, e.g. a *St. Sebald* at Munich (S. 1672), and the same type of work is seen in several other full-length figures of saints, e.g. a *St. Jerome* in the British Museum (S. 1527 a), a popular subject, to judge from the existence of two other versions at Magdeburg (S. 1527) and Weimar (S. 1527 b).

[1] See pp. 372, 374.

Another name which occurs on even cruder cuts is that of HANS PAUR, e.g. on a large and amusing sheet, the *Stock in Trade of a Married Couple* (S. 1991, Munich), on the *Creed, the Apostles and Prophets* (S. 1852, Stuttgart), while the *Lord's Prayer* of 1479 signed *h.p.* (S. 1851, Munich) is probably by the same hand, which is more likely to be the cutter than the designer.

JORG GLOCKENDON is another Nuremberg craftsman who signed various woodcuts which date about the turn of the XV and XVI centuries (if indeed there are not actually two cutters of the name), e.g. the *Virgin and Four Saints* (S. 1162, Berlin, with the original block from the Derschau Collection), *The Youth and Death* (S. 1898, Bamberg), the *Vision near Constantinople* (S. 1944, Munich Library), the *St. Christopher and St. John Baptist* (Metropolitan Museum, New York, from the McGuire Collection; Heitz, *Einbl.*, vol. lxv., pl. 23) and two maps and plans already noted.[1]

The name of CASPER (or CASPAR) occurs on other cuts of the same period, and is probably that of a Regensburg or Nuremberg cutter.[2] A *Virgin and Child and St. Anne* at Stockholm (S. 1191) and the *Influence of Venus* (S. 1975 a, Berlin) are signed *Casper*, while on a *Crucifix with Signs of the Passion* (S. 943, British Museum)[3] and a *St. Francis and the Stigmata* (S. 1423 a, Munich Library) the signature is spelt *Caspar*. Dr. Rosenthal has noted a further signed cut, *St. Florian*, and its unsigned pendant, *St. Wolfgang*,[4] and has made various probable attributions. The variety of style shown in the signed cuts renders it almost certain that he was a cutter and not a designer. A variety of dialect shown on the various cuts again probably implies that he was following text as well as designs supplied him as a journeyman cutter.

An earlier cutter, definitely belonging to Regensburg, LIENHART (WOLFF?), has already been noted among the authors of block-books.[5]

LANDSHUT

Of considerably greater interest than the five craftsmen just mentioned is MAIR OF LANDSHUT. He has been generally called Nicolaus Alexander

---

[1] See p. 316. See also p. 265 for an undescribed series of cuts by Jorg Glockendon.

[2] See Erwin Rosenthal, *Casper* (Beiträge zur Forschung: Studien aus dem Antiquariat J. Rosenthal), Munich 1929.

[3] Another version was signed by Firabet ze Raperswil (see p. 324).

[4] The *St. Florian* and *St. Wolfgang* now in the Metropolitan Museum, New York, from the McGuire Collection, and reproduced on pls. 25 and 30 of Heitz, *Einbl.*, vol. lxv.

[5] See p. 257.

Mair, but the most recent study of his work [1] finds no grounds for his identification with the painter of that name, though he was himself probably also a painter, and identical with the *Mair Maler von Freising* who occurs in the Munich 'Stadtsteuerbuch', 1490, and the painter of a work in Freising Cathedral. The *Alexander* might also be based on a confusion with Alexander Mair, a later Augsburg engraver (1559–1620). Only three woodcuts bearing his name are known, *Christ disputing with the Doctors* (dated 1499), *The Scourging of Christ* (fig. 181) and *St. Barbara*, dated 1499, the first known in two impressions (Paris and the British Museum), the other two only in the British Museum. [2] There is also a fourth woodcut after Mair's design, and only known in the British Museum impression, the *Reception at the Door of a Gothic House* (the same design as Mair's line-engraving, P. 13), [3] which is signed by the woodcutter HANS WURM, whom we have already mentioned for his block-book of the *Art of Wrestling*. [4] It is very probable that Mair's fellow-citizen, Hans Wurm, may also be the cutter of the three other subjects. In three of the cuts considerable portions of the background are left black: and the same practice of printing on tinted paper and heightening with white is found as in the case of Mair's line-engravings. In fact the *St. Barbara* is the only uncoloured impression. Mair's style of design has a certain mannered simplicity, his figures archaic in flavour for their date (and reminiscent of such designs as those in the Ulm *Buch der Weisheit*, printed by Lienhart Holle, 1483), [5] and his architecture that of doll's houses.

A woodcut *Pedigree of the Counts Palatine and Dukes of Bavaria*, belonging to a book entitled *Chronik und Stamm der Pfalzgrafen bei Rhein und Herzoge in Bayern*, printed by N. Wurm at Landshut, 1501, [6] is of a similar character and possibly also cut by Hans Wurm, though there is no reason to regard him as the designer of this subject any more than of the *Art of Wrestling* block-book. Mair may quite possibly be his designer in each case.

---

[1] Franz Schubert, *Mair von Landshut*, Landshut 1930. Cf. Max Lehrs, *Geschichte und Kritischer Katalog des Deutschen Kupferstiches*, vol. viii., 1932, p. 282.

[2] See Dodgson, *Catalogue of Early German and Flemish Woodcuts in the British Museum*, vol. i. p. 148, A. 143-45.

[3] See Dodgson, vol. ii. p. 263.   [4] See p. 261.

[5] Cf. e.g. *Reception at the Door of a Gothic House* with *Buch der Weisheit*, Sig. i. iii. (reproduced Schramm, vii. fig. 84).

[6] Edited by G. Leidinger, Strassburg (Heitz) 1901. Leidinger attempts to identify the printer N. Wurm with Hans Wurm. Schreiber regards him as probably Hans Wurm's father.

Fig. 181. Mair of Landshut. The Scourging of Christ.

PASSAU

The last German town which we shall pass in our survey before crossing the borders of Austria is Passau[1] on the Danube. But there is nothing of greater note than the cuts in two works printed by JOHANN PETRI, the plants in his *Herbarius* of 1485 (S. 4206, H. 8445), copied from Schoeffer's Mainz edition of 1484, and a stiff design of Leopold, Duke of Austria, in J. F. de Pavinis, *Defensorium Canonisationis S. Leopoldi*, n.d., about 1490 (S. 4903, H. 12536).

Fig. 182. Portrait of Mahomet II. S. 4557.

On Austrian territory (according to the old borders) the first printer to interest us is ALBRECHT KUNNE (of Duderstadt, near Göttingen), who printed books for the publisher HERMANN SCHINDELYP of Trent about 1475–76, not for any actual book-illustration, but for a single cut with accompanying text, a *Portrait of Mahomet* (S. 4557, Munich), probably intended for Mahomet II., the conqueror of Constantinople.[2] The text, of which a part is preserved, is a supposed letter

[1] See Albert Schramm, *Bilderschmuck des Frühdrucke*, xvi., Leipzig 1933.

[2] The patterned background should be compared with the pavement design in a curious cut of *Two Monkeys doing Circus Tricks on Horseback* (with revolving monkeys) at Zürich (S. 1985 n), of which there is another, perhaps earlier, version without the pattern at Nuremberg (S. 1985 m).

of the Turkish Emperor, in a type of Italian character, used by Schindelyp and probably printed by Albrecht Kunne. It was probably issued originally as a broadside, or folding sheet, but it is preserved with the incomplete text printed on the reverse of the cut.

It is possible that the Munich sheet may have been printed by Kunne in Italy, and at least certain that the design came from an Italian source. The portrait should be compared with the Florentine engraving *El Gran Turco* at Berlin,[1] and for the Venetian type of design with the *Portrait of Scanderbeg* in M. Barletius, *Historia Scanderbegi*, Rome, n.d., though the latter is a considerably later work belonging to the early xvi century.[2]

Another contemporary woodcut of the *Sultan*, lettered *der türgisch Kayser* (S. 2008, British Museum), seems more fanciful as a portrait if intended to represent Mahomet II. It is probably Upper German work of about 1480.

From about 1480 Albrecht Kunne was settled for some years at Memmingen, and issued a small portrait of the author in his edition of Paolo Attavanti, *Breviarium Decretorum*, 1486. But this is only a copy from the original cut in the Milanese edition of 1479.

Vienna

Apart from Kunne's *Mahomet* there are few cuts of any interest issued on Austrian territory during the xv century.[3] One of the earliest is an illustration in the *Legend of St. Roch*, issued without printer's name at Vienna, 1482 (Gollob, *Verzeichnis*, No. 226), only known in the copy at the Abbey of Melk.

Most of the other occasional cuts in Viennese books of the end of the xv century were printed by JOHANN WINTERBURGER, e.g. a *Sick-room with two doctors and two patients* in Steber, *A Malafranczos morbo Gallorum Praeservatio*, n.d. (Gollob 242), and the *Author writing at his desk* in Augustinus Datus, *Elegantiae Minores*, 1499 (Gollob 81). But in these early years of his press, the best woodcuts used by Winterburger are the initials and borders, generally in white on black ground after the Venetian style of

---

Bear-baiting and bull-baiting in Elizabethan times frequently ended with the 'pleasant sport of the horse and the ape' (see *Shakespeare's England*, Oxford, 1917, ii. p. 430), and the prints may represent a diversion of the same kind.

[1] See Lippmann, Pr. Jahrbuch, ii. 215, for reproduction, and notes of other portraits.

[2] Reproduced by Essling, part ii. No. 2317, as a Venetian cut.

[3] See Hedwig Gollob, *Der Wiener Holzschnitt in den Jahren von 1490–1550*, Vienna 1926; *Systematisches Verzeichnis der mit Wiener Holzschnitten illustrierten Wiener Drucke*, 1482–1550, Strassburg 1925.

Ratdolt and others. The title border to his *Practica auf dis jar 1497* (Gollob 216) is an attractive floral design on black ground.

BRÜNN—OLMÜTZ

We have already mentioned the cuts in Johannes de Thwrocz, *Chronica Hungarorum*, printed by CONRAD STAHEL and MATHIAS PREUNLEIN at Brünn, 20th March 1488, in relation to the other blocks of the same subject in Ratdolt's edition of three months later.[1] The illustration of the *Tartars marching into Hungary in the time of Bela IV.* is a clumsy but spirited piece of work.

A woodcut of *St. Wenceslas* which appeared in the *Olmütz Psalter*, printed by Conrad Stahel alone, Brünn 1499 (S. 5029, H. 13503), of which there are other versions in Grüninger's *Olmütz Breviary*, Strassburg 1499 (S. 3611), occurred later on the title of Augustinus Moravus, *De Secta Waldensium*, printed by CONRAD BAUMGARTEN, Olmütz 1500 (S. 3397, H. 11614).

KUTTENBERG—PRAGUE

A *Bohemian Bible*, printed at Kuttenberg by MARTIN OF TISCHNIOWA, 1489 (S. 3468, H. 3162), and a *Bohemian New Testament*, printed anonymously at Prague about 1497–98 (S. 5336), are both illustrated with cuts, but they are crude works and only merit a passing notice.

BIBLIOGRAPHY

BURLINGTON FINE ARTS CLUB. Catalogue of a Collection of Woodcuts of the German School, XV and XVI Centuries. London 1882.

MUTHER, Richard. Die ältesten deutschen Bilder-Bibeln. Munich 1883.

MUTHER, Richard. Die deutsche Bücher-illustration der Gothik und Frührenaissance (1460–1530). 2 vols. Munich and Leipzig 1884.

BARACK, Carl August. Elsässische Büchermarken. Strassburg 1892.

SCHORBACH, Karl. Seltene Drucke in Nachbildungen, mit einleitendem Text. 5 vols. Leipzig and Halle 1893–1905.

    i. Die Historien von dem Ritter Beringer. Strassburg 1495 (S. 3427, Nuremberg).

    ii. Dietrich von Bern. Heidelberg (Knoblochtzer) 1490 (S. 3822, Berlin).

    iii. Ecken Auszfart. Augsburg (H. Schawr) 1491 (S. 3885, Berlin).

    iv. Laurin. Strassburg 1500 (S. 5152, *Rosengarten König Laurins*; Berlin).

    v. Die Geschichte des Pfaffen vom Kalenberg. Heidelberg 1490 (S. 4409, *Kalenberg-Pfaffe*; Darmstadt).

---

[1] See p. 303. For Bohemian and Moravian books in general, see J. Volf, *Geschichte des Buchdruckes in Böhmen und Mähren*, Weimar 1928.

COCKERELL, S. C. Some German Woodcuts of the xv Century. London 1897.

HEITZ, P., and SCHREIBER, W. L. Die deutschen Accipies und Magister cum Discipulis Holz-schnitte als Hilfsmittel zur Inkunabel-Bestimmung. Strassburg 1908.

HEITZ, P., and SCHREIBER, W. L. Christus am Kreuz. Kanonbilder der in Deutschland ge-druckten Messbücher des xv[ten] Jahrhunderts. Strassburg 1910.

WORRINGER, Wilhelm. Die altdeutsche Buchillustration. Munich 1912 (3rd ed., 1921).

MURRAY, C. Fairfax. Catalogue of a Collection of Early German Books in the Library of C.F.M. 2 vols. London 1913.

EINBLATTDRUCKE DES xv[ten] JAHRHUNDERTS. Ein bibliographisches Verzeichnis. Herausgegeben von der Kommission für den Gesamtkatalog der Wiegendrucke. Halle 1914.

VOULLIÉME, E. Die deutschen Drucker des xv[ten] Jahrhunderts. Berlin 1916 (2nd ed., 1922).

SCHRAMM, Albert. Der Bilderschmuck der Frühdrucke. Leipzig, fol.

   i. Die Drucke von Albrecht Pfister in Bamberg. 1922.

   ii. ,,   ,,   Günther Zainer in Augsburg. 1920.

   iii. ,,   ,,   Johann Baemler in Augsburg. 1921.

   iv. ,,   ,,   Anton Sorg in Augsburg. 1921.

   v. ,,   ,,   Johann Zainer in Ulm. 1923.

   vi. ,,   ,,   Konrad Dinckmut in Ulm. 1923.

   vii. ,,   ,,   Lienhart Holle, Johannes Reger, Johann Schaeffler and Hans Hauser in Ulm. 1923.

   viii. Die Kölner Drucker. 1924.

   ix. Die Drucker in Esslingen, Urach, Stuttgart, Reutlingen, Tübingen, Blaubeuren. 1926.

   x. ,,   ,,   in Lübeck. (1) Die beiden Brüder Brandis. 1927.

   xi. ,,   ,,   ,,   (2) Steffen Arndes. 1928.

   xii. ,,   ,,   ,,   (3) Ghotan; (4) Mohnkopfdrucke. Die Drucker in Magde-burg. 1929.

   xiii. ,,   ,,   in Leipzig and Erfurt. 1930.

   xiv. ,,   ,,   in Mainz. (1) Fust und Schoeffer; (2) Johann Numeister; (3) Peter Schoffer. 1931.

   xv. ,,   ,,   ,,   (4) Erhard Reuwich; (5) Jacob Meydenbach; (6) Peter Fried-berg. 1932.

   xvi. ,,   ,,   in Speier, Würzburg, Passau, München, Ingolstadt, Zweibrücken, Freis-ing, Memmingen. 1933.

   xvii ,,   ,,   in Nürnberg. (1) Anton Koberger. 1934.

SCHRAMM, Albert. Die illustrierten Bibel der Inkunabelzeit. Leipzig 1922.

SCHRAMM, Albert. Illustrierte Gebetbücher des xv[ten] Jahrhunderts. Wolfenbüttel 1928.

WEIL, Ernst. Die deutschen Druckerzeichen des xv[ten] Jahrhunderts. Munich 1924.

JUCHHOFF, Rudolf. Drucker- und Verlegerzeichen des xv[ten] Jahrhunderts in den Niederländen, England, Spanien, Böhmen, Mähren und Polen. Munich 1927.

JAHN, Johannes. Beiträge zur Kenntnis der ältesten Einblattdrucke. Strassburg 1927.

GEISBERG, Max. Die Deutsche Buchillustration in der ersten Hälfte des xvi Jahrhunderts. Munich 1930, etc. (in progress).

CHAPTER VI

BOOK-ILLUSTRATION AND CONTEMPORARY SINGLE CUTS IN ITALY

WE have already noted how the Venetian woodcutters and playing-card makers in 1441 essayed to protect their trade against foreign competition; and how in consequence regulations were made forbidding the import of every kind of print.[1] But this does not seem to have interfered with the continued influence of the foreign craftsman, which became even more marked in the early years of book-printing in Italy. The pupils of the earliest German printers soon realised the extensive field that lay before them, and many turned South, preferring the places where they would be pioneers rather than remaining among many competitors in their own country. It is probable also that they took with them their own cutters, or they may even have ventured to undertake block-cutting themselves when free from the restrictions imposed by the guilds in their own country.

ROME

The earliest series of illustrations known with Italian printed text seems to be that of the dotted prints, the so-called *Stoeger Passion*, which has been described in an earlier chapter.[2] This was a set of German metal-cuts, probably issued in Italy by some travelling printer from Mainz or Bamberg. But the first book-illustrations, cut on wood, in Italy, appeared in the edition of Turrecremata's *Meditationes*,[3] printed at Rome by ULRICH HAN in 1467 (H. 15722), i.e. two years after the first dated book printed in Italy (the *Lactantius*, printed by SWEYNHEYM and PANNARTZ at Subiaco). They were thoroughly German in linear character, though they were certainly derived from Italian designs. According to the text the cuts, chiefly illustrations from the Old and New Testaments, were based on a series of frescoes (no longer extant) in St. Maria sopra Minerva, Rome, and the dignified character of the design, poorly seconded by the crudeness of the cutting, entirely supports the claim.

[1] See pp. 82-83.   [2] See p. 192.
[3] Cardinal Turrecremata (Torquemada), the Abbot of the Benedictine Monastery of St. Scholastica of Subiaco, was no doubt partly responsible for the introduction of printing in Italy, for it was in his convent that Sweynheym and Pannartz set up their first press.

There are thirty-one cuts in the first edition, of 1467 (e.g. Manchester, Vienna and Nuremberg), the extra three cuts in the Nuremberg copy being inserted later. The second edition, of 1473 (H. 15724, e.g. Manchester, Vienna), contains thirty-three cuts, three subjects being added, i.e. the *Fall* (f. 3, verso), the *Flight into Egypt* (f. 8, verso), the *Trinity* (f. 25), and one omitted, i.e. the *Last Judgment* (which occurred on f. 33, verso of the first edition). The same cuts appeared in Han's third edition,

Fig. 183. Procession of the Eucharist, from Turrecremata, *Meditationes*, Rome 1467.

1478 (H. 15725, Pierpont Morgan Library, lacking f. 26 with the cut of the *Dominican Tree*), and in that of 1484 printed by his successor Stephan Planck (Reithling 1100, Dyson Perrins No. 34). Stephan Planck also issued an edition in 1498 (H. 15728) with small copies of somewhat delicate cutting (about $2\frac{3}{4} \times 3$ inches), in which the first cut is surrounded by a border (white scroll on black ground with a *putto* at the foot) similar in style to the ornament of the Naples *Aesop* of 1485.

Adaptations of the same subjects printed by J. Neumeister at Mainz in 1479 have already been described.[1]

[1] See p. 194.

Fig. 184. Initial G, from Barberiis, *Opuscula*, Rome, about 1481–83.

Sweynheym and Pannartz used no woodcut decoration in their books printed at Subiaco (1465–67), but used a woodcut bar and capitals in occasional copies of Suetonius, *Vitae Caesarum*, printed at Rome in 1470 (e.g. in the Pierpont Morgan copy, Catalogue, vol. ii. No. 245). These capitals were used later at Rome by the printers GEORGIUS TEUTONICUS and SIXTUS RIESSINGER (1481–83) and OLIVERIUS SERVIUS (1484).[1] The bar, like the capitals, is in outline branch-work on a black ground, printed by hand after the text, probably in the rubricator's shop, and intended as a basis for hand colouring.[2] The same practice of using outline woodcut as a basis for rubrication is also seen in certain books printed by JOHANNES and VINDELINUS DE SPIRA, NICOLAUS JENSON and BARTHOLOMAEUS CREMONENSIS at Venice between 1469 and 1472.[3]

---

[1] Very close replicas of the same capitals were used in books printed by Johann Müller (Regiomontanus) at Nuremberg, about 1474 (see p. 369). Careful comparison of the capitals in Teutonicus and Riessinger's with those in Müller's books leads me to conclude that Müller's were probably for the most part (if not all) metal casts from the original blocks. In the cases where the original capital lacked its left border (intended for use against a border), this is repeated in Müller's version. If they had been woodcut copies it is more likely that the capital would have been completed with its four borders. Moreover, the Müller versions combine a very exact relation to the originals with small flaws which appear like faulty casting. On the other hand, occasional dots in the background differing in position suggest copies, made perhaps from tracings or from prints.

The following letters can be compared in Italian and German versions in the British Museum:

S (*a*) Teutonicus and Riessinger. *Ad Peccatorem Sodomitam*, n.d. IB. 19245.

    (*b*) Müller. Marcus Manilius, *Astronomica*, n.d. (H. 10703). C. 16. h. 6.

I (*a*) Teutonicus and Riessinger. *Decisiones Novae Rotae Romanae*, n.d. (H. 604). IB. 19237.

    (*b*) Müller. Manilius, *Astronomica*, n.d. (H. 10703). C. 16. h. 6.

P (*a*) Teutonicus and Riessinger. Philippus de Barberiis, *Opuscula*, n.d. IA. 19241.

    (*b*) Müller. J. Müller, *Tractatus contra Cremonensia*, n.d. (H. 13805). IB. 7885.

E (*a*) Oliverius Servius. Boethius, *Topica*, 1484 (H. 3429). IB. 19259.

    (*b*) Müller. Basilius, *Opusculum ad Juvenes*, n.d. IA. 7883.

On the question of metal casts cf. Index of Subjects (under *Casts*).

[2] See p. 534, for a certain Francesco Rosselli, described as *miniatore e stampatore* (illuminator and printer), who, judging from his son's inventory, was no doubt the owner of a large stock of copper plates and wood blocks.

[3] See A. W. Pollard, *Woodcut Designs for Illuminators in Venetian Books*, 1469–73, Bibliographica, iii., 1897, 122. Nothing is known of the famous printer Jenson, apart from his activity at Venice, except that he was French and a native of Sommevoire (Aube). Tradition makes him

The design is generally more in the nature of a 'branch' pattern in the 'white vine' style, as it is usually termed in regard to contemporary manuscript illuminations. The borders are for the most part composed of several blocks arranged in various ways, for two, three or four sides; and small pieces of pattern could be adapted by repetition to whatever spaces they were required to fill.

The chief books noted by Essling and elsewhere as containing such borders are as follows:

(*a*) Printed by JOHANNES DE SPIRA (d. 1470) and VINDELINUS DE SPIRA:
  Pliny, *Historia Naturalis*, 1469. H. 13087, E. 2.
  Augustinus, *De Civitate Dei*, 1470. H. 2048, E. 72.
  Virgil, *Opera*, 1470. E. 52.
  Livy, *Decades*, 1470. H. 10130, E. 32.
  Petrarch, *Sonetti*, etc., 1470. H. 12753, E. 74.
  Sallust, *Opera*, 1470. H. 14197, E. 43.
  Cicero, *De Officiis*, 1470 and 1472. H. 5257-8, E. 7 and 8.
  Cicero, *Epistolae ad Familiares*, 1470 and 1471. H. 5166-7, E. 20 and 22.
  Appianus, *De Bellis Civilibus Romanis*, 1472. H. 1306, E. 220.
  Georgius Trapesuntius, *Rhetorica*, 1470. H. 7608, E. 118.
  Curtius, *Historia Alexandri Magni*, c. 1470. E. 119.
  Valerius Maximus, *De factis dictisque mirabilibus*, 1471. H. 15775, E. 211.
(*b*) Printed by NICOLAUS JENSON:
  Eusebius, *De Evangelica Preparatione*, 1470. H. 6699, E. 71.
  Quintilian, *Institutiones Oratoriae*, 1471. H. 13647, E. 130.
  Cicero, *Epistolae ad Familiares*, 1471. H. 5168, E. 21.
  Leonardus Bruni (Aretinus), *De Bello adversus Gothos*, 1471. H. 1559, E. 219.
  Suetonius, *Vitae Caesarum*, 1471. H. 15117, E. 207.
  Pliny, *Historia Naturalis*, 1472. H. 13089, E. 3.
(*c*) Printed by CHRISTOPHORUS VALDARFER:
  Cicero, *Orationes*, 1471. H. 5122, E. 218.
(*d*) Printed by BARTHOLOMAEUS CREMONENSIS:
  Virgil, *Opera*, 1472. E. 53.
  St. Jerome, *Vita et Transita*, 1473. H. 8637, E. 122.

at some period Master of the Mint at Troyes or Paris, and sends him at the behest of Louis XI. on a secret mission to Mainz to find out about the newly discovered methods of printing.

(e) Printed by JACOBUS RUBEUS (JACQUES LE ROUGE):
　　Ovid, *Metamorphoses*, 1474. H. 12138, E. 222.
(f) Printer unknown:
　　Cicero, *De Oratore* (V. de Spira?), *c.* 1470. H. 5096, E. 115.
　　Petrarch, *Sonetti*, etc. (N. Jenson?), n.d. H. 12757, E. 75.

The Grenville copy of the Virgil (British Museum), of which a re-production is here given (fig. 185), is of particular interest as it shows the woodcut uncoloured, but with the remains of an outside border-line of yellowish paste, probably the ground work (adhesive material) for a gold border to the illumination. The paste border has set off on the opposite page, and a fragment of a simple black-leaf border prepared for the top and left side of the page also shows clearly in the offset, though it has almost disappeared on the original page.

That Sweynheym and Pannartz intended to use woodcut illustration is shown by the spaces left in Nicolaus de Lyra, *Postilla super Bibliam*, 1471–72 (H. 10363), with headings *hic figura*, *sequitur figura*, etc. No copies are known with cuts, but a few contain drawings.[1]

After Turrecremata's *Meditationes* no subject illustrations are known in Roman books until those in the various editions of Philippus de Barberiis, *Opuscula*, printed in and about 1481, with illustrations chiefly of *Sibyls* and *Prophets*.

There is an edition printed by J. P. DE LIGNAMINE and dated 1st December 1481 (British Museum, from the Malcolm Collection) in which thirteen subjects, i.e. the twelve *Sibyls* and the figure of *Proba*, are printed from five blocks. They are rudely cut, in strong outline and little shading, within a thick border-line, and measure about $4\frac{1}{4} \times 2\frac{7}{8}$ inches in size.

A second edition printed by Lignamine, n.d. (H. 2455), includes twenty-nine illustrations printed from twenty-three blocks, all being newly cut except the *Proba*. To distinguish them from the earlier edition, many of the figures stand under round arches; they are as crudely cut, and even broader in line. The subjects added to the *Sibyls* and *Proba* were twelve *Prophets*, *Plato*, the *Man of Sorrows*, a *Nativity*[2] and *St. John the Baptist*. Despite the rudeness of the cutting, there is something attractive in the designs of both these editions.

A rough and angular title-block to Horace, *Carmen Saeculare*, n.d., about 1484 (issued by the printer of Manilius, *Astronomicum*), is certainly

---

[1] See p. 282.
[2] The *Man of Sorrows* and the *Nativity* based on engravings by the German Master E.S.

P. VIRGILII MARONIS BVCOLICA.
AEGLOGA PRIMA: INTERLOQVTORES.
MELIBOEVS ET TITYRVS AMICI.   ME.

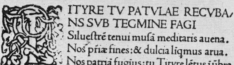

ITYRE TV PATVLAE RECVBA/
NS SVB TEGMINE FAGI
Siluestrē tenui musā meditaris auena.
Nos priæ fines: & dulcia liqmus arua.
Nos patriā fugius: tu Tityre lētus iūbra
F ormosam resonare doces amaryllida siluas.   TI
O Meliboee deus nobis hæc ocia fecit
N anq; erit ille mihi semper deus: illius aram
S æpe tener nostris ab ouilibus imbuet agnus
I lle meas errare boues (ut cernis) & ipsum
L udere quæ uellem calamo permisit agresti   ME
N on equidem inuideo: miror magis: undiq; totis
V sq; adeo turbatur agris: en ipse capellas
P rotinus æger ago: hanc etiam uix Tityre duco.
H ic inter densas corylos modo nanq; gemellos
S pem gregis ah silice in nuda cōnixa reliquit.
S æpe malum hoc nobis si mens non leua fuisset
D e cælo tactas memini prædicere quercus.
S ed tamen iste deus qui sit da Tityre nobis   TI
V rbem quam dicunt Romam Meliboee putaui
S tultus ego huic nostræ similē: quo sæpe solemus
P astores ouium teneros depellere foetus.
S ic canibus catulos similes: sic matribus hædos
N oram; sic paruis componere magna solebam.
V erum hæc tantū alias inter caput extulit urbes
Q uantum lēta solét iter uiburna cupressi.   ME
E t quæ tanta fuit Romam tibi causa uidendi?   TI
L ibertas quæ sera tamen respexit inertem
C andidior: postq tondenti barba cadebat.
R espexit tamén & longo post tempore uenit
P ostq nos amaryllis habet galathea reliquit
N anq; fatebor enim dum me galathea tenebat
N ec spes libertatis erat nec cura peculi.
Q uáuis multa meis exiret uictima septis
P inguis: & igratæ premeretur caseus urbi
N ō unqua grauis ære domū mihi dextra redibat

Fig. 185. Half-border and Initial T, from Virgil, *Opera*, Venice 1472.

by the same cutter as the second edition of Lignamine's *Opuscula* of Barberiis.

Better known in design though still weak and angular (and also probably German) in cutting, are the blocks in the edition printed by GEORGIUS TEUTONICUS and SIXTUS RIESSINGER, between 1481 and 1483 (H. 2453). Here the subjects are limited to the twelve *Sibyls* and *Proba*, and there is no economy in using blocks for more than one subject. There is considerable grace in several of the *Sibyls* and a certain classical dignity in the *Proba*, which is here reproduced (fig. 186). The beautiful capitals in strap-work on black ground, used in this and other books by Teutonicus and Riessinger, came from the stock of Sweynheym and Pannartz.

Fig. 186. Proba, from Barberiis, *Opuscula*, Rome, about 1481–83.

Another book printed by J. P. de Lignamine, the *Herbarius* of Lucius Apuleius, n.d., about 1483–84 (H. 1322), is certainly one of the earliest, if not actually the first, among printed herbals.[1] It contains a hundred and thirty-one illustrations of plants, about 4 × 3 inches, simply designed and cut, making good use of broad black lines and spaces.

Two other Italian herbals printed in the XV century may be mentioned

[1] Schreiber dates it about 1493 in his facsimile edition of Schoeffer's *Gart der Gesuntheit*, 1485 (*Hortus Sanitatis Deutsch*, Munich 1924), but the dedication of one issue to Cardinal Gonzaga, who died 21st October 1483, is witness to the earlier date. The British Museum copy is dedicated to Giuliano della Rovere, and is probably after the Cardinal's death. See A. C. Klebs, Papers, Bibliographical Society of America, Chicago, xi., 1917, p. 82, and see above, p. 348.

here as their simple cutting of plants shows little individuality of style, and does not call for special reference in our local sections, i.e. the *Herbolarium*, printed by Leonardus Achates and Gulielmus of Pavia, at Vicenza, 1491 (H. 8451), and *De Virtutibus Herbarum* printed by Bevilaqua at Venice in 1499 (H. 1807). Both of these books may be found variously described under the title of *Aggregator*, or the name of Arnoldus de Villa Nova. They each contain 150 woodcuts of plants and derive from the Mainz *Herbarius Latinus* of 1484.

By the same draughtsman and cutter as the illustrations in Planck's edition of Turrecremata, *Meditationes*, of 1498,[1] are the little cuts in Thomas Ochsenbrunner, *Priscorum Heroum Stemmata*, printed by JOHANN BESICKEN,[2] 1494 (H. 11934), and the frontispiece to Bernardus Granollachs, *Lunarium*, printed by Planck, about 1497 (H. 7863). The latter subject is freely adapted from the frontispiece to the Florentine editions of the *Lunarium* printed by Morgiani, 1496, with suggestions from the cut of the *Astrologer in his Study* at the end of the Florentine edition.

The subjects in the *Priscorum Heroum Stemmata* (mostly about $1\frac{3}{8} \times 1\frac{7}{8}$ inches; one or two $2\frac{3}{8} \times 1\frac{7}{8}$ inches) represent for the most part Roman and later heroes issuing half-length from decorative stems. Whether by a German or Italian cutter, these little blocks and the other works by the same hand are far more delicately cut than any of the other Roman blocks hitherto mentioned.

The Florentine frontispiece is in its turn closely related to the title cut of Anianus, *Compotus*, printed by ANDREAS FREITAG at Rome 1493 (H. 5596) and might be copied from it (unless there is a lost earlier edition of the Florentine version, which would give it the priority). The *Compotus* block is surrounded with a black-ground *passe-partout* border, with children tilting on pigs, which is copied from one used by Morgiani and Petri at Florence.[3] The first suggestion of the *Compotus* and *Lunarium* subjects was the frontispiece in B. Granollachs, *Sommario dell' arte di astrologia*, Naples, about 1485 (F.-B. 65).

The only other illustrated book printed in Rome during the xv century that demands our attention is the *Mirabilia Romae* (or, in its German editions, *Wie Rom gepauet ward*). We have already described these popular guide-books to the Papal city, for its first edition was a block-book.[4]

Of the very numerous type-printed editions in the last fifteen years of

---

[1] See p. 397.

[2] For another book recently attributed to Besicken, see my Additions in vol. i., p. 265.

[3] See No. 6 in my list of Florentine *passe-partout* borders, p. 533.   [4] See p. 258.

the xv century there are two distinct classes: (1) those with black-line cuts, based more or less closely on the block-book illustrations; (2) those with cuts within black-ground borders, with additional subjects of the Virgin and Child, the Crucifixion and various saints.

Of the first class the German edition of STEPHAN PLANCK, 20th November 1489, reproduced by the Wiegendruckgesellschaft, Berlin, 1925 (ed. C. Hülsen), is a good example; the Latin edition of Andreas Freitag, 1492, contains much cruder copies of the original cuts.

Of the second class Planck's Latin issue of about 1497 (H. 11177) is perhaps the best in quality, while much poorer copies of Planck's illustrations occur in the editions printed by Johann Besicken (e.g. that of 29th January 1500 in Latin, H. 11203).

It has already been noted that one of the earliest type-printed editions, formerly attributed to Planck, contains illustrations cut from the blocks of the original block-book. The British Museum Catalogue of xv-Century Printed Books (part iv. p. 144) describes it as by an unknown printer, not before 1485, remarking on the similarity of the type to that used at Gaeta in 1487 by Andreas Freitag, who, as we have seen, printed an edition with crude copies at Rome in 1492.

NAPLES

The leading spirit in the production of illustrated books at Naples[1] was the humanist FRANCESCO DEL TUPPO. It has only been recently established that SIXTUS RIESSINGER, the earliest of printers at Naples, and certain 'Germani fidelissimi', JOHANN TRESSER, MARTINUS DE AMSTERDAM, and CHRISTIAN PRELLER, used Tuppo's own press in various books. Tuppo was evidently the publisher, and after the printers mentioned had severed connection with him, it is known that works were still issuing from his press in 1498.

The earliest of these illustrated books was the Boccaccio, *Filocolo* (*Florio e Biancofiore*), printed by Sixtus Riessinger, 8th March 1478 (H. 3299, F.-B. 46). The illustrations, very simply cut in outline with little shading, are German in style, and though considerably inferior to the average of contemporary German work, possess a certain naïve charm. Sixtus Riessinger's own device, which appears at the end of the volume, is probably by the same designer and cutter, and displays greater refinement of execution than the illustrations (fig. 187).

[1] Mariano Fava and Giovanni Bresciano, *La stampa a Napoli nel xv secolo*, Leipzig 1911–13 (Hefte 32-34 of C. Dziatzko and C. Haebler, Sammlung Bibliothekswissenschaftlicher Arbeiten).

It may be noted in passing that ARNALDUS DE BRUXELLA had evidently intended using woodcuts in his edition of Lucianus, *Vera Historia*, 6th March 1475/76 (H. 10259, F.-B. 91), as there are spaces left for illustrations: but these were never filled up.

Another interesting early Naples book is Franchinus Gafurius, *Theorica Musicae*, printed by FRANCESCO DI DINO, 8th October 1480 (H. 7404, F.-B. 170). It contains two subject illustrations, *Figures at an anvil (Tubal Cain)*, and an *Organist playing*. The block of the organist was reprinted in the Milan edition of 1492, and as Gafurius was a Lombard, and the style of the design Milanese or Brescian in character, it is almost certain that he had the block cut in Lombardy.[1]

Fig. 187. The Mark of the printer Sixtus Riessinger, Naples.

But by far the most important Naples book is the Aesop, *Vita et Fabulae*, with Tuppo's Italian paraphrase.[2] It was printed in 1485 on Tuppo's press by the 'Germani fidelissimi' already mentioned. The illustrations are framed in richly decorated *passe-partout* borders, of which there are several varieties. These borders show a combination of black line and white on black ground, and are characteristic of Neapolitan tendencies in the Oriental richness of their design.[3] The border at the beginning of the Fables is a handsome design on a black ground, scroll work with a cupid attacking a lion's head with a lance in the right border, and with two cupids at the foot flanking a wreathed circular space left blank for the insertion of arms.[4] The same border was used at Soncino by the publisher Joshua Solomon in his *Hebrew Bible* of 1488, and later the same block, cut up and

---

[1] See p. 516 and fig. 281.

[2] For a recent study of the illustrator of this Aesop, see Lamberti Donati, *Di Alcune ignote zilografie del XV secolo nella Bibl. Vaticana*, Gutenberg-Jahrbuch, Mainz, 1934, p. 86. Donati derives the designer's origin from the Netherlands.

[3] If there are actually any Islamic elements in the design (which is not beyond question), they would probably have come to Naples through Sicily, just as Spain derived similar elements through Moorish channels (Hispano-Mauresque).

[4] A modified version of the same design in which a cow's head is added in the upper border, and in which the cupid on the right armed with sword and buckler attacks a large lion rampant, appears in Hebrew books printed at Naples by ISAAC BEN JUDAH (Moses ben Nachman, *Commentarius in Pentateuchum*, 1490, H. 11671, F.-B. 268; and David Kimchi, *Liber Radicum*, 1491, H. 6034, F.-B. 272). It is somewhat coarser in cutting than the *Aesop* version.

rearranged with the side-pieces on the reverse sides to fit the reversed order of the Hebrew book, was printed in his edition of Jacob ben Ascher, *Arba Turim*, 1490 (H. 1880).

A fairly close copy of the 1485 *Aesop* border appeared in the Aesop, *Vita et Fabulae*, printed at Aquila by Eusanius de Stella, Johannes Picardus de Hamel and Louis de Masson, 1493 (H. 355, Paris and Pierpont Morgan). This Aquila edition contains eighty-eight copies of the original illustrations, and a cut of *Master and Pupils* on the title page, of which I have not identified an earlier version.

Fig. 188. Aesop's introduction to the house of Xanthus, from his *Vita et Fabulae*, Naples 1485.

The subject designs of the 1485 *Aesop* were very probably cut, if not designed, by an artist from Northern Europe; they are angular in style, exhibit strong emphasis on the inner contours of the face, and are characterised by the use of a very regular system of short lines in parallel series, and ribbons of close parallel shading against the outlines of drapery. The borders are more possibly the design of an Italian artist. The illustrations of the Life of Aesop are on the whole more clumsy in design than those of the Fables; they certainly show the northern craftsman in his more independent vein, as he had no Italian models for this part of the work. He probably knew the cuts to Johann Zainer's Ulm edition of about 1475-76, which included a Life, but he did not follow them in his designs. In the Fables he borrowed largely from the inventions of the Verona *Aesop* of 1479,

Fig. 189. The Ox and the Frog, from Aesop, *Vita et Fabulae*, Naples 1485.

though he modified his originals with great freedom, and occasionally showed entirely independent designs. Further notes about *Aesop* illustrations in general will be added in relation to the Italian *editio princeps* of Verona.

Kristeller very rightly compared the style of the Naples *Aesop* cuts with illustrations signed I.D. in books published at Lyon,[1] and with certain cuts in Spanish books. It is necessary, however, to specify more definitely the incidence of the comparison. The subject cuts in the *Aesop*, on the one hand, are certainly near in character of design and cutting to I.D.'s signed work at Lyon, Toulouse, and in Spain.[2] On the other hand, the border at the beginning of the Fables is undoubtedly related in style to such Spanish borders as that first used by the printer Spindeler in his 1490 edition of *Tirant lo Blanch* (Kurz 252, Haebler 639), and to the woodcut of *King in Council* in the *Usatges de Barcelona e Constitucións de Cataluña*, printed by Pere Miguel and Diego de Gumiel, Barcelona, 28th February 1495 (K. 98, H. 652, Olschki, *Le Livre illustré*, 1926, No. 89).[3] But I would nevertheless hesitate to go so far as to identify the woodcuts of the *Aesop* with the Master I.D., and even less to assume his later activity in Spain. But neither conjecture is unreasonable, as the Naples cutter, who was probably a wandering craftsman from the North, whose style shows much kinship with Netherlandish woodcut, might well have continued his wanderings in Spain and France. But there was later work at Naples comparable with that of the *Aesop*, e.g. another fine border with scroll work, children and stags,[4] which was used by the publisher Joshua Solomon in his *Hebrew Bible*, n.d., about 1490-91 (H. 3028, F.-B. 270; fig. 190), and in his *Pentateuch* which is dated 1491 (H. 12574, F.-B. 271), and in a reversed copy by Ayolfo de Cantono in his edition of Leonardo Bruni (Aretino), *L'Aquila*, 1492 (H. 1577, F.-B. 188);[5] and the illustrations in Marino Gionata (Angionese), *Il Giardino*, 28th June 1490 (F.-B. 178), and in the Aesop, *Fabulae*, n.d., about 1495 (F.-B. 179 *bis*), both printed by Christian Preller, who was one of Tuppo's 'Germani fidelissimi', show a continuation of a similar style of subject design, less skilfully cut. So that an alibi might be urged against the identification of the Aesop Master with I.D.

---

[1] See pp. 614-616.   [2] See p. 754.   [3] See p. 746.

[4] The animals in the scroll-work of this border, somewhat heraldic in character, may possibly derive from Islamic designs.

[5] The title cut of *L'Aquila* (an eagle within a border) is in the manner of various heraldic cuts in Spanish books, another slight link with Spain in Naples woodcuts.

אַחֲרֵי מוֹת מֹשֶׁה עֶבֶד יְהֹוָה וַיֹּאמֶר יְהֹוָה אֶל־יְהוֹשֻׁעַ בִּן־נוּן מְשָׁרֵת
מֹשֶׁה לֵאמֹר: מֹשֶׁה עַבְדִּי מֵת וְעַתָּה קוּם עֲבֹר אֶת־הַיַּרְדֵּן הַזֶּה
אַתָּה וְכָל־הָעָם הַזֶּה אֶל־הָאָרֶץ אֲשֶׁר אָנֹכִי נֹתֵן לָהֶם לִבְנֵי
יִשְׂרָאֵל: כָּל־מָקוֹם אֲשֶׁר תִּדְרֹךְ כַּף־רַגְלְכֶם בּוֹ לָכֶם נְתַתִּיו
כַּאֲשֶׁר דִּבַּרְתִּי אֶל־מֹשֶׁה: מֵהַמִּדְבָּר וְהַלְּבָנוֹן הַזֶּה וְעַד־הַנָּהָר
הַגָּדוֹל נְהַר־פְּרָת כֹּל אֶרֶץ הַחִתִּים וְעַד־הַיָּם הַגָּדוֹל מְבוֹא
הַשָּׁמֶשׁ יִהְיֶה גְּבוּלְכֶם: לֹא־יִתְיַצֵּב אִישׁ לְפָנֶיךָ כֹּל יְמֵי חַיֶּיךָ
כַּאֲשֶׁר הָיִיתִי עִם־מֹשֶׁה אֶהְיֶה עִמָּךְ לֹא אַרְפְּךָ וְלֹא אֶעֶזְבֶךָּ: חֲזַק
וֶאֱמָץ כִּי אַתָּה תַּנְחִיל אֶת־הָעָם הַזֶּה אֶת־הָאָרֶץ אֲשֶׁר נִשְׁבַּעְתִּי
לַאֲבוֹתָם לָתֵת לָהֶם: רַק חֲזַק וֶאֱמַץ מְאֹד לִשְׁמֹר לַעֲשׂוֹת בְּכָל־
הַתּוֹרָה אֲשֶׁר צִוְּךָ מֹשֶׁה עַבְדִּי אַל־תָּסוּר מִמֶּנּוּ יָמִין וּשְׂמֹאל
לְמַעַן תַּשְׂכִּיל בְּכֹל אֲשֶׁר תֵּלֵךְ: לֹא־יָמוּשׁ סֵפֶר הַתּוֹרָה הַזֶּה
מִפִּיךָ וְהָגִיתָ בּוֹ יוֹמָם וָלַיְלָה לְמַעַן תִּשְׁמֹר לַעֲשׂוֹת כְּכָל־הַכָּתוּב
בּוֹ כִּי־אָז תַּצְלִיחַ אֶת־דְּרָכֶךָ וְאָז תַּשְׂכִּיל: הֲלֹא צִוִּיתִיךָ חֲזַק
וֶאֱמָץ אַל־תַּעֲרֹץ וְאַל־תֵּחָת כִּי עִמְּךָ יְהֹוָה אֱלֹהֶיךָ

ח

Fig. 190. Border, from the *Hebrew Bible*, Naples, about 1490-91.

Valturius (who was on Sigismondo's council), there is no documentary evidence in its support. Though Matteo de' Pasti is known to have painted the *Triumphs of Petrarch* for Piero di Cosimo de' Medici at Venice in 1441,

Fig. 192. The Youth and Thais, from *Aesop*, Verona 1479.

and to have worked with Giorgio Tedesco and others on a Breviary for Lionello d' Este (between 1441 and 1446), these works are either lost or perished, so that comparison with painted work is not available.[1] Moreover, Valturius himself, who designed engines of war, must have invented his own illustrations, and may well have been capable of embellishing his designs with figures. We have already noted early adaptations of Valturius's designs in Vegetius Renatus, *Von der Ritterschaft*, printed at Augsburg by J. Wiener about 1475. Two later Verona editions with reduced copies of the original woodcuts were printed by BONINUS DE BONINIS in 1483

(H. 15848, 13th February 1483, in Latin; H. 15849, 17th February 1483, in Italian). They contain (in book XI.) an interesting new subject representing *Three Soldiers in a Tent*, which appeared later in Antonio Cornazano, *Opera Bellissima del Arte Militar*, Venice (C. de Pensis) 1493 (E. 723).

In very much the same style of cutting as the Valturius are the illustrations to the first edition printed in Italy of Aesop's *Fables* (in Latin and

[1] Essling and Müntz (*Pétrarque*, Paris 1902, p. 136) identified Matteo's *Triumphs of Petrarch* with the paintings (*Fame, Religion, Love* and *Death*) on a circular box preserved in the Uffizi. Their identification is not, however, generally accepted, as the paintings appear to be Florentine, and Matteo's *Triumphs* are more likely to have been miniatures (see P. Schubring, *Cassoni*, Leipzig 1915, p. 271, Nos. 208-11, and pl. xlvi for description and reproduction).

Italian verse) issued by Giovanni and Alberto Alvise, 26th June 1479 (H. 345, GW. 428). And the figures are sufficiently similar in character to render it possible that if Valturius had been helped by a figure draughtsman, it was the same man who designed the *Aesop* cuts. They are charming and lively inventions, and the cutter, though hardly precise as a craftsman, sufficed to support the simple linear style of design, made even simpler by a frequent and fitting use of black spaces. The printer used a variety of small blocks of decorative designs, technically known as 'printer's flowers', with which he made up his border decoration, the various designs being no doubt multiplied by casting. The same 'flowers' are also used decoratively at various places throughout the text, at the beginning and end of sections and lines, etc., in this and other books from the same press, e.g. in Capranica, *Arte di bene morire*, 28th April 1478 (H. 4398) and Hieronymus Manfredi, *Prognosticon Anni 1479* (H. 15848). Reference has already been made to the Naples *Aesop* as largely dependent on the present edition for its designs. Regarding the Verona *Aesop* as the *editio princeps* of the Fables in Italy, I would add some further comparative notes on *Aesop* illustrations. In the first place the designer of the Verona cuts must have known those of Johann Zainer's Ulm edition (of about 1476–77), but his illustrations seldom show more than general points of comparison, and even in the examples of closer resemblance show originality of rendering.

The Brescia edition of 1487, printed by Boninus de Boninis (H. 348, GW. 430), is very closely modelled on the Verona edition. There is variety in the *passe-partout* borders, but the frontispece and the subjects themselves are for the most part copies in reverse, far inferior to the originals in draughtsmanship and cutting. The Venice editions, which are of two families, printed respectively by BERNARDINUS BENALIUS and MANFREDUS DE BONELLIS, deserve more attention. They are two distinct series of cuts, deriving from both Verona and Naples editions, but more from that of Naples.

The subjects of the edition printed by Benalius in 1487 (E. 358, GW. 431) are framed within *passe-partout* borders on a black ground with three variant designs in the arch above. The cuts themselves are variable in quality, rather heavy and unsensitive in line, and considerably inferior to either the Verona or the Naples edition.

The series first printed by Manfredus de Bonellis, 31st January 1491 (E. 360, GW. 432), are of finer quality. Their author, who is nearly related to (if not identical with) the designer of the Malermi Bible of

1493, has a fine classic sense, and is well served by the delicate draughtsmanship of his cutter. The frontispiece with *Aesop and his Commentators* is an

independent design, and the illustrations of the fables are framed within a variety of attractive scroll and figure borders in black line. In the later issue of 1497 (E. 363, H. 351) the original frontispiece is replaced by a poorer cut of the same design with parallel shading within a border repeated from Lucan's *Pharsalia* (1495), but the other blocks are reprinted with slight differences in the borders. Bonellis also issued editions of the *Life of Aesop* in 1492 (E. 611, H. 354, GW. 445) and 1493 (E. 612,

Fig. 193. The Rat and the Frog, from *Aesop*, Venice 1491.

GW. 612) with cuts derived from those of Naples, and repeating the frontispiece from his 1491 edition of the Fables.

POJANO

The only book printed at Pojano (*Rure Polliano Verona ad lapidem jacente quartum*, i.e. four miles from Verona, as it appears in the colophon) is an Italian translation of Petrarch, *Libro degli Uomini Famosi*, issued from the press of FELICIANUS (ANTIQUARIUS) and INNOCENS ZILETUS in 1476 (H. 12808). It contains two outline strap-work borders of attractive design, of which one or the other is repeated at the beginning of each section (see fig. 194).

There are two copies of the book in the British Museum, one in which the borders (which never surround any text) are left uncoloured, the other in which the borders are covered in opaque colours and the blank centre filled with drawings of the various heroes in pen and light washes of water-colour. The drawings are evidently by a hack draughtsman, who found especial difficulty with his mounted figures. It is probable that the printer intended the whole edition to be illuminated in this way, as the borders served no other purpose.

VENICE [1]

ITS EARLIEST BOOK-ILLUSTRATION
AND THE SO-CALLED BLOCK-BOOK PASSION

Like the borders already noted, the earliest subject illustrations in Venetian books were cut chiefly in outline, and no doubt in the first place intended as bases for illumination. An isolated example is the series of six small cuts to the *Days of Creation* in the *Italian Bible* printed by ADAM DE AMBERGAU on 1st October 1471 (E. 131, H. 3148), but it is curious that the only copy in which the cuts are noted (and in that case illuminated) is the Spencer copy in the John Rylands Library, Manchester. In other copies, such as that of the British Museum, the spaces are left blank.

---

[1] For Venetian books the indispensable work of reference is Prince d'Essling (Victor Masséna, Duc de Rivoli), *Études sur l'art de la gravure sur bois à Venise, Les Missels imprimés à Venise de 1481 à 1600*, Paris [1895] 1896; *Les Livres à figures vénitiens de la fin du XV⁰ siècle et du commencement du XVI. I⁰ Partie: Ouvrages imprimés de 1450 à 1490 et leurs éditions successives jusqu'en 1525*, tome i. Nos. 1-530 (1469-90), Florence, Paris 1907; tome ii. Nos. 531-1255 (1491-1500), Florence, Paris 1908; II⁰ Partie: *Ouvrages imprimés de 1501 à 1525*, (1) Nos. 1256-1950 (1501-17); (2) Nos. 1960-2307 (1517-25); Nos. 2308-2585 (n.d., early XVI century), Florence, Paris 1909. III⁰ Partie: *Les Origines et le développement de la xylographie à Venise*, Revision; Appendix; Tables, Florence, Paris 1914. It should be noted that successive editions of each work are given after its first edition. The work entirely supersedes the same author's *Bibliographie des livres à figures vénitiens* (1469-1525), Paris 1892. See also Prince d'Essling, *Études sur l'art de la gravure sur bois à Venise, Les Missels imprimés à Venise de 1481 à 1600*. Paris [1895]-1896; Paul Kristeller, *La xylografia veneziana (a proposito dell' opera del Duca di Rivoli*, Archivio Storico dell' Arte, v., 1892, 95; P. Kristeller, Review of Essling, I⁰ Partie, tom i., in *Mitteilungen der Gesellsch. für vervielfältigende Kunst*, 1907, p. 12; C. Castellani, *L' arte della stampa del rinascimento italiano, Venezia*, Venice 1894; also works specifically on the Venetian Block-book, footnote to p. 416.

After this apparently abortive experiment no subject cuts appear in Venetian books until the *Crucifixion* subject (the Canon cut) in certain Missals, again in outline, and mostly found coloured by hand. Such are the several blocks of different sizes, each in the same style, in the Missals printed by Octavianus Scotus, i.e. the *Missale Romanum*, in quarto, 29th December 1481 (E. 18), and in folio, 31st August 1482 (E. 21), and the *Missale Ordinis Praedicatorum*, in quarto, 24th December 1482 (E. 248, H. 11289). The large cut in the folio Missal is by far the finest of the three blocks (fig. 195).

Apart from these early illustrations in Bibles and Missals, Venetian woodcuts are seldom coloured, even though their style is predominantly outline. This devotion to purity of line

Fig. 194. Border, from Petrarch, *Libro degli Uomini Famosi*, Pojano 1476.

in woodcut was more marked, and persisted longer, in Venice than elsewhere, only yielding to a fuller system of shading in the early xvi century.

Some orientation in regard to the earliest work of Italian block-printed illustration, the so-called *Block-book Passion* at Berlin[1] (S. iv. p. 325), is offered by the appearance of later impressions from the same blocks in a Venetian book, i.e. Bonaventura, *Meditazioni sopra la Passione*, printed in

[1] Paul Kristeller, *Ein venezianisches Blockbuch in Berlin*, Pr. Jahrbuch, xxii., 1901, 132; Victor Masséna, Prince d'Essling, *Le Premier Livre xylographique imprimé à Venise vers 1450*, Paris

1487 by HIERONYMUS DE SANCTIS and his partner CORNELIO. Though examples of the loan and transfer of blocks from one locality to another are recognised,[1] nevertheless it is more natural to assume that the blocks remained in the place of their origin, and comparison of their style with early Venetian art in general, with its Gothic architecture and sculpture in particular, a comparison which has been developed in detail by Kristeller, fully supports the assumption.

In spite of its usual designation, the *Passion* series is not a block-book in the strict sense of the word, though it might have originally been issued as one. As preserved in the unique set at Berlin it includes eighteen subjects (each about $8\frac{5}{8} \times 5\frac{5}{8}$ inches) printed in black ink, probably in an ordinary printing-press, on both sides of nine sheets. Three lines of Latin text from the Bible, cut in Gothic letters, appear

Fig. 195. Christ on the Cross, from *Missale Romanum*, Venice 1482.

below each subject on a scroll held by two angels. The prints are heavily illuminated, and no watermark can be deciphered.

1903 (in shorter form in Gazette des Beaux-Arts, 3e pér., xxx., 1903, pp. 89, 243); Paul Kristeller, *Eine Folge venezianischer Holzschnitte aus dem XV^{ten} Jahrhundert im Besitze der Stadt Nürnberg*, Graphische Gesellschaft, ix., Berlin 1909 (a series of Venetian copies from the Block-book series); Paul Kristeller, *Das italienische Blockbuch des Kupferstichkabinetts zu Berlin*, Monatshefte für Bücherfreunde und Graphiker, i., 1925, 331.

[1] See Index of Subjects (*Blocks, Transfer of*).

Fig. 196. Christ before Pilate, from the Venetian *Block-book Passion*.

A series of early Venetian copies in the Germanic Museum, Nuremberg, came from a miscellaneous collection of early cuts pasted on an altar-piece in the Church of St. Catherine, in the same town.[1] It is equally possible that the original set might have been intended for church decoration rather than for issue in book form, but there is no evidence on one side or the other.

That the Berlin set was early in Germany or in German hands is proved by the German manuscript inscriptions above and below each subject, which appear to be nearly contemporary with the prints. But this does not in any way invalidate the attribution of the designs or the cutting to Venice.

As issued in Bonaventura's *Meditazioni sopra la Passione*, the

Fig. 197. The Raising of Lazarus, from Bonaventura, *Meditazioni*, Venice 1487.

blocks were cut down to about $6\frac{1}{2} \times 5\frac{1}{4}$ inches, taking away the lettered scrolls, and leaving the supporting angels' heads in meaningless isolation. This rare

[1] The prints related to the Berlin block-book were described and reproduced by P. Kristeller, Graphische Gesellschaft (see Bibliography in footnote to p. 416). These copies were made from the lettered blocks, but as preserved are cut down like the later state of the originals. There is a second copy of the *Entombment*, with Cross added behind the tomb and buildings in the background, in Paris (S. 516, Bouchot 51, Lemoisne, xxxi.; about $10\frac{1}{2} \times 7\frac{1}{2}$ inches).

An early notice of the Nuremberg altar-piece is in Passavant, i. p. 33, No. 24, where it is stated that it was removed from the Church of St. Catherine to the Burg in 1811. Further description and reproduction of miscellaneous cuts apart from the Venetian series are given by W. Stengel,

book, of which copies are known in the British Museum (from the Huth Collection), Rome (Bibl. Casanatense), Ferrara and Modena, contains eleven cuts, ten from the Berlin series, and an additional subject, the *Raising of Lazarus*, which is used as the frontispiece (fig. 197). This additional cut is in precisely the same style and shows the isolated angels, so that it evidently belonged to the original series.

Fig. 198. The Martyrdom of St. Sebastian. Miniature from the
Mariegola dell' Arte dei Verrieri di Venezia.

The series of copies at Nuremberg, to which reference has already been made, includes twenty-five subjects in all, but lacks the *Christ washing the Disciples' Feet* (Berlin) and the Bonaventura *Raising of Lazarus*. The additional subjects are six scenes from the *Life of Christ* (the *Annunciation, Nativity, Circumcision, Adoration of the Magi, Massacre of the Innocents*, and *Christ disputing with the Doctors*), and two scenes after the Resurrection, *Christ appearing to the Magdalene*

Unedirte Holzschnitte im Nürnberger Kupferstichkabinett, Strassburg (Heitz, *Einbl.*, 37) 1913. Stengel states that the watermark on three of the Venetian series is Briquet 13618, noted about 1426–1446 and chiefly in North Italy, so that Stengel appears to regard these 'copies' as earlier than the Berlin block-book. Most of the miscellaneous cuts are crude work rather in the style of the German block-books, *Decalogus* and *Septimia Poenalis*, and can hardly be much later than 1450. Stengel suggests that they were cut in the Katharinenkloster.

and the *Incredulity of S. Thomas*. It is probable, therefore, that the original series was a *Passion*, preceded by a select number of scenes from the *Life of Christ*, certainly including twenty-seven subjects, and possibly a few more.

The copies [1] at Nuremberg show greater refinement than the originals in both cutting and draughtsmanship, and Kristeller has rightly compared them with the allegorical woodcut in Sacro Busto, *Sphaera Mundi* of 1488, which is known from the colophon verses to have been cut by Hieronymus de Sanctis after the invention or design by JOHANNES SANTRITTER.[2] As de Sanctis was in possession of the blocks of the original series (for it was he who published the *Meditazioni*), it is reasonable to suppose that as a woodcutter himself he may also have been responsible for the copies. It is curious, however, that they are not known in any of his publications.

The Berlin series is vigorous and crude in character, with strong plastic qualities, and from its style probably dates about 1450. It is not far removed in general character from painted work by Michele Giambono (e.g. panels illustrating the story of St. Mamas, Exhibition of Italian Art, Royal Academy, London, 1930, No. 23-27).

Another link with Venice is offered by the close kinship in style to a miniature of the *Martyrdom of St. Sebastian* in the *Mariegola dell' Arte dei Verrieri di Venezia* (Members' List of the Guild of Glass Makers) of 1436, discovered by Kristeller in the Archivio di Stato, Venice (fig. 198).[3]

The relationship is equally marked in various single cuts of the period, of which the largest collection is preserved in the Biblioteca Classense, Ravenna,[4] which now demand our attention.

---

[1] For contention that they are too early to be the copies, see p. 420, footnote.

[2] See p. 463 for other work attributed to De Sanctis.

[3] See Essling, Gazette des Beaux-Arts, 3ᵉ pér., xxx., 1903, 255.

[4] For reproduction of the Ravenna cuts see W. L. Schreiber, *Einzel-Formschnitte des XV^{ten} Jahrhunderts in der Bibl. Classense, Ravenna*, Einbl., Band 68, Strassburg (Heitz) 1929. For other notes on the series see (1) the articles by Kristeller on the Berlin block-book; (2) Essling, *Les Livres à figures vénitiens*, 3ᵉ partie, 1914; (3) Kristeller, *Holzschnitte des Meisters des Abendmahls in Ravenna*, Festschrift für Max Friedländer, Leipzig 1927, p. 3 (which gives a careful classification of the prints).

All the Ravenna cuts except one occur in a xv-century Codex (No. 485, *Consilia Jurisconsultorum*). Until recently it appeared to contain forty impressions from thirty-eight blocks, a few of which may be German, including a criblée print of *St. Roch* (S. 2722); but Heitz has noted in his introduction to Schreiber's volume that two new subjects have been found concealed behind S. 1414 and 1248, which have still not been reproduced. An additional subject (the *Trinity with the Virgin and Child and Saints*, S. 749 f) came from a different source, the Abbazia di Porto, and the Archivio Communale.

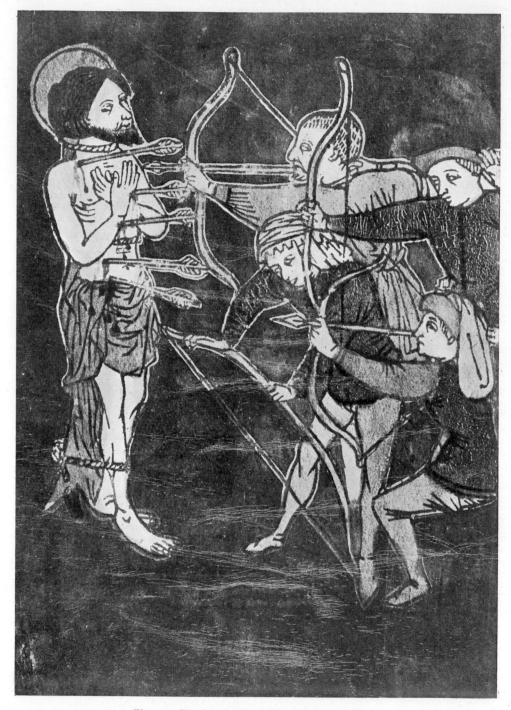

Fig. 199. The Martyrdom of St. Sebastian. S. 1676.

SINGLE CUTS OF VARIOUS SCHOOLS

The most striking comparison with the Venetian *Mariegola* miniature is afforded by the woodcut of the *Martyrdom of St. Sebastian* at Ravenna (S. 1676). There is the same type for the Christ, and the same costume and character in the other figures. And similar analogies in style of design and cutting are manifest in the Berlin block-book.

Unfortunately most of the woodcuts pasted in the Ravenna Codex have been much mutilated or obscured. In some, the figures have been cut round like silhouettes and mounted; in nearly all, the backgrounds have been so darkly coloured that practically nothing can be seen of this part of the design. Happily, certain photographs have been taken by transparency, rendering the background visible. One of these, and the

Fig. 200. St. Anthony of Padua. S. 1233.

finest cut of the whole collection, the *St. Anthony of Padua* (S. 1233; fig. 200), shows buildings in the background based on the Santo at Padua, and I am glad to have Prince d'Essling's permission to give a reproduction from a photograph, obtained by transparency, first used in his father's *Livres à figures vénitiens*, 3ᵉ partie, 1914.

Like most of the others, it shows great simplicity in the linear design, which is left, as in the Verona *Valturius* and *Aesop* cuts, without any shading, but it surpasses the rest in the structural quality of draughtsmanship displayed, e.g. in the rendering of head and hands. The only direct evidence in regard to the dating of any of the series is offered by the *Martyrdom of St. Simon of Trent* (S. 1970), which cannot be before 1475, the date of the event, and can hardly be much later.[1]

From the manuscript inscription *Sktarina* on S. 1316, Schreiber surmises that the original owner was a German. One at least of the prints in the collection is German, i.e. the criblée *St. Roch* (S. 2722), and it is possible that others are either German or cut by German craftsmen in Italy, e.g. the *Last Supper* (S. 169) and *St. Martin* (S. 1619), which Kristeller regarded as Ulm work of about 1450–70, christening the author of a series of cuts which he grouped round these as the 'Master of the Ravenna Last Supper'.[2] He was certainly right in regarding the *Death of the Virgin* (S. 710, British Museum) as by the same hand, and possibly so in his attribution of the *St. Nicholas of Tolentino* (S. 1637, Vienna), but less near the mark in placing the *St. Christopher* at Weimar (S. 1348) in the same group.

German characteristics appear also in the *Stigmatisation of St. Francis* (S. 1423), and the *St. Bernardino of Siena* (S. 1279),[3] both of which show the slight shading and angular drawing of the *Last Supper*, but here Kristeller was justified in comparing the style with Brescian illustration, and accepting them as Italian. I incline to the same conclusion in regard to the supposed Ulm group. *St. Martin* in particular seems to me unlike German work, and it should be noted that the *St. Nicholas of Tolentino* at Vienna (S. 1637)[4] corresponds in its presentation of the title along a strip across the centre with another certainly Italian example from the Ravenna group, the *St. Joseph* (S. 1575).

In most, the design is in outline, and the drapery drawn in a simple system of parallel lines tending to break into curves rather than angles, and the general style of several of the somewhat static figures of saints

---

[1] Two other Italian woodcuts of this subject, which must be nearly contemporary with the event, are preserved in the Vatican (S. 1969, and 1969 a). They are both crudely cut in outline, the one allegorical, the other naturalistic in treatment.

[2] See p. 421, note 4, and W. Cohn, *Untersuchungen zur Geschichte des Deutschen Einblattholzschnitts.* Strassburg 1934, p. 29.

[3] A transparency (Essling, iii., 1914, p. 39) shows the saint standing in a garden before a battlemented wall, essentially Italian in conception.

[4] Its date (1446) refers to the canonisation of the saint.

Fig. 201. St. Clara. S. 1380.

Venice[1] and a *Madonna di Loreto* (Virgin and Child and Angels under a small domed building) in the collection of Baron Edmond de Rothschild, Paris (S. 1104)[2]. A cut of similar design to the latter occurs in the *Miracoli della Gloriosa Maria*, printed by BAPTISTA DE FARFENGO, at Brescia, 1490 (Reichling 630, Naples),[3] and the same motive appears in a line-engraving of about the same date in the Liechtenstein Collection (P. v. 15, 9).

The leaf border of the *St. Nicholas of Tolentino* is found in several of the illuminated borders used by Venetian printers, e.g. Vindelinus de Spira, Jenson, and Bartholomaeus Cremonensis, between 1469 and 1473,[4] and occurs also in a North Italian line-engraving, representing the *Month of March* at Vienna (P. V. 116, 84), and in the large *Virgin and Child with the Infant St. John* at Hamburg (S. 1137) which is more probably Florentine (see p. 448 and fig. 211).

A woodcut of *St. Albert of Trapani* (S. 1184 a, Berlin), which is pasted inside a box, is of the same style as several of the figures of saints at Ravenna (e.g. the *St. Philip of Florence*, S. 1651), and certainly Italian of about 1470. Of other cuts of similar character two may be noted, which, if not Italian, are at least based on Italian originals, i.e. a *St. Bernardino of Siena* once at Maihingen (S. 1278 a),[5] and a *St. Benedict and two seated Monks* (S. 1268) at Vienna.[6]

One of the most beautiful of Italian cuts of the period, probably produced in North Italy between 1490 and 1500, is the *Annunciation* (S. 29 m, Oxford, and Rothschild). Its inscription *Annuntiata Fratrum Carmelitarum Conventus Bgomi* connects it with Bergamo, though the block might of course have been commissioned elsewhere (fig. 203).

By some designer influenced by the Paduan school or Carlo Crivelli, is a *Virgin and Child* preserved in fragmentary condition at Berlin (S. 1041, fig. 204). It is characterised by the hanging festoons, and by the border of geometrical patterns, such as are seen in the decorative cuts of the same

[1] Paul Kristeller, *Un blocco d' una silografia antica italiana*, Bollettino d' Arte, iii., 1909, 429.

[2] *Xilografia italiana inedita posseduta e descritta da Luigi Arrigoni*, Milan 1884. See p. 448 for possibility of identification of the *St. Nicholas* and *Madonna di Loreto* with Florentine blocks.

[3] The cut occurred in a copy in the possession of E. P. Goldschmidt & Co., London 1928.

[4] See p. 399. It occurs on the Virgil border reproduced, in the part which is clearly seen only in the offset.

[5] Karl and Faber, Auction xi, Munich, May 7, 1935, No. 24. Cf. a similar, but much inferior, cut on the reverse of the title of S. Bernardinus, *Sermones de Evangelio*, Basle (N. Kesler), about 1494 (S. 3428, H. 2828).

[6] For the motive of the seated monk in the background cf. a cut of *St. Bernardino and two monks* in St. Bernardino, *Confessiones*, Venice (B. Benalius), n.d., about 1493 (Essling 730).

Fig. 203. The Annunciation. S. 29 m.

uncertain whether the latter is also identical with the line-engraver Zoan Andrea of the Mantegna school, who appears to have worked later at Milan.[1] Another cutter who has sometimes been confused with one or other of the Zoan Andreas is the author of the signature l a.[2]

Better is a large *Virgin and Child on a Crescent* (S. 1047), of which only the lower half is preserved (11 × 15 inches, so that the entire composition would be about 22 × 15 inches) The Virgin holds a circle containing the view of a church by a lake. The block of this subject appears to be among those now in the Galleria Estense at Modena. The style of cutting, in which considerable use is made of the white line, is rather like that of the copy of Pollaiuolo's *Battle of Naked Men* by Johannes of Frankfurt,[3] and probably dates about 1500–10. The complete subject of S. 1047 occurs in a copy of about half the size, which may be of about 1520, also in the Berlin Print Room.

The large collection of original blocks at Modena, acquired about 1890, had long belonged to the Soliani, a family which had been active as printers in Modena between about 1645 and 1870.[4] They range in date from about 1500 to about 1800; some, as we have seen, known in old impressions; the majority poor in quality; a few of known designers of the xvi century, such as FRANCESCO DI NANTO; others with genuine monograms; an occasional date of the xvi or xvii century; many bearing monograms or signatures which appear to have been added with fraudulent intent in the xix century.

A *Last Judgment* (S. 598), generally found in late impressions with the signature MF, preserves a dignified design under the influence of Mantegna or Giovanni Bellini, and is probably North Italian about 1500. There is a still later state, with a border added, in the Museo Civico, Pavia, where the block itself is also preserved. An early state before the monogram was once noted by Kristeller in the collection of G. B. Venturi at Reggio.

An ill-drawn but naïvely attractive *St. George* in the collection of the late Mr. Henry Oppenheimer[5] is very definitely established as Venetian by the orthography of its title ·S·ZORZO·CHAVALIERO· With its white-line background, influenced by Florentine work, like many examples of Venetian book-illustration in the early xvi century, it probably dates near 1500. Another cut by the same hand (similar in style of drawing and in the design

---

[1] See A. M. Hind, *Catalogue of Early Italian Engravings in the British Museum*, 1910, p. 382.
[2] See pp. 433, 469, 489, 500, and 502. [3] See p. 450.
[4] See Achille Bertarelli, *Di alcune falsificazioni moderne eseguite cogli antichi legni della tipografia Soliani di Modena*, Il Libro e la Stampa, Bolletino Ufficiale della Società Bibliografica Italiana, ii., Milan 1909, p. 64. [5] Now belonging to Mr. W. M. Ivins, Jr., New York.

of border and background) is the *Christ on the Cross between the Virgin and St. John* (inscribed CHROCIFISO·DE·FRA·MINORI·DI·VINEZIA·) in the Guildhall, London (S. 417 m; C. Dodgson, Graphische Gesellschaft, xx., 1914, No. 11, pl. x.). And the fragment of a third, *St. Barbara with Christ Child*, is at Berlin (S. 1264).

L' Hora Passa, an allegory on the transitoriness of life, with hour-glass and a naked child leaning on a skull (Paris, S. 1896, Hirth and Muther, 31), is another example which appears to be Venetian in design, though evidently related to the Florentine manner in its white scheme on black ground.

One of the few known woodcutters working in Venice about 1500 is JACOB OF STRASSBURG (JACOBUS ARGENTORATENSIS). His developed manner of cutting with clear outline, and shading in close parallels, achieving qualities of tone which imitate line-engraving, undoubtedly originated in the school of woodcutters who worked for Johann Grüninger at Strassburg, in the style first seen fully developed in the *Terence* of 1496.

Jacob's only dated work, the *Triumph of Caesar* (P.I. 113, 1), signed at Venice *MDIII Idibus Februarii* (i.e. probably 1504 in present calendar), is shaded in fairly open parallels, as if at that time he had not developed the 'Grüninger' style, and with its angular drawing and crude cutting, appears to be an early work. The design forms a procession made up of twelve sheets, and is evidently inspired by Mantegna's famous paintings, now at Hampton Court. It is not altogether outside the grounds of possibility that he is identical with the cutter **I a** who signed numerous blocks in Venetian books, from 1497 onwards, chiefly in the 'shaded' style, for the letters of the signature are never divided by stops and very probably refer to some Jacobus.[1] The fact that some of the earliest of these (in the Ovid of 1497) are in the outline style does not preclude the possibility, as a cutter would in most cases merely follow his designer.

His other cuts are much nearer to the Grüninger style, and more developed in their tonal qualities. The *Istoria Romana*, a large oblong cut signed *opus · iacobi* (P. I. 133, 3), may be derived from some Roman sarcophagus relief, but it is entirely Mantegnesque in treatment, and probably due to some designer of Mantegna's school such as Giovanni Antonio da Brescia.[2]

Jacob of Strassburg was also responsible for a series of roundels illustrating the *Passion*, which has already been noted for its decorative use in St. Damiano, Assisi.[3] The series is incompletely represented at Berlin and in the British Museum, and one original is preserved in the Museo Civico, Padua. The designs show considerable dependence on other artists (e.g.

[1] See p. 469.   [2] See p. 438.   [3] See p. 76.

Schongauer in *Pilate washing his Hands*, and Mantegna in details of the *Descent from the Cross*), and Jacob himself may have been capable of designing as well as cutting so derivative a work.

But his most important woodcut, in which the signatures specifically assign him the rôle of cutter, is the large *Virgin and Child with St. Sebastian and St. Roch*, after BENEDETTO MONTAGNA (Paris, and British Museum; P. v. 159, 53, P. i. 133, 2). Nevertheless, as the inscription is *Benedetto Pinxit Jacobus Fecit*, it is possible that Jacob made the design in his own convention after a painting, a work of no mean skill in so ambitious a subject. Possibly details, such as the thirteen little panels of the *Passion*, above the throne and on its base, may have been added to a simpler composition by Montagna, which unfortunately is not identified.[1]

Another contemporary woodcut gives the same composition in simpler and modified form (S. 1147), which occurs in Berlin with a border, only partially preserved, containing portraits of the Jewish kings, and in an impression once at Dresden (Sammlung Friedrich August II.),[2] with the imprint in type *In Verona Per Bortolamio Merlo*. Benedetto Montagna, the son of the better known painter Bartolommeo Montagna of Vicenza, is chiefly known as a line-engraver, and his work dates from about 1500 (or a little earlier) until after 1540.

Another North Italian painter and line-engraver who designed woodcuts is the Venetian JACOPO DE' BARBARI,[3] whose work interested Dürer on his first visit to Venice about 1494. He was born at Venice about 1450 (if not before, as he is referred to in a document of 1511 as 'old and infirm'); worked in Germany between about 1500 and 1508, and was later in the service of the Archduchess Margaret in the Netherlands, where he died before 1516.

The three large woodcuts attributed to Barbari are not actually signed, but have all the marks of his style. Jacopo de' Barbari frequently added the *caduceus* (Mercury's wand) to his signature, and this mark alone serves as signature on most of his line-engravings. Its occurrence in actual elements of the design in the woodcuts may have appeared to Barbari sufficient indication of his authorship. The most important is a large *Bird's-eye View*

[1] A painting by Benedetto Montagna of a *Virgin and Child with St. Sebastian and St. Roch* is recorded as signed and dated 1533 and once on an altar in St. Rocco, Vicenza. It was later in the Academy, Venice, but it cannot now be traced (see Tancred Borenius, *The Painters of Vicenza*, London 1909, p. 120).

[2] Boerner Sale, 4th-6th May 1927, No. 52 (with reproduction).

[3] See Paul Kristeller, *Engravings and Woodcuts by Jacopo de' Barbari*, International Chalcographical Society, 1896; A. M. Hind, *Catalogue of Early Italian Engravings in the British Museum*, 1910, p. 442.

Fig. 205. Jacob of Strassburg, after Benedetto Montagna. The Virgin and Child with
St. Sebastian and St. Roch.

of Venice (P. III. 142, 33) dated 1500. It is printed from six blocks, the four outside portions measuring about $26\frac{1}{2} \times 35\frac{3}{4}$ inches, the two inner portions about $26\frac{1}{2} \times 39\frac{1}{4}$ inches, making when complete a surface of about 4 ft. $4\frac{1}{2}$ in. $\times$ 9 ft. $\frac{1}{2}$ in. (see fig. 206).

The head-piece of the upper central block is formed by a figure of Mercury with the *caduceus*, the inscription *Mercurius preceteris huic fauste emporiis illustro*, and *VENETIE MD*.

A fine impression in the British Museum, from the Mitchell Collection, has the six parts complete with separate border-lines; it is in the first state, dated 1500, and shows the flat temporary roof placed on the Campanile after a fire in 1489. In the second state, which is also represented in the British Museum, the date is removed, and the Campanile is shown with the restored pyramidical roof, which was done between 1511 and 1514. There is a third state in which the original date and temporary roof are replaced, and the original blocks still exist in the Correr Museum, Venice.

There is documentary evidence, in the four years' copyright granted him by the Signoria in October 1500, that the plan was published at the expense of Anton Kolb, a Nuremberg merchant (and friend of Dürer) resident at Venice, but no mention is made therein of Barbari by name.

The figures (the Mercury, Neptune, and the faces of the Winds) are entirely in Barbari's manner, so that this part at least was probably cut in facsimile after his design on the block. The actual view itself is a remarkable achievement, with many side-issues of interest in addition to the excellently drawn buildings, notably in the representation of ships and a regatta. It is conceivable that the topographical details were provided by another hand, but if not by Barbari himself, it must have required an artist of great talent to fuse them into this splendid sheet.

The other cuts attributed to Barbari actually form one subject, the *Battle between Men and Satyrs* and the *Triumph of Men over Satyrs* (P. III. 141, 31 and 32), the former on a large block about $15\frac{1}{4} \times 21\frac{1}{4}$ inches, the latter from three blocks each about $11\frac{1}{2} \times 16\frac{7}{8}$ inches. Two figures in the left portion of P. 32 carry tall Mercury wands. The motto on a banner in the central portion of P. 32 (*Virtus excelsa cupidinem ere regnantem domat*) shows that the subject is an allegory on the Triumph of Virtue over Lust, or of Civilisation over Barbarism. Here too the style of drawing the figures with their sinuous outlines and shading is so characteristic of Barbari that the cutter might be translating in facsimile the master's design. There is no clue to the identity of the cutter, who was almost certainly not Barbari himself.

Among North Italian artists of the earlier XVI century to whom woodcuts

Fig. 206. Jacopo de' Barbari. Part of the Bird's-eye View of Venice.

have been attributed is GIOVANNI ANTONIO DA BRESCIA, well known as a line-engraver, educated in the school of Mantegna.[1] One of these cuts, an *ornament panel*, bearing his signature (B. XIII. 330, 22), is merely a woodcut copy of a line-engraving by G. A. da Brescia.[2] The other woodcut bearing a signature corresponding to his, IO · AN · BO, and dated 1538, a large *Ecce Homo*, is partially in a white-line manner resembling that of GIUSEPPE SCOLARI. But the signature might apply to another Giovanni da Brescia who was working as a painter in Venice about 1512–31, or it might even be a later falsification (like many of the names on the blocks at Modena).[3]

The majority of the larger Venetian woodcuts of 'pageant' and miscellaneous subjects belong to the XVI century, but one exceedingly fine example, recently acquired by the British Museum from the collection at Gotha,[4] probably falls just within the XV century, as it represents a fight between Turkish and Venetian ships which took place in 1499, the *Battle of Zonchio*. The Turkish ship was commanded by a famous corsair, Kemal Ali; the Venetians were defeated; one commander, Andrea Loredano, fell on his burning ship; the other, Albano Armer, was taken prisoner and put to death in Constantinople. The decorative character of the woodcut is heightened by the brilliance of the contemporary colouring (see fig. 207).

In regard to several of the artists just noticed we have exceeded the strict limits of our study, i.e. the XV century. But it is impossible and perhaps inconvenient to preserve perfect consistency, as certain of these artists who worked before the influence of the greater masters of the XVI century might escape notice in a survey of woodcut of the High Renaissance.

Another designer of woodcut who might be mentioned, as he is generally studied as a line-engraver in company with XV-century artists, is DOMENICO CAMPAGNOLA.[5] But as a designer of woodcuts he is so essentially a representative of the Titian influence that he is best left for study in this later phase.

More appropriately considered here is the artist who uses the signature ·I·B·.[6] Zani stated[7] that he had reason to identify the monogrammist with

---

[1] Cf. above, p. 433.

[2] A. M. Hind, *Catalogue of Early Italian Engravings in the British Museum*, 1910, p. 362.

[3] See G. Ludwig, Pr. Jahrbuch, 1905, Beiheft, pp. 112-17.

[4] Boerner Sale, Leipzig, 2nd and 3rd May 1932, No. 187. The only known impression, measuring $21\frac{1}{2} \times 31\frac{5}{8}$ inches. See British Museum Quarterly, vii. p. 32 (Sept. 1932).

[5] A. M. Hind, *Catalogue of Early Italian Engravings in the British Museum*, 1910, p. 501.

[6] See F. Lippmann, *The Woodcuts of the Master I B with the Bird*, International Chalcographical Society, 1894; A. M. Hind, *Early Italian Engravings in the British Museum*, 1910, p. 535; J. Byam Shaw, Print Collector's Quarterly, xix. (1932), 273; xx. (1933), 9, 169.

[7] *Materiali*, 1802, p. 134, note 56.

Fig. 207. The Battle of Zonchio. British Museum.

a Modenese engraver Giovanni Battista del Porto, who is mentioned in Vedriani's *Raccolta de' Pittori Modonesi*, 1662 (p. 45). There was nothing improbable in the conjecture, and it might have been supported by various points of contact in his style with the work of the line-engraver Nicoletto da Modena,[1] but later research has failed to add anything along the lines of Zani's theory, beyond noting the activity of a certain goldsmith and die-cutter Battista del Porto at Modena about 1529–39.

Far more probable, and indeed practically convincing, is the suggested identity, recently advanced by J. Byam Shaw, with JACOPO RIPANDA of Bologna. He was known as Jacopo Bolognese, and as *ripanda* is Italian for a water-bird, the signature ·I·B· is aptly explained. He is mentioned in the XVII and XVIII centuries as *intagliatore in legno*,[2] and his documented work in fresco, notably the series of the *Punic Wars* in the Palazzo dei Conservatori, Rome, harmonises with the monogrammist's prints.

·I·B· is known as line-engraver as well as designer of woodcuts, and one of his copper plates is dated 1503.

In style of design he is something of an eclectic, his work reminding one now of Mantegna, now of Nicoletto da Modena, now of Sodoma, now of Baldassare Peruzzi, now of Francesco Francia. Landscape and accessories are marked by Bolognese character, and it is in Bologna that Kristeller was inclined to place him.

As in the case of the young Marcantonio and many of the Italian engravers of the early XVI century, there is constant borrowing from Dürer, particularly in motives of landscape background.

This description of his style, made before Byam Shaw's identification, falls into line with what is known of Ripanda's life and work.[3] He is said to have been born at Bologna, and to have worked between 1490 and 1530. Philotheo Achillini, a Bolognese poet, associates him with Marcantonio in his *Viridario* of 1504 (published in 1513).[4] By 1507 he was settled in Rome, and probably painted his Capitol frescoes within the next six years. Apart from the frescoes, there are several drawings of a similar character, one in the Louvre, possibly an *Allegory of the Third Punic War*, having been engraved by Marcantonio (B. XIV. 173, 213, as 'Triumph of Titus'). And finally some sheets of a small sketch-book at Lille, signed by a

---

[1] Whose signature actually occurs on a reworked state of the line-engraving of *Leda* by ·I·B· (Hind, *loc: cit.* p. 538, No. 2).

[2] A. Masini, *Bologna perlustrata*, 1666; M. Oretti, *Notizie di professori del disegno*, XVIII-century MS. at Bologna.   [3] See Giuseppe Fiocco, L' Arte, xxiii., 1920, 27.

[4] See A. M. Hind, *History of Engraving*, 1923, p. 92.

Fig. 208. The Master ·I·B· (Jacopo Ripanda?). Apollo and Daphne.

Berlin), which was tentatively assigned by Kristeller to the Lombard school.[1] I am more inclined to regard it as Ferrarese under the influence of Francesco Cossa, and would compare the style of a line-engraving at Bologna of *St. John the Evangelist seated*.[2]

More probably Milanese is the fine cut of *St. Martin and the Beggar in a Tiled Courtyard*, now in the Masson Collection at the École des Beaux-Arts, Paris.[3]

Harder in linear style, and even more characteristic of the Milanese school of the last quarter of the xv century, especially in the profile portraits of the kneeling figures, is the *St. Nicholas of Tolentino*, once in the Schreiber Collection (S. 1636).

Similarly characteristic is the *Head of a Man in Profile* at Berlin, S. 2013 (fig. 209). Schreiber compares with Florentine profile drawings such as one attributed to Paolo Uccello in the Uffizi (Berenson, *Florentine Drawings*, No. 2766, and pl. xii.), but the outline drawing seems less subtle than one would expect from a Florentine, and finds closer analogies in a North Italian drawing from the Wauters Collection (reproduced F. Lees, *Art of the Great Masters*, London 1913, frontispiece, and Sale Catalogue, Muller, Amsterdam, 15th and 16th July 1926, No. 109). It is unique in its technical style among prints of the period, and in its appearance anticipates chiaroscuro woodcut, though it is only printed from a single block. Lippmann [4] expressed the opinion that its effect was entirely achieved in the press. I am on the whole inclined to think that the background silhouetting the contour of the head is printed, but that the delicate modelling of the face was largely done with delicate touches of the brush in a greyish bistre, possibly also with slight use of chalk. The background is nearly black, but the general appearance is brownish, partly from the tone of the paper.

A Miracle of St. Martha in the collection of Baron Edmond de Rothschild (S. 1618; Lippmann, p. 196 and reprod. p. 163) has been rightly compared by Lippmann with Milanese illustrations such as that printed by the brothers Le Signerre (*Specchio dell' Anima*, 1498, *Tesauro Spirituale*, 1499) and with the *St. Jerome* in Vivaldus, *De Veritate Contricionis*, issued by the same printers at Saluzzo, 1503. The style of the border decoration, which is nearly related to the *St. Jerome*, emanates from the school of Mantegna, and is represented at Milan by ornament panels such as are seen in the

---

[1] P. Kristeller, *Die Lombardische Graphik*, Berlin 1913, p. 28 and pl. xi.

[2] Kristeller, *Le gallerie nazionali ital.*, ii., 1896, 166.

[3] Kristeller, *Die Lombardische Graphik*, pp. 27-28 and pl. x.

[4] *Italian Wood-Engraving*, p. 170.

Fig. 210. Christ bearing the Cross. S. 919.

well-known Florentine painter, Cosimo Rosselli, contains record of a large assortment of miscellaneous goods, including numerous books, volumes of maps and views drawn and engraved, playing-cards, miscellaneous prints, as well as original copper plates and wood blocks. A certain number of the original plates can be identified with Florentine line-engravings of the xv century, but the majority of references are not sufficiently specific for identification. In addition to the entry already quoted, here are a few others definitely referring to wood blocks:

1º *Giuoco d' Apostoli chol Nostro Singnore, in sette pezze, di lengno.*

1ª *Santa Maria di Loreto, in due pezi di lengno.*

1º *Vergine Maria* (as quoted above).

1º *Giuoco di sete virtù in 5 pezi, di lengno.*

4º *Forme da roste in 2 pezi, di lengno.*

1ª *Vergine Maria d' un foglio qumane, di lengno.*

10 *Pezzi di forme di lengno d' uomini famossi, cioè pezi dopi e uno cienpio.*

1ª *Stampa di San Nicholo da Talentino in dua fogli chomuni.*

1º *Cenacholo di foglio chomune, la Nostra Donna da l'altra banda, di lengno.*

1º *San Gristofano e uno uomo famoso, di lengno.*

1º *San Michele, e San Nicholo da Talentino di lengno.*

It is probable that *foglio comune* is a small size, possibly the same as the *ordinary* paper noted by Briquet (*Dictionnaire des filigranes*, 1907) from standard Arabian sizes, i.e. 142×213 mm. = about $5\frac{1}{2} \times 8\frac{1}{2}$ inches. To judge from one of the identified line-engravings (the *Deluge* in the Broad Manner, B. xiii. 71, 3) a *foglio reale* is 268×400 mm., i.e. about $10\frac{1}{2} \times 15\frac{1}{2}$ inches.

On this scale it should be noted that the *San Nicholo di Talentino in due fogli chomuni* would fit well with the dimensions of the print already noted as probably North Italian, about $11\frac{3}{4} \times 8\frac{1}{4}$ inches (see p. 426), while the *Santa Maria di Loreto* would probably be too large (being on two blocks) to be identified with the cut also noted in the same place. But such subjects must have been sufficiently common to render conjectured identifications dangerous.

It is of interest, however, to note that the *Virgin and Child with the Infant St. John* at Hamburg (S. 1137; fig. 211), which is generally regarded as Florentine, has the same border design as the *St. Nicholas of Tolentino*, though this actual design seems more usual in North Italy. This print is one of the most beautiful of early Italian woodcuts, and is undoubtedly

Fig. 212. The Flagellation.

the design of some more than ordinary painter, and it is strange that his identity should elude the student. Lippmann's suggestion of the influence of Raffaellino del Garbo does not appear to me entirely satisfactory.

Recently discovered by Dr. Ugo Procacci [1] inside the binding of a xv-century Venetian book in the *Biblioteca dell' Accademia Etrusca* at Cortona is an interesting woodcut of the *Flagellation*, within a border with white scroll decoration on a black ground, and with white line, characteristic of Florentine work, in the rendering of the ground with its grass and plants. The design reflects the influence of Filippino Lippi, and is comparable with a smaller *Flagellation* woodcut in Bonaventura, *Meditazioni sopra la Passione*, printed by Miscomini, Florence, about 1494.[2]

Somewhat later is a *Nativity and Annunciation to the Shepherds* (S. 86, Paris; Hirth and Muther, pl. 42), rather in the manner of Lorenzo di Credi. From its technical character, with close parallel shading related to the conventions of line-engraving, it may confidently be dated in the early years of the xvi century.

A *Tobias and the Angel* (S. 1702, Paris) [3] derives its design from some good Florentine painter of about 1480, and should be compared with such pictures as those in Turin (Venturi, *Storia dell' arte italiana*, VII. i. p. 566, A. and P. Pollaiuolo) and in the National Gallery (No. 781, Tuscan School). But the woodcut in its coarsely shaded manner might be as late as 1500. Similarly crude, but without shading, is a *St. Jerome* (S. 1555, and VI, pl. 26; Paris); and here again a good Florentine design of about 1480 is the source. Both cuts are only known in the late impressions at Paris (both inscribed 1562 in MS.), which probably do injustice to the cuts in their original condition.

A roughly cut *Nativity*, preserved at Bremen (S. 85), may also be placed somewhat in the same category.

JOHANNES OF FRANKFURT may be mentioned here as he is only known for an early woodcut copy of Pollaiuolo's famous line-engraving of the *Battle of Naked Men*.[4] The copy (P. 1. p. 132), which is signed *Johānes de franc-*

---

[1] See Ugo Procacci, *Due incisioni fiorentine del' 400*, Rivista d' Arte, xvi., 1934, No. 3 (July-September). The book in which it was found is Robertus Caracciolus, *Specchio della Fede*, Venice (Jo. Rubeus) 1495 (H. 4494, E. 833).

[2] See p. 539.

[3] Reproduced, Delaborde, *La Gravure en Italie avant Marcantoine*, p. 206.

[4] For the original engraving, which probably dates about 1470, see A. M. Hind, *Catalogue of Early Italian Engravings in the British Museum*, 1910, p. 192, No. 1. Dr. Panofsky has recently suggested that the subject represents *Titus Manlius Torquatus in combat with a Gaul.*

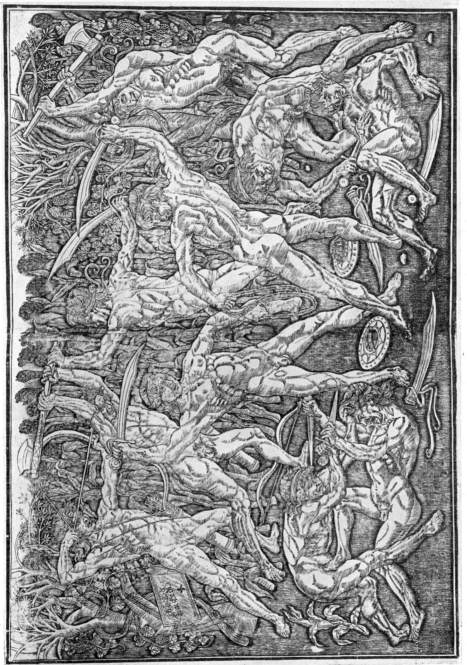

Fig. 213. Johannes of Frankfurt. Battle of Naked Men, after Pollaiuolo.

fordia, and is practically of the original size (about $16\frac{3}{4} \times 24$ inches), follows the engraving in its contours and shading of the figures, but renders the dark background in its own convention, a series of white perpendicular lines and of dots on a black ground. The resemblance of this convention to Florentine woodcut makes it probable that the cutter worked at Florence. A certain *Hans von Frankfurt* is mentioned in documents at Würzburg, where he painted a crucifix in 1470, and his activity extended to 1501, and other painters of the same name are recorded in the later xv and early xvi centuries at Strassburg, but there is no clue to identify any of them with the woodcutter.

A true Florentine, on the other hand, is LUCANTONIO DEGLI UBERTI,[1] but his work falls largely in the xvi century, though its beginnings may come within the last years of the xv century. The description of his work has been obscured by Passavant, who added to it somewhat promiscuously from cuts in books issued by his Florentine namesake, Lucantonio Giunta, who was the most prolific publisher in Venice between about 1490 and 1510. As Uberti occasionally appeared himself as a printer of books the confusion was an easy pitfall.

His signature occurs in most explicit form on one of the five series of woodcuts of the *Triumph of Faith*, of which Titian did the designs, according to Vasari, in the year 1508.[2] It is signed *Opus Luce Antonii ubertii i venetiis ĩpreso* (early impressions at Florence and Gotha; late impressions in the British Museum and at Bassano). A large cut of *St. George and St. Catherine* at Copenhagen (P. v. 64, 7) is signed *Opus . Luce . Atonii . v . f.*, and a full-size copy of Pollaiuolo's *Battle of Naked Men*, OPVS LVCE M FLORENTINI ED INPLESA IN STRAGVA (P. v. 64, 8). Both these cuts from their style are certainly by Uberti, but I cannot explain the *v.* in the former, nor the M or IN STRAGVA in the latter. INPLESA is probably in error for *impreso*.

Explicit again as to printer and cutter is the *Opus lucha ãtonio de uberti fe i vinetia* on the last block of the *Libro d' Abacco*, a popular ready-reckoner, first issued at Venice in 1520. He is also probably the *Lucantonius Florentinus* who printed a few books at Verona in 1503 and 1504.

In addition to these more fully signed works, a considerable number of line-engravings and cuts signed LA, LA*, LAF (in various forms) may be

---

[1] See Kristeller, *Early Florentine Woodcuts*, London 1897, p. xli; A. M. Hind, *Catalogue of Early Italian Engravings in the British Museum*, 1910, p. 209.

[2] See P. Kristeller, *Il Trionfo della Fede*, Graphische Gesellschaft, i., 1906, Berlin (the version D).

Fig. 214. Attributed to Lucantonio degli Uberti. Part of a View of Florence.

attributed to him with fair certainty on the basis of their style. Of single cuts may be mentioned:

(1) The series of four blocks after designs by Domenico Campagnola (*Procession and Adoration of the Magi* and the *Massacre of the Innocents*), of which the *Adoration of the Magi* bears the signature LA*, and the *Massacre of the Innocents* the date 1517 and imprint of the publisher, *In Venetia Il Vieceri* (P. v. 63, 5, and D. Campagnola, P. 4, a and b, and Galichon, 1-4).

(2) A copy of Baldung's *Witches*, dated 1516, printed as a chiaroscuro in the German manner, with key-block and a single tone-block (P. v. 64, 9, after B. vii. 319, 55); signed LA*.

(3) *A woman seated in meditation, with a Child*, based on motives from Marcantonio after Raphael (P. v. 64, 10; Gotha).

Another very large woodcut subject which bears the same imprint as No. (1), *In Venetia Il Vieceri*, i.e. the *Martyrdom of the Ten Thousand Christians* (British Museum), is signed L*, and might well be another work of Uberti, the differences in style being easily accounted for by difference of designer.

On the other hand, caution is necessary even with cuts signed LA*, for the *Virgin and Child with St. John the Baptist and St. Gregory* (P. v. 63, 6), which bears the imprint and date *Gregorius de Gregoriis* MDXVII, would appear to be by the same hand as one of the versions of Titian's *Triumph of Faith* (Kristeller, version B) which is inscribed *Gregorius de Gregoriis excussit* MDXVII. As we have already seen, another version of the same subject bears Uberti's full signature, so that the unsigned version B is hardly likely to be his.

Essling attributes to Uberti a great variety of monograms occurring on cuts in Venetian books, chiefly in the early half of the xvi century, L, LA, LA*, LF (in various forms), and Kristeller has noted certain cuts signed LA in Florentine books (e.g. a *St. Anthony and St. Stephen* in the *Historia di S. Antonio di Padova*, 1557, P. K., 'Early Florentine Woodcuts', No. 32, and cut 193). From its condition the Florentine cut was probably only in a late issue in 1557, but it seems likely that Uberti returned to Florence after a prolonged stay at Venice.

A series of six large upright sheets in the Bibliothèque Nationale, Paris, representing the *Ages of the World* (Courboin, 'Catalogue de la Réserve', 416; with inscriptions *Vis Imaginaria, Humana Christi Genealogia*), is unsigned but might reasonably be attributed to Lucantonio as cutter. The procession is shown in five of the sheets against an architectural background with angels playing musical instruments above: the last subject has a landscape background with river in hilly country of distinctly Tuscan character.

Finally there is the large woodcut *View of Florence*, only known in the impression at Berlin, which has been attributed by Kristeller to Lucantonio.[1] Measuring in all about 23 × 52 inches, it appears to be printed from eight blocks, two on the left being narrower than the rest. The whole is surrounded by a border composed of chain and padlock, such as one might imagine the border which Vasari had in mind in describing Pollaiuolo's line-engraving of the *Battle of Naked Men* (though the latter is not known in that form).[2] Lippmann dated the view before 1489, as it does not show the Palazzo Strozzi, whose building was begun in that year. It has been found that the woodcutter merely copied an earlier line-engraving, of which only the upper left portion is preserved in an impression belonging to the Società della Columbaria at Florence. Though the original portion which might include the Strozzi Palace is not known, it may be assumed from the closeness of the copy of the one part that the Strozzi Palace was not shown on its section, and that the argument for dating must apply to the original and not to the woodcut, which can hardly be before 1500. The line-engraving is undoubtedly the *Firenze di sei fogli reali* which occurs in the Rosselli inventory which we have already mentioned.[3]

In technical character the woodcut is in the Venetian manner typified by Jacob of Strassburg, if not actually introduced by him from the North. Comparison of its figures with subjects such as Jacob's *Istoria Romana*, with its strong outline and close parallel shading, shows the resemblance most clearly. The by-play of the subject (the ferry-boat, the naked fishermen with drag net, and workmen driving piles into the weir) adds human interest to a view of great topographical importance.

In line-engraving it may perhaps be assumed that Lucantonio's work was in part at least original,[4] and on that score the poverty of his achievement is evident. As a woodcutter he no doubt worked chiefly after the designs of

---

[1] See F. Lippmann, *Italian Wood-Engraving*, London 1888, p. 30, for description and reproduction; see also P. N. Ferri, Rivista d' Arte, viii., 1912, 103; and C. Hulsen, Pr. Jahrbuch, 1914, p. 90, for a discussion of the original line-engraving.

[2] Vasari, ed. Milanesi, vol. iii. p. 295, *ignudi . . . e di quelli tutti, cinti d' una catena, intagliò in rame una battaglia.*

[3] And it was probably this line-engraving which was the source of the woodcut views in the *Supplementum Chronicarum*, Venice (Rizus) 1490, and the *Nuremberg Chronicle* of 1493.

[4] Though his most important plate reproduces the fresco of the *Last Supper* in St. Onofrio, Florence.

others, and as a craftsman he was respectable, perhaps the best word that can be said for his productions.

With a passing reference to an earlier section in which we described certain Italian woodcuts of more purely decorative character,[1] we will retrace our steps, and continue the survey of book-illustration in Venice.

VENICE

(continuation)

While the discussion of the large *View of Florence* is fresh in our minds, I would mention the two books which are chiefly noteworthy in our study for their topographical cuts, i.e. Werner Rolewinck, *Fasciculus Temporum,* and Jacobus Philippus Foresti (Bergomensis), *Supplementum Chronicarum.* The general scheme of illustration of the Italian editions of the *Fasciculus* corresponds with that of the German editions on which they were based,[2] including woodcuts of *Noah's Ark,* the *Tower of*

Fig. 215. The Ducal Palace, Venice, from the *Fasciculus Temporum*, Venice 1480.

Babel and of the *Redeemer,* and various views of towns. In the first two Italian editions, that of Georgius Walch (evidently a Northern craftsman) of 1479 (H. 6924, E. 276), and Erhard Ratdolt of 1480 (H. 6926, E. 277), the cuts are German in character and crude in execution. In the 1480 edition the cuts are somewhat the better, and the little *View of Venice with the Ducal Palace* (at f. 37, verso) is decorative in quality (fig. 215), while a few further views added in Ratdolt's edition of 1481 (H. 6928, E. 278) show an attractive simplicity in landscape design.

A distinct advance in topographical study is made in the 1486 edition of the *Supplementum Chronicarum*, printed by BERNARDINUS BENALIUS (H. 2807, E. 342). Here the *Genoa*, at f. 50, and certain other views look as if based on drawings from nature, but that does not hinder the printer using the same block again as a *View of Rome*, on f. 79. The cuts are also more Italian in character than those published by Walch and Ratdolt, and the same character, as well as a continued improvement in topography, may be

[1] See pp. 73-77.   [2] See p. 357.

noted in the editions printed by BERNARDINUS RIZUS in 1490 (H. 2808, E. 343) and subsequent years. The *View of Rome* is of particular interest, and is certainly one of the earliest printed views of the city of any claim to accuracy; while that of *Venice* is pictorially even more attractive. In the various editions the views always occur at particular dates in the history of the world, and as an aid to finding those I have mentioned in other editions, I would add that *Genoa* illustrates the year 1507 B.C., *Rome* the year 751 B.C., and *Venice* A.D. 456.

Fig. 216. View of Genoa, from the *Supplementum Chronicarum*, Venice 1486.

The edition of Benalius is notable for its inclusion on the first three leaves of three subject cuts, the *Creation of Eve: a Roundel* (based on the cut in the Cologne Bible), the *Fall and Expulsion from Paradise* and the *Story of Cain and Abel.* The *Fall and Expulsion* is certainly by the same designer and cutter (Hieronymus de Sanctis) as the frontispiece in Sacro Busto's *Sphaera Mundi* of 1488, a subject to which I shall recur later.[1]

Rizus' editions contain the same blocks, and an additional *Building of the Tower of Babel* (fig. 217) which offers an attractive illustration of building operations taken from contemporary Italian life.

The edition printed by Rizus, 15th February 1492/93 (H. 2809, E. 315), is further embellished by a border twice used, first as a frontispiece including the cuts of the *Six Days of Creation* (from the Malermi Bible of 1490), and then round the first page of text. The border itself (with eight children at the vintage in the lower part) appeared a few months earlier in Jacobus de Voragine, *Legenda Aurea*, issued by Bonellis, 10th December 1492 (E. 678), and in St. Jerome, *Vitas Patrum*, printed by CAPCASA in February 1493/94 (cf. E. 569, of February 1492).

[1] See p. 463.

of Part I. of Appianus, *Historia Romana* (*De Bellis Civilibus*), 1477, folio (H. 1307, E. 221). A three-sided border of similar design but closer pattern and smaller branch-work, and with empty wreath of scale-like pattern in the lower panel, was prefixed to Part II. of the same work. The third version of the second design was a fairly close repetition in smaller size of the first version, and used in Dionysius Periegetes, *Cosmographia*, 1477, quarto (H. 6226, E. 255).

The third design, also a complete four-sided border, and the most delicate of all, formed of branch-work and foliage, crossed shields in circle in the lower panel, appeared with a beautiful capital Q of the same design on the first page of Coriolanus Cepio, *Gesta Petri Mocenici*, 1477, quarto (H. 4849, E. 254).

The fourth design, somewhat bolder than the preceding, consisting of branch-work with oak-leaves and acorns, and an empty wreath in the lower panel, appeared in Celsus Maffeus, *Monumentum Compendiosum pro Confessionibus Cardinalium*, 1478 (E. 275; fig. 219). Altogether these borders form an incomparable series, those on black ground unsurpassed in later Venetian work, as in the whole field of book-decoration.

Matching the borders in style were various series of initials, of which examples are here reproduced from the outline set used with the first border (fig. 220); black ground branch-work capitals corresponding to the Appianus border (fig. 221), and black ground branch-work with oak-leaves and acorns corresponding to the fourth design (fig. 222). The partnership which produced these beautiful works was too soon dissolved, the cause no doubt being a severe epidemic of plague in Venice in 1478, visitations which so constantly accounted for the rapid changes of fortune noted throughout the century in the history of the different printers. Ratdolt only retained part of the stock (some of the type and initials passing into the hands of Renner), and though he used many of the initials, he only reprinted one of the borders, the three-sided version of the second design (in some copies of his 1482 *Euclid*, British Museum, IB. 20513, variant of H. 6693, E. 282). And he only added one further border to his stock in these later years (chain-work on black ground, with a seven-pointed shield at the foot), used for example in Johann Müller, *Calendarium*, 1482 (H. 13777, E. 250). Ratdolt carried some of his stock of initials back to Augsburg, an example such as the Q reproduced in fig. 222 being also used in his *Augsburg Obsequiale* of 1487.[1]

In his later years at Venice, Ratdolt was chiefly interested in the publication of astronomical and mathematical books, and decoration in itself was

[1] See p. 300.

Suo Reuerendiſſimo patri & Domino.D.B.Ze
no diuina miſeratione preſbytero Cardinali ſan
cte Marię i porticu.Celſus Mapheus uetonenſis
canonicus regularis congregationis Lateranenſis
Salutem ęternam & cõmendationem peroptat.

I reuerendiſſime pater & domine
dixerimus quia peccatum non ha
bemus iuxta Iohannis apoſtoli ſen
tentiam noſmetipſos ſeducimus &
ueritas in nobis non eſt.Ideo pie ac
recte a ſancta matre eccleſia inſtitutũ arbitror: ut
omnis utriuſcʒ ſexus ſemel ſaltem i anno propria
cõfiteat peccata:quo per huiuſmodi confeſſionis
humilitatẽ auctori noſtro reconciliari mereamur
cum quo peccando inimicitiam contraxeramus.
A quo quidẽ ſalutari precepto nec uos qui eccle
ſiaſtica preeminentia inſigniti eſtis: exemit. Cũ
magis deceat eos qui excellentiori fulgent digni
tate etiã puriori conſcientia nitere:Cęteriſcʒ qui
bus preſunt fidelibus non ſolũ bene uiuendi pre
cepta tradere: ſed etiã exempla monſtrare. Tuo
itacʒ precipuo hortatu & iuſſu ac nõ nulloʒ alioʒ
patrum in hoc breui ſcrutat riolo aliqua congeſſi

a

Fig. 219. Title-border to Celsus Maffeus, *Monumentum* Venice 1478.

(5) John Estwood (Eschuid), *Summa Astrologiae Judicialis*, Venice (J. L. Santritter for F. Bolanus) 1489 (H. 6685, E. 450): with a map of the world with wind faces.[1]

(6) Cherubino da Spoleto, *Spiritualis Vitae Compendiosa Regula*, Venice, n.d., n.pr. (B. Benalius) (E. 1268): cut of the saint holding books and flowers.

(7) *Fior di Virtù*, Brescia (B. Farfengo) 1491, and Brescia (B. Misinta) 1495: with cut of student at his desk. Cf. p. 507.

The frontispiece of the *Sphaera Mundi* and the *Fall and Expulsion* from the *Supplementum Chronicarum* are in a classic style, influenced by Mantegna, foreshadowing the *Ovid* of 1497 and the *Hypnerotomachia Poliphili* of 1499. Certain details of design which occur in both *Sphaera Mundi* and the *Fall*, i.e. the ground with flowers and rabbits, will be met again in the *Petrarch*, printed by Bernardinus Rizus in 1488, though the cutting of the latter is distinctly more angular in character.[2]

I have already alluded to the *popular* and *classic* styles in Venetian woodcut. The distinction is vital to the understanding of book-illustration in Venice, and seems to indicate the existence of two master designers, who are probably to be found among the miniaturists and painters, and not among the craftsmen who cut the blocks. I will speak of these designers respectively as the '*popular*' *designer* or the *Illustrator of the Malermi Bible of 1490* and the '*classic*' *designer* or the *Illustrator of the Malermi Bible of 1493*. Nicolò Malermi (*b.* 1422) was the author of the Italian translation, and the issue in 1490 of this *Biblia Vulgar Istoriata*, printed by GIOVANNI RAGAZZO for Lucantonio Giunta (H. 3156, E. 133), was the earliest illustrated edition.[3] The edition of 1493 (E. 135) was printed by GULIELMUS ANIMA MIA (Tridinensis, de Monferrato).[4]

---

[1] A still earlier woodcut map of the world appeared in Pomponius Mela, *Cosmographia*, Venice (Ratdolt) 1482 (H. 11019, E. 274).

[2] See p. 484.

[3] The earliest edition of Malermi's Bible was printed by Vindelinus de Spira, 1st August 1471 (H. 3150), and the new version was also adopted half-way through the printing of the Bible issued by Adam de Ambergau, 1st October 1471 (H. 3148, E. 131).

[4] For notes on both editions see F. Weitenkampf, *The Malermi Bible in the Spencer Collection*. Bulletin of the New York Public Library, November 1929. Later editions of the 1490 Bible, with variations and additions in the cuts, were printed by Ragazzo for Giunta in 1492 (H. 3157, E. 134), and Jo. Rubeus for Giunta, 1494 (H. 3158, E. 136). Certain differences between the cuts and their arrangement in the Bible of 1493 (E. 135) from either the 1490 or 1492 editions inclined Mr. A. W. Pollard to assume the possibility of a lost Ragazzo-Giunta edition of about 1491. The 1493 Bible was not reprinted, so that it was evidently less popular. A

It may be assumed that Lucantonio Giunta, who was the most enterprising publisher in Venice between 1490 and 1510, was chiefly responsible for the form of the 1490 edition. It is a medium-sized folio printed in two columns, illustrated by numerous little cuts of column width (the average dimension of the blocks being $1\frac{3}{4} \times 2\frac{7}{8}$ inches). Its form became a pattern for a great number of Venetian illustrated books of the succeeding two decades. Such small illustrations have often been described as sign-posts to help the reader find his place without page headings or index; and they are certainly valuable as memorisers of the main episodes of a long text. But for all that they are very true illustrations, vividly drawn, though seldom of original invention. As illustrations they do not always claim to be more than typical of incident; so that one block will frequently serve for more than one story. The general elements of the compositions were to a large extent borrowed from the woodcuts of the

Fig. 224. Frontispiece to Johannes de Sacro Busto, *Sphaera Mundi*, Venice 1488.

small selection of its cuts appeared in *Fioretti della Bibbia*, printed by Antonio e Rinaldo di Trino, 1493 (E. 159). A limited number of the cuts from the 1490 Bible also appeared in the *Latin Bible* printed by Bevilaqua, 1498 (H. 3124, E. 138).

Cologne Bible of about 1478–79,[1] which had become a model for the majority of Bible-illustrators of the period. But the designer adopted his originals with great independence, using contemporary costume, and imparting thereby a sense of surprising reality to his little illustrations. They are almost entirely in outline: they tend to a certain angularity of drawing, in which bearded faces resemble the designer's characteristic stubbled ground, made up of short parallel and nearly perpendicular strokes.

The *Malermi Bible* of 1493 was based closely on the edition of 1490, both in its form as a book and in the design of its woodcuts. But the style of the illustrations was entirely transformed from the vernacular into a classic rendering inspired by the influence of Andrea Mantegna. Contemporary costume yielded to a more typical classic; the angular gave way to a more rhythmic and curving treatment of fold and figure; the figure itself was not hidden by its clothes, but often rendered with considerable science beneath a more clinging drapery. This description may sound as if I magnify the *classic* designer to the detriment of his *popular* rival, but this is far from my intention. As an illustrator the popular designer possesses by far the more vivid touch; he is not shy of indecencies, which the classical designer discreetly covers (e.g. in Potiphar's wife); moreover, the cuts of the classic designer are often blunted renderings, wanting in life, for all their greater science in drawing.

And it is seldom that the designer of the Bible of 1493 shows real independence from his predecessor in invention (one of the few examples being the illustration to the *Building of the Tower of Babel*, where both designers drew directly from contemporary building operations). But where he does exert independence, he generally achieves the better and certainly more dignified result, e.g. in the *Death of Abel*, and in such revisions of the poorer designs of the 1490 Bible as *Christ preaching from the Boat* (Matthew xiii.).

Even the greater science displayed by the classic designer is not always seconded by the cutters, who are certainly several, and of very varying quality. In general there is more regularity and excellence in the cutting of the blocks in the 1490 Bible than in the 1493 edition, though the best cutter of the latter edition is equal to the best of 1490.

In the 1493 Bible the style of drawing is more consistent than the quality of cutting, so that it may perhaps be inferred that all the illustrations are due to one draughtsman. On the other hand, in the 1490

[1] See p. 358.

Bible the woodcuts certainly disclose two designers, and my designation the 'Illustrator of the Malermi Bible of 1490' must be referred to the chief designer. Most of the Old Testament subjects are the work of this master, the chief exceptions being contained in 'Solomon's Song', the 'Wisdom of Solomon' and 'Ecclesiasticus'. This poorer designer was also responsible for a great part of the New Testament. The difference, moreover, consists in style, and not merely in quality of cutting (though each designer may be affected by the latter contingency).

Many of the cuts of the 1490 Bible are signed *b* or ·*b*·, and as this is found on examples by both designers, it can definitely be assigned to cutter and not designer.[1] One of the cuts (Deuteronomy xxv.) has the two signatures *b* and ·*b*·, the second signature ·*b*· being perhaps added, as the former might have been confused with the ground; in any case this example seems to show that *b* is identical with ·*b*·. The one other signature is ·M*b*·, found once only on Apocalypse xvii. The majority of the cuts are without signatures, and these include many of the finest quality, equal to the best of those signed *b*, and probably cut by the same hand. It is difficult to explain the irregularity of signature. It is possible that a considerable number of subjects might have been cut on a larger block, and divided before printing, and in this case the cutter might have economised in his signatures.

The only signature on the cuts in the 1493 Bible is *N*, and this not nearly so frequently as the *b* in the 1490 Bible. Apart from those signed *N*, there are certainly various hands among the cutters; a good craftsman (including *N*); an inferior cutter, and a third craftsman of very poor talent (responsible for such crude cuts as Deuteronomy xviii. and xxi.).

The natural inference is that there were two distinct woodcutters' workshops, those of the master *b*, and the master *N*, each with various craftsmen.

Cuts signed *b* in Venetian books of the period are all, as far as I can find, in the 'popular' style, except the examples in the *Hypnerotomachia Poliphili*. Those signed *N* on the other hand are consistently of the 'classic' style. This might incline one to think that the workshops included a designer; but it seems to me more in keeping with the general history of the art to think that the designers were painters or

---

[1] There is a slight possibility that these letters have some workshop signification distinct from the individual cutters. My further references to the Master *b,* etc., must be read with this potential qualification.

illuminators outside the cutters' shops, and that the designers, who would probably be appointed by the publisher or printer for the illustrations, would tend to employ particular workshops for the cutting of their blocks.

A careful tabulation of cuts in the two styles used by the various printers and publishers reveals little in the way of exclusive relations between certain printers and one or the other workshop. I do not know that Anima Mia, Luere or Aldus used any but the 'classic' style; while Ragazzo, B. Benalius, Capcasa, Plasiis and Pensis chiefly favoured the 'popular' manner. The publisher Giunta used illustrations of both kinds, and the same may be said of other printers, such as Gregoriis, Jo. Rubeus, Bonellis, Locatellus, and J. Hamman.

It would seem, therefore, that the cutters' shops were independent of the printers, and worked for any printer or designer who commissioned them, and that the designers were more attached to particular cutters than were the printers. The same independence was certainly exemplified in the cutters of the outline borders used as a basis for illumination between the years 1469 and 1472, for the same atelier of illuminators and cutters supplied these borders, as we have seen, to several publishers indiscriminately.[1]

Moreover, an examination of the borders of the last decade of the century seems to show that the woodcutters' workshops must have kept some of their miscellaneous stock, hiring it out as occasion required to any publisher according to his requirement.[2]

These considerations have differentiated our treatment of Venetian woodcut illustration from that of most German towns, where we had more often been able to arrange our description of book-illustrations under the various printers.

Other signatures which appear on cuts of the 'popular' style are:

> *i* (e.g. *Malermi Bible*, printed by Ragazzo for Giunta, 1492, E. 134; S. Jerome, *Vitas Patrum*, Ragazzo for Giunta, 1491, E. 568, and later editions; Jacobus de Voragine, *Legenda Aurea*, Bonellis, 1492, E. 678).
>
> *F* (e.g. *Malermi Bible*, Ragazzo for Giunta, 1492, E. 134; *Legenda Aurea*, E. 678, and Livy, *Decades*, Jo. Rubeus for Giunta, 1493, E. 33; *Trabisonda Istoriata*, Pensis, 1492, E. 661; Petrus de Crescentiis, *De Agricultura*, Capcasa, 1495, E. 842).

[1] See p. 399.   [2] See pp. 502-504.

£ (Jerome, *Vitas Patrum*, Ragazzo for Giunta, 1491, E. 568, and later editions).

Mɣ (*Malermi Bible*, 1490 and 1492, E. 133 and 134).

The only other signature apart from *N* found at all frequently on the cuts in classic style is **1a** (e.g. Ovid, *Metamorphoses*, printed by Jo. Rubeus for Giunta, 1497, E. 223; *Officium B.V.M. Virginis*, printed by J. Hamman, 1497, E. 462; and *Breviarium Romanum*, B. Stagninus, 1498, E. 919, in which the shaded style is used). The letters of this signature are not divided by stops, so that it more probably indicates some Jacobus (Giacomo), and the possibility that it might be Jacob of Strassburg has been already mentioned.[1]

My remarks have shown that I regard the designers of Venetian book-illustration as distinct from the cutters, and of greater artistic importance in our history. It would be of far greater interest to identify any of these designers than find an explanation for any of the monograms of cutters which we have cited.

The style of the 'classic' designer or designers is strongly influenced by Andrea Mantegna, possibly through the medium of such painters as Cima and Benedetto Montagna. Cima studied under Benedetto's father, Bartolommeo Montagna, in Vicenza, and was later under the influence of Giovanni Bellini. He painted various little mythological pictures somewhat after the manner of Bellini's five *Allegories* in the Academy, Venice, but nearer in style to the more angular manner of his Vicentine master, and of the line-engravings of his master's son Benedetto. The woodcuts which are nearest in style to Benedetto Montagna's line-engravings, containing certain correspondences in design, occur in the edition of Ovid's *Metamorphoses*, printed by Jo. Rubeus for Giunta, 1497 (H. 12166, E. 223), e.g. the *Apollo and Marsyas* at f. 49, verso (fig. 225), and the *Apollo and Pan* at f. 93, comparable respectively with B. Montagna, B. 31 and 22. Only a few paintings by Benedetto Montagna are known, and it seems more than probable that as an engraver of small subjects he may also have been supplying Venetian printers with designs for woodcuts. There are a few woodcuts signed *b. M*[2] (a *Sibyl beneath an Arch* in Valerius Probus, *De Interpretandis Romanorum Litteris*, Venice, printed by J. Tacuinus, 1499, H. 13378, E. 1179, the *St. John the Baptist with the Lamb*, one of Tacuinus's printer's marks,

---

[1] See p. 433.

[2] The signature on the *Sibyl* is certainly *b. M*. In the *St. John the Baptist* an *o* above the *M* makes *b. Mo*, or it may only be part of the ground. It is reproduced in Lippmann, *Wood-Engraving in Italy*, 1888, p. 127.

Kristeller 328, not used until the early years of the XVI century,[1] and the large and powerful cut of *St. Michael* in the *Camaldolensian Missal* printed by Antonius de Zanchis, 1503 (E., *Missals*, 235), which are not unlike the Vicentine's style), but this is more likely to represent a cutter than a designer, and it is improbable that the painter and line-engraver Benedetto Montagna would have practised woodcutting as well. On the other hand,

Fig. 225. Apollo and Marsyas, from Ovid, *Metamorphoses*, Venice 1497.

if any of the Venetian illustrations are Benedetto Montagna's design, nothing is more likely to be his than the Ovid.

The style of the 'popular' designer does not seem so nearly related to any of the well-known painters as that of the 'classic'. Though the best work of the kind is certainly that of a very talented hand, yet he might well belong to the company of illuminators, of whom so few are identified, rather than the panel painters. Benedetto Bordone[2] is one of the known illuminators of the period who has been compared with some of the 'popular' illustrations (e.g. Essling has compared his work with the New Testament cuts in the Malermi Bible of 1490, and with the two illustrations in Marco

---

[1] It appears in Cicero, *De Officiis*, Venice 1506.

[2] See notice of his work in Thieme-Becker, *Künstler-Lexicon*. He worked in Venice from about 1480 to 1539. There is a Missal illuminated by his hand, about 1525, in the British Museum (Add. MS. 15813).

dal Monte S. Maria in Gallo, *Libro de la Divina Lege*, printed by Nicolaus de Balaguer de Castilia, 1486, E. 355), but I see no real case for identification, and the *b* that recurs on the cuts is again more likely to denote cutter than designer.

If any of the greater painters might be mentioned as showing something of the spirit of the 'popular' designer it would perhaps be Carpaccio, but I find no real relation in style of draughtsmanship, in which he is in fact nearer to the 'classic' side.

The clearest indication of the two styles is given in the

Fig. 226. Jacob's Blessing, from the *Malermi Bible*, Venice 1490.

illustration of *Jacob's Blessing* taken from the Malermi Bibles of 1490 and 1493 (figs. 226, 227), and the general origin for the composition of both may be seen in the *Cologne Bible* (fig. 168). In the 1493 edition the figures show greater stability, drawing of a more structural character and costume of a more classic, or fanciful classic, tendency; but they lack the vivid qualities of the earlier designer. The cuts in the 1493 edition are slightly smaller than those of 1490, but are made up to column breadth by decorative border-pieces at the sides, and generally provided with upper and lower borders as well.

Fig. 227. Jacob's Blessing, from the *Malermi Bible*, Venice 1493.

The column itself is about a quarter of an inch wider in the 1493 edition, and the general appearance of the page, with less careful printing and a somewhat untidy effect from the combinations of little cuts and borders, by no means so satisfying as the 1490 Bible.

I have already spoken of the greater variety in the quality of the cuts in the 1490 Bible. Of the examples here reproduced, the cuts of *Jacob's Blessing* (fig. 226), of *Nicolò Malermi in his Study* (fig. 228), of *Solomon's Messengers before King Hiram*, of the *Monks and Choristers singing*, signed *b* (fig. 229),

Fig. 228. Nicolò Malermi in his Study, from the *Malermi Bible*, Venice 1490.

are by the better designer, while *Christ in the House of Martha and Mary*, signed ·*b*· (fig. 230), is by the weaker master.

From the 1493 Bible the illustration of *Heliodorus driven from the Temple* (fig. 231) shows a powerful design with skilfully foreshortened figures but somewhat careless cutting; while the cut of *Solomon in his Court* within the same border as was used in the frontispiece and first page (fig. 232) is a most masterly piece of design, almost worthy of Mantegna himself. The border itself is one of the most beautiful of all the outline borders of the time, and the panel at the foot with Tritons and Nymphs is again thoroughly Mantegnesque in vein.

Two *Latin Bibles* (*cum postillis N. de Lyra*),[1] printed by B. LOCATELLUS for O. Scotus in 1489 (H. 3168, E. 132), and by PAGANINIS in 1495 (H. 3174, E. 137), contain a few woodcuts, but mostly mere diagrams (of the ark, the temple and its treasures, etc.), and little of artistic

Fig. 229. Monks and Choristers singing, from the *Malermi Bible*, Venice 1490.

interest except the *Creation of Eve* in the 1489 edition. In style of figure and design this illustration is more classic than the woodcuts of the 1490 Malermi Bible, and nearer to the cut of the *Fall and Expulsion from Paradise* in the *Supplementum Chronicarum* of 1486,[2] rather than to the classic designs of the 1493 Bible. But in manner of cutting, with its delicate line, it is certainly related to the 1490 Bible.

Another book with cuts comparable with the Malermi Bible of 1490 is

[1] Cf. p. 370.   [2] See p. 457.

Bonaventura's *Devote Meditazioni sopra la Passione* printed by CAPCASA, 27th February 1489/90 (E. 405). The majority of the cuts are in the same manner as the poorer illustrations in the Malermi Bible, exemplified by many in the New Testament,

Fig. 230. Christ in the House of Martha and Mary, from the *Malermi Bible*, Venice 1490.

and are probably by the same designer. But three stand out from the rest, the *Christ before Pilate*, the *Flagellation* and the *Mocking of Christ* (fig. 233), and are probably by the Master Illustrator of the 1490 Malermi Bible. The *Mocking of Christ* is excellent in its study of character, while the *Flagellation* has a dignity in both figure and setting which places it among the best illustrations of the time.

The 1490 Malermi Bible was twice reprinted for the original publisher, L. A. Giunta, with a few additional cuts (some signed *F* and *i*), by Ragazzo

Fig. 231. Heliodorus driven from the Temple, from the *Malermi Bible*, Venice 1493.

in 1492 (E. 134), and by Jo. Rubeus in 1494 (E. 136), which proves its greater popularity than the edition of 1493. Many of the cuts from both Malermi Bibles are also found reprinted in various other books of the period, e.g. numerous illustrations from the 1490 Bible in the *Epistole et Evangeli* issued by Anima Mia about 1492 and in 1494 (E. 185 and 187), by Capcasa in 1493

(E. 186) and by Manfredus de Bonellis in 1495 (E. 188), and in the *Vita della preziosa Vergine Maria* printed by Jo. Rubeus for Giunta in 1492 (E. 630); and cuts from the 1493 Bible issued by their original printer, Anima Mia, in his *Epistole et Evangelii* of 1494 (H. 6642, E. 187). The fact that Anima Mia, the printer of the 1493 Bible, was also using some

Fig. 232. A page from the *Malermi Bible*, Venice 1493, with Solomon in his Court.

of the cuts of Ragazzo's 1490 Bible while Ragazzo was still active in printing, shows clearly how promiscuously the woodcutters must have supplied their blocks to the printers.

I will mention the more important books with illustrations by the 'popular' designer, nearly all column cuts of the same size and form as those of the 1490 Bible.

St. Jerome, *Vitas Patrum*, printed in 1491 by Ragazzo for Giunta (H. 8624, E. 568), contains nearly four hundred illustrations and on the front page an attractive larger cut of *Episodes in the Life of the Hermit St. Paul* within the border from the 1490 Bible (fig. 234). Another lively example, of a *Story of the Abbot Daniel of Egypt*, where the child points to its father, most delicate in line and subtly expressive,

Fig. 233. The Mocking of Christ, from Bonaventura, *Devote Meditazioni*, Venice 1489/90.

is in the best style of the 'popular' designer. Capcasa's edition of February 1493/94 (E. 569), which has the border from the *Supplementum Chronicarum* printed by Rizus, 1492 (E. 345), reprints the same small cuts. Jacobus de Voragine, *Legenda Aurea*, in Malermi's Italian translation (*Legendi di Sancti vulgare storiado*), first printed by Manfredus Bonellis, 1492 (E. 678, Modena), and in 1494 by Capcasa (E. 679), include numerous cuts of the same character.

Capcasa's edition, which contains well over two hundred illustrations, is largely independent of the earlier issue. Two excellent initials, P with Jacobus de Voragine (fig. 235) and a smaller E with Nicolò Malermi, appear on the first leaf. The *Transportation of the Body of St. Lucy* at f. 14 (repeated at f. 164, *de Sancto Lamberto*) is an unusual example in this kind of illustration of a composition with many small figures (fig. 236). It looks as if it were based on some picture by Gentile Bellini, comparable with his *Discovery of the Relics of the Cross* in the Academy at Venice,[1]

[1] Reproduced Venturi, *Storia dell' arte italiana*, vii. (4), fig. 134.

INCOMINCIA IL PRIMO LI
BRO DE LE VITE DE SANCTI
PADRI COMPILATO DA SAN
TO HIERONYMO E PRIMA DI
SANCTO PAVLO PRIMO HE
REMITA COME LASSO IL MO
NDO.   CAPITVLO PRIMO.

EL TEMPO DI
Decio e di Valeria
no iperatori psecu
tori de fideli christi
ani: Nel quale tem
po Cornelio a Ro
ma: e Cipriano a car
thagine furon martyrizati: fuo grande
persecutione & ocisione di Christia
ni in Thebayda & in egypto: e uedendo

il tyranno che signoregiaua i quelle con
trate li Christiani con grande deside
rio riceuere il martyrio per lo nome di
Christo istigato dal diauolo trouo noui
& inusitati tormenti: ne quali tardi mo
rissero: e molto con tedio se tormentas
sero uolédo per questo modo prima oc
cidere lamima chel corpo facendogli ne
gare Christo per lo cui amore uolen
tieri moriuano pur che tosto fossero:
occisi. Ma comme scripse il predicto
Cypriano : ilquale dal predicto tyran
no receuete il martyrio. La crudelita
de dil quale tyranno e la graueza de la
persecutione: accio che meglio se con
nosca per li infrascripti duoi memorabi
li exempli manifesto uenendo a mano
del predicto tyranno uno christiano ua

Fig. 234. Episodes in the Life of the Hermit St. Paul, within the border from the *Malermi Bible*
of 1490, a page from St. Jerome, *Vitas Patrum*, Venice 1491.

Fig. 235. Initial P from *Legenda Aurea*, Venice 1494.

or by one of his immediate followers (e.g. G. Mansueti, or Lazzaro Bastiani).

A good example, with figures in the usual scale, is the *Group of Monks standing in a Portico (S. Sabba Abbate)*, on f. 222, verso. Another interesting illustration of a *Group of Monks* (in this case seated, and with the injunction SILENTIUM) may be referred to in comparison, in St. Bernardus, *Sermones de Tempore*, printed by J. Emericus, 1495 (H. 2849, E. 806).

A third group of rather similar composition, *St. Thomas Aquinas lecturing*, in Thomas Aquinas, *Commentaria in libros Aristotelis*, printed by Otinus de Luna for A. Calcedonius, 1496 (H. 1495, E. 897; reprinted in Petrus Bergomensis, *Tabula Operum Thomae Aquinatis*, 1497, Jo. Rubeus, H. 2820, E. 914), may be noted here, though its design is in the 'classic' manner.

A book entirely suited to the vein of the 'popular' designer, with his naïve and occasionally naughty wit, was Boccaccio's *Decameron*, which he illustrated with his usual small cuts in the editions printed by Joannes and Gregorius de Gregoriis, June 1492 (H. 3277, E. 640, dated; E. 641, undated). They were reprinted by Manfredus de Bonellis, 1498 (H. 3278, E. 642). One of the two larger cuts which occur at the heads of the 'Giornate', with two charming groups, is here

Fig. 236. Transportation of the Body of St. Lucy, from *Legenda Aurea*, Venice 1494.

reproduced (fig. 237).[1] Equally attractive is the illustration of the whole company seated in a garden, framed within the border that surrounds the first page.

[1] The example reproduced occurs throughout E. 641, and at the fourth, seventh and tenth days in E. 640. The other example appears at the head of the other days in E. 640.

The same border and a certain number of the small cuts from the *Decameron* recur in the same printers' edition of Masuccio's *Novellino*, July 1492 (H. 10888, E. 668), with many new illustrations of a similar character (fig. 238). The little cuts of the *Cobbler* (f. 1, verso; fig. 239) and the *Preacher, Frate Hieronimo da Spoleto*, with its excellent rendering of a crowd, are among many vivid renderings of contemporary life.

Another work by the 'popular' designer, as lavishly illustrated as the *Vitas Patrum*, is the Livy (*Deche di Livio vulgare historiate*) printed by Jo. Rubeus

Fig. 237. From Boccaccio, *Decameron*, Venice 1492.

for L. A. Giunta, 1493 (H. 10149, E. 33; reprinted in Latin by Philippus Pincius, 1495, H. 10141, E. 34). One of its best illustrations, inscribed BOOZ, used for more than one subject (e.g. Decas III. lib. viii. c. 50, lib. ix. c. 22, and Decas IV. lib. iii. c. 32), was originally intended to represent *Boaz seated with his Kinsmen and Elders at the City Gate* (fig. 240), and appeared at the head of Chapter IV. of *Ruth* in the Malermi Bible of 1492 (H. 3157, E. 134), though it did not figure in the original edition of 1490. The faces are most expressive and the figures equally significant in gesture and pose. The cuts made for the *Livy* are about $2\frac{1}{8}$ inches high (see fig. 241), while others which belonged originally to the 1490 Bible are within 2 inches.

Fig. 238. A page from Masuccio, *Novellino*, Venice 1492, with the author presenting his book.

Cuts of a similar character, including many battle scenes, had appeared in *Trabisonda Istoriata*, printed by Pensis, 1492 (H. 15585, E. 661). Several were used again in the *Livy*. The average quality is high, an illustration of a *Banquet* on sig. pp. v being one of the most interesting.

Fig. 239. The Cobbler, from Masuccio, *Novellino*,
Venice 1492.

Among other cuts by the popular designer is that of a *Monk gathering flowers in a walled garden* which appears in various editions of the *Fior di Virtù* (Capcasa, 3rd April 1490, E. 389; Ragazzo, 30th December 1490, E. 390; Capcasa, 14th July 1492 and 3rd June 1493, E. 391 and 393). The reproduction given shows it in its second state, in which the clouds and star, which somewhat disturb the composition as it appears in the 1490 edition, have been cut away (fig. 242). The book also contains small column cuts of fables, and a larger cut of *Four figures at a farm* on the end page.

Several of the cuts from the *Fior di Virtù* and the *Livy* reappear in Petrus de Crescentiis, *De Agricultura*, printed by Capcasa, 1495 (H. 5839, E. 842). The larger cut of a *Farmstead*, under the title, is specially interesting from its subject, as are numerous illustrations of country occupations, e.g. that of *Threshing* on sig. L. vi. verso (fig. 243).

Plutarch's *Lives*, printed by Ragazzo for Giunta, 1491 (H. 13129, E. 594; re-

Fig. 240. Boaz and his Kinsmen at the City Gate, from
the *Malermi Bible*, Venice 1492.

printed by B. Zanis, 1496, H. 13130, E. 595), contains another of the best designs in the same style, that of *Theseus and the Minotaur*.

The *Vita de la preciosa Vergine Maria* (Jo. Rubeus for Giunta, 1492, E. 630) has an attractive cut of *Joachim's Offering* on the first page, a little upright *Annunciation*, and among numerous little oblong cuts several from the 1490 Malermi Bible.

Fig. 241. The Roman Navy, from *Livy*, Venice 1493.

An unusually large woodcut in the style of the 'popular' designer (but with parallel shading rarely found in his work) is the *Seated Figure of a Man* from whose head and hands sprouts a tree of consanguinity in Joannes Crispus de Montibus, *Repetitio Tituli de Heredibus*, printed by J. Hamman 19th October 1490 (H. 11607, E. 527; fig. 244). The figure is generally printed in brown, the text in red, and the leaves coloured (either by printing or stencil) in green.

Similar again in style and in its shading is the larger woodcut in St. Augustinus, *De Civitate Dei*, printed by B. Locatellus for Octavianus Scotus, 1489 (H. 2065, E. 73).

Of other works in the manner of the 'popular' designer I would mention illustrations in:

Joannes Climacus, *Scala Paradisi*, printed by [B. Benalius and] Capcasa, 1491 (H. 5468, E. 565; the same and other cuts in ed. Pensis, 1492, H. 5467, E. 566).

Miracoli della Madonna, printed by B. Benalius and Capcasa, 1491 (E. 605).

St. Augustine, *Sermones ad heremitas*, printed by V. Benalius, 1492/93 (H. 2004, E. 695) (with an interesting cut of a Baptism).

Processionarium, printed by Emericus, 1494 (H. 13381, E. 751).

Pulci, *Morgante Maggiore*, printed by M. de Bonellis, 1494 (H. 13588, E. 759).

S. Caterina, *Dialogo della Divina Providenza*, printed by Capcasa, 1494 (H. 4692, E. 738).

Robertus Caracciolus, *Specchio della Fede*, printed by Jo. Rubeus, 1495 (H. 4494, E. 833) (with an attractive cut of Fra Roberto preaching).

An illustration of a school class in Nicolaus Perottus, *Regulae Sypontinae*, printed by PENSIS, 1492/93 (H. 12682, E. 622; 1493/94, H. 12683, E. 623; 1495, H. 12688, E. 624), is particularly entertaining (fig. 245),

and one of the printer's marks used by Tacuinus, with centaurs and nymphs, is another excellent example of the work of the 'popular' designer (fig. 246). Another interesting illustration of a *School Class* is contained in the border of Guarinus Veronensis, *Grammaticales Regulae*, printed by NICOLAUS DE BALA-GUER, 1488 (E. 315). This is probably by the 'popular' designer, while a corresponding copy in the border of Augustinus Datus, *Elegantiolae*, printed by J. B. SESSA, 1491, is probably by the designer of the New Testament and poorer illustrations of the 1490 Malermi Bible. Still another example of a border containing an illustration of a

Fig. 242. A monk gathering flowers, from *Fior de Virtù*, Venice 1493.

school is J. E. B. Pylades, *Grammatica*, printed without date by BERNARDINUS VENETUS DE VITALIBUS (E. 861).

The best books are often the least happy in their illustration, and there is no exception in the three chief editions of Dante's *Divine Comedy*, printed with woodcuts in the xv century, those of Brescia, 1487 (printed by Boninus de Boninis, H. 5948), and of Venice (printed by B. Benalius and Capcasa, March 1491, H. 5949, E. 531; and by Petrus de Plasiis, November 1491, H. 5950, E. 532).

All go back either directly or indirectly to Botticelli's designs, of which only the first nineteen, for Cantos i.-xix. of the *Inferno*, were engraved on copper for Landino's *Dante*, printed at Florence, 1481 (H. 5946).[1] The Venice designers may have known the Florentine edition, but probably used the Brescia edition as their immediate source. The illustrations of the Brescia edition, which precede each canto up to *Paradiso* i., where they cease, are all full-page within

Fig. 243. Threshing, from Petrus de Crescentiis, *De Agricultura*, Venice 1495.

black-ground borders of two patterns (see fig. 247),[2] somewhat in the style of the Venice *Petrarch* of 1488. The cuts are for the most part done with parallel shading, a practice which only became common in North Italian book-illustration in the last years of the century, and some are much more crudely cut than others (e.g. *Inferno* xxi., and many of the *Purgatorio*). The best designs are in the earlier part of the *Inferno*, where the Florentine engravings would be available as models. Great deterioration is noticeable in the later illustrations, so that the designer could hardly have known any of Botticelli's unpublished drawings. Benalius and Capcasa's edition contains full-page cuts within outline borders at the head of each book, and only small cuts (about $2\frac{1}{2}$ inches square) for each canto (see fig. 248); Plasiis' edition has only the small cuts (about $3\frac{1}{4}$ inches square; see fig. 249). The cuts in both are very much of the same character and quality, and, considering the close relationship of their designs and the small interval of six months between the two editions, it seems almost more

[1] See A. M. Hind, *Catalogue of Early Italian Engravings in the British Museum*, p. 83. For Botticelli's drawings at Berlin and in the Vatican, see F. Lippmann, Berlin 1887, and J. Strzygowski, Berlin 1887.

[2] Pattern (*a*)—Cherub's head (below), candelabra (sides), grotesque head (above) (fig. 247); pattern (*b*)—dolphins (below), candelabra (sides), scroll (above).

likely that the cuts to both were provided by the same firm of cutters, rather than that the designer or cutter of the later edition copied the earlier. The illustrations of both are nearly related in style to the work of the 'popular' designer, though for the most part very inferior in quality, especially, as in the Brescia edition, in the later parts of the work.

Petrarch is somewhat better served in the three chief Venetian editions of his *Trionfi*, printed respectively by Rizus, 1488 (H. 12787, E. 76; see

Fig. 244. Seated Man, from Crispus de Montibus, *Repetitio Tituli de Heredibus*, Venice 1490.

fig. 250), Plasiis, 1490 (H. 12771, E. 77; reprinted 1492, H. 12773, E. 78), and Capcasa, 1492/93 (H. 12774, E. 79; see fig. 251).[1] The six designs to the 'Triumphs' in each of these editions are full-page cuts within decorative borders, those of Rizus and Plasiis being on black ground, and Capcasa's the same outline border which had been used in the *Dante* of March 1491. The illustrations of the 1488 edition have already been compared in certain details (the ground with rabbits and flowers) with the *Fall and Expulsion* in the *Supplementum Chronicarum* of 1486 and frontispiece of the *Sphaera*

[1] For Petrarch illustration in general see Essling and Müntz, *Pétrarque*, Paris 1902.

Mundi of 1488, and their general style is allied to the Venetian designers of the 'classic' school, though somewhat more angular in cutting. The cuts of the 1490 edition are different designs, freely copied from the Florentine line-engravings, and preserving the same method of shading in open parallels.[1] This imitation of line-engravings in the 'Broad Manner' no doubt had some influence in developing the 'shaded' manner of Venetian woodcut. The adaptation might have been made by the 'popular' designer, or one of his school.

Fig. 245. A School Class, from Perottus, *Regulae Sypontinae*, Venice 1492/93.

The Florentine designs are again followed in Capcasa's issue of 1492/93, probably through the medium of the 1490 edition. In style they are nearly related to the 'classic' designer of the Malermi Bible of 1493, but if by the same hand they are not his best performance. They were reprinted by Zanis in 1497 (H. 12776).

Fig. 246. Printer's mark of Tacuinus, Venice.

I have already described and illustrated the Venetian edition of *Aesop* in connection with the Verona *editio princeps* of 1479.[2] The better of the two Venetian series of cuts is that first issued by Manfredus de Bonellis in 1491 (E. 360, GW. 432), and their author is possibly identical with the 'classic' designer of the 1493 Malermi Bible. An interesting cut of similar

---

[1] See A. M. Hind, *Catalogue of Early Italian Engravings in the British Museum*, 1910, p. 115.

[2] See p. 413.

Fig. 247. Inferno, Canto II., from *Dante*, Brescia 1487.

character is that of *St. Aloisius at his forge* prefixed to Giordano Ruffo, *Arte di cognoscere la Natura dei Cavalli*, printed by PETRUS DE QUARENGIIS, about 1493 (H. 14034, E. 692). And not unlike the Bonellis *Aesop* designs is the woodcut of *Master and Pupil* in *Lucidario* (*Libro del Maestro e del Discipulo*), printed by Bonellis, 1st March 1495 (E. 812), which is copied in a much cruder manner in the edition issued with the same printer's name, but probably at Milan, on the 12th July 1495 (E. 813).[1]

The same classic style is shown

Fig. 248. Inferno, Canto III., from *Dante*, Venice (Benalius and Capcasa) 1491.

in the woodcuts to the *Terence* printed in 1497 by SIMON DE LUERE for L. SOARDIS (H. 15429, E. 864), and reprinted by SOARDIS alone in 1499 (H. 15430, E. 866). The small illustrations (measuring about $2 \times 3\frac{1}{4}$ inches), which are in many cases based on those of the edition printed by Trechsel at Lyon in 1493, are well designed, chiefly in outline, but somewhat carelessly cut. Their effect is somewhat spoilt by the printing or stamping of the names of the characters (or abbreviations for the same) in ordinary

Fig. 249. Inferno, Canto I., from *Dante*, Venice (Plasiis) 1491.

[1] See p. 522.

Fig. 250. Triumph of Chastity, from Petrarch, *Trionfi*, Venice 1488.

type on the woodcut impression, which introduces a heavier tone than the woodcut line. More important are the two fine full-page frontispieces, representing *Terence and his Commentators in a Classic Hall* and the

Fig. 251. Triumph of Love, from Petrarch, *Trionfi*, Venice 1492/93.

Performance in a Theatre (fig. 252).

Somewhat more Vicentine in style are the numerous and excellent cuts of the *Metamorphoses* of Ovid, printed by Jo. Rubeus for Giunta, 1497 (H. 12166, E. 223), and re-printed by F. MAZALIS at Parma, 1505. The style of design is consistent through-out, but the quality of the cuts varies considerably, several hands taking part, as is evidenced by the two signatures ı a and N. Those by ı a, whose signature occurs here for the first time, are among the best and most firmly cut. The possibility of Bene-detto Montagna be-ing the designer of the Ovid has already been discussed.[1] I would here note how in general character they lead on to that masterpiece of the classic style in Venetian illustration, the *Hypne-rotomachia Poliphili*, by Francesco Colonna, printed by Aldus in 1499.[2]

[1] See pp. 469, 470.
[2] Albert Ilg, *Ueber den kunsthistorischen Werth der H. P.*, Vienna 1872; C. Popelin, *Le*

Whoever the designer, he is not far removed from the author of the *Ovid* woodcuts, and his work is in direct descent from cuts such as the *Fall and Expulsion from Paradise* in the *Supplementum Chronicarum* of

Fig. 254. Ruined Temple, from *Hypnerotomachia Poliphili*, Venice 1499.

1486,[1] a relation particularly noticeable in the style of drawing faces and mouths. In general the influence of Giovanni Bellini is evident, but its specific expression, with a tendency to sharp folds and straight lines at the foot of long drapery, is Vicentine rather than purely Venetian. One thinks again of Benedetto Montagna, or Cima, and on occasion of Carpaccio (e.g. sig. E. 1, verso), but no definite clue has been found to fix the identity of a designer who is manifestly an artist of charming invention and sensitive genius. Certain of the illustrations seem to disclose a knowledge of the work of Botticelli, possibly of the drawings to Dante,[2] e.g. the cut of *Poliphilus in a wood* (sig. a iii, verso; fig. 253), and *Poliphilus and Polia walking by an arched trellis*. He has a good understanding of classic decoration, a remarkable faculty for beauty of architectural design (e.g. in the *Ruined Temple*, sig. p iii; fig. 254), and a fine sense of rhythm in figure drawing (e.g. *Poliphilus and the Dragon*, sig. d iii, verso). And the book is ennobled by the pure beauty of type and printing that char-

[1] See p. 456.   [2] See p. 483.

acterises most of Aldus's work. A decorative design of a *Siren* (sig. n iv) and one of the outline initials, which occur in the book, are also reproduced (figs. 255 and 256).

The *Hypnerotomachia* is the only book Aldus issued with numerous illustrations.[1] Apart from woodcut capitals, head- and tail-pieces (generally in delicate tendril and leaf pattern), there is seldom more than a single cut, and that only in occasional books. His main interest was centred in the printing of classical, especially Greek texts, and this richly illustrated book must

Fig. 255. A Siren, from *Hypnerotomachia Poliphili*, Venice 1499.

have been entirely due to Leonardus Crassus of Verona, who in his address of the Duke of Urbino states that he financed the undertaking.

The greater connoisseurs of the period cared for books for their literary contents and printing, and not for the illustrations, which they despised as vulgar substitutes for their more precious illuminations.

Fig. 256. Initial letter P, from *Hypnerotomachia Poliphili*, Venice 1499.

It is noteworthy that the presentation copy of Landino's *Dante* (Florence 1481) to the Signoria, which is preserved in the National Library, Florence, is without any of the engraved illustrations; and the contempt for engraved or woodcut illustration was sometimes accompanied by a complete contempt for all printed books, for it is known that none was admitted to the library of Federigo, Duke of Urbino.[2]

Other woodcuts in the style of the illustrations of the *Hypnerotomachia Poliphili* occur in:

Constitutiones Fratrum Ordinis B.V.M. de Monte Carmelo, printed by Johannes Emericus for Giunta, 1499 (H. 5652, 13242, E. 1182).

---

[1] See A. A. Renouard, *Annales de l'imprimerie des Aldes*, Paris 1834.

[2] See the *Lives* of the bookseller Vespasiano da Bisticci, translated by William George and Emily Waters, London 1926, p. 104: "In this library all the books are superlatively good, and written with the pen, and had there been one printed volume, it would have been ashamed in such company".

be doubted that these woodcuts are the invention of a painter of genius.

The first of the new illustrations, the frontispiece, shows the professor, *Petrus de Montagnana in his pulpit*; the second, *Petrus, his students and an*

attendant with a flask of urine; the third, a *Doctor's visit to a plague patient* (fig. 257); the last, a *Lesson in Dissection*. The last subject is sometimes found printed in colours in the same manner as simpler examples, already quoted, by the printer Ratdolt,[1] and there is a fine impression in the British Museum copy, printed from three colour-blocks in red, green and yellow, in addition to the outline in black. It has sometimes been suggested that the colour might have been achieved by stencils, but the mottled yet regular quality of the pigment proves that it was printed, and probably by hand pressure.

Fig. 258. S. Lorenzo Giustiniani, from his *Doctrina della Vita Monastica*, Venice 1494.

There were three later editions during the succeeding few years, all in Latin, printed respectively on the 15th October 1495 (H. 9775, E. 587), 28th March 1500 (H. 9776, E. 588) and 17th February 1500/01 (H. 9777, E. 589). The third subject, the *Doctor's*

[1] See p. 462. Other copies, beside that in the British Museum, with the *Lesson in Dissection* printed in colour, are in the Pierpont Morgan and Dyson Perrins Collections. See B. Berenson, *Three Essays in Method*, Oxford 1927, p. 32, for reference to the change of fashion indicated by the plain coloured hose in the 1493/94 edition, and striped hose of the 1500 edition (cf. E. P. Goldschmidt & Co., London, Catalogue III., No. 14). Colour-printing is only found in certain copies of the 1493/94 edition; colour, if it occurs in the later edition, is added by hand.

Visit, occurs in a second state in the edition of March 1500, the block being cut about ¾ inch along the foot, and the cat being removed. The fourth subject, the *Lesson in Dissection*, is re-cut on a new block for the edition of 1495, and an elderly Petrus de Montagnana replaces the younger man of the Italian edition in the pulpit. Moreover, the left-hand window, which was only slightly open on the first block, is now completely open, showing a view of buildings on the waterside. This new block is cut down along the foot for the edition of March 1500, similarly to the third illustration, and the basket beneath the table disappears.

Another book printed in the same year as the *Fascicolo di Medicina*, the *Doctrina della Vita Monastica*, by S. Lorenzo Giustiniani (B. Benalius, 20th October 1494; H. 9477, E. 757), contains a woodcut definitely known to be based on Gentile Bellini (fig. 258). It is the portrait of Lorenzo Giustiniani, who was Patriarch of Venice, 1451–56, and canonised in 1690, walking, preceded by an acolyte bearing a cross, which renders in reverse[1] and in modified form Gentile's picture of 1465 now in the Academy, Venice. The modifications, especially in the background and figure of the acolyte, are considerable, and it is possible that Gentile may have provided the new design for the woodcutter. Comparable with the Ketham and Giustiniani cuts are certain large woodcuts of single figures of Mantegnesque design, i.e. a *Christ with the Instruments of the Passion* signed by the cutter *N* in Bonaventura, *Devote Meditazioni*, n.d., n.pr., about 1493 (E. 411), the figures of the famous warriors, in the books of *Guer(r)ino chiamato Meschino*, printed by Pensis, 1493 (E. 715; reprinted by J. Alvisius, 1498/99, H. 8145, E. 716), and of *Altobello*, printed by J. Alvisius, 1499 (H. 884, E. 1187). The figure of *Altobello* is perhaps the best of these, and his book is interesting as well for its smaller cuts, some, in the popular style, taken from *Trabisonda Istoriata* (Pensis, 1492),[2] others newly designed in the classic style, and showing a draughtsman of considerable power (fig. 259).

The *Guerino* subject was reprinted by Pensis in 1494 in the *Libro della Regina Ancroia* (H. 965, E. 740), in which a woman's head was pieced into the old block.

An example of movable pieces in a block is seen in a large woodcut of *St. Gregory*, which is certainly a Venetian work, though it appears in certain copies of St. Gregory's *Moralia in Job*, originally issued by Nicolaus Laurentii (Alamannus) at Florence in 1486 (H. 7935, E. 321, Kristeller 211). This work was the last book printed by Laurentii, and as the woodcut

---

[1] The reproduction in Lippmann, *Wood-Engraving in Italy*, 1888, p. 105, appears to be erroneously reversed.   [2] See p. 480.

can hardly date much earlier than 1500, and is accompanied by a title printed in red in a type such as was used by Emericus at Venice, it was undoubtedly an insertion, procured from Venice, made by some distributor of Laurentii's stock after the original issue. Both St. Gregory's head and the

Fig. 259. From *Altobello*, Venice 1499.

church held in his hand show in the impressions as separate pieces, a fact which proves that the cutter was evidently prepared to supply other saints at request with economy to himself, though I have not found examples of the figure differently used.

Other examples in which the printer exercised economy by the use of composite blocks (like Grüninger, at Strassburg) are the woodcuts of classical authors and their commentators, in which names and parts of the blocks are changed to suit the occasion, e.g. in Juvenal, *Satires*, printed by Tacuinus, 1494/95 (H. 9710, E. 784), Persius, *Satires*, Tacuinus, 1494–95 (H. 12738, E. 794), Ovid, *Fasti*, Tacuinus, 1497 (H. 12247, E. 1124), and Horace, *Opera*, printed by J. Alvisius, 1498 (H. 8896, E. 1164).

One other work in the classical style may be mentioned, i.e. the frontispiece to Johann Müller (Regiomontanus), *Epitoma in Almagestum Ptolemaei*, printed by Johannes Hamman, 1496 (H. 13806, E. 895). Ptolemy and Müller are seated in a landscape beneath a large planisphere, the subject being enclosed within a black-ground border of leaf and strap-work design. Müller must have been a well-known figure at Venice (though information is lacking about the dates of his visits to Italy), and he may well have been represented in an actual portrait.

We have already referred to certain missals printed by Octavianus Scotus in 1481–82 for their outline woodcuts.[1] In the last decade of the century a large number of liturgical and devotional books were produced in Venice, printed chiefly by the German settlers, Johannes Hamman, and Johannes Emericus of Speier.

[1] See p. 416.

The form of the *Officium Beatae Virginis Mariae*, or the 'Hours of the Blessed Virgin' (*Horae*), would seem to have originated in France, where it was the most popular book of devotions throughout the xv century.[1] The earliest printed examples issued in Paris with woodcut illustrations appeared about 1485–1486, and Venice followed soon after with an edition of 23rd July 1489 printed by ANDREAS TORRESANUS (E. 451, Venice), and another of 1490 printed by Johannes Hamman (E. 452, Parma).

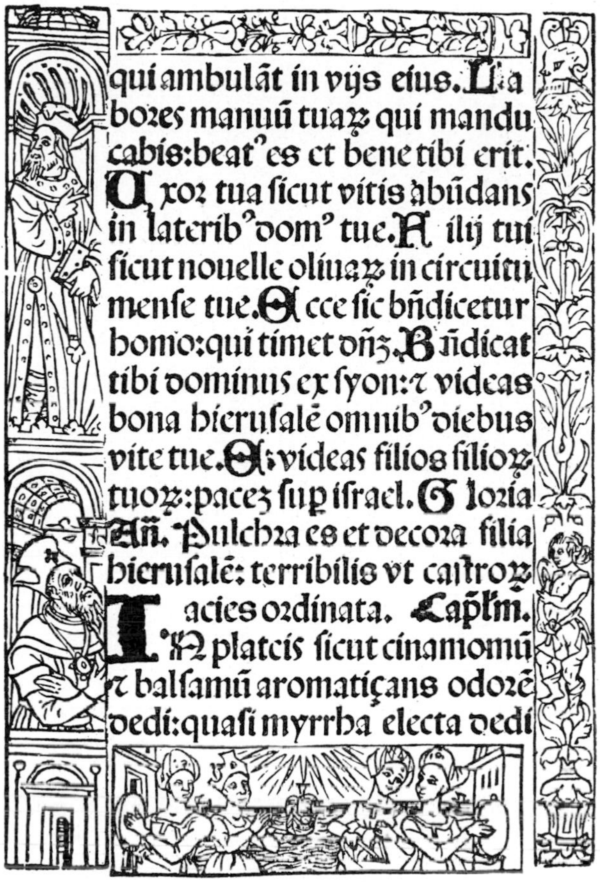
qui ambulāt in vijs eius. La
bores manuū tuaꝝ qui mandu
cabis: beat⁹ es et bene tibi erit.
Uxor tua sicut vitis abūdans
in laterib⁹ dom⁹ tue. Filij tui
sicut nouelle oliuaꝝ in circuitu
mense tue. Ecce sic bñdicetur
homo: qui timet dñz. Bñdicat
tibi dominus ex syon: ꝛ videas
bona hierusalē omnib⁹ diebus
vite tue. Et videas filios filioꝝ
tuoꝝ: pacez sup israel. Gloria
Añ. Pulchra es et decora filia
hierusalē: terribilis vt castroꝝ
acies ordinata. Capl'm.
In plateis sicut cinamomū
ꝛ balsamū aromatiçans odorē
dedi: quasi myrrha electa dedi

Fig. 260. From *Officium B.V. Mariae*, Venice 1493.

The borders and illustrations to these two editions of Torresanus and Hamman are entirely French in character, and might both have been produced by craftsmen from the school of Jean Dupré, whose other relations with Venice will be noted below.[2] Especially near to Dupré's *Horae* of about 1488 in the British Museum (IA. 39817),[3] not only in style, but in details of design, is the Hamman edition, E. 452.

Two subsequent *Horae* issued by Hamman (3rd December 1491, E. 453, Paris; E. 454, 4th February 1492, Paris), and others printed by Emericus of Speier 6th May 1493 and later issues (E. 455, Paris; E. 458, 459, Paris; E. 460, Modena), are without the complete borders, and the little cuts, largely in outline, are Italian in character, and comparable with the illustrations in the Naples editions of 1486 and 1487, which seem to be the earliest of the Italian *Horae*.[4]

[1] See p. 676. [2] See pp. 500 and 628. [3] See p. 683.
[4] See p. 410.

Then Hamman produced a few very beautiful *Horae* with borders, and with some suggestions from French designs, but largely Italian in style, e.g. that of 1493 (E. 456, B.M., IA. 23362; fig. 260), and 1st October 1497,

Fig. 261. From *Sarum Horae*, Venice 1494.

for Scotus (E. 462, Parma). Some of the cuts in the latter are signed **1 a.** A Sarum *Horae*, not described by Essling, still smaller in form, was printed by Hamman for London booksellers, G. Barrevelt and F. Egmont, in 1494 (Duff, 181, S.T.C. 15874, only known in fragments, e.g. B.M., IA. 23403; fig. 261). The *Annunciation* shown in the reproduction also occurs in E. 456, so that other cuts as well were probably used in both editions.

Purely Venetian in design is the *Officium* printed by Hieronymus de Sanctis in 1494 (E. 457, Paris; see fig. 262), its woodcut borders and subjects being among the most delicate achievements of Italian illustration. The designer of this edition was also in part at least responsible for the designs to Hamman's issue of 1st October 1497 (E. 462, Parma).

In the early XVI century the French style again appears, and several of the Venetian prayer-books show borders with black ground after the model of the majority of Paris *Horae* about 1500, the first noted by Essling being published by the Giunta in 1501 (E. 465). And the black-line style of Dupré recurs in editions by Zuan Ragazzo for B. Stagnino, 24th October 1504 (E. 467, Vienna), and by Gregorius de Gregoriis (E. 472, Berlin), and a comparison, which I have been unable to make between these two editions and the Dupré-Caillaut group,[1] might show that not only designs, but actual blocks from Dupré's workshop were used.

To the Missals, which are for the most part larger folios, the late Prince d'Essling devoted a special volume of his work on Venetian illustration.[2]

[1] See p. 683.   [2] *Les Missals imprimés à Venise de 1481 à 1600*, Paris 1896.

They are generally limited in illustration to a large cut of the *Christ on the Cross* at the *Canon of the Mass* (usually called on that account the *Canon* cut), but occasionally have fine borders, and more frequently attractive initials.

Among the pictorial initials those in the Roman Missal printed by Emericus for Giunta, 10th November 1497, are among the best (fig. 263). Similar initials had been used earlier in the *Processionarium* printed by Emericus in 1494 (E. 751). Other subjects most usually found in Italian Missals are the *Annunciation* and a little roundel of the *Agnus Dei*, but a variety of Old and New Testament subjects also occur. Though Germany may claim priority by a year, and France by some three months, in Missals illustrated with woodcuts,[1] Venice was perhaps the most important centre in their production during the xv century, and continued to print liturgical books for many foreign dioceses well into the xvi century. Nevertheless, Paris and Lyon vied with Venice in the number of their

Fig. 262. From *Officium B.V. Mariae*, Venice 1494.

illustrated Missals during the xv century, and began their publication in the same year, 1481. Later in the xvi century Antwerp, and the Plantin press in particular, gradually absorbed the trade.

The large folio Choir Book (*Graduale*) printed by Emericus for Giunta in 1499 and 1500 (H. 7844, E. 1208) is one of the most interesting of the larger Venetian service books of the xv century for its series of historiated initials (fig. 264). They were used again in Giunta's smaller folio *Graduale* of 1513–15 (E. 1209), in which two full-page cuts also appeared, a *Christ on the Cross with the Virgin, St. John, and the Magdalene* (copied from ·I·B·),[2]

---

[1] See pp. 283 and 628. [2] See p. 442.

Fig. 263. Initial used as E, in *Missale Romanum*, Venice 1497.

and a *Death of the Virgin*, the latter signed ꞁ a. The initials are in the same style as the larger cuts, and it is possible that the cutter ꞁ a may be responsible for them all. The larger cuts may have been done for the edition of 1499–1500, but they do not occur in the only two copies known (British Museum and Venice). They are all in the shaded style, comparable to the work of Jacob of Strassburg, a style which was becoming general in Venetian woodcuts by the beginning of the XVI century.

The turn of the century also saw a certain reflection of the Florentine style, in an increased use of white line on black ground. A few of the illustrations in the *Hypnerotomachia Poliphili* show this manner in the treatment of the ground (e.g. *Europa and the Bull*, at sig. k iv), and an edition of Ovid, *Epistolae Heroides*, printed by TACUINUS, 1501 (E. 1136), offers similar and more frequent examples. Comparison of two editions of A. Cornazano, *Vita de la Madonna*, those of Bonellis, 1495 (E. 821), and of Sessa, 1502 (E. 823), illustrates the same change in style.

Fig. 264. Initial letter S, from *Graduale*, Venice 1499.

I have said little about the *borders used in Venetian books* during the last decade of the XV century, reserving them for separate treatment, chiefly because the same blocks were used by various printers in different books. I have already referred to this practice as an argument in favour of the independence of the woodcutters from the printers in Venice.[1] I add here, in two groups,

[1] See p. 468.

a list of the more important borders, and the principal books in which they occur:

A. BLACK-LINE BORDERS

(1) *Two Cupids on horses* (below); *pilasters with medallion heads* (sides); *two eagles flanking lunette* (above). Folio. Fig. 234.

    (*a*) *Malermi Bible*, Ragazzo for Giunta, 1490 (H. 3156, E. 133). With dove in lunette.

    (*b*) St. Jerome, *Vitas Patrum*, Ragazzo for Giunta, 1491 (H. 8624, E. 568). With God the Father in lunette (as reproduced in fig. 234).

    (*c*) Plutarch, *Vitae*, Ragazzo for Giunta, 1491 (H. 13129, E. 594).

    (*d*) Livy, *Decades*, Jo. Rubeus, 1493 (H. 10149, E. 33). With scholar standing at desk in lunette.

(2) *Two Cupids supporting shield* (below); *columns with sphinxes and naked youths* (sides); *lions flanking lunette* (above). Folio. Fig. 251.

    (*a*) *Dante*, Benalius and Capcasa, March 1491 (H. 5949, E. 531). With God the Father in lunette.

    (*b*) Petrarch, *Trionfi*, Capcasa, 1492–93 (H. 12774, E. 79).

    (*c*) Voragine, *Legenda Aurea*, Capcasa, 1494 (E. 679).

    (*d*) Marsilio Ficino, *Epistole*, Capcasa, 1495 (H. 7059). In *c* and *d* with four additional outside border-pieces.

(3) *Cupids on rams* (below); *columns with putti and lions* (sides); *putti and dolphins flanking lunette, and putto playing viol in lunette* (above). Folio. Fig. 238.

    (*a*) Boccaccio, *Decamerone*, Gregoriis, June 1492 (H. 3277, E. 640).

    (*b*) Masuccio, *Novellino*, Gregoriis, July 1492 (H. 10888, E. 668).

    (*c*) Boccaccio, *Decamerone*, Bonellis, 1498 (H. 3278, E. 642).

(4) *Eight children at Vintage* (below); *columns* (sides); *sphinxes flanking lunette* (above). Folio.

    (*a*) Voragine, *Legenda Aurea*, Bonellis, 1492 (E. 678).

    (*b*) Foresti, *Supplementum Chronicarum*, Rizus, 1492/93 (H. 2809, E. 345). With the dove in lunette.

    (*c*) St. Jerome, *Vitas Patrum*, Capcasa, 1493/94. With God the Father in lunette.

(5) *Tritons and Nymphs* (below); *ornament panels* (sides); *cupid and vases* (above). Folio. Fig. 232.

    (*a*) *Malermi Bible*, Anima Mia, 1493 (E. 135).

(6) *Putti on griffins* (below); *naked youths with torches* (sides); *sirens* (above). Quarto.

> (*a*) *Vita de la Preciosa Vergine Maria*, Jo. Rubeus for Giunta, 1492 (E. 630).
> With Man of Sorrows above.
> (*b*) Niger, *De Modo Epistolandi*, Capcasa, 1492 (H.C. 11867, E. 671).
> (*c*) *Trabisonda Istoriata*, Pensis, 1492 (H. 15585, E. 661).
> In *b* and *c* with scholar writing at desk above.
> (*d*) *Lucidario* (*Libro del Maestro e Discipulo*), Bonellis, 1495 (E. 812).
> With vacant space above.

(7) *A second block of same design as No. 6, but less well cut.* Quarto.
> With Man of Sorrows above.

> (*a*) *Vita de la Madonna Storiada*, Tacuinus, 1493 (E. 631).
> (*b*) *Epistole ed Evangeli*, Anima Mia, 1494 (H. 6642).

B. BLACK-GROUND BORDERS

(1) *Nymphs on centaurs supporting medallion head* (below); *candelabra* (sides); *dolphins and head* (above). Fig. 250.
> Petrarch, *Trionfi*, Rizus, 1488 (H. 12787, E. 76).
> The style of borders (1) and (2) similar in style to the two borders used in the Brescia *Dante* of 1487 (H. 5948; see fig. 247 and p. 483).

(2) *Two cupids playing viol and pipe* (below); *candelabra* (sides); *sphinxes* (above).
> Petrarch, *Trionfi*, Plasiis, 1490 and 1492 (H. 12771, 12773; E. 77 and 78).
> Plutarch, *Vitae*, B. de Zanis, 1496 (H. 13130, E. 595).

(3) *Panel with the Choice of Hercules* (below); *candelabra* (sides); *panel with satyr and ram* (above). Fig. 265.
> Herodotus, *Historiae*, Gregoriis, 1494 (H. 8472, E. 735).
> St. Jerome, *Opera*, Gregoriis, 1498 (H. 8581, E. 1170).

(4) *Eagle, cornucopiae and winged animals* (below); *candelabra* (sides); *grotesque head* (above); similar in style of design to No. 3.
> Lucianus, *Vera Historia*, Bevilaqua, 1494 (H. 10261, E. 747).

(5) *Two lions seated back to back* (below); *candelabra* (sides); *scroll-work* (above).
> Lucan, *Pharsalia*, Bonellis, 1495 (H. 10248, E. 851).
> Mandeville, *De le più maravigliose cose del Mondo*, Bonellis, 1496 (H. 10656, E. 907).

HERODOTI HISTORICI INCIPIT.
Laurentii Vallen, conuerfio de Græco in Latinum.

ERODOTI Halicarnafei hiftoriæ explica-
tio hæc eft: ut neq; ea quæ gefta funt: ex rebus
humanis obliterentur ex æuo: neq; ingentia &
admiranda opera: uel a Græcis edita: uel a Bar
baris gloria fraudétur:cum alia: tum uero: qua
de re ifti inter fe belligerauerüt. Perfarü eximii
memorät diſſenfionü auctores extitiſſe Phœ-
nices qui a mari quod Rubrum uocatur:in hoc noftrum proficif-
centes:& hanc incolentes regionem:quam nunc quoq; incolunt:
longinquis continuo nauigationibus incubuerunt: faciendiſq;
Aegyptiarum & Aſſyriarum merciü uecturis in alias plagas: præ-
cipueq; Argos traiecerunt. Argos &enim ea tempeftate omni-

Fig. 265. First Page with border, in *Herodotus*, Venice 1494.

Fig. 270. Printer's mark of Hieronymus Blondus Florentinus, Venice.

Here the earliest woodcut illustrations
reflect the style of Cosimo Tura, the most
characteristic, and in some respects the
most mannered, of the xv-century Ferrarese
painters. The earliest of these, representing
a *Pope seated between two Cardinals* (fig.
272), appeared in Bonifacius VIII., *Sextus
Liber Decretalium*, printed by AUGUSTINUS
CARNERIUS, 1478,[1] and in the *Constitutiones*
of Clement V., issued by the same printer, in
1479. The next in order known to me is the
woodcut of *St. Maurelius standing beneath
an Arch* prefixed to the *Leggendario e vita
e miracoli di S. Maurelio*, printed by LAUREN-
TIUS DE RUBEIS
(ROSSO), 1489 (H.
10918). It is a
dignified subject,
somewhat carelessly
cut (fig. 273).

Gruyer cites a
variant edition in
the Ferrara library
with the title
*Leggenda de sancto
Maurelio*, which
contains a second
cut on the verso of
the last leaf of the
volume represent-
ing *St. George and
the Dragon*. It ap-
pears to be by a
different hand from
the other, and more
nearly related to the
Venetian cuts in the
'popular' style. The

Fig. 271. The Virgin and Angels, from *Miracoli della Gloriosa Maria*,
Brescia 1490.

[1] My reference is taken from Katalog No. 1 of Dr. Ignaz Schwarz, Habsburgergasse 3,

design might have been suggested by Tura's panel of *St. George*, of 1469, in the Cathedral at Ferrara (once an organ wing), but it is not near enough in detail to render the relation at all certain.[1]

Another woodcut entirely under the same influence of Tura, with the characteristic bulging folds of drapery, is that of *Alfraganus and his editor* ('Heremita') in Alfraganus, *Rudimenta Astronomica*, printed by ANDREAS BELLFORTIS, 1493 (H. 822).

Contrasting with the cuts in the style of Tura is another group more nearly related to the work of the 'popular' designer at Venice. Among these

Fig. 272. Pope between two Cardinals, from Bonifacius VIII., *Sextus Liber Decretalium*, Ferrara 1478.

may be mentioned a *Virgin and Child standing beneath a Canopy, within a border of classic design*, the frontispiece to Petrus Pallagari Tranensis, *De Ingenuis Adolescentium Moribus*, printed by L. de Rubeis, 1496 (H. 15597). Similar in style are also the little outline cuts in the *Officium* printed by L. de Rubeis, 1497 (H. 11972), and in the *Corona Beatae Virginis*, n.d., by the same printer, which is appended to the *Officium* in the British Museum copy. There are some delicate figured capitals in the *Officium* (e.g. a *D* with David playing the Harp).

The most attractive of all the Ferrarese illustrations are contained in the

Vienna 1919, No. 11, where the cut is described as appearing on f. 5 of the Bonifacius book. My illustration was kindly supplied me by Dr. G. Agnelli (Director of the Biblioteca Publica, Ferrara), who confirms Gruyer's description of the *Constitutiones* as of 1479.

[1] Tura's painting is reproduced in Venturi, *Storia dell' arte italiana*, vii. (3), fig. 398. Dr. G. Agnelli, Director of the Ferrara library, informs me that the second edition with the cut of St. George was actually printed by Franciscus de Rubeis (son of Laurentius) in 1544. See p. 74 and fig. 33, for a book-cover design with a similar subject.

Epistles of St. Jerome, printed by Laurentius de Rubeis, 12th October 1497 (H. 8566). Their author is evidently inspired by the 'popular' designer at Venice, in particular by the cuts in his *Vitas Patrum* of 1491 and *Legenda Aurea* of 1494.[1] They are small column cuts of similar form and dimensions, and in the same outline style. They have a certain roundness in linear character which distinguishes them from the Venetian designer, and a characteristic emphasis of the black pupil of the eye, which adds to their vivacity of expression. The artist is a most conscious humorist in the wonderful variety of facial expression he gives to St. Jerome's lion, offering its naïve comment on the various episodes of the saint's life (fig. 274). As illustrations of contemporary custom,

Fig. 273. St. Maurelius, from *Legendario di S. Maurelio*, Ferrara 1489.

the woodcuts in the last section of the book, dealing with the rules of monastic life, are peculiarly interesting (fig. 275).

Less humanly attractive, but more individual in their technical manner, are the woodcuts in Jacobus Philippus Foresti (Bergomensis), *De Claris Mulieribus*, issued a few months earlier by the same printer, 29th April 1497 (H. 2813). They are a series of illustrations of the famous women

[1] See p. 475.

of history and fable, in which a few contemporary examples are undoubtedly portraits. Most of the cuts have backgrounds in white line, probably suggested by the Florentine practice. Several of the blocks serve to repre-

sent more than one character, e.g. the *Proba Poetrix* (f. 115, verso; as *Angela Nugarola*, f. 149, and as *Isota Nugarola*, f. 151), which is one of the few examples chiefly in black line, and the *Marcella Romana* (f. 116, verso, who also appears as *Paula Gonzaga*, f. 142, verso, *Genebria Cambare*, f. 150, and *Hippolyta*, *wife of King Alphonso of Naples*, f. 159, verso). Among the contemporary person-

Fig. 274. St. Jerome and pupils, from his *Epistole*, Ferrara 1497.

ages which appear to be based on portraits from the life are *Bianca Maria Sforza* (f. 153, verso), *Catherina Countess of Forlì and Imola* (f. 160), *Leonora of Aragon, wife of Ercole d' Este* (f. 161, verso),

Fig. 275. Visit to a Convent, from St. Jerome, *Epistole*, Ferrara 1497.

and *Damisella Trivulzia* (f. 167; see fig. 276). The *Damisella Trivulzia* is certainly based on a Milanese painting or drawing.

The *Medusa* (f. 24) is one of the most excellent of the illustrations as decorative design (fig. 277). The black-ground (white-line) woodcuts make a good balance to the heavy Gothic type of the text.

Two attractive outline borders in the Venetian style, by the same designer as the St. Jerome illustrations, appear in both the *St. Jerome* and the *De Claris Mulieribus*. One of them (with four children below, little cavaliers at the sides, and six children making music, flanking a lunette, above) bears a date 1493, but I have not found it in any book before the two in question. The second contains sirens and two children with trumpets (below), children on griffins (sides), and children playing viol and pipe, flanking a lunette (above). Each shows certain differences of state, according as *God the Father* (in the final border), the *Resurrection*

Fig. 276. Damisella Trivulzia, from Foresti, *De Claris Mulieribus*, Ferrara 1497.

(in the second border), or merely lettering, appears in the respective lunettes.

In the *De Claris Mulieribus* the first border is used on the back of the title to contain a cut of the author presenting his book to Beatrice of Aragon, Queen of Hungary and Bohemia, and also to surround a second frontispiece with *Scenes from the Life of the Virgin*.

Though a few years beyond the limits of my study, I would refer to the large outline cut of *St. Christopher*

(6 × 4 inches)[1] in the *Carthusian Missal* issued by the Carthusian Monastery at Ferrara in 1503; it is closely related to Venetian style, and probably by the designer of the St. Jerome illustrations. On the other hand, the *Canon* cut of the *Christ on the Cross* in the same missal is in the white-line manner, somewhat crude in execution. There are some good figured initials, e.g. an M with a Priest celebrating Mass.

MILAN—SALUZZO—MONDOVÌ —PAVIA—MANTUA

Milanese woodcut achieved no individual position during

Fig. 277. Medusa, from Foresti, *De Claris Mulieribus*, Ferrara 1497.

[1] Reproduced in the Dyson Perrins Catalogue, No. 166.

the xv century comparable with the schools of Venice or Florence. There were probably fewer workshops devoted in any special way to either line-engraving or woodcut, and what was done, as Kristeller rightly observed, shows the variable quality that would denote occasional work by craftsmen engaged in other fields.

The same remark applies to Lombardy and Piedmont in general, and the book-illustration of all this region is most naturally treated as a single group.[1]

As in painting, the most distinguished Milanese achievement in woodcut was in portraiture. The earliest book-illustration to which I can refer (apart from woodcut initials) is the *Profile Portrait of Paolo Attavanti* (fig. 278), which appears in his *Breviarium totius juris canonici*, printed by PACHEL and SCINZENZELER, 28th August 1479 (H. 7159, P.K. 38), and later in the same year in the same author's and printer's *Quadragesimale de reditu peccatoris ad Deum* (H. 7166, P.K. 39), and *Comento volgare e latino del psalmo lxxxx*,

Fig. 278. Paolo Attavanti, from his *Breviarium totius juris canonici*, Milan 1497.

and in his undated *Modo utile di Confessione* (Reichling IV. 1309, P.K. 40). The letters at the foot, M.P.F.O.S.S., can be interpreted as *Magister Paulus Florentinus Ordinis Sancti Spiritus*. The block shorn of its pediment appeared soon after in the *Penitential Psalms* (Latin and Italian), printed without date or printer's name, but almost certainly by Ratdolt at Venice, about 1480 (H. 7165, British Museum).[2]

A most attractive little composition is the *Portrait of Bernardo Bellinzone*

---

[1] See Paul Kristeller, *Die lombardische Graphik der Renaissance*, Berlin 1913 (including catalogue of books printed at Milan, Como, Pavia, Turin, Asti, Savona, Saluzzo and Mondovì); Paul Kristeller, *Books with Woodcuts printed at Pavia*, Bibliographica, vol. i., 1895, 347.

[2] Copies appeared in editions of the *Breviarium Decretorum* printed by Matthias Hus and Jean Battenschue of Lyon, 1484, and by Albrecht Kunne, at Memmingen, 1486.

which appears in his *Rime*, printed by PHILIPPUS DE MANTEGATIIS, 1493 (H. 2754, P.K. 52; fig. 279). There is a line-engraving of the same subject, known in only one impression, now in the collection of Baron Edmond

Fig. 279. Bernardo Bellinzone, from his *Rime*, Milan 1493.

de Rothschild,[1] from which the woodcut may be copied, unless both are based on the same original. The figure is evidently drawn from nature with its rendering of an easy and unconventional attitude, and Kristeller's suggestion that Leonardo da Vinci might have been responsible for the drawing is by no means unreasonable.[2] Bellinzone, who died in 1491, was, like Leonardo, a Florentine engaged at the court of Lodovico Sforza, and they must have frequently met.

Two other notable Milanese woodcut portraits fall just outside the limits of our date, i.e. in the early years of the XVI century, but they demand some reference, i.e. the large *Portrait of Bernardino Corio seated writing*, which appeared in his *Patria Historia*, issued by Alexander Minutianus, Milan 1503 (P.K. 116; measuring over $11 \times 6\frac{1}{4}$ wide),[3] and the striking *Profile Portrait of the Marquis of Saluzzo* (fig. 280), in J. L. Vivaldus, *Opus Regale*, printed by JACOBUS DE CIRCHIS and SIXTUS DE SOMASCHIS, Saluzzo 1507 (P.K. 365).

Another book of J. L. Vivaldus, *De Veritate Contricionis*, printed by the brothers GUILLERMI LE SIGNERRE at Saluzzo 1503, contains a *St.*

[1] Reproduced Kristeller, *Lombardische Graphik*, pl. ix.
[2] See André Blum, *Léonard de Vinci graveur*, Gazette des Beaux-Arts, August 1932.
[3] A folio book which also contains a fine classical design of a figure of Virtue.

Fig. 280. The Marquis of Saluzzo. from Vivaldus, *Opus Regale*, Saluzzo 1507.

Jerome kneeling before a Crucifix, within a fine classical and heraldic border, which is one of the most decorative of Lombard woodcuts.

Returning on our tracks, one of the earliest Milanese cuts appears to be

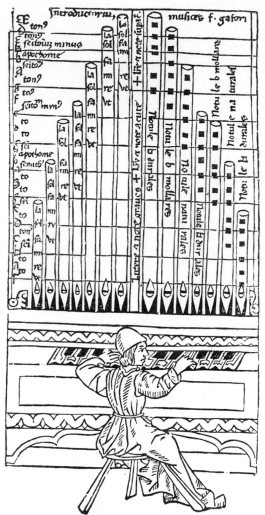

Fig. 281. The Organist, from Gafurius, *Theorica Musicae*, Milan 1492.

that of the *Organist* (fig. 281) in Franchinus Gafurius, *Theorica Musicae*, printed by Philippus de Mantegatiis, 1492 (H. 7406, P.K. 161). The block was issued earlier in an edition printed by Francesco di Dino at Naples in 1480 (H. 7404, Fava-Bresciano, 170),[1] but the style was unlike anything else in Neapolitan book-illustration, and the Lombard musician Gafurius, who only stayed about two years at Naples (1478–80), no doubt had the block cut in his own province. The style shows kinship to Brescian work, like most of the earlier Milanese illustration. The other illustration in the Naples edition of 1480, *Figures at an Anvil (Tubal Cain)*, was re-cut in the Milan edition.[2]

In their somewhat loose style of drawing and shading the Gafurius cuts are not unlike the allegorical title-cut in Baptista Fulgosius, *Anteros*, printed by Leonardus Pachel, 1496 (H. 7393, P.K. 160).

Another work by Gafurius, the *Practica Musicae*, printed by Le Signerre, 1496 (H. 7407, P.K. 162), has one of the most attractive borders. From 1484 Gafurius, who was priest as well as musician, directed the music in the Cathedral at Milan, and he is shown in the

[1] See p. 405.

[2] For another block first used at Naples and printed later in Lombardy (at Soncino), the border to Tuppo's *Aesop* of 1485, see p. 405.

LIBER TERTIVS.

De Contrapuncto & eius elementarijs vocibus.   Caput primum.

Armonici modulaminis Genus auctore Baccheo est mos vniuersum quid subindicans diuersas in se habens ideas idest exemplaria:seu diuersas cantilenæ compositiones: quod quidem contrapunctum vocamus:quasi concordem concentum extremorum sonorum inuicem correspondentium contrapositis notulis: arte probatum.Hunc enim & si certis est regulis institutus: tanto tamen pulcherrimum æstimari licet:quanto euenerit vsui nobiliori .   Est itaq; contrapunctus ars flectendi cantabiles sonos proportionabili dimensione & temporis mesura:Nãq; Melodia ex vocibus constat & interuallis atq; temporibus.   Vocum autem Alia pedestris qua.s.orationes legimus & loquimur.Alia equestris qua poetica carmina secundum Arsim & thesim enuntiamus.Alia modulata qua & naturaliter & in instrumêtis secudum harmonicam canentes aliquid operamur.Heæ enim voces certa dimensione determinata habent interualla.Pedestres indiffinita.Equestres vero quasi quodammodo ex vtrisq; commixta.   Interuallorum Alia æquisonis vocibus extremis dupla dimensione intercludûtur.Alia consonis hemiolia & epitrita.Alia ex vtriusq; commixtis tripla dispositione atq; quadrupla.Alia(minima quidem)sesquioctaua.Alia rursus incerta irrationaliq; dimensione extremis vocibus concluduntur interualla: quorum longiorem in harmonia instrumentali prosequemur enarrationem:De his item Guido sic scribit.Ditonus & Semiditonus atq; semitonium & si voces ad canendum coniungunt nullam tamen recipiunt diuisionem.   Irrationalia igitur & incerta dicimus huiusmodi interualla : quæ in chordotono a tribus primis multiplicibus seuincta sunt:& a prioribus duabus superparticularibus segregata:cum omnem potissime melodicam consyderationem vel multiplicitati vel superparticularitati ipsi ascripserint Pythagorici.Hæc enim sunt huic arti con

Fig. 282. Page with Border, in Gafurius, *Practica Musicae*, Milan 1496.

border training his choir (fig. 282). The border occurs before the first and third books, while a second border with Amphion, Orpheus and Arion, and cupids supporting a shield, is prefixed to books two and four.

Fig. 283. Frontispiece to *Antiquarie prospetiche Romane*, Milan, about 1499–1500.

The interesting frontispiece to the *Antiquarie prospetiche Romane composte per prospectivo Melanese depictore*, n.d., n.pr. (P.K. 21, Munich, Rome, Casanatense; fig. 283),[1] is related to Brescian work in the resemblance of its border to that of the frontispiece of the Brescia *Aesop* of 1497 (GW. 419, see p. 507), but in its subject, the nude figure amid Roman architecture, is very near in style to Bramantino. Whether the author of these curious verses on the 'Mirabilia Romae', who calls himself *Prospectivo Melanese depictore* and signs the frontispiece with the initials P M, is Bramantino or some similar stylist is still unsolved. The verses dedicated to Leonardo da Vinci contain references which support a date of about 1499–1500.

Another attractive cut, of *Two Lovers*, is described and reproduced by Kristeller from Fossa Cremonese, *Inamoramento di Galvano*, printed without date by Petrus de Mantegatiis (P.K. 152), but another version, which may be the earlier block, appeared in Aeneas Sylvius Piccolomini (Pius II.), *Historia di due Amanti*, printed by ALEXANDER DE PELIZONIS, 1500.[2]

---

[1] The book described and frontispiece reproduced by G. Govi, *Intorno a un opusculo rarissimo della fine del secolo XV*, Rome 1876 (Reale Academia dei Lincei, 16th January 1876). For a recent attribution of the book to the printer J. Besicken at Rome, see my additions, Vol. I. p. 265.

[2] First described and reproduced by E. P. Goldschmidt & Co., Catalogue VIII., No. 11.

Two editions of Bernardino de Busti, *Mariale*, contain attractive little cuts of the *Virgin and Child*, no larger than initial letters, and printed at the beginning of sections like initial letters. Two designs occur in the *Mariale*, printed by Uldericus Scinzenzeler, 1492 (H. 4159, P.K. 81 a), each several times repeated. They are simple outline cuts, of excellent classical design, and give the impression of being based on larger works of painting (see fig. 284).

Fig. 284. The Virgin and Child, from *Mariale*, Milan 1492.

In the edition of the *Mariale* printed by Leonardus Pachel, 1493 (H. 4160, P.K. 81 b), the *Virgin and Child* is a white-line metal-cut. The same edition also contains a little outline *Annunciation*, repeated many times like the *Virgin and Child*. The *Annunciation* lacks clear linear quality, and I am inclined to think that it might be printed from metal casts of a wood-block, as an economy in printing where so much repetition was required, as with initials.[1]

Another Lombard book with metal-cut illustrations is the Aesop, *Vita et Fabulae*, printed at Mondovì (Piedmont) by DOMINICUS DE VIVALDIS, 1481 (Paris, H. 295, P.K. 3a). They are rough metal-cuts somewhat in the manner of Neumeister's edition of Turrecremata, *Meditationes*, 1479.

It has been suggested by Kristeller (*Lombardische Graphik*, p. 48) that the *Portrait of Attavanti*, mentioned above, might be cut in metal. It seems to me unlikely that metal would be used for direct cutting in outline work of this delicate line, but metal casts, on the other hand, might have been made from the original block for purposes of repeated printings.

Among other small cuts of delicate outline style in Milanese books may be mentioned a *Pietà* in Busti, *Defensorium Montis Pietatis*, printed by Scinzenzeler, about 1497 (H. 4167, P.K. 86), and a little *Annunciation* in St. Bernardus, *Sermones de Tempore*, printed by Leonardus Pachel, 1495 (H. 2850, P.K. 59), and later in the *Miracoli della Madonna*, printed by P. de Mantegatiis, 1496 (P.K. 224). The *Sermones* also contains a full-page cut in a broader style representing *St. Bernard in his Study*, which also appears in his *Epistole*, Pachel, 1495 (H. 2873, P.K. 60). In its strong outline and parallel shading it is not unlike the style of the *St. Jerome before a Crucifix* in St. Jerome, *Vita et Transita*, printed by P. de Mantegatiis, 1495 (H. 8650, P.K. 178).

---

[1] See Index of Subjects (under *Casts*).

Fig. 285. The Triumph of Fame, from Petrarch, *Trionfi*, Milan 1494.

Interesting in relation to the use of wood and metal at Milan is the edition of Petrarch, *Trionfi*, printed by ANTONIUS ZAROTUS, 1494 (H. 12762, P.K. 279 b; fig. 285). The six Triumphs are derived from the Florentine broad-manner line-engravings, in part directly and in part through the medium of the woodcuts in the Venetian edition, printed by Plasiis, 1490 (H. 12771, E. 77). The Triumphs of Love and Chastity are woodcuts; the others are white-line metal-cuts. They are all enclosed in black-ground borders of two types: (*a*) with cupids playing musical instruments, below, (*b*) with tritons and nymphs, below. The first three have border (*a*), which is certainly cut on wood; the last three have border (*b*), which appears to be on metal.

Another series of the 'Triumphs of Petrarch', copied from the Venice edition of Plasiis, was issued by Scinzenzeler, 1494 (H. 12775, P. 279 a). These are all on wood, and one of them, the *Triumph of Divinity*, also appeared in Bernardus, *Sermoni sopra la Cantica*, 1494 (H. 2861, P.K. 58).

The *Missale Ambrosianum*, printed by Leonardus Pachel, 1499 (P.K. 247 c), also contains a metal-cut copy from a Florentine broad-manner engraving, i.e. the *Annunciation* (after P. v. 51, 1, Hind, B.I. 1). Among other cuts, it contains a *Christ on the Cross* which appeared earlier in the *Missale Ambrosianum* printed by Zarotus, 1488 (H. 11256, P.K. 247 a), and a *St. Ambrosius with SS. Protasius and Gervasius*, nearer in style to Pavia woodcuts of the early XVI century.

Though woodcut is manifestly more suited to book-illustration than line-engraving, as intaglio plates would require printing in a separate press, it is noteworthy that the earliest book-illustrations, both at Milan and Florence, were from intaglio plates, i.e. at Milan in Fra Pacifico de Novara, *Summula de pacifica Conscientia*, printed by FILIPPUS DE LAVAGNIA, 24th March 1479 (H. 12259), and at Florence in Bettini, *Monte Santo di Dio*, printed by NICOLAUS LAURENTII, Alamannus, 1477 (H. 1276). Though the practice was not continued at Milan, and only repeated, then only partially, in the *Dante* of 1481, at Florence, it probably offers some evidence that engraving on metal was in more general vogue than woodcut in both these places before 1480.

A considerable proportion of Milanese woodcut of the last decade of the XV century is characterised by heavy outlines, regular parallel shading, and crude and somewhat angular design. It is German in manner, though often based on Venetian originals.

Several books originally printed by Bonellis at Venice appear in Milanese type, e.g. that of Scinzenzeler, and with Milanese woodcut decoration, though in some cases the name of Bonellis still appears (in what exact signifi-

printed for a bookseller, Nicolaus de Panibus, at Casale Monferrato (between Vercelli and Alessandria), so that the block was probably a Lombard or Piedmontese work. It has also been noted in a book probably printed at

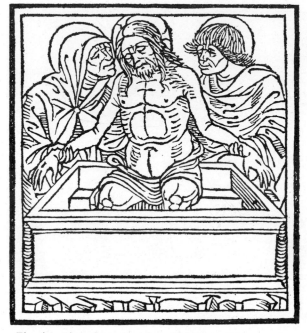

Fig. 287. Pietà, from *Quaedam Auctoritates*, Mantua 1485.

Rome,[1] and in another printed at Paris,[2] but none of the references explain the letters I.G.S.

Of other Lombard towns, Mantua may be mentioned for a woodcut *Pietà* (Christ in the Tomb supported by the Virgin and John), which occurs on the last page of *Quaedam Auctoritates ad misericordiam inducentes*, issued without printer's name in 1485 (B.M.L., IA. 30674; fig. 287). It is cut in strong outline, and a somewhat exaggerated Mantegnesque style of design, comparable in certain respects with woodcuts, which will be noted below, in books printed at Modena by Dominicus Rocociolus.

PARMA—FORLÌ—MODENA—BOLOGNA

Before coming to Florence, which was the only other centre of comparable artistic importance with Venice in xv-century book-illustration, we will pass in rapid review the unimportant production of a few towns of the Emilia. Venice was not infrequently called on for the loan of blocks, e.g. in the Ovid, *Metamorphoses*, printed by FRANCISCUS MAZALIS at Parma, 1505 (reprinted from the Venice edition of Jo. Rubeus, 1497),[3] and in

---

[1] *Soleñis repetitio . . . per . . . Franciscum de Pepis Florentinum . . . edita Romae . . . per Fabianum de Giocchis* (Munich).

[2] *Lectura aurea . . . Petri de Bellapertica . . . super librum Institutorum . . . Parisiis sub signo duorum cygnorum . . . impensis Nicolai Vaiautierii et Charoli Dudecii* (Olschki, Catalogues LIII, No. 405, and LXII, Florence 1906).

[3] See pp. 469, 470, 489. Mazalis describes himself as *calcographus* in the colophon, which must not be confused with its other technical use as line-engraver. It implies no more than

Nicolaus Ferrettus, *De Structura Compositionis*, printed by HIERONYMUS MEDESANUS at Forlì in 1495 (H. 6974), with two borrowed blocks, the *School Class*, from the *Regu-*

Fig. 288. Adoration of the Magi, from *Legenda Sanctorum Trium Regum*, Modena 1490.

lae Sypontinae printed by Pensis, 1492/93,[1] and *Theseus and the Centaur* from the edition of Plutarch, printed by Ragazzo, 1491.[2]

At Modena a few woodcuts appeared in books printed by DOMINICUS ROCOCIOLUS, by far the most attractive being the *Adoration of the Magi* in the *Legenda sanctorum trium Regum*, 1490 (H. 9399; fig. 288). Kristeller has attributed its design to the author of the frontispiece to Alfraganus, *Rudimenta Astronomica*, issued at Ferrara in 1493. There is certainly a relationship in manner, but it seems to me less immediately inspired by Cosimo Tura than by some such master of the Lombard school as Vincenzo Foppa. It is a design of real strength and dignity.

A *Madonna and Child seated beneath an Arch*, which appeared in Antonio Cornazano, *Vita di Nostra Donna*, 1490 (H. 5726), with hard outline

printer (a 'writer in metal-type'), and other instances of its use may be noted with Bartholomaeus Cremonensis in his colophon verses in Hain 13035 (Venice 1472), and with Benedictus Hectoris in Hain 14868 (Bologna 1498).

[1] See p. 482 and fig. 245.   [2] See p. 480.

for the reproduction of his designs to *Dante*, printed by Nicholaus Laurentii in Landino's edition of 1481 (H. 5946).[1] Line-engravings in the same style had been successfully used in Antonio Bettini's *Monte Sancto di Dio* issued by the same printer in 1477.[2] But in that volume there were only three illustrations, and the trouble of separate printing for the copper plates was in consequence small. The same condition in relation to the numerous plates proposed for the Divine Comedy (one for each Canto) was no doubt partly the cause of the breakdown of the project, and after the nineteenth plate no further progress was made, and the blank spaces remained in the printed copies, as a record of thwarted intention. Only a very few copies contain all the illustrations done, the majority having no more than the first two plates; and as token of the small regard paid to the illustrations, the copy on vellum presented to the Signoria, and now in the National Library at Florence, was entirely without plates.

A more successful venture in illustration with copper plates was Berlinghieri's *Geographia*, with its numerous engraved maps, printed by Laurentii about 1480–82. The same medium was used in the two other contemporary series of maps (Ptolemy, *Cosmographia*, of Bologna 1477, and Rome 1478), but separate printing would be essential with large folding maps, whether from wood or copper, so that the same objection did not exist. After these publications no illustrated books appeared in Florence for some eight or nine years, and the woodcut illustration with which we have to deal falls entirely within the last decade of the century.

There were comparatively few fully illustrated books: the exceptions being three works printed for Piero Pacini, the *Epistole e Evangelii* of 1495, the *Aesop* of 1496, and Pulci's *Morgante Maggiore* of 1500/01, and if we trespass slightly into the succeeding century, Frezzi's *Quadriregio* of 1508 (also done for Pacini).

Most of the books are small quartos, within $8\frac{1}{2} \times 6$ inches; the *Epistole e Evangelii* and Frezzi's *Quadriregio* are exceptionally large examples with a page of about 11×8 inches.[3] Few had more than two woodcuts, at beginning and end, and a large proportion only a frontispiece, or small cut

---

[1] See A. M. Hind, *Catalogue of Early Italian Engravings in the British Museum*, 1910, p. 83.

[2] *Ibid.*, 1910, p. 81. These illustrations were copied with considerable freedom in woodcut in the edition printed by Lorenzo Morgiani and Johannes Petri, 1491 (P.K. 60), the *Christ in a Glory* reappearing in D. Cavalca's *Frutti della Lingua*, issued by the same printers in 1497 (P.K. 96).

[3] Another of the larger-size Florentine books with woodcuts is the edition of the *Monte Sancto di Dio*, mentioned in the preceding note.

beneath the title. The cuts themselves are very uniform in size and shape, by far the greater number being small oblongs about 3 × 4 inches in size, nearly adapted to the width of the type surface, whether a single column of prose, or two narrow columns of verse.

There is far less fine printing and careful book-making at Florence than at Venice, but in spite of a certain amateur character in book production, there is no lack of artistic sense in the balance of the page of type and the woodcut illustration.

The books themselves are largely of popular character, poetry, romance and religious tracts. Technical books were seldom provided with illus-

Fig. 290. Piero Pacini's marks, from Frezzi, *Quadriregio*, Florence 1508.

trations as at Venice, a point on which the Florentines may have been guided by their artistic sensibility.

It is the very cheap and popular character of the books (often no more than pamphlets in extent) that has rendered them so scarce. They were disregarded by connoisseurs of the period, and few reached the libraries of great collectors, and the well-worn pages may have largely ended in the waste-paper basket within a few decades of their production.

PIERO PACINI DA PESCIA published (through various printers) a large proportion of the best of the Florentine illustrated books, and he evidently aimed at producing attractive books, but in general there is evidence that those who desired production of greater efficiency, at least as regards the text, went to Venice. Marsilio Ficino was amongst them, as is clear from his *Epistole* printed by Capcasa at Venice in 1495 (H. 7059), with its references on ff. 146 b and 177 a to Alopa's Florentine edition of his translation of Plato (1484–85, H. 13062), and the Venetian edition printed by De Choris in 1491 (H. 13063).

Moreover, the most notable publisher in Venice at this period, Lucantonio Giunta, was a Florentine, who probably chose his residence for its provision of better printing.

Fig. 291. From *Lucidario*, Florence 1494.

A considerable number of the Florentine woodcuts appear in the books of more than one printer, so that it is no more feasible here than at Venice to order one's descriptions according to printers. Another difficulty is presented by the frequent lack of dates in the books, and the absence of the printer's name adds a further obscurity in description. The study of types, chiefly promoted by Robert Proctor, has resulted in assigning a great part of the anonymously printed books to BARTOLOMMEO DI LIBRI (for only eight of his books from a total of about one hundred and twenty contain his name).

There are indications that certain editions have been lost, e.g. a *Fior di Virtù* of about 1492, and a xv-century *Ninfale Fiesolano*.

The earliest edition of the *Fior di Virtù* which is preserved is that printed by the SOCIETAS COLUBRIS (COMPAGNIA DEL DRAGO) in 1498,[1] but a cut which was manifestly made for this work appeared in the *Lucidario* printed by Miscomini in 1494 (fig. 291), and reasons have been given above[2] for thinking that the original edition of the *Fior di Virtù* was issued before 20th March 1492.

Boccaccio's *Ninfale Fiesolano* is only known with the Florentine cuts in the edition of 1568 (P.K. 66, Paris; Met. Museum, New York; fig. 292),

[1] B.M.L., IA. 28049. Kristeller, 150 a, confuses with that of Bonaccorsi and Francisci, 1488 (H. 7108).

[2] See p. 527.

but their style is that of the xv century (or at least not later than Frezzi's *Quadriregio* of 1509) and the inspiration that of Botticelli, no doubt through the medium of some less notable designer.

The descriptions of Florentine editions in Hain and Kristeller are so frequently ambiguous that wherever possible I will add references from the British Museum Catalogue of Books printed in the xv Century.

Fig. 292. From Boccaccio, *Ninfale Fiesolano*, Florence 1568.

No doubt the printers, or the publishers, dealt with various independent ateliers; but there is no evidence as to whether they commissioned the painter-designers, or dealt with the wood-cutters direct. They probably took either course according to opportunity.

The chief printers who issued books with cuts were ANTONIO DI BARTO-LOMMEO MISCOMINI; BARTOLOMMEO DI LIBRI, who printed the largest number of Savonarola tracts, and plays sacred and profane;[1] FRANCESCO BONACCORSI, and LORENZO MORGIANI, in part with JOHANNES PETRI (Giovanni di Piero da Maganza), who also printed many of Savonarola's works. A few illustrated books only were issued at the beginning of the last decade of the century by FRANCESCO DI DINO, and at the end by the SOCIETAS COLUBRIS (COMPAGNIA DEL DRAGO), and by three partners, ANTONIO TUBINI, LORENZO (DE ALOPA) VENEZIANO, and ANDREA GHIRLANDI, of whom the first and last had belonged to the Societas Colubris.

Florentine woodcut illustrations have a special character in being nearly always enclosed within a narrow border on the block itself, while broader *passe-partout* borders are used when occasion demands to adapt the usual small type of woodcut to fill a whole page. The artist evidently aimed

---

[1] There is a useful understanding between certain American University libraries with regard to their collection of early books. Thus the Widener Library, Harvard, makes a special point of collecting *Savonarola* tracts and *Sacre Rappresentazioni*, and reproductions of the same. Princeton, on the other hand, specialises in *Virgil*, and Cornell in *Petrarch* and *Dante*.

at presenting something of the illusion of a framed picture in his little woodcuts.

In the earlier illustrations the borders are for the most part a simple design of three-lobed leaf either in outline or on a black ground: the black ground sometimes sufficing for the limitation of the border, and later more often defined with separate outer and inner border-lines. The corner-pieces contain some simple pattern, such as five dots or a star.

In the *Epistole e Evangelii* printed by Morgiani and Petri for Pacini in 1495 [1] there are as many as fourteen different border designs.

Of the broader *passe-partout* borders the following are the most important designs:

(1) Flower, scroll, and shield (below); candelabra (sides); wreaths (above). Black ground. $4\frac{1}{4} \times 3\frac{1}{8}$ inches.

     Augustinus, *Sermones* (Dino), 1493. H. 2009; P.K. 11; B.M., IA. 27707.

(2) Man of Sorrows and two angels (below); candelabra (sides); Veronica napkin (above). Black ground. $6\frac{3}{4} \times 4\frac{7}{8}$.

     Fior di Virtù (Societas Colubris), 1498. B.M., IA. 28049. (Probably appeared in an earlier edition before 20th March 1492.)

(3) Four cupids holding wreaths about escutcheon (below); candelabra (sides); I.H.S. and two grotesque heads (above). $6\frac{3}{8} \times 4\frac{1}{4}$.

     Sogni di Daniel Profeta (Morgiani), n.d. B.M., IA. 27920.

     Pietro Bernardo, *Compendio di Contemplatione* (Tubini), n.d. B.M., IA. 28075.

(4) Veronica napkin (below), scroll (sides), God, Father and Dove (above). $5 \times 3\frac{3}{8}$.

     Savonarola, *Trattato dell' Umiltà* (Miscomini), n.d. H. 14372; B.M., IA. 27250.

     Savonarola, *Trattato dell' Umiltà* (Libri), n.d. H. 14373; B.M., IA. 27506.

(5) Eagles (below), scroll (sides), tritons (above). Black ground. $6\frac{3}{4} \times 4\frac{3}{8}$. P.K., fig. 17.

     Passavanti, *Specchio di Vera Penitenza* (Libri), 1495/96. H. 12435; B.M., IA. 27317.

     Savonarola, *Predica dell' Arte del bene morire* (Libri), n.d., after 2nd November 1496. B.M., IA. 27321.

     Angelo da Vallombrosa, *Lettera ai Signori e popolo Fiorentino* (Libri), n.d., after 1st January 1496/97.

             [1] See p. 538.

GW. 1911; B.M., IA 27324.

Savonarola, *Trattato contra gli Astrologi* (Libri), n.d., H. 14378; B.M., IA. 27512.

(6) Children tilting on pigs (below); candelabra (sides); hare and hounds (above). Black ground. $6\frac{7}{8} \times 4\frac{3}{4}$. P.K., fig. 13.

This border cannot be later than 1493, when it was copied in Anianus, *Compotus*, printed by Andreas Freytag, at Rome.

Canzone per andare in maschera per carnesciale, fatte da più persone (by Lorenzo de' Medici and others) (Morgiani and Petri), n.d. (about 1493–97). P.K. 284; B.M., IA. 27887.

Ippolito Buondelmonti e Dianora de' Bardi (Morgiani and Petri), n.d. (about 1493–97). GW. 575; P.K. 72 a; B.M., IA. 27935.

Uberto e Filomena, n.d., n.pr. P.K. 421 a (Erlangen).

(7) Cupids on deer (below); candelabra (sides); cupids supporting medallion with profiles of man and girl (above). Black ground. $6\frac{7}{8} \times 4\frac{1}{2}$. P.K., fig. 15.

Storia di Bradiamonte, n.d., n.pr. P.K. 70 (Erlangen).

Apart from the borders and *passe-partouts* the purely decorative features of Florentine book-illustration are scanty. Woodcut initials are not so common as at Venice, nor so varied or interesting. A good representative example is the capital F from St. Augustine, *Sermones*, printed by Francesco di Dino, 1493 (H. 2009, P.K. 11 b, B.M., IA. 27707).

The woodcut designs show a remarkably high level in invention and composition. In subjects which admit of dramatic rendering there is no lack of expressive representation, made all the more vivid by the limitation of the means at the draughtsmen's disposal. In stories of sentiment, the reader is touched by motives of gentle reserve and unaffected charm; while religious themes are accorded their pictures of grave, yet harmonious dignity.

The designers were undoubtedly painters, and in many illustrations one finds reflection of the style of the greater artists of the time, and of Botticelli and Ghirlandaio in particular. But there are no woodcuts whose character claims by indubitable signs such exalted paternity. The probabilities are all in favour of lesser artists under their influence devoting their energies to woodcut design, and perhaps only a small number, as the variety of style shown in the cuts of this decade is not very large.

Thus Mr. Berenson[1] has ventured to attribute the larger proportion

[1] See Burlington Magazine, i., 1903, 6. The *Master with Seven Pupils* reproduced in our fig. 294 is among the many so attributed.

of the cuts of about 1490–1500, reproduced by Kristeller, to his Alunno di Domenico, now identified as BARTOLOMMEO DI GIOVANNI, a painter who is known to have done the *predelle* to Ghirlandaio's *Adoration of the Kings* in 1488. It is the same painter to whom the late Mr. Herbert Horne attributed the design of the line-engraving, the *Triumph of Bacchus and Ariadne*, only known in the British Museum.[1] There is unfortunately no evidence beyond that of style, and the inevitable difficulty of comparing the painter's style with the modified reflection in work of another convention adds another obstacle.

Mr. A. W. Pollard certainly voiced more scientific opinion in his scepticism of undocumented attributions, but such attributions do not thereby lose their value, for they at least place the illustrations near their probable artistic milieu, and may at any time help to find the link required.

Another possible clue might be found in research of the unidentified work of FRANCESCO ROSSELLI, the little known brother of Cosimo Rosselli. A *Map of the World* engraved by him on copper after Giovanni Matteo Contarini in 1506 (the first-known printed map showing the Discoveries of Columbus) was recently acquired by the British Museum.[2] Apart from this line-engraving nothing is known of his work beyond conjectures based on the inventory of his son ALESSANDRO DI FRANCESCO ROSSELLI, 1528, which contains a large number of engravings and woodcuts of the most various character.[3] Several of the known line-engravings of the xv century figure in the list, and it is extremely probable that Francesco Rosselli, who is described as an illuminator of prints (*miniatore e stampatore*) was the engraver of some of these in addition to the Contarini Map. It is equally probable that he was woodcutter as well, and responsible for many of the woodcuts described. Whether any of these are book-illustrations is uncertain, though entries such as *7 Lisime di fogli stampati in sonetti e in chomedie* imply the possibility that he was among the makers of woodcut illustrations. But I can do no more than suggest a possible direction for research.

Another link might be offered by drawings such as a sheet of studies by an anonymous Florentine artist in the Uffizi,[4] which contains a variety of studies for narrow borders, and is probably on that account by a designer

---

[1] A. M. Hind, *Catalogue of Early Italian Engravings in the British Museum*, 1910, p. 44, A. II. 11.

[2] Published with description and facsimile by the British Museum, 1924.

[3] See I. del Badia, *Miscellanea fiorentina*, vol. ii. No. 14, p. 24 (Florence 1894); A. M. Hind, *Catalogue of Early Italian Engravings in the British Museum*, 1910, p. xxix.

[4] The reverse of Schönbrunner and Meder, 277. Both sides reproduced by O. Fischel, *Die Zeichnungen der Umbrer*, Berlin 1917, p. 40, figs. 40, 41.

who worked for woodcut illustration (fig. 293).[1] One of the figures is nearly related to Donatello's *St. George*; others appear to be based on subjects of the heroes of antiquity done by Ghirlandaio, probably with the collaboration

of Perugino, in the Palazzo della Signoria at Florence about 1482. But of the dozen designs for borders on this sheet, I have only connected two with published work. The topmost pattern occurs (*a*) in the cut of the *Master with Seven Pupils* in C. Landinus, *Formulario*, printed by Miscomini, 1492 (P.K. 230 b, H. 9862, B.M., IA. 27203), which also appears in *Flores Poetarum*, printed without date or printer's name (P.K. 153), and in Nicolaus Valla, *Ars Metrica*, n.d., printed by Bonaccorsi (B.M., IA. 27651, fig. 294);

Fig. 293. Sheet of Studies. Pen drawing in the Uffizi, Florence.

and (*b*) in borders in the *Aesop* printed by Bonaccorsi for Pacini, 1496 (P.K. 137 a, H. 1350 a, and later editions). The second example, four rows from the foot of the drawing, i.e. the series of triangles, corresponds with borders of certain cuts in Frezzi's *Quadriregio* of 1508, and there are unmistakable Umbrian characteristics in these illustrations as

[1] But it must be remembered that armourers used similar border designs, and panels of trophies such as appears as one of the drawings (cf. armour illustrated in the Bulletin of the Metropolitan Museum of Art, New York 1930, p. 93).

well as in the drawing. Nevertheless this correspondence in character is not enough to support any conclusions.

The last clue to authorship is the signature LV which occurs in the first illustration of Frezzi's *Quadriregio* (fig. 295), which is repeated on sig. B. 2.

Fig. 294. Master with Seven Pupils, from Valla, *Ars Metrica*, Florence.

It has been connected with Luca Signorelli (*Luca Venturi*), but though certain subjects, such as the *Battle of Naked Men* (f. 68, verso), are reminiscent of his style, there is little foundation for the conjecture. Inference from other examples of signed cuts and the general practice of the period [1] renders it far more probable that the LV denoted the cutter rather than the designer, and it is not beyond reason that it might be the cutter Lucantonio degli Uberti, only his usual initials were LA, and it seems probable that in the few years preceding 1508 he was out of Florence.[2]

Our indications have thrown little illumination on the possible authorship of Florentine woodcuts, but in spite of paucity of results they are set down in the hope that they may lead other researchers to some solution.

I will conclude this section with a short survey of the more important Florentine books, beginning with the few more fully illustrated examples.

[1] See Index of Subjects (under *Designer and Cutter*).   [2] See p. 452.

One of the most attractive of these in the earlier style of pure outline, is Filippo Calandri, *Arithmetica*, printed by Morgiani and Petri, 1491/92 (P.K. 77 a, H. 3156, B.M., IA. 27782). There are borders to the tables throughout, of charming scroll and figure design, and even the pages of problems have their appropriate illustrations, and nothing could be imagined more alluring to the young student of arithmetic (fig. 296).

Jacobus de Cessolis, *Libro di Giuoco di Scacchi*, printed by Miscomini, 1493/94 (P.K. 101, H. 4900, B.M., IA. 27205), contains, under the guise

Fig. 295. Frontispiece to Frezzi, *Quadriregio*, Florence 1508.

of the game of chess, a picture of the various occupations of men, in a frontispiece and thirteen other illustrations. The frontispiece of the *Game of Chess* (fig. 297) is one of the finest of Florentine illustrations, and, added to its sensitive draughtsmanship, has a certain largeness of style which is remarkable even amid the high average attained by Florentine work of the period. It is nearly related to Botticelli, and undoubtedly the design of a painter, and of a really gifted artist. The remaining illustrations are good, but lack the rhythmic quality of the frontispiece, and can hardly be by the same designer.

The most considerable achievement of xv-century Florentine book-illustration is contained in the *Epistole e Evangelii*, printed by Morgiani and Petri, for Pacini, 27th July 1495 (P.K. 135 b).[1]

Only two copies of the original edition of 1495 are known, one in the Corsini Library at Rome (see fig. 298), the other belonging to Mr. C. W.

Fig. 296. Page with border, from Calandri, *Arithmetica*, Florence 1491/92.

Dyson Perrins. The latter, which came from the collection of Richard Fisher, was reproduced in facsimile by the owner for presentation to the Roxburghe Club, with descriptive text by Mr. A. W. Pollard, in 1910. Unfortunately it had suffered by fire; the full-page frontispiece being considerably damaged and made up, and a few of the other small cuts also having suffered. In addition to the frontispiece,[2] it contains 144 illustrations of the standard Florentine size (i.e. about 3 × 4 inches, a small number being uprights), with some fourteen varieties of border design, as well as twenty-five small half-lengths of prophets, evangelists, and epistle-writers, and a little St. Sebastian. The colophon emphasises the numerous leaves and woodcuts, no doubt to compare the achievement favourably with the less ambitious Venetian edition of the same work.[3]

---

[1] The complete title is *Epistole e Evangelii è Lectioni vulgari in lingua toschana*, i.e. the Epistles, Gospels and Lessons as read in the Mass.

[2] The inset cuts of the Evangelists, from small blocks which also occur in the text, differ in the later editions. For other woodcuts comparable in style with this frontispiece, see p. 74.

[3] See p. 473. It is noteworthy that another Florentine edition which appeared a few months after Morgiani's issue, printed by Bartolommeo di Libri on the 24th October 1495

Some of the cuts are in outline, such as the *Last Supper*, f. 47 b (with its inevitable reflection of the versions in fresco by Castagno and Ghirlandaio), the *Flagellation*, f. 60, and the *Mocking of Christ*, f. 49, verso (with something of the style of Pollaiuolo), and the *Last Judgment*, f. 22 a (fig. 299), the

Fig. 297. Frontispiece to Cessolis, *Libro di Giuoco di Scacchi*, Florence 1493/94.

last being a design of great dignity; but the majority are in the usual Florentine manner, with white-line ground. A few of the cuts had appeared in Bonaventura, *Meditazioni sopra la Passione*, printed by Miscomini about 1494 (P.K. 69 a; B.M., IA. 27248), and it is from this edition that I reproduce the *Christ entering Jerusalem* (fig. 300).

There were later editions of the *Epistole e Evangelii* in 1515 (P.K. 135 c, Victoria and Albert Museum, Biblioteca Riccardiana), and in 1551 (Dyson

(P.K. 135 a, Essling 189, Florence), was illustrated entirely with Venetian blocks, e.g. from Jacobus de Voragine, *Legendario di Sancti*, 10th December 1492 (Essling 678, Modena).

Fig. 298. Frontispiece to *Epistole e Evangelii*, Florence 1495.

Perrins, W. M. Ivins, Jr.) and 1559/60 (British Museum). Some of the cuts also appeared subsequent to 1495 in other works, e.g. the *Feast of the Prodigal Son* in the *Rappresentazione del Vitello Faggiato*, n.pr., n.d. (P.K. 434, Oxford, etc.), the *Agony in the Garden* and *Christ bearing the Cross* in Savonarola, *Sermone dell' Orazione*, Morgiani and Petri, n.d. (P.K. 382 c, B.M., IA. 27956), and the *Agony* alone in Savonarola, *Esposizione del Pater Noster*, Morgiani and Petri, n.d. (P.K. 384 a, B.M., IA. 27953), and eleven cuts in Bernardo Pulci, *La Passione del Nostro Signore*, n.pr., n.d. but before 1559 (P.K. 340, British Museum).

Only two copies of any xv-century Florentine edition of Aesop's *Fables* are cited by Kristeller, those of Prince Trivulzio and the Biblioteca Riccardiana, Florence (printed

Fig. 299. Last Judgment, from *Epistole e Evangelii*, Florence 1495.

by Bonaccorsi for Pacini, P.K. 137 a). But some of the sixty-five cuts of this edition reappear in editions of 1514 and 1520 (P.K. 137 b and c). A variant of the last edition from the Fairfax Murray Collection is now in the library of Mr. Wilfred Merton,[1] and it is from this copy that I reproduce the *Sick Vulture and his Mother* (fig. 301), a design of fine decorative quality. The subjects show a general dependence on the editions of Verona (1479) and Naples (1485), but other sources may well have been used in designs of such traditional character.

Pulci's *Morgante Maggiore*, published by Piero Pacini 1500/01 (P.K. 347,

[1] The cuts of Mr. Merton's copy are reproduced in *Aesop's Fables: Samuel Croxall's Translation with a bibliographical note by Victor Scholderer*. Arranged by Bruce Rogers for the Limited Editions Club, 1933.

Vienna; Berlin, incomplete), contains some 149 cuts, of which 14 also appear in other books (mystery plays and romances). Mr. Scholderer has identified the printers with the *Societas Colubris* or *Compagnia del Drago* (Antonio Tubini and Antonio Ghirlandi).[1] The cuts show a variety of styles, some near to that of the earlier Florentine illustration, others in the more angular and piquant manner of the *Epistole e Evangelii* and of many books of about 1495, and the largest group in an apparently later style in which the

Fig. 300. Christ entering Jerusalem, from Bonaventura, *Meditazioni sopra la Passione*, Florence, about 1494.

figures are in general shorter and drawn with more rounded contours and delicate lines (see fig. 302). Kristeller has compared the style of this last group with Piero di Cosimo.

Frezzi's *Quadriregio del Decorso della Vita Umana* of 1508 (P.K. 164), which has already been mentioned in the discussion of possible authorship of Florentine woodcuts in general,[2] is the last of the books with more copious illustration which demands our attention (see figs. 295 and 303). It was printed for Piero Pacini, in part at least by Filippo Giunta, but

---

[1] By comparison with an edition of Perottus, *Rudimenta Grammatica*, 1500, which contained the imprint of the Societas Colubris, and the device of the Dragon with initials A A for Antonio Tubini and Antonio Ghirlandi (the only known copy submitted to Mr. Scholderer by Mr. E. P. Goldschmidt in 1930).   [2] See p. 536.

a change in type half-way through the book complicates the typographical problem. It is one of the larger-size Florentine books, the verses being

Fig. 301. The Sick Vulture and his Mother, from *Aesop*, Florence.

printed in double column on a page of about 11 × 8 inches. Its illustrations (title-border and 116 subjects) are remarkable for their general high

Fig. 302. From Pulci, *Morgante Maggiore*, Florence 1500/01.

level of quality; many are very beautiful in design, and full of life and motion, while the black and white lines are perfectly combined in the

cutting. Here is certainly the culmination in the development of Florentine
woodcut illustration both in design and technical quality; some of the charm
of the earlier woodcuts may have been lost in a more uniform achievement,
but I cannot agree with Kristeller's conclusion that 'in their conventional
correctness, in the lifelessness of the scratchy lines, in their tedious repetitions of the same forms and movements and of the background, these and
other similar cuts are very far removed from the simple illustrations of the
xv century, which were full of spirit, character, and artistic life.' [1]

Fig. 303. The Pursuit of Cupid, from Frezzi, *Quadriregio*, Florence 1508.

The earliest type of Florentine illustration seems to be seen in the *Christ
on the Cross with the Virgin and St. John* (P.K. cut 2) and the *Man of Sorrows
with two Angels* (P.K. cut 3; fig. 304) which appeared in various books
about 1490-92, both occasionally within the same border of interlaced
pattern. They are good designs, roughly cut in outline and parallel shading,
in a style that probably had its source in the Broad Manner line-engravings.
In the impressions known the blocks already seem worn, so that they were
possibly done earlier, either as separate cuts or for books which were not
issued or of which no copies remain.

Both subjects in their earlier state have a border of interlaced pattern,

[1] *Early Florentine Woodcuts*, p. xxxix.

the border of the Crucifixion subject having a rosette in each corner, that of the Man of Sorrows a leaf. In the books in which they occur the blocks, inclusive of the border, are too large for the page, and they are found cut or masked in the impression, another fact which favours the probability that they were done for some earlier works. The *Christ on the Cross* appears with its border in D. Cavalca, *Specchio di Croce*, printed by Dino, Florence 1490 (P.K. 95 b, Florence), and in Savonarola, *Trattato del Sacramento*, printed by Miscomini, Florence, n.d. (P.K. 391 a), and with its border cut away in Savonarola, *Trattato dell' Amore di Jesu*, Miscomini, Florence 1492 (P.K. 374 f).

Fig. 304. The Man of Sorrows, from Savonarola, *Dell' Umiltà*, Florence 1492.

The *Man of Sorrows* is only known in Savonarola, *Trattato dell' Umiltà*, printed by Miscomini, Florence 1492, where it appears with its border (P.K. 394 d).

Then between 1490 and 1495 a considerable number of cuts appeared in a much more sensitive style of draughtsmanship, largely in outline. One of the finest examples occurs in Jacopone da Todi, *Laude*, printed by Bonaccorsi, 1490 (P.K. 220), the *Virgin adored by the Author* (fig. 305), a cut similar in quality to the *Last Judgment* in the *Epistole e Evangelii* of 1495 (fig. 299). Others of the same group (though probably by a variety of designers) are:

Christ standing with Cross and Chalice in a Niche, in Thomas à Kempis,

Imitatio Christi (Miscomini), 1493 (P.K. 227 b), and Passavanti,
Specchio di Vera Penitenza (Libri), 1495/96 (P.K. 323);
Christ standing with Cross and Chalice in a Landscape, in Thomas à
Kempis, *Imitatio Christi* (Libri), n.d. (P.K. 227 a);

Fig. 305. The Virgin adored by the Author, from Jacopone da Todi, *Laude*, Florence 1490.

The title-cut of Granollachs, *Lunare* (Morgiani), 1491 and 1496
(P.K. 210 a and b) (P.K. cut 11);
St. Francis receiving the Stigmata (P.K. cut 27), in S. Francesco,
Fioretti, n.d. (P.K. 155 a, Vatican), and the *Rappresentazione di
S. Francesco* by Antonia Pulci (Libri), n.d. (P.K. 158 a);
The Agony in the Garden, in Savonarola, *Sermone dell' Orazione*, n.d.

(P.K. 382 a), and *Dell' Orazione Mentale* (Libri), n.d. (P.K. 383 a), comparable with another representation of the subject in the *Epistole e Evangelii* of 1495;

St. Augustine in his Study, turned to the left (fig. 306) in St. Augustine, *Soliloquii* (Morgiani), 1491 (P.K. 10 a), and as *St. Antoninus* in Antoninus, *Confessionale* (Morgiani), 1493 (P.K. 25);

Fig. 306. St. Augustine in his Study, from his *Soliloquii*, Florence 1491.

St. Augustine in his Study, turned to the right in St. Augustine, *Sermoni volgari* (Miscomini), 1493 (P.K. 11 c);

Master with Seven Pupils (fig. 294, $5\frac{7}{8} \times 4$ inches), in C. Landinus, *Formulario di Lettere* (Miscomini), 1492 (P.K. 230 b); *Flores Poetarum*, n.d. (P.K. 153); Nicolaus Valla, *Ars Metrica* (Bonaccorsi), n.d. (B.M.);

Smaller subject of a *Master with Seven Pupils* ($4 \times 3\frac{1}{4}$ inches) in C. Landinus, *Formulario di Lettere* (Libri), n.d. (P.K. 230 a), and N. Perottus, *Regulae Sypontinae* (Libri), n.d. (B.M.);

Master and Pupil in *Lucidario* (Libri), n.d. (P.K. 244 a), and F.
Berlinghieri, *Protesto alla Signoria* (Libri), n.d. (H. 2826);
Young Man at a Desk (P.K. cut 22) in Luca Pulci, *Epistole* (Libri),
n.d. (P.K. 342);
Turbaned Sage at a Desk in *Il Savio Romano* (Morgiani), n.d. (B.M.);

Fig. 307. Confessions in a Church, for Capranica, *Arte del ben Morire*, Venice (?) 1490.

Astrologer in his Study in Pietrobono Advogario, *Pronostico dell' Anno*
1496 (Morgiani) [1495–96] (P.K. 332), *Pronostico dell' Anno* 1497
(Morgiani) [1496–97] (P.K. 333), Granollachs, *Lunare* (Morgiani),
1496 (P.K. 210 b), and Giuliano Dati, *Prete Janni* (Prester John)
(Morgiani), n.d. (P.K. 122 a);
Prester John in Giuliano Dati, *Prete Janni* (Morgiani), n.d. (P.K. 122 a);
The Mount of Piety (freely adapted from the large Florentine line-

engraving in the Broad Manner, B. xiii. 88, 7), in Marco del Monte Santa Maria, *Tavola della Salute* (Miscomini), 1494 (P.K. 257), and the same author's *Libro dei Commandamenti di Dio*, 1494 (P.K. 258);

Confessions in a Church (with two Confessors), which, though printed probably at Venice, in Capranica, *Arte del ben morire* (Clein and Himel) 1490 (Essling 271; H. 4402), is likely to be Florentine work (fig. 307), and the original of which there is a modified copy in Antoninus, *Confessionale: Summa omnis mortalium cura* (Libri), n.d. (B.M.) (P.K. cut 108).

Confession in a Church (with one Confessor) in Antoninus, *Confessionale: Curam illius habe* (Morgiani and Petri) 1493 (P.K. 25), and Antoninus, *Tractato volgare intitolato Defecerunt* (Morgiani and Petri), 1496 (P.K. 26).

One of the most important groups of Florentine illustrated books is that of the Savonarola tracts.[1] Illustrations from several of these have already been mentioned (see pp. 532, 541, 545, 546, 547), and I would now add a list of the other sermons and tracts which contain the chief woodcuts, mostly examples in which a greater use of white line is seen:

Predica dell' Arte del ben morire (Libri), n.d. (about 1496)[2] (P.K. 375 c and d): Title cut within a border, and three other cuts.

Compendio di Rivelazione (Morgiani and Petri), 1st September 1495 (H. 14335): four cuts (one repeated), with a most vivid representation of *Savonarola preaching* (fig. 309).

De Simplicitate Christianae Vitae (Morgiani): two editions, 1496 (P.K. 392 a and b), and *Epistola a tutti gli eletti* (P.K. 379; Corsini), containing a cut representing *Savonarola writing in his Cell* (fig. 308).

---

[1] See Gustave Gruyer, *Les Illustrations des écrits de Savonarole publiés en Italie au XVe et au XVIe siècle*, Paris 1879. The Widener Library, Harvard University, has added to its original Savonarola tracts a large collection of facsimiles. Cf. p. 531, footnote 1.

[2] Facsimile, Wiegendruck Gesellschaft, Berlin 1926 (Einleitung von Erich von Rath). The facsimile is made from P.K. 375 c (Berlin). The same cuts appear in two slightly varying editions in the B.M. (IA. 27321 and 27320) which Kristeller includes under his 375 d. Kristeller 375 a, printed, according to von Rath, by Morgiani and Petri (Stuttgart, Paris; not in the B.M.), contains three cuts, variants on the last three cuts in 375 c and d, with the first repeated on the title. It is only the later issue of this variant, P.K. 375 b (printed by Tubini and Ghirlandi, after 1500; B.M., 3905 dd. 118), which contains the *Triumph of Death* cut from Petrarch, *Trionfi* of 1499 (P.K. 328) on the title. The three blocks in these editions seem to me inferior to Libri's, but it is difficult to say whether they are modified copies of Libri's blocks, or based on the same original drawings.

Sopra i dieci Commandamenti (Morgiani), n.d. (P.K. 377 a), containing
cuts (*a*) *Savonarola presenting his book to kneeling nuns in a chapel*; (*b*)
another oblong subject of *Monk and Nuns*, at the end.

{ *Predica e Rivelazioni* (Libri), 5th September 1495 (H. 14380),
Sopra i dieci Commandamenti (Libri), 24th October 1495 (P.K. 377 b),
Epistola a un amico (Libri), n.d. (P.K. 380 a), with the upright

Fig. 308. Savonarola in his Cell, from his *De Simplicitate Christianae Vitae*, Florence 1496.

subject of *Two Monks receiving Nuns* (P.K. cut 32) which occurs in
various other tracts printed by Libri.

Tractato del Sacramento (Libri), two undated editions: H. 14352 and
14353 (B.M., IA. 27498 and 27552), with two woodcut versions
of the *Elevation of the Host* (one being reproduced by Kristeller,
cut 109).

Dell' Orazione Mentale (Libri), n.d. (P.K. 383), and *Regola del bene
vivere* (Libri), 1498 (P.K. 389), with a subject of a *Monk kneeling
before the Altar* (P.K. cut 42).

Trattato contra gli Astrologi (Libri), n.d. (P.K. 376), with a cut of
Monk and Astrologer.

Another group of great interest is offered by the *Sacre Rappresentazioni*,
or Mystery Plays, published in such numbers by the Florentine printers.[1]

---

[1] See Colomb de Batines, *Bibliografia delle antiche rappresentazioni italiane sacre e profane
stampate nei secoli XV e XVI*, Florence 1852; Alessandro d' Ancona, *Sacre rappresentazioni dei
secoli XIV, XV e XVI*, Florence 1872, and *Origini del teatro in Italia*, Florence 1877. Cf. p. 531
footnote.

xv-century editions are rare, but the popularity of such plays is evidenced in the numerous reprints of the xvi century. Many of the later editions contain cuts printed from the original blocks, and in the absence of early issues may be of considerable interest. Several collected editions containing numerous plays (which had no doubt in most cases been printed separately) are known, with a special lettering or signature affixed to each play and

Fig. 309. Savonarola preaching, from his *Compendio di Rivelazione*, Florence 1495.

index to the series added. Two of these *collectanea*, issued by the Giunta, are preserved in the Museo Poldo-Pezzoli, Milan, *Il Primo Libro di Rappresentationi et Feste, di diversi Santi e Sante*, 1555, and *Il Secondo Libro di Feste et Rappresentationi*, 1560, and titles occur in the same collection for *Il Terzo Libro di Feste, Rappresentationi, et Comedie Spirituali*, 1578, and for another series of 1591.

Most large collections such as that of the British Museum show various late issues in which the signatures occurring on the title-pages show that they had belonged to one or another of such collected editions.

The title nearly always contains a cut of the *Angel of the Annunciation*, generally placed above another woodcut illustrating the play. The text of the play occasionally contains further illustrations.

The earliest type of this *Angel of the Annunciation* is in outline within a border of trefoil on black ground, with the lower border removed, probably for convenience of space. A good example is seen in the *Rappresentazione di San Panunzio*, by Feo Belcari, printed by Libri, n.d. (P.K. 321; fig. 310). The same design of angel is found in xvi-century editions

without the border, and a third design, in which the figure is shaded in
parallel lines, is also commonly found.

A very beautiful *Annunciation* (fig. 311) appears on the first page of the

Fig. 310. Title-cuts to Feo Belcari, *Rappresentazione di San Panunzio*, Florence.

Rappresentazione della Festa della Annunziazione (Libri), n.d. (P.K. 365 a),
and another excellent cut probably by the same hand is the *Last Judgment*
on the title-page of the *Rappresentazione del Dì del Giudicio* by Antonio
Araldi (?) (Libri), n.d. (P.K. 206a).

From the numerous *Sacre Rappresentazioni* issued in Florence in the xv and xvi centuries, I would also note the following as among the more important examples of which there are editions of the xv century, or

Fig. 311. The Annunciation, from the *Rappresentazione della Festa della Annunziazione*, Florence.

the early years of the xvi century (collections are only cited when early editions are not in the British Museum):

La Rappresentazione

di *Santa Agata*, n.d. (P.K. 7 a, Oxford);
di *Santa Cristina* (Libri), n.d. (P.K. 115 a);
della *Natività di Cristo* (Libri), n.d.;
della *Regina Esther*, n.pr., n.d. (P.K. 138 a);
di *Santa Felicita Hebrea*, n.d. (P.K. 144 a);
del *Figliuol Prodigo*, n.d. (P.K. 148 a);
di *San Francesco*, by Antonia Pulci (Libri), n.d. (P.K. 158 a);
di *San Giorgio* (Libri), n.d. (P.K. 195 a, Oxford);

di San Giovanni Battista, by F. Belcari (Libri), n.d. (P.K. 199 a);

di San Giovani e Paolo, by Lorenzo de' Medici (Libri), n.d. (P.K. 285 a);

di San Giovanni Gualberto, n.d. (P.K. 203 a);

d' un Miracolo del Corpo di Cristo (Libri), n.d. (P.K. 180 a);

Fig. 312. The Death of Lucretia, from the *Storia e Morte di Lucrezia*, Florence.

d' un Miracolo di Nostra Donna (Libri), n.d. (P.K. 270 a);

di Santa Orsola, n.d., P.K. 309 d. (good early cut of a Martyrdom of Six Saints, in ed. 1554, B.M.);

di San Valentino e Santa Giuliana, n.d. (P.K. 422 a, Florence).

Sometimes the title, as with novels, will be *Storia* or *Historia*, and *Festa* is often added, e.g.:

La Hystoria e Festa di Susanna, n.d. (P.K. 408, *bis*);

La Hystoria di Sancta Maria Magdalena e Lazaro e Martha, n.d. (P.K. 250 c, Corsini).

Many of the editions described in Kristeller without name of printer may have been issued by Libri, who printed more of these plays than any other Florentine printer in the xv century. A certain number of such plays were also printed at Siena, more particularly those about Saint Catherine of Siena.

Novels and romances, in prose and verse, form another large group of the Florentine illustrated books, and two of the most attractive examples appeared in the *Storia di Ippolito Buondelmonti e Dianora Bardi* (Morgiani), n.d. (P.K. 72 a), and in the *Storia e Morte di Lucrezia* (Morgiani), n.d. (P.K. 245 a, fig. 312), the latter being very typical of Florentine work in its vivid and expressive quality.

Fig. 313. Market Scene, from *Contrasto di Carnesciale e la Quaresima*, Florence.

The following *novelle* might also be noted (Erlangen being one of the richest collections of the rare early editions):

Novella di due preti et un cherico innamorati duna donna, n.pr., n.d. (P.K. 300, Kupferstichkabinett, Berlin; Erlangen).
Storia di Maria per Ravenna, n.pr., n.d. (P.K. 272, Erlangen).
Novella della figliuola del Mercante, n.pr., n.d. (P.K. 299, Erlangen).
Storia di Bradiamonte, n.pr., n.d. (P.K. 70, Erlangen) (woodcut within the *passe-partout* border, described as No. 7 on p. 533).
La Nencia de Barberino, n.pr., n.d. (P.K. 282 a, Erlangen).
Storia di Uberto e Filomena, n.pr., n.d. (P.K. 421 a, Erlangen) (woodcut within the *passe-partout* border, described as No. 6 on p. 533).
Novella di Gualtieri e Griselda, n.pr., n.d. (P.K. 215 a, Erlangen).

I will conclude this section on Florence with reference to various other illustrations of interest:

Monte dell' Oratione (Bonaccorsi), 1496 (P.K. 288 a, Florence) (the first cut reproduced, Delaborde, *Gravure en Italie*, p. 219).

Chapel scene, in *Laude facte da piu persone* (Libri), n.d. (P.K. 232 a and b, and cut 73).

Scene at a Banker's, in Chiarini, *Libro di Mercatanzie* (Libri), n.d. (P.K. 104); reprinted in the *Rappresentazione di Agnolo Hebreo*, 1554.

Domestic and Market Scenes, in *Contrasto di Carnesciale e la Quaresima* (Morgiani), n.d. (P.K. 85 a; fig. 313).

Monk arguing with two other monks and five laymen, in Domenico Benivieni, *Tractato in defensione della Doctrina di Savonarola* (Bonaccorsi), 1496 (P.K. 52).

A Ring of Dancing Girls before the cornice of a building with the Medici arms (fig. 314), in Lorenzo de' Medici, Politiano and others, *Ballatette* (Libri), n.d. (about 1496) (Gamba, No. 262, Florence; the B.M. copy lacks the woodcut); the cut is reprinted in the later edition of 1568 with title *Canzone a ballo* (e.g. Metropolitan Museum, New York).[1]

The larger cut in the 1533 edition of the *Canzone a ballo* (P.K. 283 a),[2] in which the scene takes place before an archway on a squared pavement, and the young man in the foreground is on the right, instead of left ($6\frac{7}{8} \times 4\frac{3}{4}$ inches), and which contains the device of the printer Francesco di Jacopo della Spera, is based on the woodcut reproduced in fig. 314. Kristeller also describes a third and smaller version ($4\frac{1}{2} \times 3\frac{1}{8}$ inches) in an edition of 1557 (Corsini).

Carnival Scene (P.K. 284, within the *passe-partout* border described as No. 6, on p. 533; see frontispiece), in *Canzone per andare in Maschera per Carnesciale fatte da piu persone* (Lorenzo de' Medici and others) (Morgiani and Petri), n.d. (about 1493–97).

Group of Seven Men with a Dog, in Lorenzo de' Medici, *La Compagnia del Mantellacio*, n.pr., n.d. (P.K. 280 and P.K. fig. 18, Ferrara, private collection): same style as the preceding *Carnival Scene* and the *Dancing Girls* in the *Ballatette*.

The Murder of Duke Galeazzo Sforza, in *Lamento del Duca Galeazo Sforza* (B. Zucchetta), 1505 (P.K. 400 a and P.K. cut 63, Trivulzio).

---

[1] This edition was reproduced in facsimile (including facsimile of the woodcut) by Gamba, in 100 copies, at Milan 1812. The British Museum only possesses the reprint.

[2] Reproduced in Kristeller, *Italienische Buchdrucker- und Verlegerzeichen*, Strassburg 1893, pp. 18 and 19, No. 61.

Captive Youth, and a girl shooting at Cupid, in Luca Pulci, *Driadeo d' Amore*, n.pr., n.d. (P.K. 341, Oxford), and Tebaldeo da Ferrara and others, *Canzoni*, n.pr., n.d. (P.K. 411, and P.K. cut 171).

Fig. 314. Ring of Dancing Girls, from *Ballatette* by Lorenzo de' Medici, Politiano and others, Florence.

and to illustrations in the following books:

Angelo Politiano, *La Giostra di Giuliano di Medici* (Tubini), n.d. (P.K. 336 a, cuts from Pulci, *Morgante Maggiore*, 1500, and from the *Epistoli e Evangelii*, as well as others done for the book).

Petrarca, *Trionfi*, printed for Pacini, 1499 (P.K. 328, Rome, Vitt. Emman.). Facsimile, Rome 1891. The *Triumph of Death* appears

A few months later than Johann of Westphalia's printer's mark, appeared the first series of woodcut illustrations in a Netherlandish book, those in the *Fasciculus Temporum*, printed by Jan Veldener at Louvain, 29th December 1475 (CA. 1478, CN. v. 3).

In subjects these illustrations follow the pattern set by the Cologne edition of Arnold Ther Hoernen of 1474,[1] the *Christ blessing* (fig. 317) being drawn by a distinctly better hand than its original. This block is found in various other books of Veldener's press, such as the *Epistelen en Evangelien*, 1479 and 1481 (CA. 688 and 690), in the edition of 1479 above the printer's mark. Veldener's

Fig. 317. Christ Blessing, from Rolewinck, *Fasciculus Temporum*, Utrecht 1481.

Fig. 318. The Initial G, from Rolewinck, *Fasciculus Temporum*, Utrecht 1481.

second edition of the *Fasciculus Temporum*, printed at Utrecht 19th April 1481 (CA. 1479), contains additional cuts, such as the *Building of Rome* and the *Storming of a Town*, for the most part based on illustrations in that other compendium of universal history, the *Rudimentum Noviciorum* (Lübeck, Lucas Brandis, 1475, H. 4996). Of its independent cuts the most attractive is that of *St. Peter at the Gate of Heaven* (f. 76 b, reprod. Schretlen, pl. 40, B), a four-piece scroll border and large initial G (fig. 318).[2] The border and initial G also occur in his *Passionael* of 12th September 1480 (CA. 1757, Oxford, Cambridge, The Hague).

Veldener's second printer's mark (Juchhoff 55), with blank shield sup-

---

[1] See p. 357.   [2] For another initial of the same style see p. 583, and cf. also p. 725.

ported by two lions, has a border in similar scroll-work (reprod. Holtrop, pl. 39 [29], 3). The style of decoration originated in Ulm, but has its nearest counterpart in a border used by Knoblochtzer, Strassburg, e.g. in his *Aesop* (S. 3021, H. 325). The *Passionael* (CA. 1757) also contains an interesting full-page cut illustrating the *Martyrdom of Various Saints* (CN. vi. 8).

A series of thirty-nine crudely cut Bible subjects, for the most part small uprights about $3\frac{1}{8} \times 2\frac{1}{4}$ inches, appeared in Jan Veldener's edition of the *Epistelen en Evangelien*, Utrecht, 19th April 1481 (CA. 690, CN. vi. 9). This edition also contains, on its last two leaves, fragments from the block-book *Speculum Humanae Salvationis*. Mention has already been made of the appearance of such fragments in printed books,[1] and I would here supplement my earlier reference by a list of the fragments and of the books in which they were printed:

I. SPECULUM HUMANAE SALVATIONIS. Its twofold blocks, divided into their two subjects, appear in:—

Epistelen en Evangelien, Utrecht (Veldener) 1481. CA. 690, CN. iii. E (two subjects only).

Speghel onser Behoudenisse, Culenborg (Veldener) 1483. CA. 1573, CN. iii. F (all the blocks, with twelve added subjects in the same style, i.e. 128 subjects in all).

Kruidboeck, Culenborg (Veldener) 1484. CA. 918, CN. iii. G (two subjects only).

II. BIBLIA PAUPERUM (Schreiber, ed. I). Forty-four pieces cut from the blocks appear in:—

Epistelen en Evangelien, Zwolle (Pieter van Os) 1487. CA. 697, CN. i. B (The Hague).

(*Note.*—Conway states that the fragments are from his ed. B = Sotheby II = Schreiber V. I have not examined The Hague copy of the *Epistelen*, but the blocks in later books printed by Pieter van Os in the British Museum are from Schreiber I, and so presumably would be those in the *Epistelen*, 1487.)

Among the numerous books printed by Pieter van Os at Zwolle between 1487 and 1500, in which the fragments occur, may be mentioned *Die Passie ende dat Liden ons Heren*, 1489, CA. 1163.

[1] See p. 213.

III. CANTICUM CANTICORUM (ed. I). The upper half of the first subject appears in:—

Rosetum Exercitiorum Spiritualium, Zwolle (Pieter van Os) 1494. CA. 1224, CN. ii. B.

Other fragments of a similar character, which probably represent a lost block-book of the Legend of the Holy Cross (*Historia Sanctae Crucis*), appeared in the *Boec van den Houte*, printed by J. Veldener at Culenborg, 6th March 1483 (CA. 940, CN. iv. B).[1]

From the presence of the fragments of the *Speculum* blocks at Utrecht, Bradshaw inferred that the *Speculum* block-book was originally printed at the same place. But considering the way in which printers moved from place to place, and borrowed blocks from other printers, such an inference is by no means certain, either in the case of the *Speculum* and Utrecht, or of the *Biblia Pauperum* and *Canticum* in relation to Zwolle. Even the addition of blocks in a similar style need not imply the same workshop, for a careful designer might easily imitate the earlier series.

The last illustrations issued by Veldener which I would mention are 150 cuts of plants in the *Kruidboeck in Dietsche*, printed at Culenborg, 1484 (CA. 918, CN. vi. 12 A), copied in reverse from the *editio princeps*, the *Herbarius Latinus* printed by Schoeffer at Mainz (S. 4203, H. 8444).[2] As the issues come within the same year, it looks as if some arrangement had been made by which Veldener was lent proofs to copy. Veldener also printed a Latin edition about a year later (CA. 916, CN. vi. 12 B).

Another of the earliest illustrated books issued at Utrecht, 30th March 1480, was Otto van Passau, *Boeck des Gulden Throens*, with a printer's mark of a palm-tree with two blank shields and Ǵ (the initial G with a cross)[3] (CA. 1342, CN. vi. 4, Holtrop, pls. 42-44 [40-42]). They are probably by the same designer or cutter who did the additional cuts in Veldener's second edition of the *Fasciculus Temporum* (1481) and his *Epistelen en Evangelien* of 1481, and are of little artistic interest. They are curious, however, for the economy by which various figures are fitted into different Gothic architectural borders. The illustrations are conversations between an Elder and a female figure, representing the Soul.

There are six varieties of *Elder*, five varieties of the *Soul*, and four

---

[1] For reproduction and notes see John Ashton and S. Baring Gould, *The Legendary History of the Cross*, London 1887.

[2] See pp. 348-352.

[3] Read by Campbell and Proctor 8861, incorrectly, as G.L. It is the same monogram as Juchhoff 56 and 57.

varieties of the border, in addition to the first illustration, on a single block, of *Elder and the Soul with Christ enthroned*. The whole series, in which nineteen combinations are made out of the single figures and borders, are reproduced by Holtrop.

GOUDA

Much more attractive is the series of 121 small woodcuts in the *Dyalogus Creaturarum* printed by GERARD LEEUW at Gouda, 3rd June 1480 (CA. 560,

Fig. 319. Initial S and border-pieces, from *Dyalogus Creaturarum*, Gouda 1480.

CN. viii. 2), and in various later editions in Latin and Dutch (*Twispraec der Creaturen*) printed by Leeuw at Gouda and Antwerp, and by Snellaert at Delft (1481–91).

The popularity of this book of fables is evidenced by the fact that as many as nine editions were printed in the Netherlands in these years, and a French edition, with copies of the original cuts, at Lyon in 1483.

The first page of the text (sig. a. 2) has a four-piece scroll border of the same character as Veldener's *Fasciculus Temporum* of 1481, and a handsome initial S on black ground (fig. 319), in addition to the cuts of the Sun, Moon and Clouds. It is an attractively printed book in Gothic type, in which the cuts of the fables are small oblongs about $2 \times 4\frac{3}{8}$ inches (nearly the width of the text). They are simply cut, for the most part in outline, with an occasional use of white on black (e.g. for the crow, sigg. f. 6, verso, f. 8, verso, and g. 3), and by no means lacking in verve and humour (fig. 320).

The relationship of this designer, or cutter, to the block-book tradition is seen even more clearly in his full-page cuts to the *Gesten van Romen* (*Gesta Romanorum*) first printed by Leeuw at Gouda, 30th April 1481 (CA. 826, CN. viii. 6 A, Paris). Only six of the series appeared in this first edition, nine were issued in the edition (*Gesten der Romeynen*) printed by Pieter van Os at Zwolle, 1484 (CA. 828, CN. viii. 6 B), and a tenth cut (with three of the others) in *Sielentrost*, Zwolle, P. van Os, 1485 (CA. 1547, CN. viii. 6 c). In their simplicity of design and cutting they are more reminiscent of the *Apocalypse* than the *Biblia Pauperum* and *Speculum*

Fig. 320. The Fowler, from *Dyalogus Creaturarum*, Gouda 1480.

block-books. The *Story of the Emperor Conrad*, which only appears in the two editions of the *Gesten van Romen*, is reproduced from the edition of 1484 (fig. 321).

Near in style again to the *Dyalogus* and *Gesta Romanorum* woodcuts are the four illustrations[1] to the *Vier Uterste*, Gouda (G. Leeuw) 1482 (CA. 1316, CN. viii. 4, Brussels, The Hague), which were also printed (probably earlier, 1481–82) by AREND DE KEYSERE at Audenarde (*Quatre Dernières Choses*, CA. 586, Brussels, Ghent); and another set of four in the *Historia Septem Sapientum Romae* (*Die Seven wise mannen van Romen*) printed at Gouda, first (undated) by the same printer who later issued the first edition of the *Chevalier Délibéré*, possibly Gotfridus de Os (CA. 952, CN. viii. 5 A, Haarlem),[2] and about 1482 by G. Leeuw (CA. 947, CN. viii. 5 B, Cambridge, Oxford). But both these sets are inferior in interest to the Gouda books before mentioned.

---

[1] *St. Peter at the Gate of Heaven* is reproduced by Holtrop, pl. 95 (98) b, and Delen, pl. xxx.
[2] See pp. 585, 588.

Conway arranged the Netherlandish woodcuts in sections under various woodcutters whom he called the 'First Gouda Woodcutter' (i.e. the author of the *Dyalogus*, etc.), 'Second Gouda Woodcutter' (the author of the *Devote Ghetiden*,[1] etc.) and by other similar local titles. I am not following these distinctions, except for occasional reference, as I feel that the foundations of one's knowledge are too insecure. In the first place, I would prefer to make distinctions by *designer* rather than by *cutter*, but the two factors are in such constant interplay—the same designer being interpreted by various cutters, and the identity of a designer being sometimes, perhaps, obscured by bad cutting—that I would, for the most part, avoid dogmatic distinctions.

Schretlen in his study of Dutch and

Fig. 321. Story of the Emperor Conrad, from the *Gesten van Romen*, Gouda 1481.

Flemish woodcuts unites in single personalities two or more of Conway's 'sectional' woodcutters. Thus he regards the series of small cuts for a *Devote Ghetiden van den Leven ende Passie Ihesu Christi* (a book of devotions for various times and seasons, comparable to the French *Horae*),

[1] *Ghetiden* is the Dutch equivalent for *Horae* in the sense of Canonical Hours, and is used in relation to Hours of the Virgin, of the Holy Cross, of the Life and Passion of Christ, etc. Cf. pp. 566, 568, 581, 583 and 584.

which we are about to describe, as by the same artist as the *Dyalogus Creaturarum*, in the same way that he attempts to identify Conway's 'Third Gouda Woodcutter', the author of *Godevaerts van Boloen* and of the *Chevalier Délibéré*, with JACOB CORNELISZ.

Fig. 322. The Flight into Egypt, from the *Devote Ghetiden*, Antwerp, about 1484.

A series of sixty-eight small upright cuts, illustrating the Life of Christ, measuring about $4\frac{1}{4} \times 3\frac{1}{4}$ inches, first appeared complete in the *Devote Ghetiden van den Leven ende Passie Iesu Christi*, printed by Leeuw at Antwerp about 1484 (CA. 1115, CN. ix. 2 E, Leyden, Soc. de litt. néerl.; see fig. 322). Portions of the same series had appeared earlier in (*a*) *Liden ons Heren*, Gouda (Leeuw), 29th July 1482 (CA. 1156, CN. ix. 2 A, The Hague, Brussels); (*b*) *Lyden ons Heeren*, Haarlem (Bellaert), 10th December 1483 (CA. 1157, CN. ix. 2 C, Enschedè Sale, 374); and (*c*) *Epistelen en Evangelien*, Gouda (G. de Os), 23rd June 1484 (CA. 693, CN. ix. 2 D, Cambridge). And probably between (*a*) and (*b*) were issued the sheets with thirty-six of the cuts with Dutch verses (in Leeuw's type), preserved at Erlangen (CA. 746, CN. ix. 2 B).[1] Thereafter portions of the series appeared in a variety of books issued by Leeuw at Antwerp and certain other Netherlandish printers until the beginning of the XVI century.

The *Devote Ghetiden* (*getyden*) *van den Leven ende Passie Iesu Christi* is a rare form of devotional 'Hours', the regular *Ghetidenboeck* being the Hours of the Blessed Virgin. Its illustration is practically the same as would be

---

[1] Reproduced and described by M. Zucker, *Einzelformschnitte in der Kupferstichsammlung der kgl. Universitäts-Bibliothek Erlangen* (Einblattdrucke, herausgegeben von Paul Heitz), Strassburg 1913. See Schreiber, vol. i. 12, etc.

Fig. 323. Christ preaching from the Ship, and the Parable of the Sower, from Ludolphus, *Leven ons Heeren*, Antwerp 1487.

Fig. 324. The Disciples plucking the Ears of Corn, from Ludolphus, *Leven ons Heeren*,
Antwerp 1487.

required for a Life of Christ, such as that of Ludolphus de Saxonia, and
some fifty of the series appeared in Leeuw's edition of *Ludolphus*, issued in
1487, generally with two architectural side-pieces, or some other subject
block added to make up the width of page. The series may have been
originally done for a lost or unachieved *Devote Ghetiden* or even for a
Ludolphus. That there is only one copy known of the 1484 *Devote Ghetiden*
renders it quite possible that an earlier edition was completely lost. Or it
may be that before the project for the *Devote Ghetiden* was complete, part
of the series of blocks was used for works in which fewer blocks were
required.

The subjects are related to Israhel van Meckenem's line-engravings, his
Smallest Passion Series.[1] The designs must have been very popular at the
period, as numerous examples appear in a variety of forms, in line-engraving

---

[1] See M. Geisberg, *Verzeichnis der Kupferstiche I. v. Meckenem*, Strassburg 1905, p. 3,
and M. Lehrs, *Geschichte und kritischer Katalog*, ix. 62-120. Geisberg dates the Meckenem
series about 1475–78. Described by Willshire, *Early German and Flemish Prints in the British*

Fig. 325. The Disciples plucking the Ears of Corn, from Ludolphus, *Leven ons Heeren*, Delft 1488.

and woodcut, in Germany and the Netherlands, from the *Biblia Pauperum* block-book downwards.[1]

In other Netherlandish woodcuts the same designs appear in a series by the Haarlem woodcutter who worked for Bellaert, in his *Epistelen en Evangelien*, 1486 (CA. 695, CN. xi. 9 A, The Hague), reprinted in Ludolphus, *Leven ons Heeren*, Zwolle (P. van Os) 1499 (CA. 1185, CN. xi. 9 B, The Hague, Cambridge), and in the Ludolphus, *Leven ons Heeren*, Delft (Snellaert) 1488 (CA. 1182, CN. xxi. 7).

In German books with woodcuts some of the same designs appear in the *Rudimentum Noviciorum*, Lübeck (Brandis) 1475 (S. 5159, H. 4996), and *Die Nye Ee und det Passional van Ihesus und Marien*, Lübeck (Brandis) 1478 (S. 3349, H. 4061).

Museum, vol. ii. p. 339, 16, under IA. of Zwolle, and Conway's discussion (*Woodcutters of the Netherlands*, p. 44) is based on this description. Lehrs refers Meckenem's designs back to the so-called 'Master of the Martyrdom of the 10,000 Christians' (L. iii. p. 358, 8-53), and these again largely to the Master E.S.

[1] See Geisberg, *Israhel van Meckenem, Anhang*, p. 279; Lehrs, *Geschichte und kritischer Katalog des deutschen . . . Kupferstichs im XV Jahrhundert*, iii. p. 358, No. 8, etc.

of Corn; fig. 324). Here I am more inclined to regard the Delft designer as the inspirer (fig. 325). But the whole subject of these Ludolphus editions is full of difficulty, as well as interest, and I cannot pretend to have mastered its problems.

Fig. 327. Printer's mark of Christian Snellaert, Delft.

The designer of the Delft *Ludolphus* and of numerous other woodcuts printed at Delft from about 1483 by JACOB VAN DER MEER, CHRISTIAN SNELLAERT and HENRIK ECKERT of Homburg (who worked after 1500 at Antwerp), Conway's 'Second Delft Cutter', is a very distinct mannerist, and has been conjecturally identified by Dr. Max Friedländer with the painter called the 'Master of the Virgo inter Virgines'.[1]

The earliest book in which his work is recognised is the *Historie van die Seven Weise Mannen*, Delft (Meer), 13th January 1483 (CA. 953, CN. xxi. 2, Utrecht), with cuts based on Leeuw's Gouda edition of 1482 (CA. 947, CN. viii. 5 B, Oxford, Cambridge).

More interesting are the thirteen small cuts (about $3 \times 2\frac{1}{4}$ inches, within double border-lines), with single figures illustrating the game of chess, in Jac. de Cessolis, *Scaecspul*, printed by J. van der Meer, 14th February 1483 (CA. 421, CN. xxi. 3; fig. 328). They are cut with greater regularity and precision than are most of the illustrations in the Delft *Ludolphus*, as is also the *King and Ten Counsellors* on the first page of Jean Boutillier, *Somme Rurael*, printed by Van der Meer, 19th August 1483 (CA. 361, CN. xxi. 4), on which also appears an elaborate woodcut initial S on black ground.

[1] See Max J. Friedländer, *Altniederländische Malerei*, v., Berlin 1927, p. 65.

On 25th March 1486 appeared for the first time the fifty-eight small upright Bible illustrations (about 4 × 3¼ inches), based in part on the Gouda and Antwerp *Devote Ghetiden* series, in the *Vier Uterste* (Delft, Meer, CA. 1319, CN. xxi. 7 A, The Hague). They were reprinted in the same year, 29th November, in Van der Meer's *Epistelen en Evangelien* (CA. 696, CN. xxi. 7 B, The Hague), in the *Ludolphus* of 1488, already described, and in several other editions of the Epistles and Gospels, *Passionael*, *Ludolphus*, etc., by Van der Meer and Snellaert at Delft, and by Eckert at Delft and Antwerp. Further cuts of a similar character appeared in the *Passionael*, printed by Van der Meer, 1st March 1487 (CA. 1763, CN. xxi. 9, The Hague, Cambridge), and these also occur in the 1488 *Ludolphus*, and in several later *Passionael* and other books printed by Snellaert and Eckert at Delft and Antwerp, while other blocks of the

Fig. 328. The Notary, from Cessolis, *Scaecspul*, Delft 1483.

same type were cut for the first time for Snellaert's *Passionael* of 1489 (CA. 1765, CN. xxi. 15).

A series of copies from the *Ars Moriendi* block-book were printed by Snellaert in 1488 (*Sterfboeck*; CA. 1619, CN. xxi. 14), and occasional illustrations by the same Delft designer, or directly inspired by him, appeared in various Delft books till nearly the end of the century, e.g. a *Confession* in *Devotus Libellus de Modo Confitendi*, Snellaert, 14th February 1494 (not in CA.), a *Monk (St. Bernard) giving instruction* (CN. xxi. 29), e.g. in *Expositio Hymnorum*, 1496 (CA. 722), and a large *Christ on the Cross with the Virgin and St. John* in the *Missale Trajectense*, Snellaert, about 1495 (CA. 1262, CN. xxi. 30, The Hague).

The illustrations in Eckert's edition of the *Fables of Aesop* (1498, CA. 29, CN. xxi. 31) are carelessly cut copies from the series first issued at Ulm by Johann Zainer about 1476–77,[1] with eight separate side-pieces (figures and trees) used to fit the subjects to the width of the page. If the same designer as before is responsible for this series, his work has considerably suffered by the poor cutting of the blocks.

[1] See p. 306.

Dingen, 24th December 1485 (CA. 258, CN. xi. 8; fig. 331), and four slight cuts in Bellaert's edition of Otto van Passau, *Boeck des Gulden Throens*, 1484 (CA. 1343, CN. xi. 4). But more individual and varied in character are the illustrations in the two medieval romances,[1] the *Historie van Jason* of about 1485 (CA. 1092, CN. xi. 6) and the *Historie van Troyen*, 1485 (CA. 1095, CN. xi. 7), of which the only impressions to which I can refer are in the Bibliothèque Nationale, Paris. A full-page frontispiece of the *Author presenting his book to Philip the Good*, within the same border with which Bellaert surrounded his printer's mark (fig. 332),[2] and twenty half-page oblong cuts appeared in both books, and the condition of the blocks shows that the undated *Jason* is the earlier work. Then twenty-five new half-page cuts in the same form first appeared in the *Historie van Troyen*. The designs are very spirited, and here and there show a good decorative sense, as in the occasional use of white on black for the grass ground.

Fig. 330. Printer's mark of Jacob Bellaert, Haarlem.

The last two books with woodcuts by the same hand, issued by Bellaert at Haarlem, are Pierre Michault, *Doctrinael des Tyts* (CA. 1254, CN. xi. 11, The Hague), and the *Boeck vanden Pelgherijm* (CA. 1376, CN. xi. 12), Brussels, Berlin Print Room), both printed in 1486. Earlier in the same year Bellaert had issued the series of scriptural cuts in his *Epistelen en Evangelien*, to which we have already referred.[3]

The best work of the Haarlem designer, who has a natural tendency to

---

[1] First issued in the French of Raoul Le Fèvre, the English translation of William Caxton by Colard Mansion and Caxton at Bruges, about 1474–76.

[2] The frontispiece of the *Author presenting his book* appeared without the border-pieces in Pierre Michault, *Doctrinael des Tyts*, printed by Bellaert, 1486 (CA. 1254), and in *Sydrac*, printed by Hugo Janszoen of Woerden, at Leyden, 1495.

[3] See p. 569.

Fig. 331. The Birds, from Bartholomaeus Anglicus, *Boeck van den Proprieteyten der Dingen*, Haarlem 1485.

anecdote, is full of life and spirit, and the interest in landscape and architecture is characteristic of the Dutch art of the period. The cutting is not very precise, but it is in harmony with the naturalistic vein of the Dutchman's design.

Fig. 332. The Author presenting his book to Philip the Good, from the *Historie van Jason*, Haarlem, about 1485.

No books were issued by Bellaert after 1486, and his designer (whether identical with the cutter or not) probably migrated to Antwerp, for a considerable number of the illustrations in books printed by Gerard Leeuw, up to his death in 1493, and by other Antwerp printers for a few years later, are in the same style, though of varying quality.

The blocks done for Bellaert were scattered, and used by Leeuw at Antwerp, and by a variety of other Netherlandish printers. Even his printer's mark, with its original borders, reappeared without revision in the *Sydrac* (*Schoone Historie gheheeten Sydrac*), printed at Leyden in 1495, and attributed by Proctor to the printer HUGO JANSZOEN of Woerden (CA. 981). The *Author presenting his book*, and the *Creation and Fall of the Angels* in *Sydrac*, are likewise Bellaert's blocks, the former from the *Historie van Jason* of about 1486, the latter from Glanville, *Proprieteyten der Dingen* of 1485.

ANTWERP (*continued*)

The illustrations in the *Histoire de Paris et de Vienne* issued by G. Leeuw, 15th May 1487 (CA. 941, CN. xii. 1), and four days later in Dutch, *Historie van Parijs ende Vienna* (CA. 942), of which the only copies known to me are in the Bibliothèque Nationale, Paris, are in just the same style and form as the *Jason* and *Troy* cuts (see fig. 333). They were probably done at Haarlem, and might have been originally issued there, but there is no trace of an edition earlier than 1487.

We have already alluded to a section of the cuts in the Leeuw's *Ludolphus* of 3rd November 1487 as in the same style (CA. 1181, CN. xii. 3; fig. 326),[1] and the twelve illustrations in the same printer's *Hoofkyn der Devotien*, of 28th November 1487 (CA. 985, CN. xii. 4, The Hague, Cambridge), are also by the same designer.

The same hand again appears in the *Historie van*

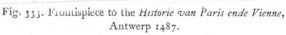

Fig. 333. Frontispiece to the *Historie van Paris ende Vienne*, Antwerp 1487.

die seven wise mannen van Romen, issued by Claes Leeuw in 1488 (CA. 954, CN. xii. 9), and by Gerard Leeuw in a Latin edition under the title *Historia Calumniae Novercalis*, 6th November 1490 (CA. 950). In the interval the blocks had been lent to Johann Koelhoff at Cologne, who printed an edition earlier in 1490.[2] The cutting is rather heavier than most of the cuts printed by Bellaert at Haarlem, so that I incline to think that Bellaert's designer continued to work for both Claes and Gerard Leeuw, but not the same cutter.

---

[1] See p. 570.   [2] See p. 362.

There are numerous little cuts of a similar character issued by Gerard Leeuw in various books of devotion, the most attractive being perhaps the *Van die gheestelike kintscheyt Ihesu*, 1488 (CA. 1074, CN. xii. 6 A), and the *Corona Mystica Beatae Virginis Mariae*, 1492 (CA. 997, CN. xii. 19).

Fig. 334. Printer's mark of Gerard Leeuw, Antwerp.

The same designer was probably also responsible for the woodcut of the *Arms of England supported by Angels* on the title-page of the *Cronycles of the Londe of Englond*, printed by Gerard Leeuw, 1493 (CA. 511, CN. xii. 20), framed within three parts of Bellaert's four-piece border (seen in fig. 332).

The woodcuts in Leeuw's edition of Aesop's *Fables*, 1486 (CA. 26, CN. xv.), are copies from the cuts in the Ulm edition of Johann Zainer,[1] and not, as described by Conway, the original German blocks. The series which appear in the Aesop printed by Eckert at Delft in 1498 were probably based on those in Leeuw's edition.

Gerard Leeuw used three printer's marks, all showing the Castle of Antwerp (Juchhoff 3-5), and the best of these is here reproduced (fig. 334; Juchhoff 3).[2] Other attractive devices used by Antwerp printers are those of GOVAERT BAC (Juchhoff 6-12, all but one showing a bird-cage), ROELANT VAN DEN DORPE (Juchhoff 13, Knight Roland), and MATHIAS GOES (*Wild man with Shield of Brabant*, Juchhoff 1, and a *Three-masted Ship*, Juchhoff 2; fig. 335). The three-masted ship is of a similar type to the ship engraved on copper by the anonymous Master W♄ (Lehrs, 1895, No. 30, and *Kritischer Katalog*, No. 41).

---

[1] See p. 306.

[2] The same block was used by later printers at Antwerp, Mathias Goes and Thierry Martens.

Mathias Goes also used an attractive series of woodcut initials (see Holtrop, pl. 100 [47] and fig. 336).

Among other Antwerp cuts I would mention the *Master and Five Pupils* (e.g. in *Cato Moralisatus*, 1485, CA. 406, CN. x. 3, and in Petrus Hispanus, *Logicalia*, 1486, CA. 1394, CN. x. 3, both printed by Gerard Leeuw), and a lengthy series illustrating the *Historie van Meluzine*, printed by Gerard Leeuw, 1491 (CA. 975, CN. x. 11, Brussels), all somewhat similar in style to the *Devote Ghetiden* series.

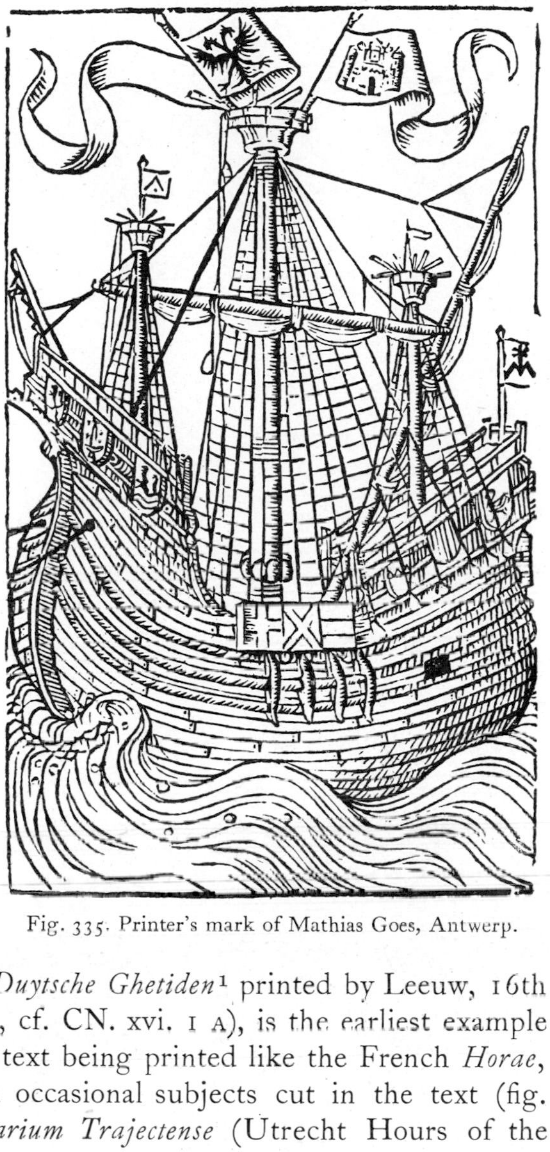

Another lengthy and interesting series of cuts was issued by Rolant van den Dorpe in the *Cronyke van Brabant* of 1497 (CA. 508, CN. xxxvii. 1, Oxford, Cambridge, The Hague), and effective designs are often made of the battle scenes with their spears and standards.

A certain number of cuts in the French style (if not actually French blocks) appeared in various small books of devotion, chiefly issued by Gerard Leeuw and ADRIAEN

Fig. 335. Printer's mark of Mathias Goes, Antwerp.

VAN LIESVELT at Antwerp. The *Duytsche Ghetiden*[1] printed by Leeuw, 16th August 1491 (B.M. IA. 49836, cf. CN. xvi. 1 A), is the earliest example to which I can refer, the whole text being printed like the French *Horae*, within four-piece borders, with occasional subjects cut in the text (fig. 337). Very similar is the *Horarium Trajectense* (Utrecht Hours of the

---

[1] This is the complete title on the first page, but the colophon expands its connotation: *Hier in desen boeck sal men vinden die getijden van onser vrouwen ende van den heylighe cruce, Een oracie van den heylighen gheest. Die vii psalmen. Die Vigilie met ix lessen. Die xv pater nr. metten ghebeden van der passie ons heeren* [etc.].

Fig. 336. Initial S, from St. Augustine, *De Virtute Psalmorum*, Antwerp, n.d.

Virgin) printed by Liesvelt, 1495 (CA. 990, CN. xvi. 1 L), which contains some of the cuts, but the borders are from a different set of blocks. The borders of both books are comparable in their alternate spaces of black and white ground with a set of cuts in the *Horae* manner in the Lyon edition of the *Mer der Hystoires*, 1491.[1]

Before leaving Antwerp I would mention a series of fifty woodcuts illustrating the *Life and Passion of Christ* which were printed at Antwerp by Hendrik Eckert of Homburg, in editions of 1500, 1503 and 1510.[2] Twenty cuts of the series have been described, on account of their two owners, as the Delbecq-Schreiber Passion (see fig. 338). These twenty impressions had been coloured and mounted in a manuscript book of devotion, and Schreiber conjecturally dates them about 1480 (S. 148, etc., now in the Bibliothèque Royale, Brussels). There are also copies of the same series at Linz and Vienna.[3] The subjects derive chiefly from the cuts of the block-book *Speculum Humanae Salvationis*, but in certain subjects they are nearer in detail to the *Devote Ghetiden* series described above.[4] Unless one could depend on more definite proof in regard to the date of the MS. to which the Delbecq-Schreiber impressions belonged, I should be more inclined to date the blocks nearer 1490 than 1480.

ZWOLLE

I have already referred to the printer PIETER VAN OS of Zwolle for his reprints from fragments of block-books, and from blocks issued earlier by Bellaert and Leeuw. He also issued copies of the *Ars Moriendi* block-book in his *Sterfboeck* printed in 1488 and 1491 (CA. 1620, 1621, CN. xvii. 7). Among work for which he was originally responsible, the *Vision of St. Bernard*, which appeared in S. Bernardus, *Sermones*, Zwolle, edd. 1484–85 and 1495 (CA. 275, 276, CN. xvii. 2; fig. 339), is the most interesting

---

[1] See p. 613.

[2] The British Museum has them in *De Leven ons heeren*, 1510.

[3] See W. Molsdorf, *Die niederländische Holzschnitt-Passion Delbecq-Schreiber*, Einbl., Strassburg 1908; G. Gugenbauer, ditto, II. Teil, Einbl., Strassburg 1913; W. L. Schreiber, Sale Catalogue, Vienna 1909, No. 65; W. L. Schreiber, *Manuel*, No. 14 a, etc., No. 148, etc.

[4] See p. 566.

and one of the best Dutch woodcuts of the period.[1] The printer's mark of an *Angel kneeling in a niche holding the shield of Zwolle* (Juchhoff 60 and 61), which occurs in the edition of 1484–85, is certainly by the same hand. Another full-page cut which occurs in the issue of 1495, the *Annunciation*, is by another hand and of harder and more angular design. It appeared earlier in the *Vaderboeck* of 1490 (CA. 938, CN. xviii. 3, The Hague, Brussels, Cambridge, Darmstadt).

A head-piece representing *Beehives and Bees* in Thomas Cantipratanus, *Der Bien boeck*, printed by Pieter van Os, 1488 (CA. 1658, CN. xvii. 6; fig. 340), is an attractive design, in which the white and black line is well combined by the cutter. Mention should also be

Fig. 337. The Annunciation, from the *Duytsche Ghetiden*, Antwerp 1491.

made of a large woodcut capital H (102 × 105 mm.) which appeared in his *Passionael* of 1490 (CA. 1766, Holtrop, pl. 92 [83]) in the style of the G used by Veldener in his *Fasciculus Temporum*, 1481, though slightly larger.[2]

DEVENTER

Little work of importance was produced at Deventer. Most of the books printed by RICHARDUS PAFRAET and JACOBUS OF BREDA were small, and few contained cuts.

Of woodcuts in Pafraet's book I would mention a *Master with five pupils*

[1] Variants of the subject are found in two dotted prints of the period, S. 2565 (Nuremberg) and 2565 a (Breslau). Cf. Dodgson, *Catalogue of Early German and Flemish Woodcuts in the British Museum*, i. p. 234.　　　　[2] See p. 560.

(CN. xxviii. 13),[1] which occurs in many of his books (e.g. in *Gemmula Vocabulorum*, 1487, CA. 792), a *Master and Youth standing* (CN. xxviii. 16), e.g. in Albertus de Eybe, *Boeck van den Echten Staete*, about 1493 (CA. 724),

Fig. 338. Christ before Pilate, from the so-called Delbecq-Schreiber Passion, Antwerp 1500.

and his two devices representing *St. Lebuin* (Juchhoff 27 and 28).

A cut on a black ground, with the *Sacred Monogram and the Signs of the Evangelists in roundels*, is found in certain of his books, e.g. Baptista (Spagnuolo) Mantuanus, *Carmen in praeconium Rob. Severinatis*, 1495 (CA. 239), and was also issued by Jacobus of Breda, e.g. in Alanus, *Doctrinale*, 1494 (CA. 56, Juchhoff 29). Juchhoff describes it as Jacobus of Breda's device, but it may be no more than a frontispiece cut. There are two other blocks of the same design, one, with the scroll of the S cutting the lower margin, and more crudely cut than Pafraet's block, used by Pieter van Os at Zwolle, e.g. in Prudentius, *Psychomachia*, n.d. (CA. 1458), and the other used by GOVAERT BAC at Antwerp, in which the eagle is on the right (in the two others it is on the left), and placed by Juchhoff among his printer's marks (10).

LEYDEN

HUGO JANSZOEN of Woerden, printer at Leyden, was one of the printers who became possessed of some of Bellaert's old blocks, and he even used Bellaert's printer's mark in its original form.[2]

Apart from this he chiefly deserves mention for his small books of devotion, though they are of less interest than those printed by Gerard Leeuw and Liesvelt at Antwerp, the blocks being for the most part cut in a hard manner. Examples of such books are the *Ghetyden van onser lieuer vrouwen*, 1495 (CA. 838, CN. xxix. 1), Bernardus, *Onser lieuer vrouwen Souter*, n.d. (C.A. 279, CN. xxx. 1 E), *Dat Leven ons liefs heren*, 1498

---

[1] Similar in general design (master on throne and the pupils grouped in lower foreground) to the cut issued by G. Leeuw (see p. 581), but the master is reading from a book, while in the latter he holds a birch.   [2] See pp. 575, 576.

(CA. 1111, CN. xxx. 1 A), and *Dat Leven onser lieuer vrouwen*, 1500 (CA. 1122, CN. xxx. 1 G). A cut of the *Annunciation* which appears in the first three of these books is in the Haarlem style, even if it did not come from Bellaert (CN. xiv. 2).

GOUDA (*continued*)

We have already considered the earliest woodcuts printed at Gouda.[1] We now return to the study of books printed at the same place under the

Fig. 339. The Vision of St. Bernard, from S. Bernardus, *Sermones*, Zwolle 1484–85.

names and initials, GOTFRIDUS DE OS, GOVAERT VAN GHEMEN and G.D., who, according to Holtrop, are possibly one and the same person. Govaert van Ghemen also printed at Leyden about 1490,[2] and from 1493 until 1510 at Copenhagen, spelling his name Gotfridus af Ghemen.

[1] See p. 563.
[2] See CA. 1256, Juchhoff 44. The printer's mark copied by the *Collacie Broeders*, Gouda 1496 (CA. 36).

both Mary of Burgundy and her consort Maximilian as *premier maître d'hôtel*.

The first edition of the *Chevalier Délibéré*, issued in Holland, was printed at Gouda between 1486 and 1490 with the printer's mark of the *Elephant and Castle* and letters G.D. (Juchhoff 34), and it is therein stated that the treatise was completed in April 1483 (CA. 1083, CN. xxv. 6, Baron Edmond de Rothschild, from the Ganay and Davillier Collections).[1] The poem and its sixteen full-page cuts were reprinted at Schiedam, about 1498–1500 (CA. 1084),[2] certainly after the *Vita Lijdwine* of 1498, where the same printer's mark is in earlier impression. The series of cuts also appeared in *Den Camp van der Doot*, issued at Schiedam in 1503. Two of the blocks were reprinted in the *Vaderboeck*, by Seversoen, Leyden 1511, and finally cut up into sections in Seversoen's *Cronycke van Hollandt*, 1517.

One of the MSS. of the poem (Bibliothèque Nationale, MS. français, 1606) gives the author's directions for its illustration, including both design and colour. These directions are closely followed in the only known copy of the first Gouda edition, in the library of Baron Edmond de Rothschild, Paris, in which the cuts are coloured. I cannot find that any of the contemporary illuminated MSS. (of which a list is given by Picot and Stein),[3] contain designs corresponding to the woodcut series in either the Dutch or French editions.

The designs of the Gouda woodcuts are the work of an artist (probably a painter) of real merit. Dr. Friedländer thinks that they belong to the local school, probably by some painter in the following of Geertgen of Haarlem, and compares the style of a picture of the *Disciples of St. John the Baptist and*

---

[1] The earliest editions printed in France are 8th August 1488 and 1493 (Cl. ii. 221), so that the Gouda issue might be the *editio princeps*. The cuts in the first two Paris editions are entirely different designs from the Gouda edition. For the work and its various editions see E. Picot and H. Stein, *Recueil des pièces historiques imprimées sous le règne de Louis XI.*, Paris (Société des Bibliophiles François) 1923, p. 305. The work must have been very popular in the xvi century, for in addition to the various French editions there were two Spanish versions printed at Antwerp in 1555, and another at Salamanca in 1560 (*El Cavallero determinado*). The Spanish version of Hernando de Acuna was translated into English by Lewis Lewkenor and issued under the title *The Resolved Gentleman*, London 1594.

[2] An edition known in imperfect copies at the Bibliothèque Nationale and the Bibliothèque de l'Arsenal, Paris, and in the Musée Plantin, Antwerp. See the reprint and facsimile of woodcuts for this edition (based on the Paris copies) with preface by F. Lippmann, issued by the Bibliographical Society, London 1898. Above the printer's mark on the last page is an excellent *Memento Mori* cut, the *Three Skulls* (CN. xxxii. 7).

[3] E.g. in the Musée Condé, Chantilly, and Fitzwilliam Museum, Cambridge.

Fig. 343. Combat between the Actor and Age, from Olivier de la Marche, *Chevalier Délibéré*, Gouda, about 1486–90.

of Christ in the J. G. Johnson Collection, Philadelphia.[1] It seems almost certain that the edition was done under the direction of the author himself, and, apart from such comparison, we might have expected that he would have

turned to some artist of the Southern Netherlands, and in some respects I feel a nearer relation in these designs to French art than in any other Dutch woodcuts. On the other hand, the cutter is more likely to have been a local craftsman, and was probably the same who worked on other books printed by Gotfridus de Os (and his doubles).

Fig. 344. St. Lydwina's Fall on the Ice, from Brugman, *Vita Lijdwine*, Schiedam 1498.

Schretlen believes that these designs are the early work of Jacob Cornelisz, but the evidence seems to me insufficient to support the conjecture.

One of the nearest relations in style to the *Chevalier Délibéré* may be seen in the woodcuts of *Les Neuf Preux* at Hamburg, of which only two of the three blocks are preserved (S. 1948, and vol. vi., 1893, pl. xvi a). Apart from the same large qualities of design, there is resemblance in details of technical method, such as the perpendicular shading of the legs.

SCHIEDAM

Allusion has already been made to the *Vita Lijdwine*, by Johannes Brugman, printed at Schiedam, 1498 (CA. 383, CN. xxxii. 5), as it bears the same printer's mark as the second edition of the *Chevalier Délibéré* (Juchhoff 53). In the *Vita Lijdwine* the mark bears the imprint *Schiedam in Hollandia* in type; in the *Chevalier Délibéré* there are further breaks in the woodcut border-lines and the imprint reads *Schiedam in Hollant*. Most of the cuts are half-page oblongs, about $3 \times 3\frac{5}{8}$ inches, and the subject of

---

[1] Max J. Friedländer, *Altniederländische Malerei*, v., Berlin 1927, p. 61, No. 37, pl. xxv.

S. Lydwina's Fall on the Ice (fig. 344) shows a Dutch designer with the gift for simple representation from daily life so characteristic of later Dutch art. Both designer and cutter might be the same as the author of the cuts in the *Historie hertoghe Godevaerts van Boloen*.[1]

SCHOONHOVEN

Near to the *Vita Lijdwine* in type of work are certain cuts in devotional books printed by the Augustinian Canons of St. Michael, near Schoonhoven, of which copies are very rare outside Holland (there are a few in the University Library, Cambridge). The *Virgin and Child in Glory* in the *Ghetidenboec* of 1498 (CA. 842, CN. xxxii. 1, Cambridge) and the

Fig. 345. Pyramus and Thisbe, from Ovid, *Metamorphoses*, Bruges 1484.

St. Augustine in the *Breviarium Windesemense* of 1499 (CA. 368, 369, CN. xxxii. 2, The Hague) may be noted.

A *Liber Horarum* of 10th March 1500 (CA. 988), one of the few Schoonhoven books in the British Museum, contains an attractive little cut of the *Annunciation* (84 × 59 mm.) of rather different character.

BRUGES

Outside Antwerp there was considerably less woodcut book-illustration in the xv century in the Southern Netherlands than in Holland. The earliest and most interesting was the *Metamorphoses* of Ovid (*Métamorphose moralisé*

[1] See p. 586.

par Maistre Thomas Waleys) issued by COLARD MANSION at Bruges in May 1484 (CA. 1348, CN. vii.).[1] It is a folio printed in two columns of large Gothic type, containing seventeen large cuts illustrating the stories (about two-thirds of the page in size, $7\frac{1}{4} \times 6\frac{1}{2}$ inches) and the same number of upright column cuts of gods and goddesses (about $4\frac{1}{2} \times 3$ inches). They are drawn in a broad and open manner, awkward and angular in cutting, but not without a certain gauche charm (see fig. 345). Very similar in character and possibly by the same designer are the cuts which appeared in *L'Abusé en Court* printed anonymously at Lyon about 1480, and in one or two other books by the same printer, e.g. in Pierre Michault, *Doctrinal du Temps passé* and the *Quatre Filz Aymon*.[2] They formed a very definite source of inspiration to the chief woodcut designer in Vérard's workshop after 1490.[3]

Mr. Henkel has demonstrated the close relationship of the designs to Flemish miniatures in MSS. at Paris (Bibliothèque Nationale, MS. français 137) and Copenhagen (Royal Library, MS. Otto Thott 399). There are probably many other cases unidentified where the early woodcut designer has based his work on miniatures.

Colard Mansion's only other illustrated book, if we are right in regarding it as such, is his Boccaccio, *De Casibus virorum et foeminarum illustrium* of 1476, but there he used line-engravings, and only two copies are known with the series pasted in.[4]

BRUSSELS

Somewhat similar in their broad and angular style of cutting are the two cuts in the *Legenda Henrici Imp. et Kunegundis* printed at Brussels by the Fratres Communis Vitae[5] in 1484, representing the *Emperor Henry II. and Kunigunda seated* and the *Arms of Anthony of Rotenhan, Bishop of Bamberg* (CA. 1100, CN. xxii. 1, Holtrop, pl. 62 [74] and 63 [75]).

[1] See M. D. Henkel, *De Houtsneden van Mansion's 'Ovide Moralisé'*, Bruges 1484. Amsterdam (Koninklijk Oudheidkundig Genootschap) 1922. Bradshaw first noted two editions both with imprint of Colard Mansion and date May 1484, but the second probably printed by Jean Gossin who took over Mansion's rooms after his disappearance in 1484. The British Museum copy is of this second issue. Cf. Henkel, *Nederlansche Ovidius-Illustratien van de 14ᵉ tot de 18ᵉ Eeuw*. Oud-Holland 1921, p. 149, and *Engravings and Woodcuts after Flemish Miniatures*, Burlington Magazine, li. 209 (Nov. 1927).

[2] See p. 600.   [3] See p. 666.

[4] See my *History of Engraving and Etching*, 3rd ed., 1923, pp. 32-3. The Newbattle copy is now in the Boston Museum of Fine Arts. The other copy with the engravings is at Göttingen. There is a line-engraving at Boston of *Jason subduing the Oxen*, in the style of the Boccaccio illustrations, which shows that Mansion had originally thought of using engravings for his *Ovid* as well.   [5] Cf. p. 213.

LOUVAIN (*continued*)

By the same hand as the Kunigunda woodcuts are the illustrations in Boccaccio, *De claris mulieribus*, printed by AEGIDIUS VAN DER HEERSTRATEN, Louvain, 1487 (CA. 294, CN. xxii. 3). They are freely adapted from the woodcuts which appeared in the Ulm edition of 1473 printed by Johann Zainer,[1] and some are as good and as spirited as the originals.

Two other Louvain books may be mentioned, both printed by LUDOVICUS RAVESCOT, the *Visio Lamentabilis* of about 1487 (CA. 1745, CN. xxiii. 1), with four vivid but crude cuts representing a hermit's dream, and the adventures of the soul after death, and Petrus de Rivo, *Opus Responsivum de Anno die et feria dominicae Passionis*, 1488 (CA. 1405, CN. xxiii. 4, 5).

The most interesting of the four cuts in the latter book is the *Virgin and Child in a Church, adored by the author*, which appears on the first page, and is reproduced by Juchhoff as though it were a device of the printer (Juchhoff 52; fig. 346). It gives the impression of having been based on a painting of a similar design to the Berlin Van Eyck. Ravescot's actual printer's mark occurs in the colophon of the same book (Juchhoff 51).

Fig. 346. The Virgin and Child adored by the author, from Petrus de Rivo, *Opus Responsivum*, Louvain 1488.

[1] See p. 305.

Miscellaneous Single Cuts

In the latter part of the xv century book-illustration everywhere plays by far the most important rôle in the history of woodcut, and in the Netherlands there are few single cuts of any importance. A series of *Les Neuf Preux* (S. 1948) has already been mentioned,[1] and the only other cut of equal interest is the *Good Shepherd*, a large cut preserved in the Stadtbibliothek at Breslau (S. 838; fig. 347). The design is similar to an engraving by the Master of the Amsterdam Cabinet (Master of the Hausbuch, Lehrs 1894, No. 18), which is possibly the original on which the cut is based, though both might derive from a common source.[2] It has inscriptions in both Dutch and French, and probably belongs on that account to the Southern Netherlands, and from the dialect, according to the late M. Henri Hymans, to the region of Liége. It was preserved with a woodcut from the Lübeck *Rudimentum Noviciorum* of 1475, in the binding of an undated Missal of about 1470–80, and this is about the period to which one would assign the block.

A large and crudely cut *Christ Child in a Heart* (S. 796, Berlin) deserves mention if only for its signature, *peter de wale*, which is probably that of a craftsman of the Netherlands, or Lower Germany, in the last quarter of the xv century.

Then there is a little woodcut of *Christ on the Cross* (S. 444, Paris, Lemoisne, pl. xcvii.) inscribed *Actum Gandavi*, i.e. done at Ghent, and there are several small cuts in the British Museum and in various Dutch collections related in style to the Netherlandish illustration of the last decade of the xv century, and possibly themselves unidentified book-illustrations,[3] but they do not merit more than a passing reference.

Bibliography

Holtrop, J. W. Monuments typographiques des Pays-Bas au xvme siècle. Collection de fac-simile. The Hague 1868.

Campbell, M. F. A. G. Annales de la typographie néerlandaise au xvme siècle. The Hague 1874.

Conway, William Martin (Lord Conway of Allington). Woodcutters of the Netherlands. Cambridge 1884.

[1] See p. 157.

[2] A somewhat different treatment of the same theme is seen in S. 839 and its variants (see p. 322).

[3] See M. D. Henkel, *Holzschnitte in holländischen Sammlungen*, Einbl. 49, Strassburg 1918.

Fig. 347. The Good Shepherd. S. 838.

BRADSHAW, Henry. List of the Founts of Type and Woodcut Devices used by Printers of Holland in the xv century. Collected Papers, 1889, p. 258.

SCHRETLEN, M. J. Dutch Woodcuts, 1480–1500. *Print Collector's Quarterly*, viii., 1921, 329.

SCHRETLEN, M. J. Dutch and Flemish Woodcuts of the xv Century (with a foreword by Max J. Friedländer). London 1925.

SCHRETLEN, M. J. Het Vroege Werk van Jacob Cornelisz. Oudheidkundig Jaarboek. Utrecht v. 143 (November 1925).

DELEN, A. J. J. Antwerpsche Drukkersmerken. *Gulden Passer*. 1923.

DELEN, A. J. J. Histoire de la gravure dans les anciens Pays-Bas, Première Partie. Des origines à 1500. Paris and Brussels 1924.

JUCHHOFF, Rudolf. Drucker- und Verlegerzeichen des xv Jahrhunderts in den Niederlanden, England, Spanien, Böhmen, Mähren und Polen. Munich 1927.

NŸHOFF, Wouter. Nederlandsche Houtsneden, 1500–1550. Reprodukties van oude Nord-en Zuid-Nederlandsche houtsneden op losse bladen. The Hague 1931–35.

CHAPTER VIII

BOOK-ILLUSTRATION AND CONTEMPORARY SINGLE CUTS IN FRANCE AND FRENCH SWITZERLAND

THE story of book-illustration in France in the xv century offers peculiarly difficult problems. The various editions of numerous early works are often most confusing, a confusion which is rendered more obscure by the extreme rarity of so many. Without a first-hand survey of provincial libraries in France many problems must be left unsolved. Moreover, among French publishers and printers the practice of lending blocks was even commoner than elsewhere, and in the *Horae*, which form so important and characteristic a part of French illustrated books, the slight variations between different issues introduce many ambiguities.

Happily, the study has been very considerably clarified by the researches of the late M. Claudin contained in his monumental history of early French books, and on this basis I can at least hope to be a little more definite in my references than would otherwise have been possible.

The beginnings of book-printing and book-illustration were everywhere nearly related to the crafts of the scribe and miniaturist, but perhaps nowhere is this relation so clearly seen as in France. Several of the early printed books, such as *Les Croniques de France*, printed by Pasquier Bonhomme, 1476 (Cl. i. 172, Paris, Bibl. de l'Arsenal), and the *Valerius Maximus* in French, of about 1476 (Cl. i. 199),[1] have spaces left blank for the miniature painting, and many of the vellum copies of the finest books with woodcuts have the woodcuts almost completely covered by the opaque colours of the illuminator.[2] In certain cases we know that publishers and printers had

---

[1] *Le Livre de Valerius Maximus translaté de latin en françois par Simon de Hesdin*, n.p., n.d., n.pr. (Paris, certainly not later than 1477). There are two copies in the Bibliothèque Nationale and one in the Bibliothèque St. Geneviève (from the Moreau Collection), with miniatures; another was described in the Fairfax Murray Catalogue, H. W. Davies, 1910, No. 557. There is no copy in the British Museum.

[2] A good example in the British Museum is the *Croniques de France*, printed by J. Maurand for Vérard, 1493 (C. 22. f. 1-3). No doubt several of the illuminated vellum copies of Vérard's books in the British Museum were copies purchased by Henry VII., though the only one about which I find definite evidence is the *Grant Boèce de Consolation*, 1494 (Macf. 37), where the name of Henry VII. has been substituted for Charles VIII. in the second line of the Prologue. An uncoloured paper copy of the *Ortus Sanitatis* (Macf. 140) appears to be the copy mentioned in the Privy

been, and possibly continued to be, illuminators, e.g. the printer Pierre Le Rouge, and the publisher Antoine Vérard, and the illuminators may also have turned their hands, with the change of the times, to the designing of woodcuts.

It is natural therefore that the woodcut subjects as well as the decorative portions of various early printed books should show a close relation to miniatures, or even a direct dependence on known illuminations. This is especially true of such books as the *Cité de Dieu* of St. Augustine, printed by Pierre Gérard and Jean Dupré (Abbeville 1486), and the *Mer des Hystoires* printed by Pierre Le Rouge (Paris 1488–89). Moreover, the 'bastard' type (a cross between pure Gothic and Roman, a Gothic with its flamboyance reduced) contributed in its freer form to give the appearance of manuscript. The borders of the early *Horae* of Jean Dupré and Antoine Vérard also show fairly direct translations into wood of the illuminator's style.

Up to about 1495 this border decoration of Books of Hours was in the indigenous French tradition, but thereafter appears a gradual infiltration of classical elements in design which culminated in *Horae* printed by Geoffroy Tory. These Books of Hours form the most characteristic feature, and the finest flower of French woodcut illustration, and we shall treat them separately at the end of this chapter.

Antoine Vérard of Paris was by far the most important publisher of illustrated books in France in the xv century, though he was rivalled by Simon Vostre in the issue of liturgical books. Occasionally a colophon claims Vérard as printer (*impressum per*), but this is less likely to have been the literal truth than a publisher's licence of language in cases where he did not choose to cite the name of the printer he commissioned. Vérard undoubtedly possessed a large supply of blocks, for he was primarily interested in illustration, while in other cases it was no doubt the printers themselves who possessed their own material, type and block, and were their own publishers.

Printers from Paris occasionally helped out provincial publications with their craftsmen and material, e.g. Jean Dupré at Abbeville and

---

Purse expenses of Henry VII., 1502, 'to Anthony Vérard for two bokes called the gardyn of helth, £6'.

There are various examples of Vérard's illuminated vellum copies, done for royal presentation, in the Bibliothèque Nationale, Paris (see Cl. ii. 466). Paul Durrieu, in his *Jacques de Besançon* (Paris 1892), argued against the probability of Vérard illuminating his own printed books, and attributed most of this work in Vérard's books between 1492 and 1498 to Jacques de Besançon. But M. Durrieu's attribution of this and other works of illumination to Jacques de Besançon (including many works now ascribed to Maître François, 'Egregius Pictor Franciscus') is quite uncertain, and for the most part abandoned by the author himself since the publication of his book.

Rouen,[1] and were frequently called on to print provincial Missals.[2] An example of the loan and return of blocks from Paris has been noted by Claudin in the illustrations to the *Légende Dorée* first printed by Jean Dupré in Paris, May 1496, later by Jean de Vingle at Lyon, 1497, thereafter returning to Paris and used by N. de la Barre, 1499, but I have been unable to check his statements.[3] One instance has also been noted of a French block used at Cologne, the *Author in a Chamber*, which first appeared in Couteau and Menard's edition of the *Danse Macabre des Hommes*, Paris 1492 (Cl. ii. 176). It occurs, cut about $\frac{1}{8}$-inch along the foot, as a representation of the commentator Albertus Magnus in Aristotle, *De Anima cum comentario Alberti Magni*, printed by Quentell, at Cologne, 1499 (S. 3349, H. 1711, Schramm 493, e.g. at Berlin).[4]

It is natural that the most refined and characteristic examples of French woodcut illustration should have been produced in Paris, which was already the centre of French culture.

LYON

Lyon was equally important as a commercial centre and as a house of call on the main roads of communication between France, Switzerland and Italy, on the one hand, and Germany, France and Spain, on the other, and it is not surprising on that account that woodcut illustration should have been introduced at Lyon earlier than at Paris, and that German craftsmen should have taken a considerable part in its development.

We shall therefore begin our survey of French illustrated books at Lyon,[5] reserving the purer French style shown in Paris books for the latter part of the chapter. For the most part Lyon illustration is cruder in design and cutting than contemporary Paris work, but we shall find occasional exceptions, e.g. in the precise woodcut of the monogrammist ID, in the work of the gifted designer of Trechsel's *Terence*, and in certain Italianate cuts such as appeared in some of Sacon's books, and in Dupré's *Éternelle Consolacion* (Cl. iii. 488, Paris).

[1] See pp. 622-625. [2] See p. 631.

[3] See Cl. ii. 290-92, iv. 230. The edition referred to as printed by Jean Dupré may be that published by Vérard, 20th May 1496 (Paris). I cannot refer to the locality of the other editions. Cf. Index of Subjects (under *blocks, transfer of*).

[4] Cf. pp. 361, 362, also for comment on supposed kinship between the style of woodcut work in France and Cologne.

[5] Natalis Rondot, *Les Graveurs sur bois et les imprimeurs à Lyon au XV siècle*. Lyon, Paris 1896; Rondot, *La Gravure sur bois à Lyon au XV siècle*. Bibliographica iii. (1897) 46; Rondot, *Graveurs sur bois à Lyon au XVI siècle*. Paris 1897.

The first of the Lyon books, the *Mirouer de la Redemption* printed by MARTIN HUSS, 26th August 1478 (Cl. iii. 158), contains illustrations re-printed from the original German blocks of Richel's Basle edition of 1476.[1] The book must have been very popular, for it was re-issued by Martin Huss

Fig. 348. From *L'Abusé en Court*, Lyon, about 1480.

in 1479 and 1482, and several times later by Matthias Huss.

Some of the earliest Lyon illustrations were issued about 1480 by the anonymous printer generally known by the title of one of his books, *L'Abusé en Court* (Cl. iv. 365, B.M., C. 6. b. 9), a satirical allegory on Court life, which contains eleven woodcuts (see fig. 348).[2] Another of his books is Pierre Michault, *Doctrinal du temps passé* (Cl. iv. 375, Paris), a satire on contemporary moral instruction, in which Virtue conducts the author round various lecture-halls, illustrated in the cuts. The work was written by Pierre Michault in 1466, and dedicated to Philip the Good, Duke of Burgundy. Of curious interest in relation to the antiquity of woodcut in the region of Burgundy, is the description of the prints hanging on the walls as *aucunes histoires entaillés et gravées*.

In style these cuts show close kinship to the illustrations in the Bruges *Ovide Moralisé*, printed by Colard Mansion, 1484,[3] and it is possible they are by the same designer.

From the same press, about the same date, and with woodcuts possibly by the same hand is the *Quatre Filz Aymon*, one of the numerous romances printed at Lyon (Cl. iv. 392-93, B.M., IB. 42244; see fig. 349).[4] The

---

[1] *Spiegel menschlicher Behältnis*, see p. 325. The Lyon issue contained some 256 illustrations, about twenty-one less than the Basle edition.

[2] Facsimile reproduction of the cuts and types of *L'Abusé en Court* and the *Doctrinal*, edited by Cl. Dalbanne and E. Droz, Lyon (Association Guillaume Le Roy) 1926. Another early edition of *L'Abusé en Court* was printed by Peter Schenck at Lyon, 1485 (C. iii. 383, and iv. 360, Pellechet 24, Paris).   [3] See pp. 591, 592.

[4] Other illustrated editions of this romance were printed by Le Roy about 1484–88 (Cl. iii. 88,

most attractive part of the woodcut decoration consists of the numerous initial letters in outline, with branch and scroll patterns embellished with animals or grotesque heads (see fig. 350).

Perhaps even earlier than either of the books just mentioned is the woodcut of the *Virgin standing with the Child before a curtain* (fig. 351), which appeared as frontispiece to *L'Histoire du Chevalier Oben* (Owain), printed without date by GUILLAUME LE ROY (Cl. iii. 46). Even if the book is no earlier than about 1480, the block probably goes back somewhat earlier, as it appears already in a somewhat worn condition. Here we have a thoroughly French design, cut with a considerably thinner line than the Lyon blocks of German type, and it is one of the most attractive of the Lyon illustrations.

Fig. 349. From *Le Quatre Filz Aymon*, Lyon, about 1480.

Guillaume Le Roy was the earliest of the Lyon printers, and for the first decade of his work after 1473 his books were financed by a rich merchant, Barthélemy Buyer, whose name appeared in company with Le Roy's. Virgil's *Énéide*, 1483 (the year of Buyer's death), was the first in which Le Roy's name stood alone. It contains crude and angular cuts with some parallel shading, rather in the manner of Ulm and Augsburg illustrations.

Similarly Teutonic, and probably by the same designer and cutter as the *Quatre Filz Aymon*, are the woodcuts (two full-page and numerous half-page oblongs) in the romance of *Fierabras*, printed by Le Roy about 1485 (Cl. iii. 72; fig. 352).

The cuts in *L'istoyre du chevalier Pierre de Provence et de la belle Maguelone*, printed by Le Roy about 1485 (Cl. iii. 84), are less interesting than the frontispiece to *Fierabras* which we reproduce, but somewhat more

probably by the same designer as the *Pierre de Provence*, Cl. iii. 84, see above), and by Jean de Vingle, 1493 (Pierpont Morgan 611). The cuts in the latter are probably by the designer of Trechsel's *Terence* of 1493 (see p. 609).

Fig. 350. Initial O, from *Le Quatre Filz Aymon*, Lyon, about 1480.

advanced in drawing or more closely shaded. *Le Livre des faisz de Bertrand du Guesclin*, Le Roy, about 1487 (B.M., IB. 41544), has an attractive frontispiece representing the knight, and numerous half-page oblong cuts, some in the crude style of the *Aymon* and *Fierabras*, and others more finely drawn and cut. Probably between the latter two romances was printed Pierre Michault, *Danse des Aveugles*, which is attributed to Le Roy, about 1485 (Cl. iii. 100, Paris). The cuts were reprinted by Michel Topié and Jacobus of Herrnberg, about 1492. They probably derive from the earlier cuts illustrating the same work printed by Louis Cruse at Geneva, about 1480. The *Danse des Aveugles* printed by Le Petit Laurens, Paris, about 1495 (Fairfax Murray, Davies 277), is illustrated with cuts taken for the most part from Syber's edition of the *Roman de la Rose*, Lyon, about 1485 (Bourdillon, Ed. B).[1]

Prestre Jehan, printed by Le Roy, about 1490 (Cl. iii. 106, Paris), is of interest for the figured initial P of its title.

The printers, NICOLAUS PHILIPPI (Müller) from Bensheim and MARCUS REINHARD from Strassburg, used for the most part blocks of German character, so that they no doubt brought German craftsmen in their employ. The illustrations in their Aesop (*Fables d'Ésope*) of 26th August 1480 (Cl. iii. 120, Tours)[2] were based on the original Ulm cuts, or on one of the numerous German editions (e.g. Knoblochtzer, Strassburg, about 1480), if indeed they are not actually one of the versions printed in Germany, not yet identified. They were used later in an edition printed by Matthias Huss and J. Schabeler, 1484 (Paris). The cuts of another Lyon *Aesop*, printed by Topié and Herrnberg, about 1490, are also derived from the same source, but are much poorer in quality.

Another book of Philippi and Reinhard, Rodericus Zamorensis, *Mirouer de la Vie Humaine*, 1482 (Cl. iii. 132: Pierpont Morgan 598), contains cuts printed from the original Augsburg blocks of Günther Zainer's *Spiegel menschlichen Lebens* (about 1475–76), interspersed with certain copies from the same source, and the same series was used later still by Pablo Hurus[3] at Saragossa (1491).

[1] See below, p. 606.

[2] For reproduction and notes on this and other Lyon editions of *Aesop* see Cl. Dalbanne, E. Droz and J. Bastin, Lyon (Association Guillaume Le Roy) 1926.

[3] See p. 741. Claudin surmised that Pablo and Juan Hurus (Huss) of Constance, who printed at Saragossa, may have been of the same family as the Huss at Lyon.

Philippi and Reinhard appear to have issued the earliest Lyon edition of the Golden Legend (*Legenda Aurea*, about 1480, Cl. iii. 124-30, Fairfax Murray, Davies 589)[1] with crude cuts of German character. Other Lyon editions were printed by Matthias Huss and Petrus of Hungary, 1483 (*Légende Dorée en François*, Cl. iii. 255, 331, Lyon), with small upright column cuts, about $3\frac{1}{4} \times 2\frac{3}{8}$ inches, and by Matthias Huss alone, 1486 (*Legenda Aurea*, Cl. iii. 275, Paris, Fairfax Murray, Davies 588), with similar blocks but largely different from those in the French edition of 1483, about $3\frac{1}{8} \times 2\frac{5}{8}$ inches.

About 1482 Marcus Reinhard disappeared from Lyon, and probably returned to Strassburg to work with his kinsman, Johann Grüninger (Reinhard), and was printing independently at Kirchheim, 1490-91.[2]

Fig. 351. The Virgin and Child, from *L'Histoire du Chevalier Oben*, Lyon, about 1480.

[1] For notes on these Lyon editions of the Golden Legend see Cl. Dalbanne, *Remarques sur l'illustration de quelques légendes dorées imprimées à Lyon au XVe siècle* (Documents Palaeographiques, Monographiques, Typographiques, Lyon, Bibl. de la Ville, 1923, etc., viie fascicule, 1928); Cl. Dalbanne, *La Légende Dorée. Mathieu Husz et Pierre Hongre*, 1483. Lyon (Association Guillaume Le Roy) [1924].

[2] See p. 340, and Robert Proctor's article on Reinhard and Grüninger.

After Reinhard's departure Philippi printed an edition of Guillermus, *Postilla super Epistolas et Evangelia*, with numerous small cuts, about 1483–84 (Cl. iii. 141; locality of copy unknown to me).

Fig. 352. From *Fierabras*, Lyon, about 1485.

Martin Huss, whom we have already mentioned as the printer of the first book-illustration at Lyon, issued an edition of Jacobus Palladinus de Theramo, *Le Procès de Belial à l'encontre de Jhesus*, 1482 (Cl. iii. 173), with numerous small oblong cuts and a larger frontispiece, in a crude German style. After this year his press was carried on by MATTHIAS HUSS, from Bottwar in Würtemberg, who worked well into the XVI century. His was the first French illustrated edition of Bartholomaeus Anglicus, *Le Propriétaire des Choses*, 1482 (Cl. iii. 245), and it is one of his most interesting books, with its full-page cuts at the head of each section (see fig. 353), with its thin lines, angular design, and open parallel shading, characteristic of so much Lyon woodcut. It was reprinted by Huss in 1485, and most of the same blocks, with some replacements and new decorative work and border and initials, appeared in his edition of 15th March 1491/92 (Cl. iii. 291). The large initial *L with St. George and the Dragon* which appeared in the title was first used at Lyon by Dupré in his edition of the *Mer des Hystoires*, 1491,[1] and again by Matthias Huss in his *Grant Danse Macabre*, 1499/1500. The designs first used by Matthias Huss,

[1] See p. 612 and fig. 364.

adapted by a more powerful cutter, appeared in Jean Syber's edition of the *Propriétaire des Choses*, about 1485–86 (Cl. iii. 200; fig. 354). According to Claudin the new blocks were made for an edition printed by Le Roy, 26th January 1485/86,[1] and lent to Syber after that date (Cl. iii. 63, 202, Lyon).

Fig. 353. The Ages of Man, from Bartholomacus Anglicus,
Propriétaire des Choses, Lyon 1482.

A few cuts occur in the Boccaccio, *Livre de la Ruyne des Nobles Hommes et Femmes*, printed by MATTHIAS HUSS and JEAN SCHABELER, 1483 (Cl. iii. 256), and one to each of the books of *Le Livre de Valerius Maximus translaté en François*, Huss, 1485 (Cl. iii. 269), but of much greater interest is Huss's edition of *La Grant Danse Macabre*, 18th February 1499/1500 (Cl. iii. 318). The subject of the *Danse Macabre* will be treated at more length in the description of the Paris edition of Guy Marchant.[2] The present edition is partly based on Marchant's cuts and partly on those of Couteau and Menard's edition (1492). Its chief original interest lies in the representation of *Death and the Printers*, which is not known in the other edition (fig. 355).

Most of the subjects of the *Danse des Hommes*, and the two cuts representing *Les Trois Morts et les Trois Vifs*, are copied fairly closely from Couteau and Menard (who apparently continued no further in the work),[3] while the *Danse des Femmes*, *Death on a Horse*, the *Trumpeter of Death*, and the *Débat du corps et de l'âme*, are based on Marchant. Other illustrations,

[1] I cannot refer to locality of this edition.   [2] See p. 644.
[3] See p. 647.

i.e. *La Complainte de l'âme damnée*, *L'Exhortation de bien vivre et de bien mourir*, and *La Vie du mauvais antechrist*, are independent designs.

At the head of the section of 'Les Quinze signes' appears a late state of the woodcut by ID representing *Robertus de Licio preaching before Pope and Cardinals* with the artist's initials removed.[1]

The earliest illustrated edition of the *Roman de la Rose*[2] appears to be

Fig. 354. The Birds, from Bartholomaeus Anglicus, *Propriétaire des Choses*, Lyon, about 1485–86.

that printed by GASPARD ORTUIN and PETER SCHENCK, at Lyon, about 1480 (Bourdillon A). It contains some eighty-six cuts, the first a double subject the width of the page (fig. 356), another half-page block, the *Building of the Tower*, the rest small column cuts. Another Lyon edition with cuts derived from this edition, somewhat larger, and more expressive in drawing, was printed by JEAN SYBER about 1485 (Pierpont Morgan 601), and its blocks were reprinted by Guillaume Le Roy, Lyon, about

[1] See p. 615.
[2] See F. W. Bourdillon, *The Early Editions of the 'Roman de la Rose'*, Bibliographical Society's Monographs, xiv., London 1906.

1487 (Pierpont Morgan 606), and in Paris by Jean Dupré, about 1494 (Cl. i. 280), by Le Petit Laurens for Jean Petit and Vérard, about 1497, and by N. Des Prez for Jean Petit, and other publishers, between about 1498 and 1505, a few blocks being lost in the progress (Bourdillon B, C, D, F, G).

Another Paris edition of the *Roman de la Rose*, published by Vérard,

Fig. 355. Death and the Printers, from *La Grant Danse Macabre*, Lyon 1499/1500.

probably between 1494 and 1498 (Bourdillon E, Cl. ii. 250; printed by Etienne Jehannot?), contains an incomplete series of copies near the style of Vérard's chief designer, carelessly cut except for the subjects on the first page. It also includes numerous cuts from Petrus de Crescentiis, *Prouffitz Champestres*, and the *Cent Nouvelles Nouvelles*,[1] 1486, and from other earlier books published by Vérard.

A later edition issued by Vérard, in smaller size, about 1505 (Bourdillon H), contains another series of woodcuts, smaller than the rest, more uniform in character than his earlier edition, and better cut. The cuts for

[1] See p. 655.

this edition were also issued in Jean Molinet's prose version, *le Roman de la Rose moralisé*, also issued by Vérard (Bourdillon X). Bourdillon dates this about 1500, and regards it as the model followed by Balsarin, Macfarlane (186) and others date it about 1511.[1] In this edition the cuts were

Fig. 356. From the *Roman de la Rose*, Lyon, about 1480.

framed in a border of gothic arcading, which Vérard used in several of his later books.

Molinet's prose version was also issued at Lyon by Balsarin in 1503, with still another series of woodcuts, very wooden in character (Bourdillon Y).

Le Roman du Roy Ponthus et de la belle Sidoyne (Cl. iii. 391-94, Oxford, Proctor 8535) is another undated romance printed by Gaspard Ortuin, with blocks of more advanced design and cutting than his *Roman de la Rose*, and probably issued about 1484. There is also an edition with the same cuts, probably earlier, printed by Guillaume Le Roy in a type similar to that of his *Énéide* of 1483 (Cl. iii. 394-95, Chantilly).[2]

JOHANN NEUMEISTER, who has already been mentioned for his work at Mainz,[3] was printing at Albi about 1480–83, and from 1483 to 1498 at Lyon. His most distinguished work at Lyon is contained in two missals, the *Lyon Missal* of 1487 (Cl. iii. 360, Paris, Lyon), and the *Uzès Missal*,

[1] See p. 654.

[2] See reproduction of the 41 cuts used in the editions of G. Le Roy and Gaspard Ortuin, edited by Cl. Dalbanne and E. Droz, Lyon (Association Guillaume Le Roy) 1926.

[3] See p. 194.

Fig. 357. Initial T from the *Lyon Missal*,
Lyon 1500/1501.

which he printed in collaboration with Michel Topié in 1495 (Cl. iii. 369). Apart from the *Canon* cuts, the latter contains a fine series of pictorial initials on black ground.

The same initials were used later by Petrus of Hungary in his *Lyon Missal* of 16th April 1500/1501 (Cl. iii. 343-51, Lyon), in addition to a larger and still more interesting *Initial T with Abraham's sacrifice* (fig. 357).

The high-water mark of book-illustration at Lyon in the xv century is reached in the *Terence Comoediae*, printed by JOHANN TRECHSEL, 1493. Trechsel, who came to Lyon from Mainz about 1487, has already been mentioned for some colophon verses touching on early printing.[1] He had married the widow of Nicolaus Philippi, who died in 1488, and so came into possession of that printer's stock.

It is more than probable that the designer of the *Terence* is German or Netherlandish in origin, working in a style that recalls Erhard Reuwich's illustrations to the original Mainz *Breydenbach* of 1486.

Kristeller and Friedländer have both compared the *Terence* cuts with the Lübeck *Dodes Dantz* (1489) and *Bible* of 1494,[2] and Friedländer has suggested identity of authorship. I admit the kinship, but there is a peculiar manner of curved lines in the *Lübeck Bible* which is quite distinct. Whatever his origin, the designer's hand may perhaps be traced in various stages of progress in other Lyon books in the last decade of the century, but the series of woodcuts to Trechsel's *Terence* is his masterpiece. The book opens with a fine full-page frontispiece representing the *Theatre* (fig. 358), and the plays are illustrated with a variety of smaller oblong cuts, in which the actors are shown on the stage, disposed with a fine sense of design, and drawn with a vivid and humorous touch (see fig. 359).

Among Lyon woodcuts allied in style to Trechsel's *Terence* I would mention in the first place the illustrations to Raoul Le Fèvre, *Recueil des Hystoires de Troye*, printed by MICHEL TOPIÉ and JACOBUS OF HERRNBERG, 1490 (Cl. iv. 11-23, Paris), reprinted by JACQUES MAILLET in 1494. The

[1] See p. 209.   [2] See pp. 362-367.

Fig. 358. The Theatre, from Terence, *Comoediae*, Lyon 1493.

illustrations vary considerably in quality, possibly owing to the varying skill of the cutters, but in the best examples the peculiar virtue of the Terence designer is evident. The title contains a delightful initial *L with monkeys* (fig. 360).[1]

Topié and Herrnberg were the printers of the first French edition of Breydenbach[2] in Nicole Le Huen's version *Des Sainctes Peregrinations de*

Fig. 359. From Terence, *Comoediae*, Lyon 1493.

Jherusalem, 1488 (Cl. iv. 1), which contained copies of the Mainz blocks, nine woodcuts after the smaller subjects, the folding views being engraved on copper plates. It is conceivable that the Terence designer assimilated something of the Mainz master's character through this work, in which he might have taken part. The second French edition of Breydenbach, in the more faithful translation of Jean de Hersin, *Le saint voyage et pélerinage de Hierusalem*, was issued in February 1489/90 without name of printer (Cl. iii. 397, Proctor 8618), and has been attributed variously to Ortuin (Claudin), Maillet (Proctor) and Le Roy (Pellechet). The illustrations in this edition were printed from the original Mainz blocks.

Two further books in which the style of the Terence designer is clearly seen are Martial d'Auvergne, *Les Vigilles de la Mort du Roy Charles VII.*, n.d.

---

[1] Reprinted in Maillet's edition of Jean Boutillier, *La Somme rural(e)*, 1494 (Cl. iv. 109).

[2] See pp. 352-356.

Fig. 360. Initial L, from *Recueil des Hystoires de Troye*, Lyon 1490.

(Cl. iv. 155, École des Beaux-Arts, Paris, from J. Masson), and the Cicero, *Offices*, 1493 (H. 5236, Paris) and 1496 (Paris, Mazarin), printed by CLAUDE DAYNE (Cl. iv. 150). The earlier edition of the Cicero is without printer's name, but it has the same initials and woodcut as the later (*Cicero presenting his book to his son Marcus*), so that it is probably by the same printer.

Another book printed by Dayne, *Le Livre de Matheolus qui monstre les biens qui vieignent pour soy marier*, 1492,[1] contains on its title a characteristic *Initial L with fool and girl kissing* (fig. 361) which might also be by the Terence designer. It recurs on the title of Guy de Roye, *Doctrinal de Sapience*, printed by Dayne in 1497/98 and 1498/99 (Cl. iv. 162, Paris).

Similar again in style is the large *Initial C with a sick woman in bed* on the first page of Boethius, *De Consolatione Philosophiae* (*Commentum Duplex in Boethium*), printed by JEAN DE VINGLE, 1498 (HC. 3417). Vingle's excellent printer's mark also occurs in the same book (Meyer 69; fig. 362). And the same printer's editions of *Les Quatre Filz Aymon*, 1493, 1495, 1497 and 1499 (Cl. iv. 222; for first edition see Pierpont Morgan 611), also contains a series of woodcuts probably by the Terence designer.

Different in style from the *Terence* designs, but equally vivid in characterisation is the illustration of a *Boys' School* (fig. 363) in the *Cathon en François* printed without date by PIERRE BOUTEILLER, Lyon (Cl. iii. 433, Toulouse).

For richness of decoration one of the most notable of Lyon books is the *Mer des Hystoires* printed in 1491 by JEAN DUPRÉ,[2] who must not be confused with the Paris printer of the same name. Most of the subject cuts are copied from the Paris edition printed by Pierre Le Rouge, 1488–89, and are

[1] The wording of the colophon in the B.M. copy confirms this date. Claudin (iv. 164) places it about 1498.

[2] E.g. Paris (B.N.). This edition is wanting in the British Museum.

Fig. 361. Initial L, from *Le Livre de Matheolus*, Lyon 1492.

considerably inferior to the originals; the borders and other decorative pieces are derived in style from the same source, but show more independence and offer much of beauty and interest. Thoroughly independent are the borders to the little series in the manner of a *Book of Hours* in volume ii.; in alternate spaces of light and dark ground they are akin in character to certain Flemish Books of Devotion, printed by Gerard Leeuw and Adriaen van Liesvelt at Antwerp, 1491 and 1495.[1] I have not found them used outside the folio *Mer des Hystoires*. The large *Initial L with St. George and the Dragon* of the title-page (a variant of Le Rouge's L) appeared here for the first time (fig. 364), being used later by Matthias Huss in the *Propriétaire des Choses*, 1491/92, and *La Grant Danse Macabre*, 1499/1500.[2] Most of Dupré's blocks for the *Mer des Hystoires* were reprinted at Lyon by CLAUDE DAVOST in an edition of 1506, and many appeared later in various books issued in Paris by Enguilbert de Marnef and F. Regnault.[3] Davost's edition contains some curious initial letters, with flower and figure on black ground, which had appeared earlier in his issue of *Le Propriétaire des Choses*, 1500 (Cl. iv. 339, Paris, Bibl. du Musée d'Histoire Naturelle).

I would also mention the initial letters used by the printer JEAN CLEIN, righly designed leaf and floral design on black ground (Cl. iv. 281).

A woodcut of the *Virgin and Child in Glory*, and the *Stigmatisation of St. Francis*, which appeared on the verso of the title-page of *L'Éternelle Consolacion* (*De Imitatione Christi*) printed without date by Dupré (Cl. iii. 488, Paris), stands apart from most Lyon book-illustration and is much more nearly related to Venetian work. Another example in a similar

---

[1] See pp. 581, 582.   [2] See p. 605.

[3] The edition of the *Mer des Hystoires* published by E. de Marnef and F. Regnault about 1517 (B.M., 582. l. 7) contains cuts from the editions of both Le Rouge and Dupré.

Fig. 362. Printer's mark of Jean de Vingle, Lyon.

style, possibly by a designer from North Italy, is the small *Crucifixion* in the *Missale Romanum*, printed at Lyon by JACQUES SACON, 26th April 1500 (Cl. iv. 303, École des Beaux-Arts, Paris, from J. Masson Collection). Moreover, one of the designs used by Sacon as his printer's mark, an allegorical figure of Virtue (Silvestre 548), is copied from a woodcut in Bernardino Corio, *Patria Historia*, Milan 1503.[1]

Sacon also printed an edition of Sebastian Brant's *Stultifera Navis*[2] under the title *Salutifera Navis*, and dated 1488 (evidently in error for 1498), a translation into Latin verse by Jacques Locher from the original German *Narrenschiff*. Except for the title-cut, the blocks had appeared at Paris in 1497 in an edition printed by J. Lambert (?) for J. Philippe (Manstener) and G. de Marnef, a translation of Brant into French verse by Pierre Rivière, entitled *La Nef des Folz du monde*. Another Lyon edition of the same work, a French version by Jean Drouyn, *La Grant Nef des Folz*, was printed by BALSARIN at Lyon in 1498 and 1499. Cuts in these French editions are all derived directly or indirectly from the original Basle editions.

From other books printed by Sacon, the most interesting woodcut is perhaps that of *Five Commentators of Virgil* on the title-page of Virgil, *Opera*, 1499 (Cl. iv. 301).

WOODCUTS BY THE MASTER ID
IN BOOKS PRINTED AT LYON, TOULOUSE AND IN SPAIN

The designer who uses the initials ID holds an unimportant but unique position in book-illustration at Lyon. His work appears in the following books printed at Lyon:

[1] See p. 514.   [2] See p. 331.

Robertus de Licio (Caracciolus), *Quadragesimale Aureum de Peccatis*, printed by Trechsel, 9th February 1488/89: a small cut of *Robertus de Licio preaching before Pope and Cardinals* (Cl. iii. 83).[1]

Les Mistères de la Sainte Messe, printed by G. Le Roy, n.d. (about 1490) (Cl. iii. 82; Claudin-Ricci, No. 202, Paris): a small *Annunciation*, copied from Schongauer, B. 3, Lehrs 1 f.

Ars Moriendi, Latin text, n.d., n.pr. (about 1490) (Cl. iii. 83, iv. 436):[2] twelve cuts, including the complete series of eleven subjects copied

Fig. 363. A Boys' School, from *Cathon en François*, Lyon, n.d.

from the block-book, and a woodcut title in large Gothic letters on black ground on the last page of the volume.

---

[1] It appeared in later state, with the monogram ID removed, at the beginning of the section on 'Les Quinze Signes' in *La Grant Danse Macabre*, printed at Lyon by Matthias Huss, 1499/1500 (see p. 606).

[2] There is another Lyon series of octavo copies after the *Ars Moriendi* block-book which occurs in several editions:

    (1) [*L'Art et Disposition de bien mourir*]. Pierre Bouteiller, n.d. [about 1485], Cl. iii. 443 (in Claudin's possession, from Rosenthal, Munich, who had placed it as a Grenoble book). The eleven block-book subjects. The title was lacking in the only copy known, and is inferred from (2).

    (2) *L'Art et Disposition de bien mourir*. Jean Syber (?). After 1485. Cl. iii. 445. Chantilly.

    (3) *Ars Moriendi*. Latin text. Jean Syber (?). About 1490? Cl. iii. 209. H. 1832. R. Proctor,

Apart from books printed at Lyon, another of ID's woodcuts, the *Stoning of St. Stephen*, appeared in the *Toulouse Missal* printed by Étienne Cléblat, at Toulouse, 1490 (Cl. iii. 83, Toulouse).[1] This cut is perhaps the most interesting of all his designs, showing the saint in the centre stoned by three men, a bishop kneeling on the right, and a tiny St. Paul (*Saulus*), like a child in size and character, seated to the left on cloak and sword, watching the performance (fig. 365).

Finally a large *Christ on the Cross between the Virgin and St. John* appeared in a Spanish book of 1517, but the block probably belonged like the rest to the end of the xv century.[2]

The woodcuts of ID are Netherlandish in style, clear in design, hard in cutting, with strong outline and great regularity of shading, parallel series of short lines being often used in the background. Kristeller thought that ID was the designer of the cuts in the Naples *Aesop* of 1485, and of various blocks in Spanish books, besides the signed *Christ on the Cross*, and he regarded ID as a Northern artist (possibly from the region of Alsace) who worked successively at Naples, in France and in Spain.[3] The border to *Tirant Lo Blanch*, Valencia 1490, is certainly comparable with that in the Naples *Aesop* of 1485, and the woodcut representing the *King in Council* in the *Usatges de Barcelona e Constitucións de Cataluña* (Barcelona 1495) is equally near to the Naples *Aesop* and to the cuts signed ID, but I do not feel prepared to unite their respective authors in a single personality without more definite evidence.

Returning from this digression, I propose to continue the survey of provincial towns, all the more cursory because woodcut published in the

The Library, 2nd Ser. III., October 1902, p. 339. B.M., Paris, Auxerre, Munich. Attributed by Claudin to Jean Syber, by Pellechet to J. Dupré of Lyon, in the British Museum to Engelhard Schultis, about 1492.

The B.M. copy contains 12 illustrations from 10 blocks, i.e. copies after the whole original series except the last subject, *Triumph in face of Death*. This is replaced by a repetition of the *Inspiration of the Angel against Avarice* (*quid faciam?*), and the same cut is also repeated as frontispiece.

(4) *Tractatus succinctus de arte et scientia perfecte vivendi beneque moriendi*. Pierre Mareschal, n.d. (about 1515).

[1] Tibulle Desbarreaux-Bernard, *Çatalogue de incunables de la Bibliothèque de Toulouse*, Toulouse 1878, No. 167, and reproduction, *Figures*, fol. 22. Cf. I. van Meckenem, Lehrs 383.

[2] See pp. 752 and 754 for this, and other cuts of similar style issued in Spain.

[3] Identification with Jean de Dale, maker of playing-cards at Lyon, has also been suggested (see p. 87, and N. Rondot, *Les Graveurs sur bois à Lyon au xve siècle*, p. 133), but his signed playing-cards give no support to the suggestion.

Fig. 364. Initial L, from the *Mer des Hystoires*, Lyon 1491.

more important of these, apart from Lyon, derived directly from the fountain-head of Paris.

GENEVA

Apart from varying political relations, Geneva[1] is naturally grouped in the present study with France, as Basle had been with Germany. The output of Genevese printers is small, but a few books of some interest may be noted.

In the first place five small woodcuts, attractive in design, but primitive in their outline style, illustrating Pierre Michault, *La Danse des Aveugles*, printed by LOUIS CRUSE about 1480 (Proctor 7809). Then a striking figure of *Fierabras*, as frontispiece to the romance of that name, issued in 1483 (Proctor 7811; fig. 366), a work which also contains numerous small oblong cuts, chiefly in outline, analogous in style to the work of the Lyon *Abusé en Court*,[2] and a full-page subject of the *Emperor and his Court*, used here as Louis Cruse's printer's mark. More strictly his printer's mark is the full-page *Heraldic cut with two negresses and his name Loys M. Cruse* (Meyer 17) which appears in Rolewinck, *Fasciculus Temporum*, issued in 1495 (Proctor 7817). The *Fierabras* also contains cuts of the various subjects usual in this work.

Another edition of the *Fasciculus Temporum*, issued without printer's name

[1] See Paul Heitz, *Genfer Buchdrucker- und Verlegerzeichen*, Strassburg 1908.
[2] See p. 600.

at Geneva, in 1495 (Proctor 7820), has an interesting full-page frontispiece of the *Author at a Desk*, as well as some good initials on black ground.

A few less important cuts appeared in books printed by JEAN BELLOT, e.g.

Fig. 365. The Master ID. The Stoning of St. Stephen, from the *Toulouse Missal*, Toulouse 1490.

in the small *Missale Lausannense* of 1500, where the little cut of the *Virgin of Lausanne* is of cruder quality than the rest, and points to earlier editions.

CHAMBÉRY

At Chambéry, ANTOINE NEYRET issued a few books of interest, the first being Maurice de Sully, *Exposition des Évangiles*, 1484, with two full-page woodcuts of effective design in open linear style, *Christ on the Cross, with the Signs of the Evangelists*, and the *Resurrection*, in addition to numerous small illustrations. Then a curiously calligraphic woodcut representing *Baldwin Count of Flanders*,[1] in which the rich trappings of the horse bear the printer's

---

[1] Reproduced in A. Blum, *Les Origines du livre à gravures en France*, 1928, pl. lxxvii. It is probably based on the frontispiece of the *Fierabras*, printed by Louis Cruse at Geneva, 1483 (see p. 617).

name, occurs in *Le Livre de Baudoin Comte de Flandres*, 1485. The book contains various other smaller oblong cuts, roughly executed.

A characteristic woodcut of *Master and Pupils* appeared in Jean Dupin, *Livre de la Bonne Vie appelé Mandevie*, 1485 (H. 6460), a morality in the form of a romance, shared by *l'Acteur 'Mandevie'* (representing the Life of Man) and the virtues, vices and other characters.

And finally, there is a series of crude but interesting cuts illustrating hunting, as well as a full-page allegory, in *Le Livre du Roi Modus et de la Reine Racio*, 1486 (H. 11447), a sort of 'Chasse Moralisée' after the pattern of the more famous morality on Chess by Jacobus de Cessolis.

Albi—Toulouse

Of towns in the South of France, Albi has already been mentioned for the second impression of the series of metal-cuts illus-

Fig. 366. Frontispiece to *Fierabras*, Geneva 1483.

trating Turrecremata, *Meditationes*, 1481, which JOHANN NEUMEISTER, settled here between 1480 and 1483, had brought with him from Mainz, where he had published the first edition in 1479.[1]

Toulouse has also been noted in relation to the work of the monogrammist ID.[2] Apart from the woodcut there described, I would merely refer to a rough cut of *Christ carrying the Cross, with a kneeling Monk* in the *Imitation de Jesus Christ*, printed by HEINRICH MAYER, 28th March 1488,

[1] See p. 194; and for his work at Lyon, p. 608.
[2] See p. 616.

Fig. 367. Doctor and Patient, from *El Libro de proprietatibus rerum en romance*, Toulouse 1494.

as it is the first French edition of that famous book (H. 9120, Claudin-Ricci 633, Paris).

Mayer also printed a certain number of books in Spanish for export into Spain, one of the most notable being Bartholomaeus Anglicus, *El Libro de proprietatibus rerum en romance*, 1494. The woodcuts are naïvely crude in design and cutting, but of some interest for the style which seems to indicate a Spanish craftsman. The woodcut of *Doctor and Patient*, at the head of Book VII., *De las enfermedades*, is the most entertaining (fig. 367).

POITIERS—BRÉHAN-LOUDÉAC—DIJON

Proceeding North to Poitiers, JEAN BOUYER and GUILLAUME BOUCHET may be noted for a delicately cut printer's mark of heraldic design (Meyer 169), and the same hand was certainly responsible for the attractive little woodcut of a *Preacher* in Guillaume Alexis, *Les Faintises du Monde*, issued by the same printers about 1494 (Claudin-Ricci 448-450, G.W. 1241, Vienna).

At Dijon, I would only mention two full-page cuts of the *Vierge de*

Miséricorde and of the *Members of the Cistercian Order* which occur in Joannes de Cirejo, *Privilegia ordinis Cisterciensis*, printed by PETRUS METLINGER, 1491.

Turning North-West, I would touch at Bréhan-Loudéac (a small place near Rohan, a little south of Loudéac, in Brittany), referring to an edition of Pierre Michault, *La Danse des Aveugles*, printed by ROBIN FOUCQUET and JEAN CRÈS, about 1485, which is only known in the Pierpont Morgan Library, New York (Pierpont Morgan 621, Claudin-Ricci 1926, No. 82). The cuts are crudely executed

Fig. 368. Annunciation, from Nicolaus de Lyra, *Les Postilles*, Troyes 1492.

in outline, and based on the Geneva edition of Louis Cruse (of about 1480), or the Lyon edition of about 1485.[1]

CHABLIS—TROYES

At Chablis and Troyes, Guillaume Le Rouge published a few books with woodcuts, between 1489 and 1493, before finally settling in Paris, where we shall meet another famous member of the family, Pierre Le Rouge.[2] Interesting cuts appeared in Maurice de Sully, *Les Expositions des Évangiles*, Chablis 1489 (Monceaux ii. 47, G. Le Rouge No. 2, Claudin-Ricci 92-99, Paris), and later, with additions, in Nicolaus de Lyra, *Les Postilles et Expositions des Épitres et Évangiles* (French version by Pierre Desrey), Troyes, 30th March 1492 (Monceaux ii. 57, G. Le Rouge No. 3, Claudin-Ricci 677-679).

A remarkable full-page cut of the *Crucifixion with the Three Crosses* (reprod. Claudin-Ricci 92), and numerous column cuts, appeared in both, and a few attractive woodcuts were added in *Les Postilles*. These included

[1] See pp. 617, and 602.
[2] See Henri Monceaux, *Les Le Rouge de Chablis*, Paris 1896.

blocks. Most attractive is the full-page frontispiece, with the *Author presenting his Book* (fig. 370), designed and cut in a freer manner than the rest in consonance with the contemporary scene. The heroes themselves are

designed in a more decorative convention, powerful, if somewhat grotesque, in form, and cut in firm lines. The only exception to their flamboyant design is the subject of *Bertrand du Guesclin* himself, a bullet head which is proved to have been based on an authentic portrait tradition (fig. 371).

The most important illustrated book printed at Rouen is the first volume of Walter Map, *Le Livre des vertueux faix de plusieurs nobles chevaliers specialement du chevalier Lancelot du Lac*, issued by Jean Le Bourgeois, 24th November 1488. It

Fig. 370. The Author presenting his book, from *Le Triomphe des Neuf Preux*, Abbeville 1487.

was printed in Dupré's type, and Dupré himself printed the second volume at Paris, and his date of 16th September 1488 was no doubt an indication of the greater experience and dispatch of his own establishment (Cl. i. 272). There are half-page cuts at the head of the First and Second Parts of the Rouen volume (the second, representing a *Combat with Long Swords*, having also appeared at Abbeville in *La Cité de Dieu*, 1486–87).[1]

[1] It appeared later in Vérard's *Lancelot du Lac*, 1494.

But by far the most important illustration is the large woodcut of *King Arthur and his Knights at the Round Table*, within a four-piece border, with which the book opens (fig. 372). The outline borders are entirely in the manner of Dupré's atelier, and the fact that one of the other cuts had been used in a book in which Dupré collaborated with Gérard at Abbeville, apart from the connection with Dupré in the prints of the second volume of the work, renders it certain that Jean Le Bourgeois obtained his blocks from the same source.

Another splendid production of Rouen printing (no doubt seconded by Dupré) is the *Sarum Missal*, printed by MARTIN

Fig. 371. Bertrand du Guesclin, from *Le Triomphe des Neuf Preux*, Abbeville 1487.

MORIN, 12th October 1492.[1] In addition to the full-page subjects regularly found in French Missals at the Canon of the Mass, *Christ on the Cross with the Virgin and St. John*, and *God the Father enthroned, with signs of the Evangelists*,[2] there is a beautiful four-piece border, with branch, bird, beast and flower motives, in the style of the Paris atelier of Jean Dupré. It occurs thrice, and at its first occurrence, at sig. a. 1, encloses a woodcut of the *Mass of St. Gregory* (about $5\frac{7}{8}$ inches square) which is near the work of Vérard's chief designer, and is freely modelled on the same subject in Dupré's *Verdun Missal* of 1481.[3] The original shows white stars on a black ground behind God the Father, while the

[1] See Ed. Frère, *De l'imprimerie et de la librairie à Rouen dans les XVe et XVIe siècles, et de Martin Morin*, Rouen 1843.

[2] This second subject is not found in German or Italian missals.

[3] See p. 628.

Morin version is in black line throughout. The border is not repeated in the British Museum copy of another edition of Morin's *Sarum Missal*, of about 1497 (IC. 43967), in which the full-page Canon cuts are also different (and within architectural framework), but it occurs in certain later editions printed at Rouen (e.g. one of 1513).[1] The edition of about 1497 bears on its title-page an interesting woodcut initial M with dragon, grotesque head, and Morin's name, and below a woodcut of *St. George and the Dragon* (about $6\frac{1}{2} \times 6$ inches),[2] with king and queen looking on from the city walls on the right, and at f. 126 a *Crucifixion of St. Andrew* ($5\frac{5}{8}$ inches square). Morin's edition of 1510 (Law Society's Library) has a smaller copy of the *St. George and the Dragon* ($4\frac{7}{8} \times 3\frac{1}{8}$ inches) below the title, and Canon cuts which appear to correspond with those in the 1492 edition, but other cuts as in the edition of about 1497.

Morin's printer's mark (Meyer 178) appears framed in four attractive border-pieces in the edition of about 1497.

PARIS

In my survey of Paris books I will first deal with the independent work of certain early printers (falling largely between 1481 and 1492), then with books published by Antoine Vérard from 1485 to the beginning of the XVI century (many being by the same printers after they came into his employ, chiefly after 1492), and thirdly with other printers in their independent work during the last decade of the fifteenth century.

The independent printers of the earlier group with whom I shall be concerned are Jean Dupré, Pierre Le Rouge, Jean Bonhomme, Antoine Caillaut and Louis Martineau, Pierre Levet, Guy Marchant, Gilles Couteau and Jean Menard.

I have already spoken of JEAN DUPRÉ for his collaboration with printers at Abbeville and Rouen. Apart from the fine quality of the woodcut work which proceeded from his workshops, he is notable as the printer of the first illustrated book published at Paris. His borders and decorative pieces, largely in outline, with designs of bird, beast, branch and flower, in the best tradition of medieval French illumination, are among the most beautiful

---

[1] Reproduced, J. Lieure, *La Gravure en France au XVIe siècle: La Gravure dans le livre et l'ornement*, Paris 1927, pl. ii.

[2] This occurs later on the reverse of the title of the *Art of good lyvynge and good deyng*, published by Vérard, Paris 1503 (see p. 662).

Fig. 372. King Arthur and his Knights at the Round Table, from Walter Map, *Le Livre des vertueux faix de plusieurs nobles chevaliers*, Rouen 1488.

productions of the time. This side of his work is seen at its best in the *Book of Hours*, which will be treated separately later in this chapter.

His earliest illustrated book is the *Paris Missal* of 22nd September 1481, which he printed in collaboration with DESIDERIUS HUYM (Cl. i. 209, H.C. 11339, Pr. 7920), containing the usual *Canon* cuts in French Missals, *God the Father enthroned, with the signs of the Evangelists*, and the *Christ on the Cross with the Virgin and St. John*, each full-page, designed with a certain stiff dignity and powerfully cut, slightly arched above, and with a cross outside the border-line below.[1]

In his *Verdun Missal* of 28th November 1481 (Cl. i. 218, Paris), added to his *Canon* cuts, is a large woodcut of the *Mass of St. Gregory* within four-piece borders.[2] And the same Missal also contains a variety of smaller upright subjects, averaging about $4\frac{1}{4} \times 3$ inches (the *Adoration of the Shepherds, Presentation in the Temple, La Cour Céleste, Les Trois Morts* being reproduced by Claudin). Throughout his career (1481–1504) Dupré was printing Missals, Breviaries and Synodical Statutes for many dioceses outside Paris, among the earliest being the *Chartres Missal* of 1482 (Cl. i. 217, Paris) and the *Limoges Missal* of 1483/84 (Cl. i. 220, Limoges). In the dedication of the latter he makes the interesting statement that the work had been achieved by the help of Venetian craftsmen whom he had brought to Paris (*per Venetos arte impressoria magnificos et valde expertos completum*), adding in the colophon that it was printed in the Venetian manner (*Venetica forma*).[3] Venice was at this period the chief centre for the printing of liturgical books, and Claudin refers to a *Nantes Missal* of 1482 having been printed at Venice,[4] and several later French Missals printed at Venice are described by Essling (e.g. 149, *Paris Missal*, 1487, by J. Hamman de Landoia and J. Emericus de Spira, and 144, *Clermont-Ferrand Missal*, 1492, by Joannes Antonius Birreta).

Angers, Arras, Besançon, Meaux, Reims, Troyes, are among the dioceses for which Dupré provided liturgical books. His *Sarum Missal* of 30th

---

[1] Claudin, *Documents sur la typographie et la gravure en France*, ed. S. de Ricci, 1926, No. 242. Four copies are known, Paris (Bibl. Nat., Bibl. St. Geneviève, and Seymour de Ricci) and Oxford.

[2] Leo S. Olschki, *Le Livre illustré au XVe siècle* (Florence 1926, No. 117, and fig. 181), reproduces the *Mass of St. Gregory* within the same borders as from the *Paris Missal* of 22nd September 1481, but M. Seymour de Ricci informs me that its type is not Dupré 1 and 2 (as in the 1481 ed.), and that it is probably an issue of about 1491.

[3] For other business transactions between Dupré and Venetian printers see p. 630, note 5.

[4] Described as printed by Bartholomaeus de Alexandria (de Blavis), Andrea d' Asola (Torresanus) and Maphaeus de Salodio (Paterbonis) (Cl. i. 220). It is not described by Essling.

Fig. 373. Initial T, from the *Sarum Missal*, Paris 1500 and 1504.

September 1500 (Cl. i. 263, Duff 331, STC. 16175) shows how far-reaching was his fame. There are copies in the Law Society's Library, at Christ's College, Cambridge, and in the Cathedral Library at Ely, but the last named is the only one complete with *Canon* cut. Of the *Sarum Missal* the British Museum has a later edition printed by Dupré's heirs in 1504 (STC. 16178), with a printed note on the title-page that it was sold by booksellers in St. Paul's Churchyard (*Venales apud bibliopolas in cimyterio sancti Pauli Londoñ. invenientur*).

Besides the *Canon* cut, and a small initial T[1] on dotted ground, with a *Christ on the Cross between the Virgin and St. John* (fig. 373), it contains the *Mass of St. Gregory*, to which we have already alluded, as in Dupré's *Verdun Missal* of 1481, a *Resurrection* (about $7\frac{1}{4} \times 6$ inches), of the same design as a smaller cut in *Les Postilles* of Nicolaus de Lyra, printed by Guillaume Le Rouge at Troyes, 1492,[2] and a smaller column cut of the *Descent of the Spirit*. The illustrations noted are from the same blocks as those in the edition of 1500.

Missals and Breviaries being made for use in churches are inevitably rare in private collections. Even those compiled according to the rite of different dioceses or monastic orders, which all gave way to the uniform Roman ritual after the Council of Trent (1563), mostly remained in their respective dioceses or convents, and are as rare outside as the liturgies which remained in use. Of liturgical books it is chiefly the small Books of Hours, made for private devotion, that have been available to collectors.

Dupré's edition of Laurent du Premier Fait's translation of Boccaccio, *Les Cas et Ruynes des nobles hommes et femmes*, 26th February 1483/84 (Cl. i. 222), appears to have been the earliest illustrated book in French printed at Paris (see fig. 374). Its nine woodcuts, beginning with the *Author writing, and the Expulsion from Paradise*, which are somewhat sketchily designed and cut, were borrowed by Richard Pynson for John Lydgate's English version, the *Fall of Princes*, which he printed at London in 1494.[3]

Not unlike in character is the frontispiece, the only woodcut in Vérard's edition of Boccaccio, *Les Cent Nouvelles*, 22nd November 1485, a French version of the *Decameron* by the same translator (Cl. i. 226, Paris), and typographical reasons also favour the inference that Dupré was commissioned by Vérard to print this edition. In its loose style of handling

[1] Originally in Pierre Le Rouge's *Toul Missal*, 1492.   [2] See p. 621.   [3] See p. 732.

(contrasting with the decided line of most of Vérard's later woodcuts) it is comparable with such woodcuts as the *Translator presenting his book to the King*, which appeared in the edition of Caesar, *Commentaires* (French version by R. Gaguin), 1485, attributed by Claudin (vol. i. p. 417, Paris, Bibl. Mazarine, and St. Geneviève) to Pierre Levet, and in Sydrach, *La Fontaine de toutes Sciences*, Vérard, 1486/87 (Macf. 5),[1] and with the similar subject in the *Triomphe des Neuf Preux*, printed by Gérard, Abbeville 1487.[2]

Fig. 374. The Death of Saul, from Boccaccio, *Les Cas et Ruynes des nobles hommes et femmes*, Paris 1483/84.

To 1486 belongs Dupré's edition of St. Jerome, *Vie des Saints Pères Hermites* (Cl. i. 228), with a full-page frontispiece of *St. Jerome seated writing before a saintly assembly*,[3] numerous column cuts, well designed and clearly cut, somewhat Netherlandish in character (see fig. 375), and interesting initials with figures and grotesque heads.

The earliest French illustrated editions of the *Lives of the Saints* appear to be those published at Lyon,[4] but Dupré followed soon after with his *Légende Dorée* of 7th October 1489 (Cl. i. 264, École des Beaux-Arts, Paris, from J. Masson), with the usual small column cuts.[5] He also printed, in col-

[1] Reproduced, A. Blum, *Les Origines du livre à gravures en France*, 1928, pl. xxviii., and J. Macfarlane, *Antoine Vérard*, London (Bibliographical Society) 1900, pl. v.

[2] See p. 623.

[3] Used later by Guillaume Le Rouge at Troyes (see p. 622).   [4] See p. 603.

[5] These blocks, as well as others from his *Vie des Saints Pères Hermites* of 1486, were printed in Venetian issues of the Golden Legend in 1504 and 1514 (see Essling, *Livres à figures vénitiens*, Nos. 682 and 686), and E. P. Goldschmidt & Co., *Medieval Literature and Science*, List 5, London [1932], No. 157 A. The fact that Dupré had a second series cut for his edition of 1493/94

laboration with André Bocard, a larger folio of the same work, 10th March 1493/94 (Cl. i. 269), with a different series of cuts, and an edition of May 1496, whose blocks, according to Claudin, were printed later by Jean de Vingle at Lyon, 1497 (Cl. iv. 230), and again in Paris by Nicolas de la Barre, 1499 (Cl. ii. 290-92). I might add here that Vérard also published editions of the *Légende Dorée*, 10th February 1490/91 (Macf. 14, Vienna), 2nd June 1493 (M. 28, Paris, Pierpont Morgan 505), and 20th May 1496 (Macf. 45, Paris), and an edition of St. Jerome, *Vie des Pères*, on 15th October 1495 (Macf. 43).[1]

Fig. 375. St. Ammon, from St. Jerome, *Vie des Saints Pères*, Paris 1486.

I will here interpolate some account of the printer PIERRE LE ROUGE, returning later to other works printed by Dupré, in which he used blocks from Le Rouge's most famous book, *La Mer des Hystoires*. He belonged to a large family of scribes and illuminators, turned printers.[2] Jacques Le Rouge (Jacobus Rubeus), the earliest of the printers, friend and compatriot of Nicolaus Jenson, was working at Venice from 1470 to 1478, and in other parts of Italy till 1481 or later, afterwards returning to France, and printing a local Breviary at Embrun (Dauphiné) in 1489–90. He describes himself in this Breviary as a Frenchman of the diocese of Langres, so that Chablis, where others of his name worked, was probably the cradle of the family. Of the four other printers of the name, Jean, Pierre, Guillaume and Nicolas, only Guillaume, Nicolas and Pierre come within our survey. We have already spoken of books printed by Guillaume at Chablis and Troyes, 1489–92; and by Nicolas at Troyes (about 1496).[3] Of Guillaume's later activity in Paris, 1493–1517,

renders it probable that the original blocks had been disposed of before that date, though no Italian edition containing them has been identified before that of 1504. It should also be noted that many of the subjects (and possibly some of the blocks) from Dupré's *Books of Hours* were used in Venetian *Horae* of the early XVI century (Essling, Nos. 467 and 472).

[1] See p. 671.

[2] See Henri Monceaux, *Les Le Rouge de Chablis: Étude sur les débuts de l'illustration du livre au XVe siècle*, 2 vols., Paris 1896. The book is full of interesting material about French book-illustration in general. Its fault is the wholesale attribution of woodcut work to one or other of the Le Rouge, on purely conjectural grounds. References may frequently be given to his catalogue even though the attributions are incorrect, as it contains the fullest descriptions available of many books.   [3] See pp. 621, 622.

Fig. 376. Border-piece from the *Mer des Hystoires*, Paris 1488–89.

no books of any certain attribution belong to our period, for Monceaux's list is largely conjectural. Pierre Le Rouge (who from 1487 describes himself as 'imprimeur du Roi') remains incomparably the most important member of the family, and chiefly on account of the *Mer des Hystoires*, which he printed for Vincent Commin in two volumes, July 1488 and February 1488/89 (B.M., Paris, Pierpont Morgan Library, New York). The two large folios, with 257 numbered leaves in vol. i., and 271, in addition to 28 unnumbered leaves, in vol. ii., printed in double columns, contain an immense amount of material in historical and legendary lore, with a very large number of woodcut illustrations. The number of blocks used is far less than the number of illustrations, for the prints are often stock subjects, repeated in many different positions throughout the work.

The book itself is translated from that epitome of legend and history, the *Rudimentum Noviciorum*, first printed by Brandis at Lübeck, 1475,[1] the chronicle being continued to 1483 (the Coronation of Charles VIII.), by the anonymous translator. The illustrations are also derived to a considerable extent from the same source, but they render the originals very freely, and they include a great variety of new subjects and a wealth of new decorative material. The borders are particularly beautiful, following in outline the best traditions of the French illuminators, a charming medley of branch, leaf, bird, beast and man (see fig. 376). There are three immense decorative initials, P with the author writing, T with the Redeemer, and S in the form of a dragon, in addition to the gothic L with St. George and the Dragon of the title-page. The most important full-page cut, again very near to the illumination of the period, is the twofold subject, the *Baptism of Clovis and the Battle of Tolbiac*, at f. 214 of the second volume (fig. 377). The other full page or double folio plates are maps of the world and the Holy Land, and many genealogies designed as in the *Rudimentum Noviciorum* in the form of chains, interspersed with little scriptural and historical scenes. Then

[1] See p. 363.

Fig. 377. Baptism of Clovis and the Battle of Tolbiac, from the *Mer des Hystoires*, Paris 1488–89.

there are numerous column cuts of various sizes, largely little upright subjects, the scriptural and historical subjects being generally more elaborate and less interesting than the freshly designed scenes from contemporary life. They are all repeated time after time as stock illustrations of similar scenes and personages, for innumerable are the opportunities for using the death of a king in battle (the best and most expressive of the historical series), a battle scene, the storming of a city, a meeting of kings, king in council and the like. Among the subjects treated more completely in the vein of contemporary genre, and applied to saints, philosophers and men of learning are—a monk seated writing,[1] a monk standing reading and a woman visiting a doctor (fig. 378), a nagging philosopher, the astronomer, the lecturer, the preacher, the congregation. They are probably by

Fig. 378. Woman visiting a Doctor, from the *Mer des Hystoires*, Paris 1488–89.

the same designer as the woodcuts to *Maistre Pierre Pathelin* printed by Levet and Germain Bineaut.[2] Then two good large oblong subjects, one of the *Destruction of Pharaoh's Host* and the other a two-fold illustration of *Soldiers by a River outside a City, and Procession of Priests in a Church*. Finally, between ff. 70 and 107 in volume ii., a series of ten little cuts (measuring about $2\frac{7}{8} \times 1\frac{7}{8}$ inches) within borders, illustrating the life of the Virgin and the life of Christ (fig. 379).[3] These cuts and borders, with a woodcut surface covering about $4\frac{1}{2} \times 3$ inches, correspond in style to the Dupré-Caillaut group described below,[4] while seven of the subject-blocks are actually printed in Meslier's *Horae* of 14th February 1489/90.[5]

In a second edition of the *Mer des Hystoires* published by Vérard about 1503 (B.M., C. 7. d. 4, 5), the book is largely the same in text and illustration, with the addition of some thirty-eight folios of text in the second

---

[1] E.g. at f. 44, verso, within single border-line, measuring 74×60 mm. Another cut of a *Monk seated writing*, slightly larger and within triple border-lines (95×77 mm.), done in a more detailed setting, occurs at f. 42, and elsewhere (fig. 380), and was repeated in Vérard's *Art de bien Mourir* of 1492, and in various other books.   [2] See pp. 642, 643.

[3] Eight of these are reproduced by Claudin, i. 466-67.

[4] See p. 683.   [5] See p. 685.

volume, bringing the history down to the Italian expedition of Louis XII., in 1499–1500. A considerable number of small initial letters (Gothic calligraphy with grotesque heads) have been added where spaces were left

in the first issue for the rubricator, and a very large folding cut (about $14\frac{1}{4} \times 30$ inches) illustrating the *Battle of Fornovo* (1495) is added after f. 292 in the second volume. Reference has already been made to the edition printed by Jean Dupré at Lyon in 1491.[1] Successive editions both at Paris and Lyon, e.g. those of Davost, Lyon 1506, and of Enguilbert de Marnef and François Regnault, Paris, about 1517, bring down the history to about the time of printing. It is noteworthy that the illustrations of the edition of Marnef and Regnault are printed promiscuously from the blocks of both Le Rouge and Dupré.

The excellence of the *Mer des Hystoires* probably induced Antoine Vérard to enlist Pierre

Fig. 379. The Annunciation, from the *Mer des Hystoires*, Paris 1488–89.

Le Rouge among the various printers who worked on his publications. We have already mentioned one other independent work of Pierre Le Rouge (Nicolaus de Lyra, *Les Postilles sur le Livre des Psaulmes*, Paris, about 1490), for the woodcut of Charles VIII. enthroned (fig. 381), which had appeared earlier at Abbeville, and was used in 1493 by Dupré.[2]

Further examples of the relations between Dupré and Pierre Le Rouge may be cited in the use of various blocks from the *Mer des Hystoires* in Martial d'Auvergne, *Les Vigilles de la Mort du Roy Charles VII.*, Paris, 8th May 1493 (Cl. i. 275), and Honorat Bonnor, *L'Arbre des Batailles*, Paris, 22nd June 1493 (Cl. i. 275), both printed by Dupré. In one case two

[1] See p. 612.   [2] See p. 623.

subjects are made by dividing the oblong block of *Soldiers by a River outside a City and Procession of Priests in a Church*, noted among the illustrations of the *Mer des Hystoires*. Claudin refers to the fact that no books bear

Fig. 380. Monk seated writing, from the *Mer des Hystoires*, Paris 1488–89.

Pierre Le Rouge's name from 1483 (at Chablis) until 1488 (at Paris), and in view of the various relations we have noted between Le Rouge and Dupré at Paris and Abbeville, he conjectures that Le Rouge might have been working on blocks for Dupré during this period of 1483–87.

The conjecture is reasonable, and Pierre Le Rouge may be responsible for designing (or even cutting) such blocks as those of the Abbeville *Cité de Dieu*,[1] but it must be remembered that it is pure conjecture. Far more hypothetical are the attributions to Pierre and Guillaume Le Rouge made by Monceaux of the printing of so many of the books published by Vérard.[2] They are based chiefly on the fact that many of the cuts from the *Mer des Hystoires* are used in Vérard's books, but as they also appear in books printed independently by Dupré the argument is invalidated.[3] Monceaux's attributions equally lack support from more recent typographical research. There is, in fact, no more specific evidence of the activity of any of the Le Rouge family as designers or woodcutters than there is of Vérard himself, who from his education as scribe and illustrator might equally have designed many of the illustrations of his own books. But busy printers and publishers are more likely to have used other craftsmen for cutting their blocks.

[1] See p. 622.

[2] Monceaux describes Guillaume, who carried on Pierre's establishment in Paris after 1493, as Pierre's son and heir.

[3] Nevertheless, after Pierre Le Rouge's death in 1492, Vérard certainly commanded the use of Pierre Le Rouge's stock of illustrations more than any other printer or publisher.

Apart from the blocks from the *Mer des Hystoires*, Martial d'Auvergne,
Les Vigilles de la Mort du Roy Charles VII., printed by Dupré, 1493, contains

Fig. 381. Charles VIII. enthroned, from Nicolaus de Lyra, *Postilles
sur le Livre des Psaumes*, Paris, about 1490.

the same frontispiece of Charles VIII. enthroned used by Pierre Le Rouge
in 1490, and by Gérard at Abbeville, 1486,[1] and various new illustrations

1 See p. 623.

The book was also reprinted with the original cuts by Jean Driart for
Vérard, 1498 (Cl. ii. 331). Many of the military scenes also reappeared,
printed from the original blocks, in Robert Gaguin's French version of
Julius Caesar, *Commentaires*, 1485, attributed by Claudin to Pierre Levet
(Cl. i. 417, Paris). There is also an edition of the *Commentaires* about 1488,

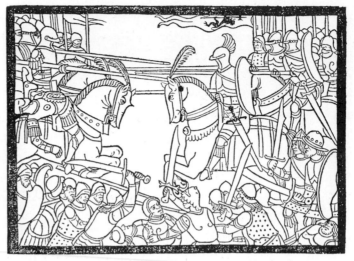

Fig. 385. Battle scene, from Caesar, *Commentaires*, Paris, about 1488.

published by Vérard, and attributed in the British Museum to the printer
Pierre le Caron (Proctor 8141), which contains three of the same blocks,
repeated to make eight illustrations (see fig. 385), and Vérard's Vegetius,
L'Art de la Chevalerie, 26th June 1488 (Macf. 6), is another book which
repeats some of the same series of cuts.

The second of Jean Bonhomme's books to which I alluded is Petrus de
Crescentiis, *Livre des Ruraulx Prouffitz*, issued 15th October 1486 (Cl. i.
190). There are a few cuts representing country occupations and sports,
but the frontispiece of the *Author presenting his book to a King* (fig. 386) is
by far the most interesting, excellent in grouping and in facial expression.
In style it is something of a French counterpart to the frontispiece group in
Schoeffer's *Gart der Gesuntheit*, Mainz 1485 (H. 8948). Jean Bonhomme
was probably also the printer of a Herbal (*Aggregator practicus de simplicibus*)
issued about 1485 (Proctor 8050, Cl. i. 195), but the 150 cuts of plants
are merely copies of the Mainz *Herbarius Latinus*, issued by Schoeffer in
1484 (H. 8444).[1]

Two books printed by CAILLAUT and MARTINEAU contain small cuts by

[1] See pp. 348-352.

a designer of a certain expressive quality, i.e. Jacques Le Grand, *Le Livre des bonnes Meurs*, 7th June 1487 (Cl. i. 306, locality not known to me), and the *Eruditorium penitentiale*, about 1490 (Cl. i. 320).

PIERRE LEVET is another of the printers who did independent work before Vérard secured his services. We have already mentioned the first edition

Fig. 386. The Author presenting his book to a king, from Petrus de Crescentiis, *Livre des Ruraulx Prouffitz*, Paris 1486.

of Robert Gaguin's translation of Julius Caesar, *Les Commentaires*, 1485, which is attributed by Claudin to Levet. The frontispiece, representing the *Translator presenting his book to the King*,[1] is designed and cut with a free touch, somewhat like the frontispiece to Dupré's Boccaccio, *Les Cent Nouvelles*, of 22nd November 1485, and the frontispiece of *Les Neuf Preux*, Abbeville 1487.[2] The frontispiece of the same subject in the second Paris edition of Gaguin's translation, published by Vérard about 1488,[3] is from a new block, and one that was thereafter used in many of Vérard's books (fig. 387).[4]

In 1486 Levet already appears to be working for Vérard, but three

[1] See p. 630.   [2] See pp. 623, 624, 654.   [3] See p. 640.   [4] See p. 656.

further independent works should be noted. In the first place a small *Latin Psalter*, 19th February 1488/89 (Cl. i. 435), with four illustrations of delicate design and cutting, *David and Goliath*, *David standing with his Harp*, the *Descent of the Spirit* and the *Flight into Egypt*. The *David with his*

Fig. 387. The Translator presenting his book to Charles VIII., from Caesar, *Commentaires*, about 1488.

Harp and the *Flight into Egypt* are also found in *Horae*, e.g. in an edition by Dupré in the British Museum (IA. 39817), and in another *Horae* issued by Vérard, 8th February 1489/90 and reprinted by Laurens Philippe, 1493 (B.M., IA. 40633).[1] Then the *Grand Testament de Maistre François Villon*, 1489 (Cl. i. 439, Paris, British Museum),[2] and the *Maistre Pierre Pathelin* of

[1] See pp. 683 and 689.

[2] Facsimile of the Paris copy edited by Pierre Champion, Paris 1925. The *Grand Testament de Villon* was also printed by Jean Trepperel in 1495 and 1497 (Cl. ii. 160); facsimile of the 1497 edition, Lille 1869. The two figures of *Villon* and *Margot* are either from the original blocks or very close copies (I have only been able to see the facsimile); *L'Évêque* and the *Three Men on the Gallows* are considerably modified.

about the same date (Cl. i. 443, Paris). The little woodcuts in both these works are well designed and expressively cut, and three single figures in the *Testament de Villon*, representing François Villon (fig. 388), his mistress, 'la grosse Margot', and L'Évêque Thibault, were copied later in Marchant's *Danse Macabre* (in edition 4, of 1490/91) and *Compost et Kalendrier des Bergiers*.[1] The blocks of *Maistre Pierre Pathelin* were reprinted by Germain Bineaut in an edition of 20th December 1490 (Cl. ii. 304, Paris). Though Levet's edition is not dated, it is proved to be earlier by the condition of the blocks. The woodcuts of *Maistre Pierre Pathelin* seem to be by the same designer as the little cuts of contemporary genre in Le Rouge's *Mer des Hystoires* (the *Woman visiting a Doctor*, and others).

Fig. 388. François Villon, from the *Grand Testament de Maistre François Villon*, Paris 1489.

GUY MARCHANT is a printer of equal importance to Jean Dupré and Pierre Le Rouge in the history of woodcut illustration in Paris, and the two books which owe their inception to him, the *Danse Macabre* and the *Compost et Kalendrier des Bergiers*, were among the most popular works of the time and illustrated with woodcuts of great interest. In quality the first series of the *Danse Macabre des Hommes* is perhaps the finest achievement of French woodcut in the xv century, designed with a fine expressive power and cut with beautiful precision (see fig. 389).

Marchant's woodcuts and verses seem to have been immediately based on two MSS. in the Bibliothèque Nationale from the Abbey of Saint-Victor (MS. lat. 14904 and MS. franc. 25550), but these are themselves derived from wall-paintings no longer extant, done in 1425 in the Cemetery of the Innocents at Paris.[2] Nevertheless the translation into line and into contemporary costume practically implies an independent work.

[1] The *Grand Testament* contains ten illustrations printed with repetitions from four blocks, the three figures in question and the *Three Men on the Gallows* illustrating Villon's epitaph. The episode of *Three Men on the Gallows* also appears in the woodcut of the *Entrance to Hell* which occurs in the *Danse Macabre* (ed. 2, 1486).

[2] See Valentin Dufour, *Recherches sur la Danse Macabre peinte en 1425 au Cimetière des Innocents*, Paris 1873 (and later editions of 1874 and 1875 with variant titles and reproductions of Marchant's woodcuts). The story of *Les Trois Morts et les Trois Vifs* also appeared in sculpture on the door of the cemetery church.

La Danse Macabre (*mirouer salutaire*) went through various editions,[1] and shows clearly the hand of two designers, the first (whom we shall call Designer A) responsible for the *Danse des Hommes*, the second, Designer B, responsible for most of the *Danse des Femmes* (see fig. 390). Designer B first appears in ed. 4. Designer A is by far the more distinguished, mordant in

Fig. 389. The Astrologer and the Bourgeois, from the *Danse Macabre des Hommes*, Paris (Marchant) 1491/92.

expression, and achieving his effects with subtlety of drawing and without exaggeration. He has something of the same style as Jean Bonhomme's designer referred to above.[2] Designer B is less sensitive in drawing and exaggerated in his types, with the angularity and the straight long noses characteristic of the designer who worked largely for Vérard.[3] In its expanded form, described from ed. 5 (British Museum, Huth), the work includes:[4]

    I. *La Danse Macabre des Hommes*: the frontispiece of the *Author at a desk* (1st version), the *Orchestra of Death* (1st version),

---

[1] See Claudin i. 236, etc.; Monceaux, P. Le Rouge, 1 (i.-x.), G. Le Rouge, 2, N. Le Rouge, 2.
[2] See p. 639.   [3] See p. 654.
[4] See *Catalogue of the Fifty MSS. and Printed Books bequeathed to the British Museum by Alfred Huth*, London 1912, Nos. xxv., xxvi.

20 cuts of the *Danse des Hommes*, and the *Author's Epilogue*, by Designer A; *Death on a Horse* by Designer B.

II. *La Danse Macabre des Femmes*: the *Author writing* (2nd version), the *Orchestra of Death* (2nd version), 18 cuts of the *Danse des Femmes*, the *Trumpeter of Death on a Tower*, the *Author's*

Fig. 390. The Chambermaid and the Matron, from the *Danse Macabre des Femmes*, Paris 1492.

Epilogue, and *Death on a Horse* (the last two repeated from Part I.). The first two cuts of the dance and the *Author's Epilogue* by Designer A; the remainder of the dance by Designer B; the *Trumpeter*, uncertain; the *Author writing* more powerfully cut than the dance of Designer B, and nearer to Vérard's chief designer. Poem of the *Author's Epilogue* further illustrated by three small figures of women, one copied from *La Grosse Margot* of *Le Grand Testament de Villon* (Levet, 1489), the others in the same style (possibly Designer B).

III. *Les Trois Morts et les Trois Vifs*: 2 cuts by Designer A.

IV. *Le Débat du corps et de l'âme*: 4 cuts, the soul represented in the form of a child, repeated to make 8 illustrations, by Designer A.

V. *La Complainte de l'âme damnée*: 1 cut, the *Entrance to Hell*, by Designer A.

Editions are as follows:

(1) 28*th September* 1485. Part I. only. Grenoble. 17 cuts: the *Author writing* (1st version), 15 cuts of the *Danse des Hommes*, the *Author's Epilogue*.

(2) 7*th June* 1486. Part I. ⎰ H. 313. Paris.[1]
    7*th July* 1486. Part II. ⎱ With title *Miroer Salutaire*, and at foot of title-page *La Danse Macabre Nouvelle*.

    Part I. The *Author at a desk* (1st version), the *Orchestra of Death* (1st version), 20 cuts of the *Danse des Hommes*, the *Author's Epilogue*, 2 cuts of *Les Trois Morts* and *Les Trois Vifs*.

    Part II. The *Author writing* (2nd version), the *Orchestra of Death* (1st version, repeated), 1 cut of the *Danse des Femmes* (Queen and Duchess), the *Author's Epilogue*, 4 cuts of the *Débat du corps et de l'âme* (repeated to make 8 illustrations), the *Entrance to Hell*.

(3) 15*th October* 1490. Latin edition. *Speculum salutare choree macabri*. Printed by Marchant for Geoffroi de Marnef. Paris. The cuts nearly as in ed. 2.

(4) 20*th January* 1490/91. Part I. ⎰ Paris.
    10*th April* 1491. Part II. | Title of Part I. *La Nouvelle Danse Macabre.*
    2*nd May* 1491. Parts III.-V. ⎱ Contents nearly as in the Huth copy, B.M.

(5) 15*th April* 1491/92. Part I. ⎰
    3*rd May* 1492. Part II. ⎱ British Museum (Huth).
    22*nd May* 1492. Parts III.-V.

The original blocks as well as certain copies were reprinted in various editions at Troyes, e.g. by Guillaume Le Rouge, 1491 (Bourges, and Comte de Lignerolles, Monceaux, G. Le Rouge 2),[2] and Nicolas Le Rouge, about 1496 (N. Le Rouge 2).[3] The blocks remained in the hands of the successors

---

[1] This edition reproduced in facsimile with introduction by Pierre Champion, Paris 1925.

[2] Claudin, ii. 126, refers to an edition by Le Petit Laurens, after 1494 (only known at Poitiers), which he describes as from the same blocks as G. Le Rouge, and as copies of the Marchant series.   [3] See p. 622.

of the Le Rouge press at Troyes until the XVIII century. An edition of Jean Garnier, 1728, may be cited which contains late impressions from both original blocks and copies.[1]

A most excellent series of copies of the *Danse Macabre des Hommes* was printed by COUTEAU and MENARD, Paris, 26th June 1492 (Cl. ii.

Fig. 391. The Astrologer and the Bourgeois, from the *Danse Macabre des Hommes*, Paris (Couteau and Menard) 1492.

174, Monceaux, P. Le Rouge 8, Paris). It contains the two subjects of *Les Trois Morts* and *Les Trois Vifs* but nothing else outside Part I. of the original series. In quality it is considerably inferior to the work of Marchant's Designer A; in style it is nearer to Vérard's chief designer, but it is cut with less angularity and force of line than in Vérard's most typical cuts. The use of white and black for the herbage is a decorative feature (see fig. 391).

The block of the *Author seated*, done in the style of Vérard's chief

[1] See E. P. Goldschmidt, London, Catalogue VIII. No. 129.

designer, was used later by Quentell at Cologne in his Aristotle, *De Anima*, 1499.[1]

As Couteau and Menard succeeded Pierre Le Rouge in printing Vérard's *Art de bien Mourir* in 1492, it is probable that their *Danse Macabre*[2] was also done at the instance of Vérard.

La Dance Macabre printed for Jean Trepperel by Nicolas de la Barre, Paris 1500, is a small book containing crude cuts in which Marchant's designs are copied very freely.

We have already described the interesting series of copies printed by Matthias Huss, at Lyon, 18th February 1499/1500.[3] The *Author seated*, the *Danse des Hommes* and *Les Trois Morts et les Trois Vifs* of this edition were copied from Couteau and Menard, but the *Danse des Femmes*, *Death on a Horse*, the *Trumpeter of Death*, and the *Débat du corps et de l'âme*, were based on Marchant, reflecting the different character of Marchant's Designers A and B in the *Danse des Femmes*. This is fairly clear proof that Couteau and Menard never completed their work, or Huss would almost certainly have used his originals throughout. The chief interest of the Lyon edition lies in its independent designs, notably the illustration of *Death and the Printers* (fig. 355).

The xv century was a time of recurrent plague throughout Europe, and moralists and preachers must have found ready listeners and readers for the vivid warnings contained in such works as *La Danse Macabre*. We have already noted other versions of the same theme in Germany,[4] and the many editions of the block-book *Ars Moriendi*, and Holbein's wonderful series of the first half of the xvi century, offer further examples of the popularity of such writings and pictures. And in the present chapter we have still to deal with Vérard's editions of *L'Art de bien Vivre et de bien Mourir*.

We should probably be wrong in thinking that these subjects suggested any exaggerated grimness in the mind of the ordinary man of the xv or xvi centuries. In Paris the Cemetery of the Innocents was a popular promenade on holidays, as cemeteries are to-day in America, and the popular enjoyment of the pomp of funerals is by no means extinct.

[1] See p. 362.

[2] Monceaux, P. Le Rouge 2, refers to two series of impressions of Couteau and Menard's *Danse Macabre* in the Bibl. Nationale, Paris, without title-page, printer's name or date, as done for Vérard in 1485, describing them as copies by P. Le Rouge, done almost immediately after Marchant's originals appeared. They happen to be without the *Orchestra of Death* which first appeared in Marchant's edition of 1492, but I find no certain evidence for the existence of an edition of 1485.

[3] See p. 605.   [4] See pp. 343 and 366.

Marchant's other great works, *Le Compost et Kalendrier des Bergiers* and *Le Compost et Kalendrier des Bergères*,[1] throw a happier light on contemporary life, and through the mouthpiece of the Shepherd offer a rich mine of lore relating to the whole existence of the countryman of the period. The former work as developed in its second edition included five sections:

(1) The Calendar proper.
(2) Tree of the Vices and the Pains of Hell.
(3) The Way of Health and the Tree of the Virtue.
(4) Physic and the Governance of Health.
(5) Astrology and Physiognomy.

Claudin was the first bibliographer, I believe, to describe the *editio princeps* of 2nd May 1491 (dated on the same day that he completed his *Nouvelle Danse Macabre*), of which only two copies are known, at Bourges and in the Bibliothèque Mazarine, Paris. It is a small folio of only thirty leaves, with far fewer woodcuts than appeared in the succeeding editions. It opens with the cut of the *Shepherd and the Stars* (which thereafter yielded its place of honour to the cut with *Five Shepherds*), includes in the Calendar proper the little border cuts with compartments of saints and signs of

Fig. 392. Figure symbolical of March, from the *Compost et Kalendrier des Bergiers*, Paris 1493.

the zodiac and the figures of the months (fig. 392), and in later sections the cut of the *Four Complexions*, a single block of the *Seven Planets in relation to the days of the week* (divided later into two parts), and two large upright cuts of *Shepherd with quadrant* and *Shepherd with plumb-line* (fig. 393).

In 1493 there were two editions, 18th April (Paris) and 18th July (Valenciennes, British Museum and Pierpont Morgan 508); they are both practically identical in contents, and added much new matter in text and illustration.[2]

[1] See Monceaux, P. Le Rouge 30, i.-vi., N. Le Rouge 3 and 13; Cl. i. 360, etc.

[2] One of two copies of the April edition in Paris is printed on vellum, illuminated and modified by Vérard, the Royal Arms covering Marchant's printer's mark and Vérard's mark superimposed on the colophon. Facsimile of 18th July 1493 (Valenciennes copy) edited by Pierre Champion, Paris 1926. The *Calendar and Compost of Shepherds*, edited by G. C. Heseltine, London 1930, is based on the cuts in the edition of 18th July 1493 (though not entirely complete), and on the English translation of R. Copland (first published by Julian Notary about 1518?) collated with the original French and revised.

The frontispiece is the *Author writing* (the second version, which appeared in *La Danse Macabre*, 1486), then the woodcut with *Five Shepherds in a Landscape* is prefixed to the prologue. Apart from the illustrations of the first edition, the most notable woodcuts are the series of the *Sept Paines d'Enfer*, introduced by the cut of *Christ in the House of Simon bidding Lazarus speak* (copied from the woodcuts in Vérard's *Art de bien Vivre et de bien Mourir*), the *Lord's Prayer*, the *Ten Commandments*, the *Commandments of the Church* (again suggested by blocks in Vérard's book), the *Ship of Life, Death on a Horse* (from *La Danse Macabre*), *Man's body as dominated by the signs of the Zodiac and the Seven Planets*, the *Planets and days of the week*, a series of the *Planets and their influences, Death in the Tombs*, and ten small and very attractive upright subjects of single and double figures (see fig. 394), of which three were based on the cuts in *Le Grand Testament de Villon*, 1489.[1]

Fig. 393. Shepherd with plumb-line, from the *Compost et Kalendrier des Bergiers*, Paris 1493.

Several editions appeared in the succeeding years, the most attractive additions to the illustrations being *January*, one of the full-page illustrations of the occupations of the months, first issued in the *Compost et Kalendrier des Bergères*, 1499, the *Trumpeter of Death* (as in the *Compost des Bergères*), and the *Lymasson* (or *L'Escargot*), with a woman and two soldiers fighting a monstrous snail, the latter being here reproduced from the *Bergiers* of 10th September 1500, in the British Museum (fig. 395).[2]

The most important of the later French editions is that of Nicolas Le Rouge, at Troyes, 1529. The illustrations are made up partly from Marchant's original blocks and partly from copies done in Vérard's workshop. The more powerfully cut blocks, e.g. the full-page *Months* (from the *Compost et Kalendrier des Bergères*, 1499), are still in good condition.

---

[1] See p. 642.

[2] The last two subjects do not occur in the British Museum copy of 18th July 1493, but Monceaux notes them in his description of edition of 18th April 1493. There are variations in most copies, so that definite statements as to when a woodcut first appeared are dangerous.

As in the case of *La Danse Macabre*, the blocks remained in the hands of the successors of Le Rouge at Troyes until the XVIII century.

Of French editions outside Paris, illustrated by different cuts, Claudin notes two printed by Jean Bellot at Geneva in 1497 and 1500, and several XVI-century editions at Lyon. He also refers to German editions printed at Lübeck, 1519, and Rostock, 1523.

There were also numerous English editions up to the earlier half of the XVII century, the first, under the title of *Kalendayr of the Shyppars*, being printed by Vérard at Paris, 1503 (STC. 22407).[1] None of the blocks is from the original series but all are from Vérard's stock: the *Christ in the House of Simon*, the *Pains of Hell*, the *Lord's Prayer*, and *Twelve Apostles* from his *Art de bien Vivre et de bien Mourir*, numerous little figures from his *Terence en françois* (about 1500), *Death with a spade in a cloister* from Robert Gobin, *Les Loups Ravissans* (Vérard, Paris, about 1503),[2] the rest being copies from Marchant's series.

Fig. 394. Schoolmaster and Boy, from the *Compost et Kalendrier des Bergiers*, Paris 1493.

The first edition printed in England (*The Kalender of Shepherdes*) was issued by Richard Pynson, 1506 (STC. 22408),[3] who borrowed most of the blocks used by Vérard in 1503, in addition to that of the *Author standing, presenting his book*,[4] which came from the *Art de bien Vivre et de bien Mourir*, 1492, and various other borders printed by Vérard. Some of the

---

[1] Reproduced in facsimile and edited by Heinrich Oskar Sommer, London 1892. The facsimile was made from the complete copy in the Library of the Duke of Devonshire. There are imperfect copies in the British Museum and at Manchester. See also E. Gordon Duff, *The First Two Books printed in the Scottish Language*, Edinburgh Bibliographical Society, 1892–93. The two books discussed are Vérard's English edition of the *Kalendayr of the Shyppars*, 1503, and the *Art of good lyvyng and good deyng*, 30th May 1503 (see p. 662), which Gordon Duff shows to have been made by a Scotsman who was at Paris in 1503. The writer who revised the translation for Richard Pynson's edition of 1506 speaks of the 1503 version as in 'corrupte Englyshe', which no Englishman could understand. And Robert Copland, who made a new translation for Wynkyn de Worde in 1508, refers to it more specifically as in 'rude and Scottysshe language'.

[2] See p. 669.

[3] The text reprinted in the work of H. O. Sommer quoted above.

[4] This appeared later in Robert Fabyan's *Chronicles*, London (Pynson) 1516 (B.M., G. 6014), and in Lawrence Andrewe's edition of Vincent de Beauvais, *Myrrour of the World* (about 1527).

Terence figures were replaced by copies. It does not include the subject from *Les Loups Ravissans*.

Many of the cuts reappeared in Julian Notary's edition (Robert Copland's translation), the *Kalender of Shepardes*, of about 1518 (STC. 22410), and in various subsequent editions.

Fig. 395. Le Lymasson, from the *Compost et Kalendrier des Bergiers*, Paris 1500.

The edition printed by Wynkyn de Worde, 1508 (The *Kalender of Shepherdes*, STC. 22409, Magdalen College, Oxford), is largely composed of poor copies of the Vérard blocks, and was no doubt immediately based, at least in part, on Pynson. But it should be noted that it contains the verses on the portentous snail (*Lymasson*, or *l'Escargot*), which did not appear in Pynson's edition.

Marchant also issued, in conjunction with the publisher Jean Petit, a *Compost et Kalendrier des Bergères*, 17th August 1499, the only edition known (H. 5590). Marchant here uses his mark of *Prestre Jehan* in place of that of the *Two Cobblers* which appeared in the *Kalendrier des Bergiers*. Much of the same illustrative material was used here as in the earlier work, the chief omission being the *Christ in the House of Simon*, the *Paines d'Enfer* and the other cuts of that section up to the *Commandments*. Of the new blocks the most important are the series of full-page illustrations of the *Occupations of the Months* (of which only the *January* ever appeared in editions of the *Kalendrier des Bergiers*), in the manner of Vérard's chief designer (see fig. 396), the two cuts of the shepherdesses *Bietrix and Sebille* and the peasants *L'un et l'autre* (fig. 397), the *Trumpeter of Death amid Flowers* (which also appears in the 1500 edition of the *Kalendrier des Bergiers*) and the little frieze of *Les Trois Morts et les Trois Vifs*. The book ends with the original *Danse Macabre des Femmes* (including the first version of the *Orchestra of Death*, eighteen subjects of the dance, and the author's epilogue) and a block of *Christ carrying the Cross, with a kneeling man*.[1]

---

[1] This block, based on a cut in Toulouse edition of *L'Imitation de Jesus Christ* (1488), was first used by Jean Lambert in his edition of *L'Imitation*, Paris, 16th November 1493; then lent to

Some of the blocks of the *Compost des Bergères* had appeared in Joannes de Sacro Busto, *Sphaera Mundi*, printed by Marchant for Jean Petit, February 1498/99, e.g. the *Hand with a Sphere*, the large *Month of May* and the *Trumpeter of Death amid Flowers*.

Of other books printed by Marchant, S. Bonaventura, *Sermones de Morte*,

Fig. 396. August, from the *Compost et Kalendrier des Bergères*, Paris 1499.

February 1494/95 (Cl. i. 397), contains a small cut of *Dives and Lazarus*, of excellent design and delicate cutting, which had appeared earlier in various *Horae*, e.g. in editions by Dupré and Caillaut in the British Museum (IA. 39817, and IA. 39507).[1]

Le Bourgeois for his Rouen edition of 1498, returning to Paris for use in the *Compost et Kalendrier des Bergères*. For note and reproduction see Claudin i. 224.

[1] See pp. 683 and 685. A different version of the same subject, with two men serving at table, and a bed in the background, occurs in the early Dupré *Horae* of about 1488–90 at Oxford (Proctor 8044).

ANTOINE VÉRARD's[1] activity as a publisher of illustrated books in the xv century seems to fall naturally into two periods, from 1485 to about 1492, when he used woodcuts of various styles corresponding to those used by Dupré, Pierre Le Rouge and other printers, and from 1492 to the end of the century.[2] He continued publishing till 1512, and died at latest in 1514. The second period, when his position as the leading publisher of books in the vernacular was assured, shows a remarkable unity in the style of his new woodcuts, which were probably designed and cut by some artist in his employ. The figures in this group of cuts are characterised by strongly emphasised types with long noses, and the drawing in general, if hard, is trenchant in characterisation and firmly cut in thick lines that would last out large editions. I have spoken of the author of the group as Vérard's chief designer. Some of the character-

Fig. 397. L'Un et l'autre, from the *Compost et Kalendrier des Bergères*, Paris 1499.

istics of drawing are already present in earlier illustrations of more delicate cutting, e.g. the series of contemporary genre in Le Rouge's *Mer des Hystoires*, and a dogmatism which tries to define the work of anonymous designers is balked by the inevitable variations in style caused by a variety of cutters. The two periods of Vérard's activity are divided by that most important work, *L'Art de bien Vivre et de bien Mourir*, issued by Vérard in 1492, which includes examples of both phases.

Boccaccio, *Les Cent Nouvelles*, a translation of the *Decameron* by Laurent du Premier-Fait, 22nd November 1485, the first book to bear Vérard's name, has already been discussed in relation to Jean Dupré, who was almost certainly the printer (Cl. i. 226, Macf. 1, Paris; see p. 641).

[1] See J. Macfarlane, *Antoine Vérard*, London (Bibliographical Society) 1900; J. Renouvier, *Des gravures en bois dans les livres d'Antoine Vérard, 1485–1512*, Paris 1859.

[2] The end of the century was a critical period for the printer, for in October 1490 his shop *Sur le Pont Notre Dame* was burnt down. After that date various addresses occur in his colophons, but Bourdillon (the *Early Editions of the Roman de la Rose*, Bibliographical Society, London 1906, Appendix A) contends that they were all actually the same house, and thereby justifies his dating of Molinet's *Roman de la Rose Moralisé* as about 1500, rather than later (see p. 608).

Then on 10th July 1486 appeared his edition of Petrus de Crescentiis, *Prouffitz Champestres et Ruraulx*, attributed to the printer Levet (Cl. i. 426, Macf. 3, École des Beaux-Arts, Paris, from Masson Collection), three months before Bonhomme's edition, to which reference has already been made.[1] It has an attractive series of cuts of country occupations, as well as an

Fig. 398. The Author presenting his book to an Ecclesiastic, from
L'Art de bien Vivre et de bien Mourir, Paris 1492.

interesting little woodcut of a *Monk seated writing in his study*.[2] To Pierre Levet again is usually assigned the printing of Vérard's *Les Cent Nouvelles Nouvelles* of 24th December 1486 (Cl. i. 428, Macf. 4, Paris), that famous series of stories compiled at the court of Louis XI. It contains a frontispiece which appears to represent *Louis XI. and the Duke of Burgundy with courtiers* (in the manner of the frontispiece to Sydrach, 1486/87), as well as a large

[1] See p. 640.

[2] 57 × 59 mm. The monk is seated on the right in a carved Gothic chair. The cut is in the same style as the little upright of a similar subject in the *Mer des Hystoires*, 1488 (see p. 634 and fig. 380). The block was frequently reprinted.

number of small column-cuts, similar in style to those in *Les Prouffitz Champestres.*

The *Author presenting his book to the King*, used as frontispiece to Sydrach, *La Fontaine de Toutes Sciences*, 20th February 1486/87 (Macf. 5, and plate v., Paris), had already appeared in an edition of Caesar, *Commentaires*, translated by Robert Gaguin and attributed to Pierre Levet.[1] Both this and the frontispiece to the first edition of *Les Cent Nouvelles Nouvelles* are in the somewhat loose and sketchy style of the frontispiece to Dupré's *Les Cent Nouvelles* of Boccaccio,[2] and probably came from the workshop of Dupré or Le Rouge.

A second cut of an analogous subject, the *Translator presenting his Book to the King*, which appeared in Vérard's edition of Caesar, *Commentaires* (Gaguin's translation), issued about 1488 (Macf. 107, Proctor 8141, attributed to the printer Pierre Le Caron),[3] was more frequently reprinted.[4] It forms a link between the earlier style of Dupré and that of Vérard's chief designer. An early and characteristic example of this designer is the *Author standing, presenting his Book to an Ecclesiastic* (fig. 398), which first appeared in Vérard's *Art de bien Vivre et de bien Mourir*, in the part entitled 'Traicté de l'Advenement de Antechrist', dated 28th October 1492.[5]

A third cut of similar character, an *Author kneeling before a King surrounded by his court* (fig. 399), a very good example by the same designer, appeared in Paulus Orosius, *Histoires*, of 21st August 1491 (Macf. 16, Paris), and subsequent editions (e.g. Macf. 92, 1509), and in the *Gestes Romaines* of about 1508 (Macf. 164). The *Caesar* (Macf. 107) also contained several of the cuts which had first appeared in Millet, *L'Istoire de la Destruction de Troye*, printed by J. Bonhomme, 1484.[6]

Vérard's illustration of the *Chevalier Délibéré* of Olivier de la Marche, first issued 8th August 1488, and probably printed by Dupré (Cl. ii. 468; Macf. 7, Vienna), is entirely independent of the Dutch edition, and by comparison a light-weight. But its twelve blocks (made by one repetition into thirteen illustrations) are attractive, and with their lettering omitted are constantly found in later books. Thus one illustration of *Le Chevalier Délibéré and*

---

[1] See pp. 630, 641. [2] See pp. 629, 641, 654. [3] See p. 641 and fig. 387.

[4] E.g. in Aristotle, *Éthiques*, 8th September 1488; Aristotle, *Livre des Politiques*, Marchant for Vérard, 1489; Paulus Orosius, 1491 (including Seneca, *Des Motz Dorez*); Josephus, *Bataille Judaique*, 1492; Bonnor, *L'Arbre des Batailles*, 1493; *Les Cent Nouvelles Nouvelles*, 2nd ed., about 1495; *Terence en François*, about 1500.

[5] See pp. 660, 662. Repeated e.g. in Josephus, *Bataille Judaique*, 7th December 1492; H. Suso, *L'Orloge de Sapience*, 1493/94; *Kalender of Shepherdes*, London, R. Pynson, 1506.

[6] See p. 639.

Fig. 399. The Author kneeling before a King, from Orosius, Paris 1491.

Accident (fig. 400) is reprinted in Josephus, *La Bataille Judaique*, 1492,[1] and more appeared in Alanus (de Insulis), *Les Paraboles*, 20th March 1492/93 (Macf. 23, Blum, 1928, p. xxxv),[2] in Boccaccio, *De la louenge des nobles et*

Fig. 400. Le Chevalier and Accident, from *Le Chevalier Délibéré*, Paris 1488.

cleres dames, 28th April 1493 (Macf. 25), in Honoré Bonnor, *L'Arbre des Batailles*, 8th June 1493 (Macf. 29), alongside other cuts of weaker design; in *Le Jouvencel*, Vérard, 27th March 1493/94 (Macf. 34), and in Raoul Lefèvre, *Recueil des histoires troiennes*, about 1494 (Macf. 123), with other cuts from *L'Arbre de Batailles* and other sources. A later edition of *Le Chevalier Délibéré* with the same blocks was printed by Jean Lambert, 1493 (Cl. ii. 221). Its title-page bears an attractive capital L with three grotesque heads (fig. 401). There are altogether about six varieties of these

calligraphic capital L's with grotesque heads in frequent use on Vérard's title-pages. Commonest of all is the one with a single head on the right, which seems to have first appeared in Heinrich Suso, *Orloge de Sapience*, 10th March 1493/94 (Macf. 33),[3] and afterwards in *Lancelot du Lac*, 1494, and Froissart, about 1495, and various other works. Then a flamboyant example with two heads on the right first occurred in the *Croniques de France*, 1493 (Macf. 30),[4] and a more perpendicular design with two heads, left and

---

[1] See p. 659.

[2] In this book the cut showing *L'Acteur* and *L'Entendement* is cut in two and used in its separate parts: when used later as a single subject there are signs of this division. The book also contains cuts from Petrus de Crescentiis, *Prouffitz Champestres*, 1486, and *Les Cent Nouvelles Nouvelles*, 1486. The small lettering on the *Chevalier* cuts was type printing superimposed, which was of course omitted in the reprints. In other cases larger lettering had been cut on the blocks, and in some instances remains and in others is cut away.

[3] It was also used by Dupré and Bocard (printing also for Vérard ?) in their edition of the *Légende Dorée*, of the same day, 10th March 1493/94 (Cl. i. 269).

[4] This appears to have been first used by Pierre Le Caron in *Les Fais de Maistre Alain Chartier*, 1489 (Cl. ii. 75). It was copied and imitated by other printers, e.g. at Troyes (*Danse Macabre*,

Fig. 401. Initial L, with three grotesque heads, from *Le Chevalier Délibéré*, Paris 1493.

right, is used in the *Lancelot du Lac*, of 1504 ('1494') (Macf. 166), and in the *Figures du Vieil Testament et du Nouvel* of about the same date (Macf. 163) (fig. 402).

A more complex design with grotesque heads and dragons appeared in Jacobus de Cessolis, *Jeu des Eschez Moralisé*, 1504 (Macf. 72), and a smaller example with grotesque head and stork in *Le Pèlerinage de l'Homme*, 1511/12 (Macf. 101).

Another interesting capital L, with design of nude woman, monkey and bird, occurs on the last leaf of *Les Ordonnances de la Prévosté des Marchands et Échevinage de la Ville de Paris*, 1500/1501, which appears to have been printed for Vérard (Cl. ii. 500, Macf. 273).

Of Vérard's other large initials with grotesque heads I would mention a remarkable P with two grotesque heads which occurred at the beginning of the Prologue of *Le Livre du Faulcon*, about 1496 (Cl. ii. 487, Paris).

In these initials with grotesque heads and other figures the designers for woodcut were following the traditions of the scribes and illuminators. A copy in the Bibliothèque Mazarine, Paris, of the first book printed by Pierre Le Rouge at Chablis, *Le Livre des Bonnes Mœurs*, 1st April 1478 (Monceaux, i. 100), shows similar calligraphic initials.

Between 1490 and 1492 Vérard commanded the services of Pierre Le Rouge, for it was he who either printed or provided part of the illustrative material to *Lucan, Suetoine et Saluste*, 22nd December 1490 (Macf. 12, Paris), *Orosius*, including the *Motz Dorez* of Seneca, 1491 (Macf. 16, Paris, and 126), and Josephus, *La Bataille Judaique*, 7th December 1492 (Macf. 21). The first two of these repeat the large initial *L with St. George and the Dragon*, and the large initials P and S from the *Mer des Hystoires*, while the Josephus includes various border-pieces from the same source. After Pierre Le Rouge's death in 1492, Vérard made constant use of his blocks, even though he may not have been the absolute proprietor.[1] I shall refer later

Guillaume Le Rouge, 1491) and at Lyon. It should also be remembered that initials and decorative cuts, which were in constant use, might have been frequently repeated in casts.   [1] See p. 636.

Fig. 402. Initial L, with two Heads, from *Figures du Vieil Testament*, Paris, about 1504.

to the remaining illustrations in the *Josephus*, but would first consider the pivotal work in Vérard's activity.

L'Art de bien Vivre et de bien Mourir is the form in which a general title for the whole work was first issued (in the edition of 12th February 1493/94), but the original edition appeared in sections beginning with *Le Livre intitule lart de bien mourir*. This first part included as its second section *Leguyllon de crainte divine pour bien mourir*, and was printed by Couteau and Menard, 18th July 1492. Then followed as Part II. the *Traicte de l'Advenement de Antechrist*, the colophon bearing Vérard's name and dated 28th October 1492. Finally as Part III. came *Le Livre de bien Vivre*, with Vérard's name and date 15th December 1492.

In the editions of 12th February 1493/94, 20th June 1496 (Macf. 46) and 15th October 1498 (Macf. 53, Paris) the general title reads *Le Livre intitule lart de bien vivre et de bien mourir*. They correspond roughly in text and illustration with the first edition, but the parts run in the order Part III., Part I., Part II.

L'Art de bien mourir contains eleven full-page cuts based on the block-book *Ars Moriendi*, within border-pieces at the sides and below, which are in the same style of decoration as those in the books of Dupré and Pierre Le Rouge. They show considerable independence of treatment and are powerfully designed and cut. The little upright cut of a *Monk seated writing* (95 × 77 mm.; sig. a. iv, verso) comes from the *Mer des Hystoires* (f. 42). *Leguyllon de crainte divine* has an upright cut with a *Saint writing, and two prophets above* (sig. d. i), but its chief cuts illustrate the *Sept Paines d'Enfer* (fig. 403) introduced by *Christ in the House of Simon bidding Lazarus speak*. The *Traicte de l'Advenement de Antechrist* contains large cuts, each with two border-pieces, illustrating the *Quinze Signes de l'Advenement*, followed by a *Last Judgment* and a full-page cut of the *Blessed in Heaven* illustrating *Les Joyes de Paradis*.[1] An upright cut of a *Sainted Bishop writing with two prophets above* (a pendant to the *Saint writing* in *Leguyllon*) comes at the beginning of the section on *Les Quinze Signes* (sig. l. ii, verso). A small column-cut

1 The original block of *Les Joyes de Paradis* came to England, and appeared in Pynson's *Sarum Missal* of 1512 (see p. 722).

of the *Birth of Antichrist* is borrowed from *Les Cent Nouvelles Nouvelles,*
1486.[1]

   L'Art de bien Vivre contains oblong blocks of the *Annunciation and
Visitation, The Virgin and Child adored by a Pope and others,* the *Lord's Prayer,*
the *Twelve Apostles* (in two cuts illustrating the Creed), the *Ten Command-*

Fig. 103. Men broken on the Wheel, from *L'Art de bien Vivre et de bien Mourir,* Paris 1492.

ments, and smaller upright cuts in two compartments showing a harmony
of subjects from the Old and New Testaments, besides separate cuts of the
Brazen Serpent and *The Crucifixion.*[2] Finally seven full-page upright cuts

---

[1] See p. 655. In the second edition of *Les Cent Nouvelles Nouvelles* (about 1495), the same cut
occurs at Nouvelles 76 and 77 but with the window and the two boys cut out of the block.
[2] The last two were repeated on smaller blocks in the 1493 edition.

illustrating the *Seven Sacraments* (fig. 404). The portrait of the *Author standing*, *presenting his Book to an Ecclesiastic*, which has been already noted and reproduced (fig. 398), appeared at the beginnings of Parts II. and III.

The illustrations of the *Quinze Signes* are below the rest in quality, possibly a difference of cutter rather than designer. Of the other woodcuts,

Fig. 404. Baptism, from *L'Art de bien Vivre et de bien Mourir*, Paris 1492.

the copies of the *Ars Moriendi*, the *Sept Paines d'Enfer* and *Seven Sacraments* are probably all by Vérard's chief designer, though the *Sacraments* show less exaggerated characterisation. The subjects of the Old and New Testament are nearer the tradition of Le Rouge, and the other smaller cuts in Part III., such as the *Lord's Prayer* and the *Twelve Apostles*, are not unlike the work of Designer A in Marchant's *Danse Macabre*, but such comparisons do not tempt me to any dogmatic attributions. Vérard also printed an English edition in 1503, under the title *The Art of good lyvyng and good deyng*, illustrated partly with the original cuts and partly with copies (Macf. 67,

STC. 791).[1] The British Museum copy is defective, but there is a perfect copy at Emmanuel College, Cambridge, which contains the original cut of the *Author presenting his Book*.[2] Other English editions are those of Wynkyn de Worde, the *Arte or Crafte to lyve well and to dye well*, 1505 and about 1506 (STC. 792, Cambridge, and 793, B.M.), with small copies

Fig. 405. Royal Hawking Party, with the Author presenting his book, from Tardif, *L'Art de Faulconnerie*, Paris 1492/93.

from Vérard and elsewhere, probably by the hand of the cutter of Wynkyn's *Castell of Laboure*, 1506.[3]

---

[1] See E. Gordon Duff, *The First Two Books printed in the Scottish Language*, Edinburgh Bibliographical Society, 1892–93 (see p. 651).

[2] This cut appeared in England, in Pynson's *Kalender of Shepherdes*, 1506, and in later English books (see p. 651).   [3] See pp. 676 and 733.

In a series of large books published by Vérard after *L'Art de bien Mourir et de bien Vivre*, the designer who may have been responsible for work such as the greater part of Marchant's *Danse Macabre des Femmes*, 1491 and 1492, the *Author presenting his Book to an Ecclesiastic* (fig. 398), and the stronger woodcuts of *L'Art de bien Mourir*, becomes more schematic in his

Fig. 406. Funeral Procession, from the *Croniques de France*, Paris (Regnault) 1514.

angular and trenchant style. In any case it is the author of this group of cuts, constantly repeated in many of Vérard's folios after 1492, whom I designate as Vérard's chief designer.

The *Bataille Judaique* of Josephus, 7th December 1492, contains borders from the *Mer des Hystoires*, and several large cuts reminiscent of the Dupré-Le Rouge manner, e.g. the *Fight in a City* (Macf. pl. xxiii.) and the *Petitioner before a King enthroned in Court*, but there are elements in both these cuts, and the same more strongly evidenced in the frontispiece, the *Reception of Charles VIII. at a City Gate, with the translator presenting his book to the King outside a tent in the background*, which seem to indicate the Vérard designer, less powerfully cut.

Already thoroughly characteristic are the *Royal Hawking Party with the Author presenting his Book* in Guillaume Tardif, *L'Art de Faulconnerie*, 5th January 1492/93 (Cl. ii. 457, Macf. 22, Paris; fig. 405), and the many new large cuts which appeared in the *Croniques de France*, 3 vols., printed by J. Maurand, 9th July–10th September 1493 (Cl. ii. 451, Macf. 30),[1]

Fig. 407. King Arthur and his Knights at the Round Table, from *Tristan*, Paris, about 1506.

La Bible des Poètes (a French version of Ovid's *Metamorphoses*), 1st March 1493/94 (Macf. 31), the *Lancelot du Lac*, 3 vols., 1st July and 30th April 1494 (Macf. 35), and the *Tristan*, about 1494 (Macf. 130).

Cuts from the *Josephus* and each successive book were constantly repeated in different context in their successors. After the issue of the *Lancelot*, large new blocks were seldom cut. Sometimes in the illuminated

---

[1] Sometimes called the *Croniques de Saint-Denys*. Covers the history to the death of Charles VII., 1461. The remarkable cut of a *Funeral Procession* (see fig. 406) is reproduced by Olschki (*Le Livre illustré au XVᵉ siècle*, 1926, fig. 160) as from this edition, but I do not find it before the edition of François Regnault, 1514, where it is used for the Funerals of Charles VII. and of Anne of Brittany, Queen of Louis XII.

vellum copies the heavy illumination not only covers but greatly modifies the design, either to suit the particular occasion or a particular decorative framework. Thus the *Fight in a City* of the *Josephus* is turned into an entirely peaceful scene in one instance where it appears in the British Museum copy of *Les Croniques de France* by covering up all the combatants in colour (vol. i. f. 60, verso), and the same copy shows illuminated architectural framework over cuts which contain no basis for such decorative design.[1]

The *Croniques de France* also contained a multitude of column-cuts, partly from earlier books, which were repeatedly being used in later works.

The *Bible des Poètes* shows most clearly the origin of the designer's style. Its illustrations are based on the woodcuts of the *Metamorphoses* printed by Colard Mansion at Bruges, 1484.[2] The designs are better drawn and more powerfully cut, but the elements of the French designer's open style are already present in his weaker predecessor, who may also have been concerned in illustration in France, about 1480, at Lyon.

Among later books in which Vérard's large cuts from 1492 to 1494 were repeated may be mentioned Boethius, *Le Grant Boèce de Consolation*, 19th August 1494 (Macf. 37); Boccaccio, *Des Nobles Malheureux*, 4th November 1494 (Macf. 38, Paris) (and the later edition, *Des nobles Hommes et Femmes Infortunez*, about 1506, Macf. 157); Boccaccio, *Généalogie des Dieux*, 9th February 1498/99 (Macf. 56, Paris); later editions of *Tristan* (about 1499, Macf. 131, Paris (Arsenal), and about 1506, Macf. 193; see fig. 407); and a later and somewhat smaller folio edition of *Lancelot du Lac* dated 1494, but certainly belonging to the year 1504 (Macf. 166). The last-named book contains the small calligraphic initials with grotesque heads constantly used by Vérard from about 1500 onwards (see fig. 408).[3]

---

[1] Another example where the illumination entirely alters the subject of the underlying wood-cuts is the vellum copy of *Le Jouvencel*, 10th March 1493/94 (Macf. 34), in the British Museum. A second copy on paper in the B.M. shows the same cuts uncoloured. Comparison of the two copies of Boethius, *Le Grant Boèce de Consolation* (1494), in the British Museum (Henry VII.'s vellum copy, C. 22. f. 8, and a paper copy, 169. k. 17), where the illuminated subjects of the vellum are entirely different from the woodcuts, shows the indentation of the paper for the line of the blocks, but hardly a trace (except in one piece of border) of inked blocks. This seems to show that in some vellum copies, intended for illumination, the blocks would be masked from inking and printed blind. Cf. p. 597.

[2] I have not been able to confirm my conjecture that the cut reproduced in fig. 407 came from an earlier edition. The Bibl. Nationale copy of the *Tristan* of about 1494 lacks vol. ii., which should contain this subject; and the block of the same subject in the edition of about 1499 in the Bibl. de l'Arsenal is different (showing trumpeters in upper r.).

[3] E.g. in his *Ortus Sanitatis en françois*, about 1500 (Macf. 140, H.C. 8958), in his edition

Fig. 408. Initial O, with grotesque head, from *Ortus Sanitatis en françois*, Paris, about 1500.

Of the larger historical works issued by Vérard in addition to his *Croniques de France* of 1493, the Froissart, *Croniques de France*, of about 1495 (Cl. ii. 481, Macf. 111), contains no illustrations, but many of the old blocks from works just mentioned reappeared in the *Miroir Hystorial* in five folio volumes, 1495–96 (Macf. 42), and in the *Croniques*, supplementary to Froissart, of Enguerrand de Monstrelet (Macf. 144). The *Gestes Romaines*, of about 1508, Livy's Third Decade, translated by Robert Gaguin (Macf. 164), also included several of the old cuts from the *Ovid* and *Lancelot*, as well as the *Author kneeling before a King* from the *Orosius*, and smaller blocks from J. Millet, *L'Istoire de la Destruction de Troye* (J. Bonhomme, 1484), and other earlier works.

In the woodcuts which appeared in Vérard's books about 1500, of different character from those of his chief designer, there are two noteworthy groups, one exemplified in his *Ogier le Danois* of about 1498 (Macf. 121, Pierpont Morgan),[1] and the other in Robert Gobin, *Les Loups Ravissans*, about 1503 (Macf. 169).

The first group shows work of an expressive designer working somewhat in the manner of the author of Trechsel's *Terence* (Lyon 1493). The subject of the *Cradling of Ogier*, the frontispiece of *Ogier le Danois* (lacking in the British Museum copy), is also reminiscent in its decorative character of the Theatre cut in Trechsel's *Terence*. Comparable work is also seen in the romance *Paris et Vienne* printed by Jean Trepperel, 1498 (Pierpont Morgan 531).

Related in style is a most interesting full-page cut representing the *Prévôt des Marchands et les Eschevins de la Ville de Paris* (fig. 409) which first appeared in *Les Faiz Dictes et Ballades* of Alain Chartier, printed for Vérard by Pierre le Caron, about 1499 (Macf. 109).[2] It was reprinted in *Les Ordonnances de la Prévosté des Marchands et Échevinage de la Ville de Paris*, January 1500/1501 (Cl. ii. 492, Macf. 273). The latter book also contains a variety of interesting little cuts illustrating the various trades of

of the *Mer des Hystoires*, about 1503 (see p. 634). Of his other series of small initial letters, the floral designs on a black ground are the most attractive. For the original and later editions of xv-century Herbals see above, pp. 348-352. The British Museum copy of Vérard's *Ortus* was probably Henry VII.'s (see above, p. 597). For this and other xv-century French Herbals see pp. 640, 670, 672.

[1] Containing 58 prints from 13 blocks.

[2] At least before 25th October 1499, as the colophon gives the address of the Pont Notre Dame.

Fig. 409. From *Les Ordonnances de la Prévosté des Marchands et Échevinage de la Ville de Paris*, Paris 1500/1501.

the city (see fig. 410), and an amusing capital L with nude woman, monkey and bird on the last leaf, to which allusion has already been made.[1]

Other examples of the group are found in the main series of woodcut illustrations in Vérard's *Terence en françois* of about 1500 (Cl. ii. 487, Macf. 152). These illustrations are based on the *Terence* printed by Grüninger at Strassburg, 1496, not on Trechsel's Lyon edition. Vérard also follows Grüninger in his composite subjects, making up his subjects by fitting together a limited number of block-pieces with figure, architecture or landscape. Most of these subjects form oblongs of the width of the text; in one case separate pieces are used to make up a full-page subject with three rows of figures (f. 156, before *Heautontimoroumenos*).

Fig. 410. Timber-haulers, from *Les Ordonnances de la Prévosté des Marchands*, Paris 1500/1501.

Coming to the second group, the characteristic cuts in Robert Gobin, *Les Loups Ravissans*, Paris (Vérard), about 1503 (Macf. 169), occur in the second part dealing with Death and Humanity (fig. 411).[2] They show a use of the swelling line, a more natural property of line-engraving, for the mere pressure of the burin in the copper would broaden the intaglio line.

Other examples occur in the *Terence*, just mentioned, in its full-page frontispiece representing the *Theatre*, and a frontispiece to *Andria*, f. 4, which is used later in *Phormio*, f. 290, both based, like the rest of the illustrations, on Grüninger's blocks.

Other woodcuts by the same designer (or cutter) occur in the following works:

> [Valerius Maximus] *Le Livre de Valère le Grant*, Paris, Vérard, about 1500 (Fairfax Murray 558).
> Livy, *Les Decades*, published by G. Eustace and F. Regnault, Paris 1515 (one cut after the *Judgment of Agamemnon* in the *Bible des*

---

[1] See p. 659.
[2] The subject reproduced in fig. 411 appeared also in the *Kalendayr of the Shyppars*, printed by Vérard, 1503. See p. 651.

LE CARON specialised in popular historical works; he was the gazetteer of current events, issuing such works as Pierre d'Urfé, *Ordonnance faicte par Messire Pierre d'Urfé pour l'enterrement du Roy Charles VIII.*, *L'Entrée du Roy Louis XII. à sa bonne ville de Paris*, 1498, and *Les Joustes faictes à Paris après l'entrée du Roy Louis XII.*, 1498 (Cl. ii. 85-88, Paris, St. Geneviève). We have already mentioned Le Caron as the first to use the capital L with two grotesque heads which was later in Vérard's hands,[1] and he also used two other varieties of such capitals which do not appear in Vérard's stock (see Cl. ii. 92, 93).

Fig. 413. Printer's mark of Thielmann Kerver, Paris.

Le Caron also issued a *Grant Herbier* between 1495 and 1500, largely based on the *Gart der Gesuntheit* (Mainz 1485), of which there is a complete copy in the Bibliothèque St. Geneviève, Paris (Pell. 1102, Cl. ii. 83).[2] It contains Le Caron's second mark (Meyer 112), which was not used before 1495. Before this date Le Caron used Vérard's mark with his own name inserted (Meyer 111).[3] There was an earlier French edition under the title of *Arbolayre* (n.d., n.p., n.pr.) which was probably printed by P. Metlinger, at Besançon, about 1487–88 (Pell. 1101, Cl. iv. 479, Paris).

LE PETIT LAURENS printed an edition of *L'Ordinaire des Crestiens* for Jean Petit, about 1497 (British Museum, IB. 40265).[4] The title-page has a capital L with two grotesque heads, and beneath it Jehan Petit's earliest printer's mark (Meyer 136). This mark was already cracked in Jean Petit's

[1] See p. 658.

[2] A perfect and uncoloured copy was recently acquired by the British Museum (see British Museum Quarterly, May 1935).

[3] For the original and later editions of the xv-century Herbals see above, pp. 348-352, and the articles by A. C. Klebs quoted in that place.

[4] This edition is described in detail, and the title-page reproduced in Catalogue VIII. No. 74 of E. P. Goldschmidt & Co., London. The B.M. copy has a mutilated title-page, but enough remains to show that its woodcuts correspond to these in the Goldschmidt copy, on which the above description is based.

edition of Joannes de Sacro Busto, *Sphera Mundi*, 1498/99 (B.M., and Fairfax Murray 492), which gives a limit for the dating of *L'Ordinaire*. Verso of the title is the cut of a *Sainted Bishop writing, with two prophets above,* which originally appeared in Vérard's *Art de bien Mourir*, 1492. A variant of this edition, without Petit's mark, and assigned to Vérard (Macf. 272, Copinger ii. 4492), is in the Bibliothèque Mazarine, Paris, so that Le Petit Lauréns probably supplied both publishers. Claudin describes another edition printed by Le Petit Laurens for François Regnault, before 1499 (Cl. ii. 118), with various cuts from *L'Art de bien Vivre et de*

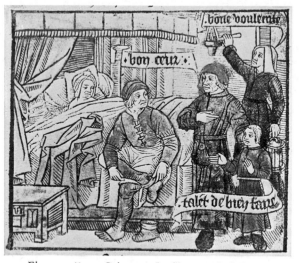

Fig. 414. From Gringore, *Le Chasteau de Labour,*
Paris 1500/1501.

bien Mourir, the full-page cut of the *Joyes de Paradis* being a modified copy.[1]

The work was an exposition of the Catholic religion for the laity, and was probably originally written in French between 1467 and 1469. Its popularity is shown by the existence of four other editions issued by Vérard between 1490 and 1495 (Macf. 11, 20, 39, 44), but except for a single cut in the first of these (Paris) they are without illustration. It was translated into English as the *Ordinarye of Crysten Men* by Andrew Chertsey, and printed by Wynkyn de Worde, 1502 and 1506, each edition with different cuts, poor copies from Vérard's *L'Art de bien Vivre et de bien Mourir*, etc. (STC. 5198, 5199).

A good series of copies of the Basle cuts illustrating Sebastian Brant's *Narrenschiff* appears to have been first used in *La Nef des folz du Monde*, printed by J. LAMBERT for J. PHILIPPE (MANSTENER) and G. DE MARNEF, 1497 (Cl. ii. 227). Proctor (8257) attributes its printing to Baligault,

---

[1] This block is printed in Julian Notary's *Golden Legend*, London 1503/04 (see p. 734), and in Hopyl's *Passionael*, Paris (for W. Houtmart, Brussels) 1505, 1507. Claudin states that it also appears in editions of the *Légende Dorée* printed by Jean de Vingle, Lyon 1497, and by La Barre, Paris 1499, and as late as 1529 by Jodocus Badius, in *Encomium Trium Mariarum.*

who must have had close relations with Lambert, for they both used the same device, *Two monkeys beneath a tree* (Meyer 82, 83, and 108, 109). The blocks were used in 1498 by J. Sacon at Lyon,[1] and again at Paris in the French edition of Badius, *Stultifera Navis*.

Fig. 415. Mark of the Publisher Antoine Vérard, Paris.

The *Stultifera Navis* of Jodocus Badius is a shorter satirical poem suggested by Brant's work, which was issued in both Latin and French editions (the French translation by J. Drouyn) in or about 1500–1501. The Latin edition, printed by KERVER for the brothers de Marnef, is dated 20th February 1500/1501; the French edition, *La Nef des Folles*, was printed by Le Petit Laurens for Geoffroi de Marnef, without date, about the same period (Cl. ii. 127). Both editions contain six new woodcuts of lively design by the author of the cuts in Vérard's *Terence*. Kerver's edition is embellished with his own beautiful device of *Two Unicorns by a Tree* (Meyer 102; fig. 413). The French issue has in addition about a dozen cuts from the editions of *La Nef des folz* of Sebastian Brant, which have just been described.

I have already referred to JEAN TREPPEREL for his romance of *Paris et Vienne* and his edition of *Le Grand Testament de Villon*, and I would here mention another popular work, *Les Quinze Joyes de Mariage* (issued about 1499), for its illustration of a *peasant family*, a woodcut of little quality, but of entertaining character.

Most attractive of all the little popular books of the end of the century is Pierre Gringore, *Le Chasteau de Labour*, printed by PIGOUCHET for VOSTRE, 1499 (Bibl. Mazarine, Paris) and 1500/1501 (British Museum). It traces the life and thoughts of a young married couple, with their joys and sorrows, the contests between the virtues and vices, and the final triumph of virtue. The book opens with two most delicate little cuts,

[1] See p. 614.

including a *garden of love*,[1] followed by a series more broadly designed showing the lovers in bed surrounded by a variety of figures with their appropriate mottoes; then seven small cuts with dotted ground representing

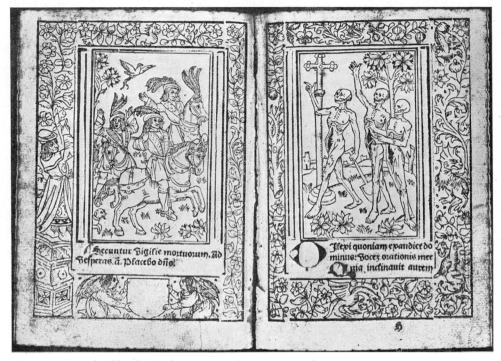

Fig. 416. Les Trois Vifs et les Trois Morts; opening (two pages) from *Horae*, Paris (Dupré), about 1488.

tourneys of the virtues and vices as mounted female figures; finally another scene of the lovers in which the husband rises from bed, visits the castle of labour, with its various employments, and returns in the end to a well-earned meal and rest in his own house. The little *Tourneys of the Virtues and Vices* are in the manner of the illustrations to contemporary *Horae*,[2] and a *Tree of Jesse* in similar style which appears on the last page is found in *Horae* issued by Vostre. The others, in black line, are near in style to Vérard's Terence designer, full of life and individuality.

Several other French editions of the *Chasteau de Labour* are known or recorded, and there were also editions in English printed by Vérard in Paris,

[1] Which came from the calendar portion of *Horae* printed by Pigouchet for Vostre (e.g. 20th March, 17th April 1496–97, B.M., IA. 40321).

[2] I have not found these blocks in Pigouchet's *Horae*, but inferior copies appeared in Vérard's *Sarum Horae* of about 1505 (B.M., C. 35. e. 4, see p. 691).

Fig. 417. Dives and Lazarus, from *Horae*, Paris
(Dupré), about 1488–90.

about 1503, and in London by Richard Pynson, about 1505 and 1506, and Wynkyn de Worde, 1506 (STC. 12379–82).[1] The woodcuts in Pynson's editions are distinctly better than Wynkyn's; in fact they are almost as well cut and as expressive as the original series. A perfect copy of Pynson's edition of about 1505 (STC. 12380) came to the British Museum from the Huth Collection. In Pynson's edition the *Tourneys of the Virtues and Vices* show some black ground without dotted work; in Wynkyn's issue these subjects are in black line only.

Pierre Gringore was also the author of *Le Casteau d'Amours*, issued by Michel Le Noir, 1500. It contains a title cut rather in the manner of the copyist of Brant's *Narrenschiff* recently mentioned, a delicate full-page of *David and Bathsheba*[2] (135 × 91 mm.) (which may have been made for a *Horae*), and Le Noir's excellent device with the two negresses (Meyer 114).

BOOKS OF HOURS [3]

Venice was the chief centre in the production of illustrated Missals, during the fifteenth century, but Paris publishers and printers first de-

---

[1] See *The Castell of Labour, translated from the French of Pierre Gringore by Alexander Barclay. Reprinted in facsimile from Wynkyn de Worde's edition of 1506*, with an introduction by A. W. Pollard, Edinburgh (Roxburghe Club) 1905.

[2] With cartouche in the centre for lettering DAVID, in the same form as cuts in Dupré's *Horae*, B.M., IA. 39817, but somewhat larger. At the foot of the block it shows Goliath overthrown by David.

[3] Apart from the general works on French woodcut books, see A. W. Pollard, *The Illustration in French Books of Hours, 1486–1500*, Bibliographica, iii. (1897), 430; Paul Lacombe, *Livres*

veloped, and perhaps originated, the little Books of Hours which form the most characteristic achievement of early French wood-cut. In manuscript form the 'Hours of the Virgin' (*Horae Beatae Virginis Mariae*) had been favourite books of private devotion in England and France from the XI to the XIV centuries and equal in popularity to the Psalter. These manuscript *Horae* generally include: (1) Kalendar, (2) Cursus Evangelii, (3) Hours of the Virgin, (4) Hours of the Cross, (5) Hours of the Holy Ghost, (6) The Seven Penitential Psalms and the Litany, (7) Office of the Dead, (8) Memoriae, or Suffrages of various Saints;[1] and the subjects which are most regularly illustrated in the wood-cuts of the printed *Horae* are the Zodiac Man, the History

Fig. 418. David and Goliath, from *Horae*, Paris (Meslier) 1489/90.

of the Virgin and of Christ, the History of Susannah, the Parable of the Prodigal Son, the Fifteen Signs of the Judgment, the Theological and Cardinal Virtues, the Seven Capital Sins, the Twelve Sibyls, and the Dance of Death. These subjects are interspersed with contemporary *genre* in the same way as medieval church sculptors mingled saints and scripture with their own translations, simple or grotesque, from everyday life. The French illuminated *Horae* of the XV century were the immediate models for the woodcut books with their complete series of borders on every page, and occasional blocks printed in the text within the borders. This became the regular form of the illustrated *Horae* printed in France, only a few of

d'heures imprimées au XVe et au XVIe siècles conservées dans les bibliothèques publiques de Paris, Catalogue, Paris 1907; H. Bohatta, *Bibliographie des Livres d'Heures,* Vienna 1900 (2nd ed. 1924).

[1] See Dr. M. R. James, *Descriptive Catalogue of MSS. in Fitzwilliam Museum, Cambridge,* 1896.

the earliest examples being without the borders. Outside France (in fact outside Paris), examples of *Horae* printed and illustrated in this form are rare. There are a few in Italy, apparently inspired by the French model,[1] rare examples in the Netherlands,[2] Germany[3] and England.[4] In Germany and the Netherlands the 'Hours' of devotion tended to centre round the Life and Passion of Christ, rather than round the Life of the Virgin. In France series of woodcuts of the Passion are in general far less common than in the North.

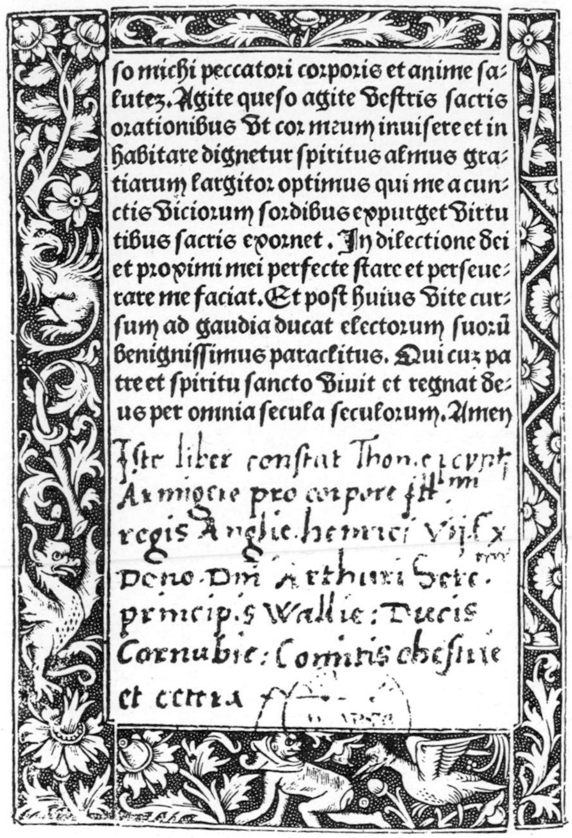
so michi peccatori corporis et anime sa-
lutez. Agite queso agite vestris sacris
orationibus ut cor meum inuisere et in
habitare dignetur spiritus almus gra-
tiarum largitor optimus qui me a cun-
ctis viciorum sordibus expurget et virtu
tibus sacris exornet. In dilectione dei
et proximi mei perfecte stare et perseue-
rare me faciat. Et post huius vite cur-
sum ad gaudia ducat electorum suorum
benignissimus paraclitus. Qui cum pa
tre et spiritu sancto viuit et regnat deus per omnia secula seculorum. Amen

Fig. 419. Last page of the *Sarum Horae*, Paris, about 1495.

It is remarkable how few copies of French *Horae* in existence correspond exactly in their contents. Apart from the special forms required by the use of the various dioceses, the publishers no doubt introduced minor differences in the text, or in the arrangement of the cuts, to answer the demands of various clients. The borders in their most regular form were printed from four blocks: in other cases they were made up by the combination of a considerable number of smaller pieces, and the disposition of such pieces would lend itself to great variety of setting. In a short survey I can do little more than sketch the general development in manner of work, citing the most important of the early editions, and referring to a few others typical of the various styles.

[1] See p. 500.

[2] See pp. 581, 584. *Ghetiden* is the Dutch equivalent for Canonical Hours (*Vigilie*), and *Ghetidenboeck* is used both for Books of Hours of the Virgin and for the Breviary (i.e. the office for the canonical hours, the daily service of the Church).

[3] See pp. 328 and 340. *Zeitglöcklein* or *Horologium* (*Devotionis*) are the usual titles.

[4] See pp. 715-719. Caxton's *Fifteen O'es*, 1491, and *Horae*, printed by Wynkyn de Worde, 1494.

The early examples are largely in black line; then a plain black ground is used to throw the design into relief (e.g. in an edition issued by Caillaut about 1490, B.M., IA. 39507)[1] and punches of various patterns (plain dots, or stars) are used to vary the design whether black on white or white on black (e.g. in edition of Dupré, 4th February 1488/89, B.M., Proctor 8045, IA. 39821); while from about 1496 a regularly dotted black ground makes an important part of the decorative character (e.g. in the edition printed by Pigouchet for Simon Vostre, 20th March and 17th April 1496, B.M., Proctor 8189, IA. 40321). The delicate line required in these little books, and particularly the manner of punching dots in a black ground, was more adapted to metal than wood, and in Dupré's edition of 4th February 1488/89 it is expressly stated that the blocks are of copper (f. 2, verso, *C"est le repertoire des histoires et figures de la bible . . . contenues dedens les vignettes de ces presentes heures imprimées en cuyure*).

Fig. 420. David and Bathsheba, from *Horae*, Paris (Dupré) 1488/89.

In the subsequent edition printed by Dupré for Vérard, 10th April 1489/90, the phrase *imprimées en cuyure* is omitted. These facts seem to imply that, both earlier and later, cuts of the sort were printed from wood blocks, but it is quite possible that here and there, even before this date, the French illustrators may have used metal for some of their delicate blocks. But they probably used metal more often for such

[1] See p. 685.

subjects as might be so frequently repeated as to justify repetition by metal casts, e.g. in initial letters and other decorative pieces. Vérard's device (Meyer 160) generally shows a bend in the upper right corner of the border-line which seems to mark it as metal rather than wood (fig. 415).[1]

Fig. 421. The Printer adoring the Virgin, from *Horae*, Paris (Dupré) 1488/89.

The best of the French *Horae* show borders spaced and laid out on the page with a perfect balance, having regard to the opening of two pages rather than the single page. The general principle of spacing which the good book-designers have followed is a gradual increase in width of margin (or border), beginning with the inner margin, and increasing with the upper, outer and lower margins respectively. This proportion is well illustrated in the opening reproduced from one of Dupré's *Horae* in the British Museum, IA. 39817 (fig. 416).[2] The borders would count as margin, so that outside the border-cut practically no margin would be left.

Most of the French Books of Hours were printed in the last decade of the xv century, and the first two or three decades of the xvi century. In view of the unity of their general character and the consistent richness of their decorative elements, these books offer most excellent material for estimating the gradual progress of Renaissance design. In the earliest examples of Dupré and others, the decoration is in the pure tradition of the medieval French illuminators; by the middle of the 'nineties there are frequent examples of Italian renaissance in candelabra and other classical inventions; by the beginning of the xvi century the Italian elements predominate, reaching their culmination in the refinement of Geoffroy Tory's books.[3]

The earliest examples, as we have noted, are mostly in black line. Then, after an intermediate stage in which dotted work predominates in

---

[1] An even more striking example of a bent border, which could only be a metal, is Richard Pynson's printer's mark (see p. 732 and fig. 466).

[2] See p. 683.

[3] See pp. 697-698.

the backgrounds, representing the most characteristic phase in the development of French woodcut *Horae*, there is a reversion to black line, and the somewhat cold severity of the Italian renaissance, as interpreted by a classicist of the pure style of Geoffroy Tory. In the middle phase borders tended to a variety of rich embellishment, decorative frills above and scroll or figured bases below (e.g. in *Horae* printed by Pigouchet for Vostre, about 1496, B.M., C. 27. e. 2, by Jehan Pychore and Remy de Laistre, 5th April 1503, B.M., Print Room, and C. 29. k. 21, and by Thielmann Kerver, 22nd June 1506, B.M., C. 29. f. 8).

Fig. 422. The Annunciation to the Shepherds, from *Horae*, Paris (Dupré), about 1490.

Most of the *Horae* are practically of pocket-book size (*Petites Heures*), the woodcut surface (which is only slightly less than the full page) varying from about $4\frac{1}{2} \times 3$ inches (e.g. Denis Meslier's edition of 14th February 1489/90)[1] to about $6\frac{1}{2} \times 4\frac{1}{4}$ inches (Vérard's edition of 8th February 1489/90).[2]

Then there is a series of somewhat larger *Horae* printed by Vérard, for the most part inscribed *imprimées par le commandement du roi*, in which the woodcut surface measures about $8 \times 5\frac{1}{4}$ inches, e.g. an edition of about 1490 (Macf. 204),[3] the work of Vérard's chief designer. These editions are generally called *Grandes Heures*, or *Heures Royales*, but not all the *Grandes Heures* are specifically printed by Royal Command,[4] while an

[1] See p. 685.   [2] See p. 689.   [3] See p. 690.
[4] E.g. that of 20th August 1490 (Macf. 202, Paris) has no reference to the Royal Command.

(4) Anonymous printer, n.d. (about 1492?). Pierpont Morgan 567. Woodcut surface about $4\frac{1}{4} \times 2\frac{3}{4}$ inches. The blocks from Dupré's stock, partly the same as in B.M., IA. 39817 (No. 1 of this group).

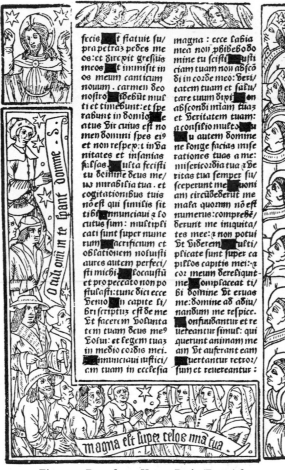

Fig. 425. Page from *Horae*, Paris (Dupré for Vérard) 1489/90.

All these four editions show four-piece black-line borders, chiefly in outline, with most attractive designs of branch, bird and beast, with an occasional figure of an angel making music and the like. They contain small subjects in about three sizes: the largest about $4\frac{1}{2} \times 3$ inches (or slightly over); the middle size about $3 \times 1\frac{7}{8}$ inches; the smallest, chiefly for single figures of saints, the size of initial letters, about $1\frac{1}{2} \times 1$ inch. The Oxford edition is entirely different in its blocks from B.M., IA. 39817, but the subjects are generally the same design with differences in detail.[1]

The Oxford borders are even more delicate than those of the British Museum edition, and a certain wiry quality of line gives it almost the character of metal even if such be not actually the case. The Caillaut edition reprints some blocks from IA. 39817, and replaces others, which may have passed into other hands (such as the *Dives and Lazarus*). In one case, that of *Les Trois Vifs et les Trois Morts*, the subject represented in two blocks in the British Museum (fig. 416) and Oxford issues is combined by Caillaut on a single block.

[1] E.g. the *Dives and Lazarus* of B.M., IA. 39817 shows a single serving-man at the table and no bed in the background; the same subject in the Oxford edition shows two serving-men and a bed in the background.

In subtle draughtsmanship, charm of decoration and harmony of page, these editions are the most perfect little books of their kind.

This pocket-book Caillaut edition must not be confused with another *Horae* of somewhat larger form (wood-cut surface about $5\frac{7}{8} \times 3\frac{1}{2}$ inches) issued by Caillaut about 1490 (British Museum, Proctor 7963, IA. 39507). The borders are narrow as in the case of the copper-plate Dupré (B.M., IA. 39821). In the calendar section they are in the style of the pocket-book Caillaut, but in the rest of the book are for the most part divided into panels with figures, largely busts and half-lengths. Most of the work is in black line, but its upper and outer corner-pieces are designed on a plain black ground. The larger subjects are partly the same as in the pocket-book edition, including the *Dives and Lazarus* from the British Museum issue of Dupré, IA. 39817.

Nearly related to the Dupré-Caillaut pocket-book group is another *Horae*, printed by Dupré

Fig. 426. The Annunciation to the Shepherds, from *Horae* (Grandes Heures), Paris (Vérard), about 1490.

for DENIS MESLIER, 14th February 1489/90, of which the only copy known to me is that of the Pierpont Morgan Library, New York, No. 565 (from the Ashburnham, No. 2023, and Bennett Collections). The borders are of similar type, delicate outline designs, chiefly of branch, bird and beast, with occasional figures; some in a single piece (e.g. round the *Annunciation* and *Crucifixion*), but mostly in four pieces. It has already been noted that seven of the little subjects, measuring about $2\frac{7}{8} \times 1\frac{7}{8}$ inches, are from the same blocks as the set of ten *Horae* subjects in the second volume of Le Rouge's *Mer des Hystoires* of the preceding year (February 1488/89).[1] The borders,

---

[1] See p. 634. The subjects which correspond are the *Visitation, Nativity, Annunciation to Shepherds, Adoration of the Kings, Pietà, Coronation of the Virgin* and *St. John the Evangelist*.

Many of the same plates (border and subject) were used in another unique edition of Dupré, issued in 1490 and printed in three colours, red, blue and green, in addition to the black type (B.M., Proctor 8047, IA. 39829). No page shows more than two colours, but as each of these would require separate printing from the black type, there is little wonder that it appears to have remained an experiment. It is without the complete borders, and the pages are made up in various combinations between the larger subjects, the side-panels with three subjects, and little upright panels of initial letter size. Some fifteen new subjects are added, chiefly from the Bible, corresponding in size to the *Death*, *Annunciation* and *Zodiac Man*, in the edition of 4th February 1488/89 (about $4\frac{3}{8} \times 3\frac{1}{8}$ inches). They are among the best subject illustrations in contemporary *Horae*, with the characteristic finesse of well-engraved metal-cuts,

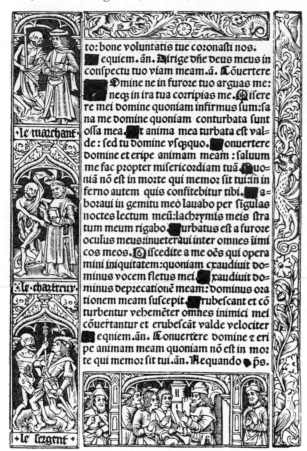

Fig. 429. Page from *Horae*, Paris (Pigouchet for Vostre) 1496/97.

and I have not found them in any other editions (see the page with the *Annunciation to the Shepherds*, which also includes a border-piece with a Siren, not known to me elsewhere; fig. 422). Another border-piece, remarkable for its vivid draughtsmanship, as if from the life, is the small lower panel with four half-figures in profile (see fig. 423). Dupré's beautiful *Printer's mark with the Two Swans* occurs in both these metal-cut editions, though my reproduction is made from a copy of Bonnor, *L'Arbre des Batailles*, of 1493 (fig. 424).[1]

[1] See p. 635.

Another slightly larger *Horae* printed by Dupré (woodcut surface about $6 \times 3\frac{3}{4}$ inches) was published by Vérard, 10th April 1489/90,[1] with the woodcut title *Les Figures de la Bible*, the L being a characteristic initial with a woman's head (B.M., Proctor 8046, IA. 39825). It carries on the style of Dupré's *Horae*, IA. 39817, with its marginal decoration of branch, bird and beast, but has new features in its designs of bare tree-trunks, and many other new subjects, religious and genre, in its borders. The borders, which are entirely in black line, are made up of pieces of various sizes and shapes, chiefly of subjects and figures in rectangular compartments. A characteristic page, sig. f. 1, verso, is reproduced in fig. 425, and in its clear and strong woodcut forms an immediate comparison with the metal-cuts reproduced in figs. 421–24. Many of the subjects, especially those in the L-shaped corner-pieces, show very vivid characteristics of face and figure, as if done from the life (e.g. sig. h. 2, verso).

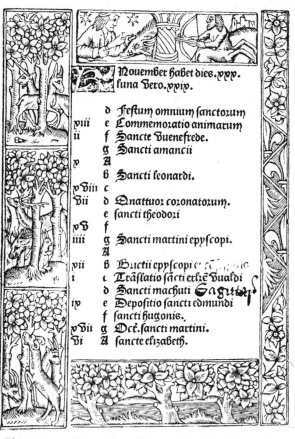

Fig. 430. Page from *Sarum Horae*, Paris (Pigouchet for Jean Richard) 1494.

Another of Vérard's *Horae*, issued 8th February 1489/90 (Macf. 199, Paris), with woodcut surface about $6\frac{1}{2} \times 4\frac{1}{4}$ inches, has attractive black-line borders, in Dupré's manner. Moreover, its Bible and other subjects in the text are for the most part the small uprights (about $3 \times 1\frac{7}{8}$ inches) which appeared in the earlier Dupré (IA. 39817), so that the same printer was probably responsible for this edition as well. The borders and other

[1] An edition 3rd April 1488/89 (Macf. 198, Toulouse) appears to be the earliest of the *Horae* published by Vérard with complete borders.

cuts of this edition were reprinted by Laurens Philippe, 1493 (B.M., IA. 40633).

I have already spoken of the *Grandes Heures* of Vérard, but would

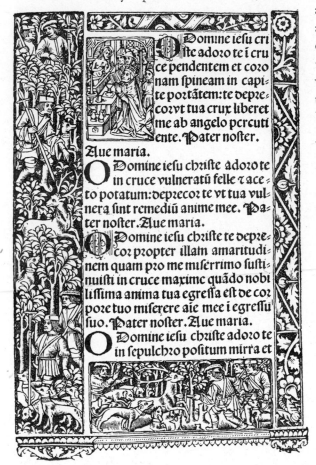

add a few further notes about the British Museum copy of about 1490 (Macf. 204, IB. 41116). In style of work its borders are near the smaller *Horae* printed by Dupré for Vérard, 10th April 1489/90, (B.M., IA. 39825), and entirely in black line, but it is less delicately cut and lacks sensitiveness in quality. It is not far removed from the harder characteristics of the later cuts of Vérard's chief designer. There is a good series of large cuts, about $4\frac{1}{2} \times 3$ inches in size, many of which had also appeared in the Dupré-Vérard *Horae* just mentioned (IA. 39825). The *Annunciation to the Shepherds, with a Country Dance* (fig. 426), and a contemporary *Funeral Service* are particularly interesting. These cuts are

Fig. 431. Page from *Horae*, Paris (Pigouchet for Vostre) n.d.

near in size and style to four which had appeared in the early Dupré-Caillaut group, but the latter generally had rectangular cartouches for inscriptions in the middle of the subject (e.g. *Dives and Lazarus*, fig. 417).

Most of the woodcuts in this edition reappeared in several other *Grandes Heures* of about the same date, e.g. one example of the *Rouen Use*[1] in the

---

[1] The *Horae* quoted may be assumed to be of the *Roman Use* (*ad usum Romanum*), and in Latin, unless otherwise described. The printer's notes and colophon are generally in French, even in the Latin *Horae*.

British Museum (IB. 41119). In general the Paris printers seem to have bestowed less care on their local *Horae* than on those of the *Roman Use*, the latter being much more frequently printed on vellum and often illuminated, no doubt on account of a richer clientèle.

I would mention one other local *Horae* published by Vérard, that of the *Sarum Use* of about 1505, with woodcut surface of about $7\frac{7}{8} \times 5\frac{1}{8}$ inches (B.M., C. 35. e. 4). There is considerable variety in quality as in all the later books of Vérard, cruder cuts of saints being mixed with some of the finer early cuts. It contains a series of *Tourneys of the Virtues and Vices* (oblong panels at the foot of page) copied from a finer set in Gringore's *Chasteau de Labour*, printed by Pigouchet for Vostre, 1499 and 1500/1501,[1] which in their turn were probably used in other *Horae*.

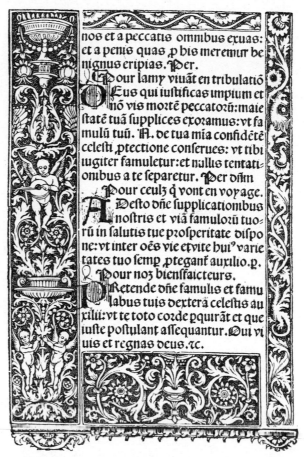

Fig. 432. Page from *Horae*, Paris (Pigouchet for Vostre) n.d.

The combination of the printer PIGOUCHET with the publisher SIMON VOSTRE[2] produced the most numerous and most typical of xv-century French Books of Hours. The earliest *Horae* printed by Pigouchet were entirely in black line in a style nearly related to the earlier issues of Vérard, and in their comparative weakness more on a level with such a book as one attributed to Denis Meslier in the British Museum (IA. 40274).[3] I refer in particular to the edition of 1st December 1491 in the British

---

[1] See pp. 674, 675.
[2] See J. Renouvier, *Des gravures sur bois dans les livres de Simon Vostre*, Paris 1862.
[3] See p. 686.

Museum, with woodcut surface measuring about $6\frac{1}{8} \times 4\frac{1}{4}$ inches, the side borders mostly in upright rectangular compartments, little figures of prophets and sibyls, etc., in the lower borders (IA. 40287). A

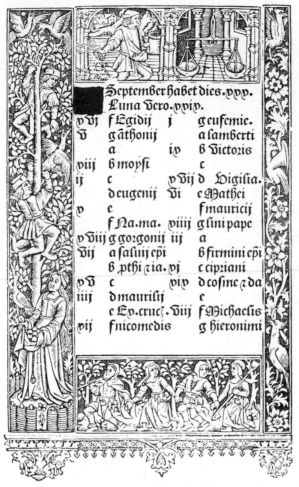

second copy in the British Museum of the same date bears the device of Marnef (IA. 40288), and most of the same blocks occur (with text set up in single instead of double column) in an edition by Geoffroi de Marnef, 20th June 1493 (B.M., IA. 40277), and in an edition of the *Troyes Use*, issued by the same publisher, 13th August 1493 (B.M., IA. 40277). Brunet described a *Horae* printed by Pigouchet for Vostre on 16th September 1488, but Claudin was unable to locate it, and the earliest Pigouchet known to him is that of 1st December 1491 just described.

Of the actual combination of Pigouchet and Vostre the earliest *Horae* which I have examined is that of 8th May 1492, of pocket size (woodcut surface about $4\frac{1}{2} \times 3\frac{1}{4}$ inches) and with

Fig. 433. Page from *Horae*, Paris (Kerver) 1506.

black-line borders of branch, bird and beast, near in style to Dupré, though hardly so good (B.M., IA. 40302). The only cut on black ground is a little *Mass of St. Gregory*, near the end. Editions dated 2nd August 1493 and 22nd August 1493 (B.M., IA. 40306 and 40308) show the same style of border decoration, but the form is larger (woodcut surface about 6×4 inches).

Pigouchet's most characteristic work for Vostre appears after the

middle of the 'nineties, e.g. in editions of 23rd January 1496/97 (B.M.,
IA. 40318) and of 20th March and 17th April 1496/97 (B.M., IA.

Fig. 434. Page from *Horae*, Paris (J. Pychore and Rémy de Laistre) 1503.

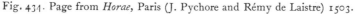

40321). They are both of the same form and size, woodcut surface about
$5\frac{1}{2} \times 3\frac{1}{2}$ inches, the borders of both are frequently made up of several
little upright panels, and both have a portion of the work (though the

lesser part) on a dotted ground, notably in the borders with the *Dance of Death*. The chief difference between the two editions lies in the calendar. In the earlier issue the lower borders contain little subjects, partly on

dotted ground: in the later issue these lower pieces contain a delightful series of children's games. These black-line woodcuts of contemporary genre are more subtle and delicate in cutting than anything in Vérard's *Horae*, just as his dotted borders, such as those with the *Dance of Death*, show an unrivalled accomplishment and finesse.

Fig. 435. Mark of the Publisher Gillet Hardouin, Paris.

A *Sarum Horae* printed by Pigouchet for Jean Richard of Rouen in 1494, of the same size, contains some different material, with attractive border-pieces such as that of unicorns, stags and goats amid trees, here reproduced (B.M., IA. 40311, STC. 15879; fig. 430). A similar series of borders appears in an undated edition of the *Roman Use* at Oxford (Proctor 8182, 8° Rawl. 1092), and adapted into larger form, made up with further border-pieces to about $6\frac{1}{4}$ or $6\frac{1}{2} \times 4\frac{3}{8}$ inches, in another issue of 20th August 1496 (B.M., IA. 40315).

The smaller form was continued in various issues in the following years. One of 8th August 1497 (B.M., IA. 40338) has a delightful addition in the border with the *Apple Harvest*; another in the British Museum, with Calendar 1502–20 (C. 29. h. 18), has additional subjects of *Stag-hunts* (fig. 431).[1] This issue has additional ornamentation in decorated bases below the lower borders, and there is considerably more decoration in the style of the Italian Renaissance (see fig. 432).

In addition to the ornate bases further frills are added at the top of the page in certain later editions, of which the British Museum possesses a handsome example with almanac covering the years 1508–28, and probably issued near the beginning of that cycle (C. 41. e. 7; complete woodcut surface about $7\frac{1}{2} \times 4\frac{1}{2}$ inches).

Besides the *Horae* in the *Roman Use*, a very large number of the local books were issued by Pigouchet and Vostre. The *Sarum Horae* of 16th May 1498, with woodcut surface $5\frac{1}{2} \times 3\frac{1}{2}$ inches, occurs in a good uncoloured example in the British Museum (IA. 40335), similar in material to IA. 40321 of 1496/97, and put together with more care than was often accorded to the local *Horae*.

[1] These appeared as early as 22nd August 1498 in the larger form (B.M., IA. 40340).

THIELMANN KERVER was both printer and publisher of *Horae*, and only less prolific than Pigouchet and Vostre. But he was far from attaining their distinction, and constantly repeated their motives in his borders, with

Fig. 436. The Rape of Deianeira: Mark of the Publishers Gillet and Germain Hardouin, Paris.

considerable loss in quality. He also divided his work fairly equally between black-line cuts and blocks with dotted backgrounds, made considerable use of Italian renaissance ornament, of frills at the top of page and ornamental bases. He is seen at his best in an edition of 22nd June 1506 in

the British Museum (C. 29. f. 8), and his versions of Pigouchet's *Apple Harvest, with a Country Dance* (fig. 433) are as strong if not as delicate as the originals. Pigouchet's hunting scenes are also repeated. One of his earliest *Horae* is that of the *Sarum Use*, printed for Jean Richard, Rouen 1497 (B.M., IA. 40487). He used an excellent device of *Two Unicorns* (fig. 413).

Among the most elaborate of the *Horae* is the edition printed by J. PYCHORE and RÉMY DE LAISTRE, 5th April 1503, with woodcut surface of about $8\frac{1}{2} \times 5$ inches (B.M., Print Room, and C. 29. k. 21; see fig. 434). The whole-page subjects, in elaborate architectural frames, exceed the space of the borders. Many of the subjects of contemporary genre are repeated from Pigouchet, but classical ornament predominates.

Fig. 437. Adoration of the Kings, from *Horae*, Paris (Tory) 1525/26.

With the publishers of the family of HARDOUIN we are further into the XVI century, their earliest *Horae* being issued in 1504/05. The edition printed by Antoine Chappiel for Gillet Hardouin, 9th January 1504/05, with woodcut surface $7\frac{1}{2} \times 4\frac{3}{4}$ inches (B.M., C. 41. e. 4), is characteristic and shows his work as inferior to Kerver, not to speak of Pigouchet and Vostre. The page is made up of a great variety of blocks, and in the foot-pieces little blocks are regularly turned sideways merely to make up space.

One of their most interesting *Horae* is the edition of a narrow upright form, commonly called the *Agenda* form, printed by Antoine Chappiel for Gillet Hardouin, 19th January 1504–05 (B.M., C. 29. k. 24). Its woodcut surface is about $8\frac{1}{8} \times 3$ inches; the cuts are largely on dotted ground, and the copy, the only one known, is an excellent uncoloured impression. Hardouin's small device of woodmen on the title-page is one of its most attractive features (fig. 435).

A larger device used by the firm, with the *Rape of Deianeira* (fig. 436), is another of their most attractive cuts, and it is here reproduced from an edition printed by G. Anabat for Gillet & Germain Hardouin, with almanac 1507–20 (B.M., C. 29. h. 8), one of their finest and most richly ornamented issues. Both in style of work, and in motives used, the cuts derive largely from Pigouchet and Vostre.

Though lying well beyond my period of the xv century, I would reproduce two pages from *Horae* published by GEOFFROY TORY[1] to illustrate the last phase of which I

Fig. 438. Death, from *Horae*, Paris (Tory) 1527.

have spoken in describing the general development of French *Horae*.

The edition printed by Simon de Colines for Geoffroy Tory, 16th January 1525/26, is the more severely classic of the two specimens in the British

[1] See Auguste Bernard, *Geoffroy Tory*, Paris 1857, 2nd ed., 1865 (English translation by G. B. Ives, Boston and New York 1909); A. W. Pollard, *The Books of Hours of Geoffroy Tory*, Bibliographica, i. (1895), 114; A. F. Johnson, *Geoffroy Tory*, The Fleuron, No. vi. (1928), p. 37. The mark of the double (Lorraine) Cross which appears on many of the cuts has recently been interpreted as referring to the woodcutter Jacquemin Woeiriot (see Albert Ohl des Marais, Byblis, x. (1931), p. 13), and it is probable that Tory himself was only the designer. A monogram with a small S within a large G surmounted by the Lorraine Cross, which appears, e.g., on a series of woodcuts of the *Labours of Hercules*, has sometimes been attributed to Geoffroy Tory, but it has recently been shown to be the mark of Gabriel Salmon, another woodcutter of Lorraine (see Albert Ohl des Marais, Byblis, x. (1931), p. 139).

state, with a blank tablet in place of a plant beneath the skull, was found at Toulouse. With it a companion print of similar character and size, and equally cut at the sides, was also acquired for the British Museum, a *Death and Assumption of the Virgin*. These two cut impressions had been folded to be used as the lining of a burse, a stiff flat case of silk used to cover the Eucharistic vessels when carried to the altar for celebration of the Mass. In a certain dignity of style I feel Italian influence, and Schreiber noted the same influence in details such as the slanting nimbus of the Christ. Considering this and the provenance of the impressions, I should be inclined to regard both subjects as productions of the South of France.

The British Museum possesses another large woodcut of *Christ on the Cross between the Virgin and St. John*, of about the same period, and measuring about $15\frac{1}{2} \times 10\frac{3}{4}$ inches, within a four-piece border of branch and flower pattern, with the name of the publisher, printer, designer or cutter *adrien de liures* in the lower piece. There are three lines of text in Gothic type between the subject and the border. The background shows a town rather like that in the *Francis receiving the Stigmata*, in Paris (see p. 702). Though large, it is not too large to have been used, at least without its border, in some Missal, but I have failed to identify it.

Another of the largest French woodcuts is a single sheet with the *Passion of Christ*, measuring about $19\frac{1}{2} \times 14$ inches (Paris, Bouchot 191; Lemoisne cxxviii.). The work is nearly related in style to illustrations in certain of Vérard's books about the end of the century, e.g. of *Ogier Le Danois*, 1498, and *Terence* of about 1500,[1] and might well be by the same hand.

A considerable number of French single cuts of about 1490–1500 are preserved, pasted in deed- and travelling-boxes.[2] An interesting example is the subject of the *Two Saints Roch, Pilgrim and Bishop, with small Votive Figures*, crudely designed and cut, but attractive in its border of branch, flower and fruit (S. 1669 m, Vienna). It was found in an alms-box with a companion print of *St. John the Baptist and St. John the Evangelist*, with a border of diamond pattern with fleur-de-lis (1518 g, Paris). The French inscriptions appear to be in the dialect of Savoy, which is probably the locality of its production.[3]

[1] See pp. 667, 669.

[2] For a general study describing and reproducing most of such prints which are known, see W. L. Schreiber, *Kassetten-Holzschnitte*, Einblattdrucke 76, Strassburg 1931. The Bibliothèque Nationale, Paris, is particularly rich in these boxes. See p. 76.

[3] Another somewhat similar print, also found in an alms-box, a *St. Anthony of Padua* (S. 1216 a = 1233 a, Oxford), has also been attributed to the same region, but I think it is more likely to be Portuguese or Spanish, and refer to it in that relation (see p. 758).

Fig. 440. Christ on the Cross between the Virgin and St. John. S. 370 i.

more German in style, and might be a work of the region of Alsace, possibly of the early years of the XVI century.

Finally, I would mention a print of *St. Bathilde kneeling in a Gothic*

Fig. 442. The Annunciation. S. 31 m.

Church, known in two impressions on vellum (Paris, Bouchot 189, and the second in the Schreiber Sale, 1909, No. 48). It is evidently printed from metal, and is described by Schreiber in his volume devoted to metal-cuts and *criblée* prints (No. 2564), but as a line-block it falls into more natural relation with the work on copper which is found in French book-illustration. It contrasts with Dupré's work on copper, in being broad and coarse in line, but as a design it possesses both refinement and charm.

BIBLIOGRAPHY

SILVESTRE, L. C. Marques Typographiques des imprimeurs en France de 1470 jusqu'à la fin du xvie siècle. Paris 1853.

RENOUARD, Philippe. Imprimeurs Parisiens depuis l'introduction de l'Imprimerie à Paris (1470) jusqu'à la fin du xvi siècle. Paris 1898 (new edition in progress in the *Revue des Bibliothèques,* Paris, from 1922).

RENOUARD, Philippe. Les Marques typographiques parisiennes des xv et xvi siècles. Paris 1926, 1928 (*Revue des Bibliothèques*, Supplement 13*).

CLAUDIN, Anatole, and LACOMBE, Paul. Histoire de l'imprimerie en France au xve et au xvie siècles. 4 vols. Paris 1900–14. Vols. i. and ii. (Paris printers); Vols. iii. and iv. (Lyon printers).

CLAUDIN, Anatole, and RICCI, Seymour de. Documents sur la typographie et la gravure en France aux xve et xvie siècles. London 1926 (700 facsimiles, with short bibliographical notes by Seymour de Ricci, from Claudin's posthumous material, relating to French printers outside Paris and Lyon).

FAIRFAX MURRAY, C. Catalogue of a Collection of Early French Books in the library of C.F.M. by Hugh W. Davies. 2 vols. London (privately printed) 1910 (the record of an extraordinarily rich collection).

BRITISH MUSEUM. Short-title Catalogue of Books printed in France and of French books printed in other countries 1470–1600, now in the British Museum. Edited by Henry Thomas. London 1924.

MEYER, Wilhelm Jos. Die französischen Drucker- und Verlegerzeichen des xv Jahrhunderts. Munich 1926.

BLUM, André. Les Origines du livre à gravures en France: Les Incunables typographiques. Paris and Brussels 1928.

MARTIN, André. Le Livre français illustré du xve siècle. Paris 1931.

CHAPTER IX

BOOK-ILLUSTRATION AND CONTEMPORARY SINGLE CUTS
IN ENGLAND

THE revolution of methods implied by the introduction of printing inevitably attracted men of enterprise and ability, and among them not the least distinguished was WILLIAM CAXTON.[1] Born in Kent, apprenticed in 1438 to a mercer in the City of London, he went abroad about 1441, and was engaged in the cloth trade on the Continent for more than thirty years before his literary interests turned him to the idea of printing.

He had lived chiefly at Bruges, and attained a leading position among his fellow-countrymen in the Netherlands. Between 1465 and 1469 he acted as Governor of the English Merchant Adventurers in the Low Countries, and was engaged in negotiating commercial treaties with Philip the Good and Charles the Bold, Duke of Burgundy, in 1464 and 1468.

It was as early as 1469 that Caxton began his translation of Raoul Le Fèvre's *Recueil des Histoires de Troye*, and he was encouraged in the work and helped to amend his 'rude English' by the Duchess of Burgundy, Margaret of York, sister of Edward IV. of England, to whose household he was attached between 1471 and 1476. He completed his translation when staying at Cologne in 1471, but whether it was here or at Bruges that he issued this first book printed in the English language is still a matter of controversy. A stanza in some verses appended to Wynkyn de Worde's English edition of Bartholomaeus Anglicus, *De Proprietatibus Rerum*, 1495,[2] refers quite definitely to the first Latin edition of this work as printed by Caxton at Cologne, and such a statement from one who

---

[1] See William Blades, *Life and Typography of William Caxton*, 2 vols., London 1861, 1863; W. Blades, *Biography and Typography of William Caxton*, London 1877 (2nd ed., 1882); E. Gordon Duff, *William Caxton*, Chicago (Caxton Club) 1905; Seymour de Ricci, *A Census of Caxtons*, Bibliographical Society Illustrated Monographs, xv., London 1909; H. R. Plomer, *William Caxton*, London 1925; Nellie S. Aurner, *Caxton*, London 1926; Rudolf Hittmair, *William Caxton*, Innsbruck 1931.

[2] The verses are entitled 'Prohemium Bartholomei' and the passage runs:

> *And also of your charytie call to remembraunce*
> *The soule of William Caxton first prynter of this boke*
> *In laten tonge at Coleyn hymselfe to avaunce.*

had been Caxton's foreman naturally demands credence. He very probably helped (and may partly have financed) the anonymous printer who issued the first edition of 'Bartholomew the Englishman' described by Proctor under his No. 1105 (Hain 2498), the printer responsible for the *Dialogi decem Auctorum* in 1473 and the undated *Flores Sancti Augustini*.

But this still leaves unsolved the place of publication of the *Recuyell*, which is printed in type used later by Colard Mansion. Blades and Gordon Duff, followed by Pollard and Redgrave, conjecturally place the printing of Caxton's *Recuyell of the Histories of Troye*,[1] at Bruges, about 1475, in collaboration with Colard Mansion (Blades 1, Duff 242, STC. 15375), while Plomer considers Cologne, about 1472–73, as the more probable place and date.

A plate representing *Caxton presenting his Book to Margaret of York*[2] is found in only one of the few known copies of the book, that of the Huntington Library, San Marino, California, acquired with the complete Caxton collection of the Duke of Devonshire at Chatsworth. The print is merely inlaid in the first blank leaf, and may have been inserted at a later date than the first publication, but there is every reason to think that it had been originally designed to illustrate the book. It is an engraving on copper done in a style closely related to the line-engravings[3] in Colard Mansion's French edition of Boccaccio, *De Casibus virorum et foeminarum illustrium*, Bruges 1476, and might be by the same hand. No woodcuts appear in any of the books with which Caxton might have been associated with Colard Mansion in Bruges.

In the autumn of 1476 Caxton returned to England, and established his press within the precincts at Westminster, issuing some eighty books, many being his own translations from French originals, between 1477 and his death in 1491.

English woodcut illustration in the xv century lags far behind contemporary work on the continent of Europe both in extent and quality, and its interest is for the most part literary and antiquarian rather than artistic.

---

[1] Caxton's translation from the French of Raoul Le Fèvre.

[2] Reproduced as frontispiece to Seymour de Ricci, *A Census of Caxtons*, 1909, and at p. 1 of A. W. Pollard, *Fine Books*, London 1912.

[3] Only known in two copies of the book, one at Göttingen and the other in the Boston Museum of Fine Arts from the library of the Marquis of Lothian (Sale, American Art Association, New York, 27th January 1932, Lot 46). See my *History of Engraving and Etching*, 3rd ed., 1923, pp. 32 and 33. For Colard Mansion and his only other illustrated work, the *Metamorphoses* of Ovid, 1484, see p. 591.

The earliest illustrated book printed in England is generally supposed to be the *Mirrour of the World*, Caxton's version of the famous *Speculum Historiale* of Vincent de Beauvais, issued about 1481 (Blades 31, Duff

401, STC. 24762).[1] There are numerous little subjects and diagrams (some with figures in circles), in thin outline and open shading, drawn and cut by a manifestly unpractised hand, no doubt in Caxton's workshop. The woodcuts of a *Master and Pupils* at sigg. a 4, c 4 and c 4 verso (fig. 443) and of a *Woman singing to the accompaniment of a man playing the flageolet* (sig. c 6) are among the more entertaining. The two

Fig. 443. Master and Pupils, from the *Mirrour of the World*, Westminster, about 1481.

versions of *Master and Pupils* which occur at sig. c 4 and c 4 verso also appear in the third edition of Caxton's *Cato parvus et magnus*, which has likewise been conjecturally dated about 1481, and is placed by Pollard Redgrave in 1480 (Blades 30, Duff 78, STC. 4852). Blades also inferred from the condition of the blocks that it was earlier than the *Mirrour*. The woodcuts in the copies of the *Cato* in the British Museum, St. John's College, Oxford, and the John Rylands Library, Manchester, are more heavily inked than the impressions in the *Mirrour*, but I find no evidence of priority of impression, and the impressions in the St. John's College copy of the *Cato* are in certain details more akin to those in the Exeter College copy of the second edition of the *Mirrour* of about 1490 (Duff 402, STC. 24763). Moreover, as the first two editions of the *Cato* were without illustration, it is more probable that the woodcuts were borrowed from the *Mirrour* series, rather than done in the first instance for the *Cato*. So that on the whole I would give the *Mirrour* priority in date.

Stronger in line, but equally poor in execution, are the sixteen blocks (repeated to make twenty-four figures) in Caxton's second edition of Jacobus de Cessolis, *Game of Chesse*, of about 1483 (Blades 34, Duff 82, STC. 4921; see fig. 444). It opens with a frontispiece representing King

[1] The work was finished 8th March 1480/81; 2nd ed., about 1490 (e.g. Cambridge). Many of the original blocks were reprinted, amid a variety of other illustrations, in an undated edition issued by Lawrence Andrewe, about 1527.

Evilmerodach, son of Nebuchadnezzar, 'a jolly man without justice who did do hew his father his body into three hundred pieces', and follows with the usual type of subject illustrating the various ranks and occupations of

Fig. 444. From Jacobus de Cessolis, *Game of Chesse*, Westminster, about 1483.

mankind. In style the woodcuts show Netherlandish influence, but there is no reason to think that they were not cut in England.

The *Aesop* woodcuts in the *Subtyl hystoryes and Fables of Esope*, issued 26th March 1484 (Blades 55, Duff 4, STC. 175, GW. 376), are derived either directly or indirectly, like nearly all fifteenth-century Aesops, from Johann Zainer's Ulm edition of about 1476–77.[1] Not only in style, but in details of design, they are much further removed from the Ulm originals than Knoblochtzer's Strassburg edition of about 1480,[2] or the first French edition, that of Philippi and Reinhard, Lyon 1480,[3] which are among the earliest series of copies. In their crude drawing and broad handling they are not far removed from the style of the woodcuts in the Oxford *Festial* of 1486.[4] Caxton states that he made his translation from the French, and he might well have used the Lyon edition of 1480, but I find no definite clue on the side of the woodcuts. The full-page frontispiece representing *Aesop* is only known in the Windsor copy (Blades, pl. xxxiv.).

[1] See p. 306.
[2] See p. 336.
[3] See p. 602.
[4] See p. 723.

In or about the same year, 1484, Caxton issued his second edition of Chaucer's *Canterbury Tales* (Blades 57, Duff 88, STC. 5083), the first to contain woodcuts (see fig. 445). The woodcuts are of the same broad line and crude execution as the *Aesop*, but these mounted figures of the pilgrims illustrating the characters as they appear in the Prologue, and repeated at the head of the respective Tales, have at least the virtue of originality. There is also an amusing cut in the Prologue of the *Pilgrims at Table* (fig. 446), which was used later by Wynkyn de Worde for a feast

Fig. 445. The Wife of Bath, from the *Canterbury Tales*, Westminster, about 1484.

of the immortals in John Lydgate, *Assembly of the Gods*, 1498 (Duff 253, STC. 17005).

It is noteworthy that a copy of Caxton's edition of Chaucer's *Troilus and Cressid* of about 1482 (Duff 94, STC. 5094) in St. John's College, Oxford, which is bound with the *Canterbury Tales*, contains an illuminated frontispiece on vellum drawn very much in a woodcutter's manner. Outline and shading are done with the pen in brown and blue, and the colour is in transparent washes of blue, green, brown and rose. If not a copy of some French or Netherlandish woodcut, it is certainly drawn in the manner of woodcutters of the Netherlands or North France, and might be by the designer responsible for Caxton's *Golden Legend*.

Caxton's English version of the *Golden Legend* was completed, according to his colophon, on the 20th November 1483, and this seems only to refer to the translation, and not to the printing, which may be assumed to have been carried through about 1484–85 (Blades 53, Duff 408, STC. 24873). It is the most extensive of his works both in text and illustration. The introductory section, which opens with an oblong heraldic design of a *Horse by a Tree* with the motto 'my truste is', the badge of William Fitzalan, Earl of Arundel (1417–1487), at whose request the translation was made, and with a full-page cut of the *Trinity adored by Saints*, contains a series of some fourteen oblong cuts (about $4\frac{3}{8} \times 6\frac{3}{4}$ inches), chiefly illustrating the life of the Virgin and of Christ. This introductory section differentiates Caxton's *Golden Legend* at once from foreign editions, which deal more exclusively with the Lives of the Saints. At a time when Lollardry was still suspect, and when the printing of Wycliffe's English Bible would have been forbidden by the Church, Caxton's short paraphrase of parts of Scripture is at least a sign of coming freedom. To judge from certain blind translations of misprints, Caxton's version of the main part

Fig. 446. The Pilgrims at Table, from the *Canterbury Tales*, Westminster, about 1484.

of the work appears to have been based on an anonymous edition, which was probably printed in North France about 1475 (B.M., Proctor 8802, IC. 46325).[1]

Then the bulk of the work is illustrated by some sixty-two column-cuts (about $4 \times 2\frac{7}{8}$ inches), with a few of the larger oblongs interspersed. Whether the author (designer or cutter) is English or not, he was at least chiefly inspired by Netherlandish woodcut in the manner of the earlier illustrations produced at Gouda (e.g. the *Liden ons Heren* of 1482)[2] and doing work comparable with the Antwerp and Delft *Ludolphus* of 1487 and 1488,[3] and the Delft *Passionael* of 1487.[4]

I am unable to identify the immediate sources used by Caxton's designer, in any of the German editions, from that of Günther Zainer of Augsburg (1472) onwards, or in the two French editions that certainly precede him, the Lyon editions, of Philippi and Reinhard of about 1480, and of Hus and Petrus of Hungary, 1483.[5] In scriptural illustration of his introductory

[1] See F. S. Ellis, *Memoranda* at end of Kelmscott Press edition of Caxton's *Golden Legend*, 1892, vol. iii. p. 1282.

[2] See p. 566.   [3] See pp. 568-572.   [4] See p. 573.   [5] See p. 603.

section he may have had recourse to the great Cologne Bible of about 1478–79, but here again the reminiscences are too general to establish any definite link. Moreover, none of the Netherlandish editions of the *Golden Legend* (*Passionael*) is illustrated.

The most interesting parts of the text concern English saints, whose

Fig. 447. The Murder of Thomas à Becket, from the *Golden Legend*, Westminster, about 1484–85.

lives do not appear in the foreign editions of Jacob de Voragine's work, and in illustrations such as the *Murder of Thomas à Becket* (fig. 447). That this woodcut has often been mutilated, or removed from copies of the book, is no doubt due to the suppression of Becket's shrine and cult in the reign of Henry VIII. The column-cuts are for the most part cruder in execution (though this seems to come from lack of care rather than difference of style), and many appear as if printed from worn blocks, though I am unable to trace their use in any earlier edition.

The British Museum copy is made up partly of the first edition and partly of a variant issue with head-lines in larger type, probably printed about 1487 (Blades 66, Duff 409, STC. 24874).[1] In both these issues initial letters are supplied by hand.

[1] This variant issue has not been found complete, so it may only have been printed to make up deficiencies.

Of a very different type, and more refined in character and more delicate in line, are the small upright cuts, measuring about $3\frac{1}{2} \times 2\frac{3}{4}$ inches, mostly within double border, in Bonaventura, *Speculum Vite Cristi*, first printed about 1486 (Blades 70, Duff 48, STC. 3259, Cambridge) and reprinted with only slight differences (e.g. *Capitulum* written in full in place of the earlier *Ca.* in the head-lines) about 1490 (Blades 71, Duff 49, STC. 3260). The lighter touch shown in these cuts is reminiscent of the work of Bellaert's chief woodcutter at Haarlem. Some of the series were not used in the *Speculum*, but appear in various books printed by Wynkyn de Worde.

Fig. 448. Christ at Emmaus, from the *Speculum Vite Cristi*, Westminster, about 1486.

Caxton's large and decorative mark appears to have been originally made for the *Sarum Missal* printed for him by Maynyal at Paris in 1487 (Duff 322, STC. 16164, Lord Newton, and Corpus Christi College, Cambridge), but is here reproduced from the second edition of the *Speculum* (fig. 449).

The *Royal Book*, Caxton's translation of the *Livre des Vices et des Vertus*[1] (Blades 67, Duff 366, STC. 21429), which appeared about 1486 or soon after, contains one cut from the *Golden Legend* (*Moses and the Tables of the Law*) and six of the *Speculum* series. Odd cuts from the *Speculum* also occur in Guy de Roye, *Doctrinal of Sapyence*, after 7th May 1489 (Blades 71, Duff 127, STC. 21431), and in the *Book of Divers Ghostly Matters*, of about 1491 (Blades 85, Duff 55, STC. 3305).

Of Caxton's woodcut initials there is an isolated rustic A (fig. 450) which occurs in the *Aesop* of 26th March 1484, and in the *Book of the Order of Chivalry* of about the same date (Blades 56, Duff 58, STC. 3326), and in Wynkyn de Worde's 1498 edition of the *Golden Legend*. Apart from certain smaller series of initials, he also used several letters of the design with leaf and flower, which figured more completely in de Worde's books (see fig. 453). Examples of this series appeared in the *Royal Book*, about 1486 (Blades 67, Duff 366, STC. 21429), in the *Governayle of Helthe* about 1489

[1] An undated edition in the British Museum, catalogued under the Italian title *Fiore di Virtù*, is conjecturally dated about 1485 (IA. 46385).

(Blades 76, Duff 165, STC. 12138, Oxford), in Virgil, *Eneydos*, after 22nd June 1490 (Blades 81, Duff 404, STC. 24796), in the *Fifteen Oes* about 1491 (Blades 82, Duff 150, STC. 20195), and the *Book of Divers Ghostly Matters* about 1491 (Blades 85, Duff 55, STC. 3305).

Fig. 449. Printer's mark of William Caxton, Westminster.

Caxton printed various editions of the *Hours of the Virgin* (*Horae Beatae Mariae Virginis ad usum Sarum*), the 'Primer' as it was commonly called in English. But these books of private devotion are exceedingly rare, and several editions are only known from fragments found in the linings of book-covers.

The two earliest editions known, that of about 1477–78 in the Pierpont Morgan Library, New York (62 leaves, vellum, covering the third part of the Primer, 'Vigils of the Dead', etc., Duff 174, STC. 15867),[1] and that of about 1480 (4 leaves, Duff 175, STC. 15868), are without cuts in the portions that remain. The fragment of a third edition of about 1490, preserved, like the second, in the British Museum (8 leaves, Duff 178, STC. 15871), contains two small cuts, an *Image of Pity* (*Christ in the Tomb, with the signs of the Passion*, 52 × 57 mm.) and a *Christ on the Cross with the Virgin and St. John* (54 × 39 mm.). A further fragment of a fourth edition, of about 1490, also in the British Museum (4 leaves, Duff 179, STC. 15872), has no woodcuts.

Even if there were no cuts in the first and second editions, when complete, it is more than probable that the third and fourth editions and others, which may have been issued during the 'eighties, contained more cuts than the two preserved. There are numerous cuts of initial size corresponding in style and dimensions with the *Christ on the Cross* of the third edition, in later *Horae* of Wynkyn de Worde,[2] and in de Worde's edition of Caxton's *Golden Legend*, and these almost certainly came from lost *Horae* printed by Caxton.

I shall speak later in more detail of Wynkyn's *Primers* of 1494 with

---

[1] See E. Gordon Duff, *The First Edition of the Sarum Primer, printed on vellum at West-minster by William Caxton*, c. 1477. 1908.

[2] E.g. in his 4to *Horae* of 1494 (see p. 719).

Fig. 450. Initial A, from *Aesop*, Westminster 1484.

woodcut borders, but I would add here note of his other *Horae* which merely contain isolated cuts, i.e. Duff 185, STC. 15878 (6 leaves, 8vo, about 1494, with two small illustrations, the *Martyrdom of St. Erasmus* and *St. Roch and an Angel*, well designed and cut, and probably by the master responsible for his edition of Bartholomaeus;[1] Corpus Christi College, Oxford); STC. 15898, 8vo, 1502 (Oxford); STC. 15899, 4to, 1503 (B.M.); STC. 15908, 8vo, 1508? (4 leaves, Cambridge); STC. 15914, 4to, 1513, *Matyns of Our Lady* (B.M.); STC. 15922, 4to, 1519, *Matyns of Our Lady* (B.M.).

The earliest English Primer known with a series of borders was printed by WILLIAM DE MACHLINIA, about 1485 (Duff 176, STC. 15869).[2] Until recently this was only known from fragments in the British Museum and various other libraries, but in 1928 a copy, bound early in the XVII century, was discovered by Mr. George Smith of the firm of Ellis, New Bond Street. It contains 100 leaves out of the complement of 108, covering the three parts of the Primer: (1) the Hours of the Virgin, (2) the Penitential Psalms and (3) the Vigils of the Dead, etc.

A considerable number of its pages are enclosed in floral scroll borders, of which there are two varieties, one of which is always used round text, the other to enclose the woodcut subjects, eight in number (see fig. 451). The impression is on vellum, the woodcut borders and subjects being lightly coloured, a few borders and initial letters being added by hand. Both borders were used later by Pynson.[3] Two other borders of similar dimensions and design appeared in books issued by Wynkyn de Worde in the early XVI century (McKerrow and Ferguson, plates 3 and 5), while a third border used by de Worde in the *Lamentacyon of Our Lady* (STC. 17537, Cambridge, McKerrow and Ferguson, pl. 6) is also near in type, but includes birds in its design and is slightly larger.

In character of design these borders are most nearly related to the work

---

[1] See p. 726.

[2] See *William de Machlinia, the Primer on vellum printed by him in London about 1484. Newly found and described by George Smith. With facsimiles of the Woodcuts.* London (Ellis, New Bond St.) 1929.

[3] See R. B. McKerrow and F. S. Ferguson, *Title-page borders used in England and Scotland, 1485-1640.* Bibliographical Society Illustrated Monographs, xxi., London 1932 (for 1931), plates 1 and 2.

of Jean Dupré, particularly in the borders of his *Horae* of about 1488 (B.M., IA. 39817) and the related group.[1] The earliest of the French *Horae* known with borders of this character is the one published by Vérard, 6th February 1485/86 (Cl. ii. 388-89), so that Machlinia's *Primer* is all the more remarkable as being among the very first examples of its kind. Machlinia's borders compare well in charm of invention (if not in precision of cutting) with contemporary French work, but the woodcut subjects are much cruder and rather Flemish or German than French in character. The designer and cutter may be the same for both border and subject, but it is evident that his talent was fully equal to decorative design, but limited in more naturalistic forms of expression. But all in all Machlinia's *Primer* is a fascinating little book, and among the most interesting monuments of English xv-century illustration.

A more important, but hardly more attractive, achievement is the *Book of Prayers*, printed by Caxton about 1491, called the *Fifteen Oes*, from the fifteen prayers each beginning with O (Blades 82, Duff 150, STC. 20195). It is an octavo of twenty-two leaves, two gatherings of eight leaves and one of six, with signatures *a*, *b* and *c*. The first page is blank, the remainder are surrounded with four-piece borders of branch, flower, bird and beast, in the manner of Jean Dupré. The second page forms a frontispiece with the subject of *Calvary* (fig. 452). The third page, the first of the text, opens with a woodcut initial O (fig. 453) of the leaf and flower series which we have already described,[2] the later initial letters in the book belonging to smaller series.

These *Prayers*, printed, as the colophon states, by the command of Elizabeth of York (Queen of Henry VII.) and of the king's mother, Margaret Beaufort, constitute a complete work in themselves, but they may have formed the supplement to a lost Primer, like the Wynkyn de Worde edition about to be described. The designer of the *Calvary* is easily the most spirited artist engaged in book-illustration in England in the xv century. He shows an individual sense of curving lines, and an incisive power of expression.

Except for a fragment of four leaves in the Baptist College at Bristol,[3] the book is only known from the British Museum copy. In several instances border-pieces are printed upside-down (e.g. f. 2), a common form of carelessness by no means confined to Caxton.

---

[1] See p. 683.   [2] See pp. 713-714.

[3] These leaves show the offset of another book with borders. Mr. Seymour de Ricci (*Census of Caxtons*) suggests that it is from part of the fourth edition of Caxton's *Horae* (see p. 714).

The same borders were used in the *Horae* printed by Wynkyn de Worde, in and about 1494 (Duff 182, STC. 15875, Lambeth Palace; Duff 183, STC. 15876, British Museum). The Lambeth copy, on vellum, is the more complete, and its last page, which contains the *Annunciation* from Caxton's *Speculum*, includes in its colophon the title applied to Caxton's

Fig. 451. The Nativity, from *Horae*, London (Machlinia), about 1485.

prayers, *These forsayd prayers as the XV Oes in Englysshe and ye other follow-yng*, also repeats Caxton's statement that they were printed by the command of Elizabeth, Queen of Henry VII., and of Margaret Beaufort. It contains the *Calvary*, and four other cuts of the same size, the *Three Rioters and the Three Skeletons* (fig. 454), the *Tree of Jesse with the Virgin and Child*, *Dives and Lazarus*, and *David* (*with Goliath above and Bath-*

sheba below).[1] The *Three Rioters and the Three Skeletons* is based on the story of *Les Trois Vifs et les Trois Morts*, which appears in most of the French *Horae*, and the design may have been adapted from one or

Fig. 452. Calvary, from the *Fifteen Oes*, Westminster, about 1491.

another of those in the Dupré-Caillaut group, corresponding to the Caillaut edition in showing the subject on one block.[2] But the com-

---

[1] Several of these blocks were used in other books of Wynkyn de Worde: The *Calvary* in his 'Golden Legend', 1493, John Alcock, *Mons Perfectionis*, 1497, and in the 'Three Kynges of Coleyn', about 1499 (Duff 398, STC. 5572, Edinburgh); both the *Calvary* and the *Tree of Jesse* in his 'Golden Legend' of 1498; the *Three Rioters and the Three Skeletons* in Richard Rolle, 'Contemplacyons', 1506 (STC. 21259); the *Dives and Lazarus* in Cordiale, 'Memorare novissima', n.d. (Duff 110, STC. 5759, Oxford), and both *Dives and Lazarus* and the *David* in Wynkyn's *Sarum Horae* of 1513.   [2] See p. 684. The Caillaut subject is reproduced in Claudin i. p. 257.

position is treated with considerable variation, so that it might be drawn from another source. The *Dives and Lazarus* is also nearly related to woodcuts in the Dupré-Caillaut group, while the *David* is a modified

rendering of the same combination of motives seen in a woodcut in Pierre Gringore, *Casteau d'Amours*, issued by Michel le Noir, Paris 1500,[1] which may have been done earlier for some *Horae*. These quarto *Horae* of Wynkyn de Worde also contain a considerable number of the small cuts of initial letter size (about 2 to $2\frac{5}{8}$ by $1\frac{1}{2}$ to $1\frac{3}{4}$ inches) to which we have already alluded as probably coming from lost *Primers* of Caxton,[2] the most attractive being a *St. George and the Dragon*, on sig. h. v. of the Lambeth and British Museum copies. There are no woodcut initials, these being added by hand.

Fig. 453. Initial O, from the *Fifteen Oes*, Westminster, about 1491.

The only other English xv-century *Horae* with complete borders to which I can refer is that of RICHARD PYNSON, printed about 1497 (Duff 192, STC. 15886, Oxford; see fig. 455). It is French in style, and except for two small border-pieces of Prophet and Sibyl, entirely in black line. Its outer and lower borders are largely divided into rectangular subjects, and the woodcut surface measures about $6\frac{1}{4} \times 4\frac{1}{4}$ inches. I have not identified the blocks in any French edition, and they may have been cut specially for Pynson's Primer. It contains a series of subject cuts in various sizes, from nearly full-page to the size of initial letters. Of Pynson's other *Primers* of the xv century, there are only fragments left, and only two of these, of about 1498 and 1500, contain woodcuts (Duff 197, STC. 15891, Cambridge; and Duff 199, STC. 15893, Durham).

A considerable number of *Horae* and Missals in the Sarum Use were printed abroad during the xv century, and I have already alluded to one or two issued at Rouen and Paris.[3] Their study should be illuminating in relation to the development of English woodcut, as it is to be expected that the decoration of foreign books produced for English use would have most influence on artists working in England.

It is an important fact that most of these imported *Horae* date before 1491, by which time both Machlinia and Caxton had issued their *Horae* with borders, and the only Sarum Missal printed abroad before the same date is the edition printed by Guillaume Maynyal for Caxton in 1487. After the *Sarum Horae* printed by Gerard Leeuw at Antwerp, about

---

[1] See p. 676.   [2] See p. 714.

[3] See pp. 625, 626, 629.

1491–92, of which there is only a single quire and single woodcut, at Brasenose College, Oxford (Duff 180, STC. 15873), the most important work is the Missal printed at Rouen by Martin Morin, in 1492.[1] The

Fig. 454. The Three Rioters and the Three Skeletons, from *Horae*, Westminster (Wynkyn de Worde), about 1494.

four-piece border, with branch and bird motives, is entirely in the style of Dupré, and perhaps came from his Paris workshop.

Then come the octavo and folio Missals printed in 1494 for the London booksellers FREDERICK EGMONT and GERARDUS BARREVELT, by Johannes Hamman at Venice: the splendid folio with a fine outline border (Essling, *Les Missels vénitiens*, p. 270, No. 215, Duff 324, STC. 16167,

[1] See p. 625.

Cambridge; the British Museum copy being very imperfect); the octavo edition with little outline initials and small *Canon* cut, but no borders (Duff 325, STC. 16168, fragments only, e.g. in B.M.), and the small *Sarum Horae* of the same printer and same year, with most attractive

Fig. 455. The Nativity, from *Horae*, London (Pynson), about 1497.

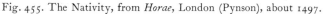

outline borders (Duff 181, STC. 15874; fragments in B.M., etc.).[1] But this Venetian art finds no reflection on English soil.

Most of the cuts in the English Missals of the late xv and early xvi centuries are based on French originals, if indeed French blocks are not used.

The *Christ on the Cross* in the *Sarum Missal* printed for Wynkyn de

¹ See p. 500.

Worde by JULIAN NOTARY and JEAN BARBIER in 1498 (Duff 328, STC. 16172) is based on the *Canon* cut which appeared first in Pierre Le Rouge's *Toul Missal* of 1492,[1] and later in the *Sarum Missal* printed by Jean Dupré, 30th September 1500 (Duff 331, STC. 16175, complete with *Canon* cut at Ely), and by Dupré's successors in 1504 (STC. 16178).[2]

The same original design is followed in another version, again without the border, in Pynson's *Sarum Missal* of 1512 (STC. 16190), a Missal which also reprints Vérard's original block of *Les Joyes de Paradis* from his *Art de bien Vivre et de bien Mourir*. The *Resurrection*, which occurs at f. 81, is a very close copy of the block in Dupré's *Sarum Missal*, Paris 1500, and in the edition of Dupré's successors, 1504.

In his earlier *Sarum Missal* of 10th January 1500/1501, the so-called *Morton Missal*, printed at the expense of Cardinal Morton, Archbishop of Canterbury, and decorated with his arms and a rebus on his name in the borders and initials (Duff 329, STC. 16173, Oxford, etc.), Pynson had used a different model for his *Christ on the Cross*, which shows the Apostle John with his hand to his face as in the *Canon* cuts in Gering and Rembolt's *Paris Missal* of 1497 (Cl. i. 107) and Wolfgang Hopyl's *Sarum Missals* of 1500 (Duff 330, STC. 16174, Oxford) and 1504 (B.M., C. 36. l. 8).

The *Morton Missal* is perhaps the finest missal printed in England at the period. The four-piece border, which is used at the head of various sections, is well designed and cut, the side-pieces in black line, the upper and lower members (each from two blocks fitted together) on dotted ground, all being in the French style of branch and bird, etc., and there are several handsome woodcut initials printed in red (see fig. 456).

Most of the English books printed abroad, and English editions of foreign books printed in England, have already been described in the sections dealing with the original editions. Apart from liturgical works, few borders with woodcuts were printed abroad for the English market during the xv century, the only one to which I can here refer being the *Cronycles of the Londe of Englonde*, printed by Gerard Leeuw at Antwerp, 1493 (Duff 100, and pl. li.; STC. 9994).[3] In the early xvi century there were various editions of the *Shepherds' Calendar*,[4] the *Art of Good Living and Good Dying*,[5] the *Ordinarye of Crysten Men*,[6] and Pierre Gringore's *Castell of Labour*.[7]

---

[1] Monceaux, i. p. 275, No. 28 (with reproduction).
[2] See p. 629. [3] See p. 580. [4] See p. 651.
[5] See pp. 662-663. [6] See p. 673. [7] See p. 676.

Fig. 456. Initial A, from the *Morton Missal*, London 1500/1501.

Another foreign printer of English books may be mentioned here, i.e. JAN VAN DOESBORGH, who followed Leeuw in his interest in the English book trade at Antwerp,[1] but his work falls entirely in the XVI century (about 1505–30), and the artistic merit of his woodcuts is very slight. Among his earliest books is the *Fifteen Tokens of the Day of Doom*, of about 1505, based on the section of *L'Art de bien Vivre et de bien Mourir* entitled *Les Quinze Signes de l'Antechrist*. He succeeded to the business of Roelant van den Dorpe, as is shown by his use of the same printer's mark of Knight Roland (Juchhoff 13) which occurs in this and other books.[2]

Resuming my survey of books printed in England, I would mention certain works issued at Oxford and St. Albans, contemporaneously with Caxton, before coming to Caxton's successors at Westminster and in the City of London.

The large folio of Lyndewode's *Constitutiones Provinciales* printed at Oxford by THEODORICUS ROOD, about 1483 (Duff 278, STC. 17102), contains a woodcut frontispiece of a *Monk seated writing at a desk beneath an architectural canopy*, with landscape and trees on either side. In style it is entirely Netherlandish, and of good average quality of design and cutting, and there seems reason to believe that it was originally intended to figure as Jacobus de Voragine in a *Golden Legend*, of which no copies are known, if it was ever published.

The other relics of this conjectured *Golden Legend* appear in the woodcuts illustrating John Mirk's *Festial*, printed by Rood at Oxford in 1486 (Duff 300, S.T.C. 17958, Oxford; see fig. 457). It is a series of oblong cuts within double border-lines, the blocks being cut down to fit the page to a width of about five inches, from an original size which was probably nearly that of the *Voragine* portrait ($4\frac{7}{8} \times 7\frac{3}{8}$ inches). They are considerably cruder in execution than the portrait, but greater care was probably spent on the frontispiece cut. Their very crudeness inclines one to accept them as by some native craftsman with little training in his art. The treatment of the blocks, and the nature of the subjects, point indubitably to the assumption of a lost Book of Saints. Two small upright cuts of *St. Andrew*

---

[1] See Robert Proctor, Bibliographical Society, Illustrated Monographs, ii., 1894.

[2] See p. 580.

with his Cross (each about $2\frac{1}{2} \times 1\frac{5}{8}$ inches) were probably done for a Book of Hours, but no Oxford Primer is known.

In addition to these subject cuts, Theodoricus Rood has a set of four large border-pieces, of branch, bird and flower design, which decorate the front page of Alexander de Hales, *Expositio Librorum de Anima* (Aris-

Fig. 457. The Murder of Thomas à Becket, from Mirk, *Festial*, Oxford 1486.

totle), of 1481 (Duff 21, STC. 314), and John Latterbury, *Commentary on the Lamentations of Jeremiah (Super Threnis Ieremiae)*, 1482 (Duff 238, STC. 15297). They are attractive in design, though somewhat weak in execution.

The press of the anonymous schoolmaster at St. Albans issued two books with woodcuts. The earlier of these, the *Chronicles of England* (generally called the *St. Albans Chronicle*), printed about 1485 (Duff 101, STC. 9995), contains a few cuts of little importance, such as a *Tower of Babel* and some diagrams. The second publication, generally known as the *Book of St. Albans*, a book on hawking, hunting and blasing of arms, by Juliana Bernes, issued in 1486 (Duff 56, STC. 3308), is of interest on account of the use of colour blocks in the section on the 'blasyng of armys' in the same manner as the early astronomical woodcuts of Ratdolt at Venice. Most of the coats-of-arms are in single colours: others are in black line with one or two colours from different blocks. In the second edition, printed by Wynkyn de Worde in 1496, the coats-of-arms are newly cut, and coloured by hand.

WYNKYN DE WORDE (Jan van Wynkyn, born at Worth in Alsace) probably came to England with Caxton in 1476, and became his foreman, succeeding to the press at Westminster after his master's death in 1491. In 1500 he removed to Fleet Street, and in 1509 opened a shop in St. Paul's Churchyard, which remained so long the centre of the London publishing and bookselling trades. His activity in the XVI century until his death at the end of 1534 or beginning of 1535[1] is outside our period, and a great deal of his work in the XV century was concerned with new editions of Caxton's books, in which the old woodcuts were largely reprinted.

Fig. 458. Printer's mark of Wynkyn de Worde, London.

One of the earliest of these new editions was his *Golden Legend* of 1493 (Duff 410, STC. 24875). In addition to a proportion of the cuts from the original edition, it contains a certain number of illustrations from other books of Caxton, e.g. an *Annunciation* on f. 112, verso, from the *Speculum Vite Cristi*, the *Calvary*, on the last page, from the *Fifteen Oes*, and numerous little cuts of initial size which no doubt belonged originally to the lost *Horae* of Caxton.[2] Moreover, he added woodcut initials; in the first place a large initial T (fig. 459), on the reverse of the first and last leaves, based on the G of Veldener's *Fasciculus Temporum*, Utrecht 1481.[3]

For his smaller initials he used here and elsewhere a set which had originally belonged to Gotfridus de Os of Gouda,[4] in addition to Caxton's leaf and flower series described and illustrated above.[5] He issued another edition of the *Golden Legend* in 1498 (Duff 411, STC. 24876), in which the *Tree of Jesse* as well as the *Calvary*, from the *Fifteen Oes* series, appeared on the last leaf.

His edition of Bonaventura's *Speculum Vite Cristi*, 1494 (Duff 50, STC. 3261), of which the only complete copy is at Holkham, is practically the same in its woodcut illustration as the original Caxton.

An interesting woodcut of the *Virgin and Child within a floral border* occurs on the title-page of Walter Hylton, *Scala Perfectionis*, 1494 (Duff 203, STC. 14042; fig. 460). The border is on the same block as the subject, and exemplifies how the lack of naturalistic power, evident in the subject, may be no detriment when applied to the decorative elements of

---

[1] His will, dated 5th June 1534, was proved 19th January 1535.
[2] See p. 714.
[3] See p. 560, and fig. 318.
[4] See p. 586, and fig. 341.
[5] See p. 713, and fig. 453.

Fig. 459. Initial T, from the *Golden Legend*,
Westminster 1493.

design, a fact noted above in relation to Machlinia's *Primer*.[1] The block is reprinted in his edition of *Dives and Pauper*, 1496.

Wynkyn de Worde's English edition of Bartholomaeus Anglicus, *De Proprietatibus Rerum* (*All the Proprytees of Thynges*), translated by John de Trevisa, 1495 (Duff 40, STC. 1536), is perhaps Wynkyn's masterpiece in illustration. The designs prefixed to each book are derived partly from Bellaert's Haarlem edition of 1485,[2] especially in the earlier part of the book, and partly from the Lyon edition of 1482, or one of the other Lyon editions closely related to it;[3] but they are in some cases adapted with such freedom as to justify our regarding them as original. Such may be said of the *Landscape* at Book XIV., *De Terra* (fig. 461), with its excellent use of white line in the trees, and of the *Workers in Field and River*, prefixed to Book XVI. (*De Lapidibus et Metallis*), in which Wynkyn's designer adds a third figure to the Lyon original. Wynkyn certainly had a competent designer and cutter, and not a fumbler, in this and a few of his other works. In this book, as in others, during the xv century, he continued to use Caxton's printer's mark. The title is cut on wood in white letters on black ground.

In his *Lyff of the olde Auncyent Holy Faders*, 1495 (Duff 235, STC. 14507), Wynkyn published the first edition of the translation of St. Jerome's *Vitas Patrum*, completed by Caxton on his deathbed. Prefixed to each of the five parts and repeated a sixth time at the end, is a full-page cut of *St. Jerome seated before a company of dignitaries of the Church*. It is sufficiently ambitious, but as poor in drawing and as crudely executed as the smaller columncuts, of which there are some forty varieties (many being repeated) throughout the book. Whether or not the designer borrowed from any earlier edition, I have been unable to establish any direct link between these subjects and the designs in any of the foreign editions, either among the German issues, from those of Strassburg and Augsburg (1477 and 1478) onwards, or among the French from that of Dupré, Paris 1486. None of the Nether-

---

[1] See p. 716.　　　　[2] See p. 575.　　　　[3] See pp. 604, 605.

landish editions before Wynkyn's have any series of woodcut designs. The title is cut in white on black as in the *Bartholomaeus*.

Wynkyn's 1496 edition of the *Book of St. Albans* (Duff 57, STC. 3309) is a finer production than the original issue of 1486. The woodcut of *Birds* on f. 1 comes from the *Bartholomaeus* of 1495, but the *Gentleman and a*

Fig. 460. The Virgin and Child, from Hylton, *Scala Perfectionis,* Westminster 1494.

Group of his Retainers on the reverse of the same leaf (fig. 462) is a new cut, and one of the best by the same designer. Better known, but somewhat cruder in character, is the *Angler*, prefixed to the *Treatyse of fysshynge with an Angle*, which was added to this edition. The book ends with a handsome full-page woodcut comprising the Royal Badge of Henry VII.

Of the same stolid character as the *Angler* is the title-woodcut in Henry Parker, *Dives and Pauper*, 1496 (Duff 340, STC. 19213). On the reverse of the title is reprinted the *St. Jerome* from the *Lyff of the olde Auncient Holy Faders* of 1495, and on the last leaf the *Virgin and Child* from Hylton's *Scala Perfectionis* of 1494. Pynson's edition of 1493 of the same work (Duff 339, STC. 19212) is without illustration. In 1498 Wynkyn reprinted Caxton's edition of Chaucer's *Canterbury Tales*, with the original

Fig. 461. Landscape, from Bartholomaeus Anglicus, *All the Proprytees of Thynges*, Westminster 1495.

woodcuts, the only perfect copy known being in the Pierpont Morgan Library, New York (Duff 90, STC. 5085).

In the same year also appeared his edition of Malory's *Morte d'Arthur*, of which only one copy is known, that of the John Rylands Library, Manchester (Duff 284, STC. 802).[1] The oblong cuts, which average about $4 \times 4\frac{7}{8}$ inches in size, crudely cut in thick line, with regular patches of parallel shading, are remarkable and somewhat bizarre in design. The violent motion seen in the illustration of *How Sir Launcelot in his madnes toke a swerde* (Book XII.) is reminiscent of certain plates in Bellaert's *Historie van Jason* and *Historie van Troyen* (Haarlem 1484 and 1485). The

[1] See *Le Morte Darthur . . . the original edition of William Caxton reprinted and edited by* H. Oskar Sommer, 2 vols., London 1889, 1892.

Birth of Sir Tristram de Lyonesse (Book VIII.) is characteristic both in its curious figures and in the originality of its landscape background, with woods and village church (fig. 463).

Some of the blocks of the *Morte d'Arthur* were used by Wynkyn in later books, e.g. in his editions of Raoul Le Fèvre, *The Recuyles of ye*

Fig. 462. A Gentleman and his Retainers, from the *Book of St. Albans,* Westminster 1496.

Hystories of Troye, 1502 (STC. 1502, Pepys Library) and about 1503 (STC. 15377).

Much less interesting are the numerous small cuts, about $2\frac{1}{4} \times 3\frac{1}{4}$ inches in size, in the Book of Sir John Mandeville (*A Lytell Treatyse or booke named Johan Maundeuyll*), 1499 (Duff 286, STC. 17247, Cambridge).

Several of the English editions of French books, to which reference has been made in the French section, were printed by Wynkyn de Worde, i.e. the *Kalender of Shepeherdes,* 1508 (see p. 652), the *Arte or Crafte to lyve well and to dye well,* 1505 and about 1506 (see p. 663), and the *Ordinarye of Crysten Men,* 1502 and 1506 (STC. 5198 and 5199; see p. 673). A few of the cuts in the earlier of the editions of the *Ordinarye* are in the same manner as the *Morte d'Arthur.* Each edition has different cuts, partly based on Vérard's *Art de bien Vivre et de bien Mourir.*

I would note here for convenience three other editions which he printed in the early XVI century, in which text or woodcuts are based on foreign books:

(1) Richard Rolle, *Contemplacyons,* 1506 (STC. 21259); with cut on

the reverse of the title copied from *Visio Lamentabilis*, Louvain (Ravescot), about 1487 (CA. 1745, CN. xxiii. 1).

(2) Sebastian Brant, *Shyppe of Fooles*, translated by Henry Watson, 1509 (STC. 3547, Paris); cuts based on the Basle designs, either directly or through one of numerous editions of copies.

Fig. 463. The Birth of Tristram, from Malory, *Morte d'Arthur*, Westminster 1494.

(3) *The Seven Wise Masters of Rome*, about 1520 (STC. 21298); cuts based on those of the edition of Claes Leeuw, Antwerp 1488.[1]

In the various editions of the *Chronicles of England* issued before 1500 there are few woodcuts. The *St. Albans Chronicle* of about 1485,[2] and the *Cronycles of the Londe of England* issued by Gerard Leeuw at Antwerp in 1493,[3] have already been mentioned. Ranulphus Higden's *Policronicon* printed by Wynkyn de Worde, 1495 (Duff 173, STC. 13439), has no woodcut subject except a repetition of the *St. Jerome* frontispiece from the *Vitas Patrum* of the same year,[4] and Wynkyn's edition of the *Chronicles of England*, 1497–98 (Duff 102, STC. 9996), reprinted in 1502, has only a *Tower of Babel*, a few diagrams like the *St. Albans Chronicle* and a view of *Towns and Country* from his *Bartholomaeus* to illustrate the *Descrypcyon of Englonde*. Nor do his later editions add anything of interest but a heraldic title-cut with Henry VII.'s badge (in two versions), while a *Town on an Estuary*, from *Bartholomaeus*, replaces the earlier view. A piece of original

[1] See p. 579.   [2] See p. 724.   [3] See p. 580, and p. 722.   [4] See p. 726.

historical illustration, the title-woodcut to Bishop's Fisher's *Funeral Sermon on Henry VII.*, printed by Wynkyn de Worde, 1509, deserves mention (STC. 10900-01, reproduced in A. W. Pollard, *Fine Books*, p. 254). The decoration and illustration of the *Chronicles* issued by Julian Notary in

Fig. 464. The Knight, from the *Canterbury Tales*, London (Pynson), about 1491.

1504 offer material of more variety, and this and Pynson's edition of 1510 will be noticed below.

We have already referred to Pynson's use of the borders from Machlinia's *Primer*, of about 1485,[1] and it is generally believed that he succeeded to Machlinia's stock about 1491. RICHARD PYNSON, who appears to have been a Norman and to have studied at the University of Paris, commissioned the Rouen printer Guillaume Le Tailleur to print him two Law books for sale in England[2] about 1490, before he began printing on his own account. In 1508 he became King's Printer,[3] succeeding William Faques, the first holder of that office. That the foreign craftsman was not entirely popular in these times is shown by the case for assault which he brought to the Star Chamber in 1500 against a certain Henry Squire and his companions, and by his statement that his workmen were so terrorised that they

[1] See p. 715.

[2] Sir Thomas Littleton's *Tenores Novelli* (Duff 275, STC. 15721) and Nicolas Statham, *Abridgment of Cases* (Duff 374, STC. 23238).

[3] About the same time Wynkyn de Worde seems to have received some official *consolatium*, for he styled himself 'Printer to the King's Mother', and after the death of Henry VII., 'Printer to the King's Grandmother'.

Fig. 465. Initial W,
from the *Speculum
Vite Cristi*, London
(Pynson), about
1494.

deserted him. Thereafter he removed to within Temple Bar, having perhaps better protection within the bounds of the City of London.

His earliest dated books belong to 1492, but his edition of Chaucer's *Canterbury Tales*, his first illustrated book, almost certainly appeared about 1491 (Duff 89, STC. 5084). Except for the woodcut of the narrator, placed at the head of each tale, the blocks with their figures on horseback are based on Caxton's designs, and even more crudely designed and cut, with broad black borders occasionally patterned with white line. The only subject which has an added decorative quality is the *Knight* (fig. 464), with the calligraphic rendering of the horse's trappings reminiscent of the frontispieces in *Fierabras* (Geneva 1483) and *Livre de Baudoin, Comte de Flandre* (Chambéry 1485).[1]

Not without reason was he dissatisfied with his local craftsmen, and for his next illustrated book, the *Fall of Princes* (John Lydgate's version of Boccaccio), 1494 (Duff 46, STC. 3175), he borrowed the blocks used in Dupré's Paris edition of 1483/84.[2]

To about the same date belongs his edition of Bonaventura, *Speculum Vite Cristi* (Duff 51, STC. 3262), with numerous small upright cuts about $3\frac{1}{4} \times 2\frac{1}{4}$ inches (or slightly larger when with double border-line), probably based on Caxton's series, and distinctly inferior and more variable in quality. Some of the cuts are of the crude and careless workmanship of Wynkyn's *Vitas Patrum*; others more carefully cut, but hard and angular in character. A *Crucifixion* which occurs at sig. n. iiii, verso ($3\frac{3}{4} \times 2\frac{3}{8}$ inches), stands apart from the rest, and is nearer in style to the designer of the Delft *Ludolphus* of 1488.[3] It is reprinted in the *Libellus qui informatio puerorum appellatur*, issued about 1500 (Duff 224, STC. 14079). The initials used in the *Speculum*, leaf, flower and grotesque faces designed in white on black, are attractive (see fig. 465). The *Informatio* also contains a woodcut of *Master and Pupils* ($5 \times 3\frac{5}{8}$ inches).

Pynson's mark (Juchhoff 66; fig. 466), as it occurs in the *Informatio*, shows a deep bend in its lower border-line, which proves its block to be of metal. In later books the indentation developed into a break.

His edition of Sir Thomas Littleton, *Tenores Novelli*, printed about 1496 (Duff 276, STC. 15722), of which the only perfect copy known is in the

[1] See pp. 617, 618, 619.   [2] See p. 629.

[3] See p. 571.

Pierpont Morgan Library, New York, contains a frontispiece of *King and Councillors*, of crude cutting but interesting design.[1]

Pynson's and Wynkyn's editions of Pierre Gringore's *Castell of Laboure* (translated by Alexander Bar-

Fig. 466. Printer's mark of Richard Pynson, London.

clay) have already been mentioned in the chapter on illustration in France,[2] and Pynson's copies are hardly less expressive than the original series. Here I would merely remark on an attractive little *View of a Town* which occurs at the end of Pynson's edition of about 1505 (STC. 12380, B.M., Huth 29; fig. 467), and is repeated to represent *Rome* in Pynson's *Chronicles of England*, 1510.

Apart from the usual diagrams, the *Tower of Babel* and the *Town on an Estuary*, from Wynkyn's *Bartholomaeus* (for the *Descrypcyon of Englonde*), Pynson's *Chronicles* of 1510 present no illustration of interest.

Pynson's finest decorative work is certainly seen in the *Morton Missal* of 1500, which has already been described.[3]

Pynson also published an English edition of Sebastian Brant's *Shyp of Folys*, translated by Alexander Barclay, 1509 (STC. 3545), with copies of the original Basle woodcuts, flanked by border-pieces with dotted ground in four varieties.[4]

WILLIAM FAQUES, whom I have already mentioned as the first holder of the office of King's Printer, and who appears, like Pynson, to have been a native of Normandy, produced one attractive little book with borders and a few woodcuts, i.e. the *Latin Psalter* of 1504 (STC. 16257). The text is surrounded throughout by four-piece borders of chain design, the most interesting of the other cuts being that of *David with his Harp*, and a good

[1] Reproduced, L. Olschki, *Le Livre illustré au XVᵉ siècle*, 1926, fig. 131.
[2] See p. 676.   [3] See p. 722.
[4] Pynson also used two other dotted border-pieces in his *Sarum Missal* of 1512.

Fig. 469. Initial W, from the *Golden Legend*, London 1503/04.

Apart from the borders the *Golden Legend* contains a series of five dotted prints, somewhat roughly executed (measuring about $2\frac{5}{8} \times 1\frac{7}{8}$ inches), *Adam and Eve*, the *Nativity*, the *Ascension*, *Pentecost* and *Christ before Pilate* (f. 1, verso of table, and ff. 4, 17, 19, verso, and 40). Their designs come from a foreign source, and are seen in prints by the Master of the Berlin Passion and his school, and in various series of dotted prints, e.g. those described by Leidinger, and now in the British Museum.[1]

Then there are a few smaller metal-cuts of initial letter size, e.g. the already-mentioned *Annunciation* (f. 71, verso), the *Nativity*, and certain single figures of Saints (e.g. f. 228, verso).

In black line, apart from the large *Assembly of Saints*, there are various column-cuts, based in part on Caxton's *Golden Legend*, and numerous smaller cuts of initial letter size, including several of the series from Caxton's *Horae* (e.g. the *Adoration of the Magi*, f. 6, verso).

There are two interesting sets of initial letters: (1) A, M and P, from a series with *Dragons*, which appear to have been brought from Paris;[2] (2) L, P, Y, W, in decorative Roman letter on black ground, in some cases flicked with white, like the series of five dotted prints (see fig. 469).

The first page of Notary's *Chronicles of England*, 1504, contains a medley of black-line woodcuts (including *St. George* and *King David*) surrounded by fifteen dotted border-pieces, of which thirteen correspond to those in the *Golden Legend*. Various pieces from the *Golden Legend* set also occur at Part IV. (*Anno Christi*), one of the narrow strips being here cut in two, at the head of the *Descripcion of Englonde* and round the printer's mark on the last page. The combination of cuts and border-pieces at the head of the *Descripcion of Englonde* again includes one of the divided pieces, adds a third new piece and includes four black-line cuts, two being figures from Vérard's *Terence*.

From the *Golden Legend* is also taken the *Adam and Eve* from the series of five dotted prints, and various black-line cuts. New black-line cuts include a *View of a Town* (with little black figures of men), used for London and Rome, and various historical subjects in the style of Vérard's chief designer and probably brought from Paris. Many of the initials of the *Golden Legend* also recur.

[1] See p. 190.
[2] They correspond to those belonging to André Bocard (Cl. ii. 146), which Claudin mentions as used also by Michel Toulouse and F. Baligault.

Notary's later edition of the *Chronicles*, 1515 (STC. 10000), has an even more jumbled medley of cuts and border-pieces on its first page, including one of Vérard's *Terence* figures, the *St. George and Dragon* from Wynkyn's *Horae* of 1494 (possibly a cut of Caxton's) and pieces of chain borders. The volume contains miscellaneous material from the earlier edition, but none of the dotted border-pieces, and of the five dotted prints only the *Nativity*, in very bad condition.

CONTEMPORARY SINGLE CUTS

The possibility that the *Grotesque Alphabet* of 1464 was produced in England, on account of English MS. inscriptions, has already been discussed and refuted.[1] And some further reference has also been made to the question as to whether any of the few English single cuts still preserved can belong to a date anterior to Caxton's earliest book-illustrations.[2] This question was also answered in the negative.

The subject has been recently treated in detail by Mr. Campbell Dodgson, partly on the basis of Henry Bradshaw's bibliographical studies.[3]

Most of these early English woodcuts are so-called *Images of Pity* (or *Piety*), figures representing the *Man of Sorrows*, generally shown half-length in the Tomb, with or without the signs of the Passion. They bear inscriptions referring to Indulgences, a purpose for which the *Mass of St. Gregory* was in use abroad. The subject may in fact be considered as a part of the *Mass of St. Gregory*, for in the woodcut of this subject in Wynkyn's *Horae* of about 1494 (Lambeth copy, at sig. r 4) the vision is actually the *Christ half-length in the Tomb*.

The subject also occasionally occurred in English *Horae*, e.g. in the fragment of the third edition of Caxton's *Primer*, preserved in the British Museum,[4] and in another version in Wynkyn's *Horae* of about 1494 (Lambeth copy, at sig. g 6).

The Bodleian Library is richest in these *Images of Pity* which have been preserved in books or manuscripts, one of the earliest being inserted in MS. Bodl. 939 (reproduced with three others in the Walpole Society,

---

[1] See p. 151. [2] See p. 159.

[3] Henry Bradshaw, *On the earliest English engravings of the Indulgence known as the 'Image of Piety'*, Collected Papers, Cambridge 1889, p. 84; Campbell Dodgson, *Woodcuts of the Fifteenth Century in the Ashmolean Museum, Oxford, with notes on similar prints in the Bodleian Library*, Oxford 1929; Campbell Dodgson, *English Devotional Woodcuts of the late fifteenth century, with special reference to those in the Bodleian Library*, Walpole Society, xvii., 1928–29, 95.

[4] See p. 714.

xvii. pl. xxxv.). Other early examples are in the British Museum (CD. 3, Schreiber 869), and in the Metropolitan Museum, New York (CD. 11 and 12, from the McGuire Collection, reproduced *Einbl.* lxv. pl. 14 and 17).

One indication of the origin of these devotional cuts is offered by the inscription *Arma Beate Birgitte De Syon* at the foot of a large *Last Judgment* (CD. 6, Schreiber 608, Walpole Society, xvii. pl. xxxvi. *a*), which with two *Images of Pity* (S. 858 and 976) occurs in the Bodleian MS. Rawl. D. 403. This must refer to the only house of the Brigittine Order in England, the Convent of Syon, near Isleworth; and the *Last Judgment*, and probably others of these devotional cuts, must have been produced for the Convent, if not within its doors.[1] The type used in the *Last Judgment* has not been definitely assigned to any printer, but has letters which are found in both Wynkyn de Worde and Pynson.[2] The cut has something of the character of the blocks in Wynkyn's Bartholomaeus, *De Proprietatibus Rerum*, 1495.[3] The design is probably original in its foreground details, but the general scheme corresponds with the subject as represented, e.g., in the Lyon *Légende Dorée*, printed by Huss and Petrus of Hungary, 1483, and in Vérard's *Art de bien Vivre et de bien Mourir*, Paris 1492.

A further clue to origin appears in the inscription *Ex domo Jhesu de Betheleem* on two cuts representing the *Arms of Jesus Christ*, or the Emblems of the Passion in heraldic form (CD. 18, 19),[4] now in the Bodleian Library, Arch. G. f. 13, 14, and detached from a *Sarum Horae* printed by Pigouchet, Paris 1495 (Duff 186). It refers to the Carthusian Priory of Sheen (Richmond), and the cuts are more likely to have been made for presentation or sale to visitors as souvenirs than as book-plates.

The same subject of the *Arms of Christ* is also found used as an Indulgence (CD. 20, York Minster), and there is another example of an Indulgence with the *Virgin and Child in Glory with the Signs of the Passion* (CD. 10, S. 1053, Oxford, MS. Bodl. 113; reprod. Walpole Society, xvii. p. 103).

Finally I would mention two large single woodcuts of very different

[1] For a line-engraving of about the same period produced for the Convent of Syon see A. M. Hind, *History of Engraving and Etching*, 1923, p. 124, footnote 1.

[2] Lt.-Colonel F. S. Isaac has recently found similar capitals in the *Myroure of our Lady* printed by R. Faques for the Abbess of Syon in 1530 (B.M., C. 11. b. 8). R. Faques succeeded about 1508–09 to the stock of William Faques. No books of William Faques are known before 1504, but as he then styled himself 'King's printer', he must have been in practice some years. The two links, i.e. the relation to the convent of Syon and the identity of capital letters, renders it more likely that the *Last Judgment* cut was printed by him rather than by Wynkyn or Pynson.

[3] See p. 726.

[4] Reproduced, Walpole Society, xvii. pl. xxxvi. b and c.

character. In the first place a sheet, measuring about 3 × 14 inches, with a *Heraldic Lion*, the arms of William Gray (Bishop of Ely from 1454 to 1478), which is pasted on a column near his tomb in Ely Cathedral (CD. 5, S. 2030). Then the *King Henry VI. invoked as a Saint* (fig. 470), inserted in a MS. English Bible on vellum, of the latter part of the xv century, in the Bodleian

Fig. 470. King Henry VI. invoked as a Saint. Fragment. Bodleian Library, Oxford.

Library (CD. 21, MS. Bodl. 277, reprod. Walpole Society, xvii. pl. xxxvii.). It is in fragmentary state, but the main part of the subject, with figures kneeling before the standing king, remains intact. Unfortunately the King's face is removed, and only a few letters of the inscription above and below remain. But from the arms and the *cu* of the lettering above, *Henricus* is evidently intended, and every detail points to the identity of the subject. It forms a most interesting historical record of the veneration paid to Henry VI. under the Tudors, of a short-lived popularity of pilgrimage to his shrine at Windsor, and of the efforts made by Henry VII. about 1490 towards his kinsman's canonisation. In style I can refer to nothing comparable in English book-illustration except the *Arundel badge* on the first page of Caxton's *Golden Legend*. It is most nearly related to the phase of North French woodcut which shows some kinship to the Flemish scheme of cutting with regular series of short lines of parallel shading, of which examples may be noted in books printed by Dupré.

BIBLIOGRAPHY

AMES, Joseph. Typographical Antiquities, being an historical account of printing in England. London 1749 (2nd ed., W. Herbert, 1785–90; 3rd ed., T. F. Dibdin, 1810–19).

BRADSHAW, Henry. On the Earliest English Engravings of the Indulgence known as the 'Image of Piety', Cambridge Antiquarian Society's *Communications*, iii. (1867), 25th February. Reprinted with revisions in H. Bradshaw, Collected Papers, Cambridge 1889, p. 84. (This deals with book-illustration as well as with single cuts.)

DUFF, Edward Gordon. Chapter on England, in A. W. Pollard, Early Illustrated Books. London 1893; 2nd ed., 1917, p. 219.

DUFF, Edward Gordon, and others. Hand-lists of English Printers, 1501–1556. 4 vols. London (Bibliographical Society) 1895–1913.

DUFF, Edward Gordon. A Century of the English Book Trade. Short notices of all printers, stationers, etc., 1457–1557. London 1905.

DUFF, Edward Gordon. The Printers, Stationers and Bookbinders of Westminster and London from 1476 to 1535. Cambridge 1906.

DUFF, Edward Gordon. The English Provincial Printers, Stationers and Bookbinders to 1557. Cambridge 1912.

DUFF, Edward Gordon. Fifteenth-Century English Books. Bibliographical Society, Illustrated Monographs, xviii. London 1917.

McKERROW, R. B. Printers' and Publishers' Devices in England, 1485–1640. Bibliographical Society, Illustrated Monographs, xvi. London 1913.

McKERROW, R. B. Border-pieces used by English Printers. Paper read before the Bibliographical Society. London 1924.

PLOMER, H. R. Short History of English Printing, 1476–1900. London 1915.

PLOMER, H. R. English Printers' Ornaments. London 1924.

PLOMER, H. R. Wynkyn de Worde and his Contemporaries, from the death of Caxton till 1535. London 1925.

SHORT-TITLE CATALOGUE of books printed in England, Scotland and Ireland and of English books printed abroad, 1475–1640. Compiled by A. W. Pollard, G. R. Redgrave and others. London (Bibliographical Society) 1926.

JUCHHOFF, Rudolf. Drucker- und Verlegerzeichen des xv Jahrhunderts in den Niederländen, England, Spanien, Böhmen, Mähren und Polen. Munich 1927.

McKERROW, R. B., and FERGUSON, F. S. Title-page borders used in England and Scotland 1485–1640. Bibliographical Society, Illustrated Monographs, xxi. London 1932 (for 1931).

HIND, A. M. Studies in English Engraving. 1. Woodcut Illustration in the xv Century. The *Connoisseur*, February 1933.

HODNETT, Edward. English Woodcuts 1480–1535. Bibliographical Society, Illustrated Monographs, xxii. London 1935.

CHAPTER X

BOOK-ILLUSTRATION AND CONTEMPORARY SINGLE CUTS IN SPAIN AND PORTUGAL

THE amount of original work in book-illustration produced in Spain and Portugal during the xv century is incomparably less than the corresponding production in Italy, Germany, France and the Netherlands. Many of the early printers in Spain came from abroad, and in many popular books they would almost be expected to use the earlier and well-known designs.

Thus the cuts in the first illustrated book issued in Spain,[1] Werner Rolewinck, *Fasciculus Temporum*, printed at Seville in 1480 by ALFONSO DEL PUERTO and BARTOLOMÉ SEGURA, was probably based on the Venice edition, printed by Georgius Walch in 1479.[2] But these woodcuts are of small artistic interest, repeating the typical subjects such as *Noah's Ark*, the *Tower of Babel*, various towns, and the figure of *Christ blessing*, which appeared in this book from its earliest German editions (about 1473) onwards.

Then PABLO and JUAN HURUS, immigrants from Constance who became the chief printers at Saragossa, issued copies of the Ulm originals in their *Aesop* of 1489 (K. 21, Haebler 6, Escorial) and Boccaccio, *Mujeres Illustres*, of 1494 (K. 69, Haebler 52, Berlin, Pierpont Morgan, etc.), while in their Rodericus Zamorensis, *Spejo de la Vida humana* (*Speculum Vitae Humanae*) of 1491 (K. 320, Haebler 579, Cambridge, Madrid, etc.) they used blocks from Philippi and Reinhard's Lyon edition of 1482 which were in part Zainer's original Augsburg blocks and in part copies from the same.[3] Other copies of foreign works issued by the same firm were Franciscus de Retza, *Defensorium inviolatae virginitatis Mariae*, about 1488 (K. 165, Haebler 190 [10]), based on a German block-book of 1470,[4] various small editions of the *Ars Moriendi*, with copies after the block-book, between about 1483 and 1493 (about 1483, K. 53, Haebler 36 bis, Escorial; about 1489, K. 54, Haebler 37, Oxford; about 1493, K. 55, Haebler 37 [5], Barcelona), Ketham, *Compendio de la*

---

[1] But cf. 748.   [2] See pp. 456 and 357.   [3] See p. 602.

[4] See W. L. Schreiber, *Defensorium* ... aus der Druckerei des Hurus in Saragossa, in Facsimile-Reproduktion. Weimar (Gesellschaft der Bibliophilen) 1910.

Salud humana (*Fasciculus Medicinae*), 1494 (K. 220, Haebler 160, Madrid), with copies after the Venetian originals, and Andres de Lí, *Tesoro de la Pasión*, 1494 (K. 40, Haebler 200, Berlin Print Room, Escorial), containing copies after the Netherlandish Delbecq-Schreiber Passion.[1]

An edition of Breydenbach, *Viaje a Tierra Santa*, Pablo Hurus, 1498 (K. 77, Haebler 75), was printed from the original Mainz blocks of 1486,[2] made up with material from other books by Hurus (e.g. from the *Tesoro de la Pasión*), and from the stock of Matthias Huss of Lyon. Other printers to use copies of well-known foreign illustrations were FRIEDRICH BIEL of Basle, in his *Aesop*, printed at Burgos, 1496 (K. 22, Haebler 7, Paris), and JUAN DE BURGOS in his Spanish edition of Ketham's *Fasciculus Medicinae* (*Epilogo en medicina y cirurgia*), printed at Burgos, 1495 (K. 221, Haebler 246, Madrid, Paris, New York Hisp. Soc.). A third series of copies of Ketham was printed at Pamplona, by Arnao Guillen de Brocar, 1495 (K. 222, Haebler 27, Paris, Madrid).

In his edition of Jodocus Badius, *Stultifera Navis*, printed by Friedrich Biel at Burgos soon after 1500 (Haebler 39), the cuts are based on the Paris edition of Kerver for de Marnef of February 1500/1501.[3]

And not infrequently woodcut illustrations are found based on line-engravings by the German Master E.S.[4] and Martin Schongauer, who must have been well known to craftsmen in Spain and in Italy in the late xv century.

Spanish and Portuguese books are particularly notable for their decorative character, in type, borders, initials and illustrative material. The quality of Spanish type-founders is evidenced in the well-known excellence of their Greek type in the early xvi century, which has never been surpassed and remains the pattern of the most modern founts.[5]

Even on the side of decoration a good deal of the earliest work is based on foreign models, and it is only from about 1490 that a genuine Spanish style may be said to emerge.

Of the borders inspired by foreign work there are in the first place a few in black-line scroll-work nearly related to the Southern German styles of Augsburg and Strassburg, e.g. those in Turrecremata, *Expositio*

---

[1] See p. 582.   [2] See pp. 352-356.   [3] See p. 674.

[4] E.g. the *Canon* cut in the Lisbon Ludolphus, *Vita Christi*, 1495, after E.S., Lehrs 31.

[5] The fount of Arnao Guillen de Brocar, first used in the great Polyglot Bible of Cardinal Francisco Ximenes, at Alcalá, 1514 (reproduced in the more developed form used in the undated *Musaeus*, in Victor Scholderer, *Greek Printing Types, 1465–1927, Facsimiles from an Exhibition*, British Museum, 1927, fig. 24).

Fig. 471. Initial D, from Diaz de Montalvo, *Compilación de Leyes*, Huete 1484.

in Psalmos, printed by Hurus at Saragossa, 12th November 1482 (Haebler 651, K. 224 b, Madrid, etc.),[1] in a *Horae* (*Officium B.M.V.*) issued by the same printer about 1490 (K. 286, Haebler 490 (5), Hispanic Society, New York), in Felip de Malla, *Pecador remut*, printed by ROSENBACH at Barcelona, about 1495 (K. 242, H. 390), and in Ludolphus de Saxonia, *Vita Christi*, printed by VALENTIN FERNANDEZ, Lisbon 1495 (K. 237, Haebler 373, Don Manuel 5). Other black-line borders which may be mentioned occur in Domenico Cavalca, *Espejo de la Cruz*, printed by ANTONIO MARTINEZ at Seville, 1486 (K. 88, Haebler 144, Madrid), in Bonaventura, *Meditationes Vitae Christi*, printed by PERE MIQUEL, Barcelona 1493 (K. 75, Haebler 67), and in Donatus, *De Octo Partibus Orationis*, printed by Friedrich Biel, Burgos 1498 (K. 126; Haebler 236 [5], present locality unknown, once Rosenthal; reprod. Lyell, fig. 60). The last is a very attractive example, representing *Children hunting and climbing a tree*, evidently inspired by subjects in

Fig. 472. Lower Border-piece, from Diaz de Montalvo, *Compilación de Leyes*, Huete 1484.

Paris *Horae*. Then a chain-work border on black ground, copied from one of Ratdolt's Venetian borders (used in his Johann Müller, *Calendarium*, 1482),[2] was used at Barcelona, e.g. by PEDRO POSA in his *Imitacio Christi*, 1482 (K. 176, Haebler 293, Paris), and Phocas, *De Partibus Orationis*, 1488 (K. 303, Haebler 549, Madrid), and by Pere Miquel in St. Jerome, *Vida e transit*, 1493 (K. 199, Haebler 682, Barcelona, Stuttgart).

Very remarkable in design is the two-sided metal-cut border-piece, partly executed in punch-work (see fig. 472), which occurs at the

---

[1] Cf. E. P. Goldschmidt, Catalogue viii. No. 96, London.

[2] See p. 460.

beginning of each of the six blocks in Alfonso Diaz de Montalvo, *Compilación de leyes y ordenanzas reales*, printed by ALVARO DE CASTRO at Huete, 1484 and 1485 (K. 109, 110, Haebler 214, 216). The six pictorial initials which occur in the same place are equally interesting. From their subjects the initials appear to have been made for the book,

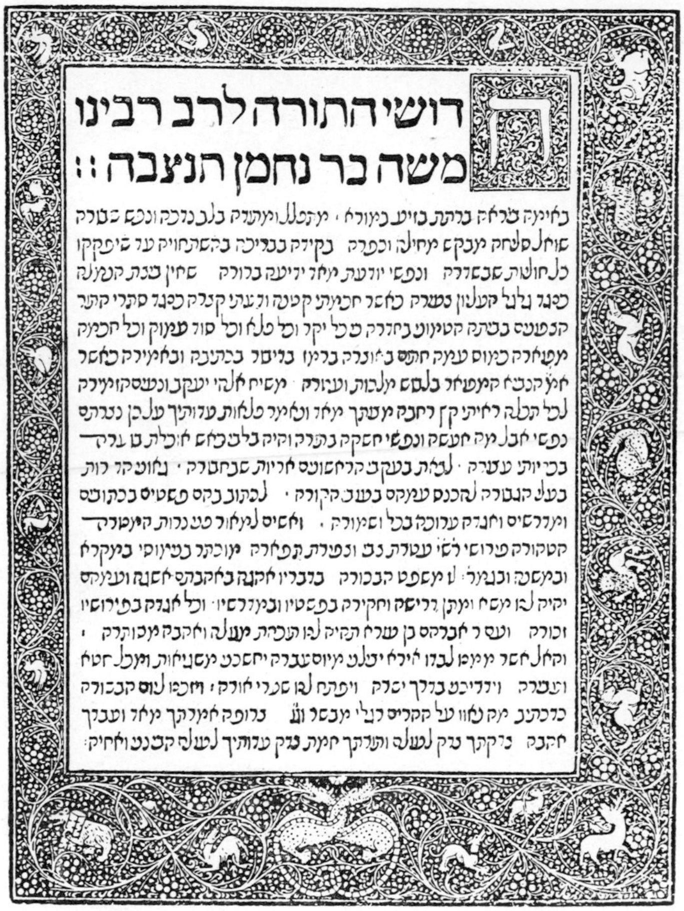
חדושי התורה לרב רבינו
משה בר נחמן תנצבה ::

Fig. 473. Page and Border, from Moses ben Nachman, *Perusch ha-Tora*, Lisbon 1489.

but it is curious that the initial reproduced in fig. 471, which from its form can be hardly other than D, is used for B(uena).

Most delicate of all the Iberian borders on black ground is that reproduced in fig. 473. It was first used by ALFONSO FERNÁNDEZ de Córdoba in his *Manuale Caesaraugustanum*, printed at Hijar, about 1487 (K. 244, Haebler 394 (5), Berlin), and later in the Hebrew books printed by the

Fig. 474. Page with border, from *Tirant lo Blanch*, Valencia 1490.

Fig. 475. Initial A, from Juan de Mena, *La Coronación*, Seville 1499.

RABBI ELIEZER at Lisbon, i.e. Moses ben Nachman, *Perusch ha-Tora* (*Nuevas de la ley o comentario sobre el pentateuco*), July 1489 (K. 278, Don Manuel 3), and David Abu-Derahim, *Comentario sobre el orden de las oraciones*, November 1489 (K. 102, Don Manuel 4). In its combination of delicate tendril and scroll, with animals and conventional grotesque, it shows definite Islamic influence, and is characteristic of Hispano-Mauresque design. It is comparable with Ratdolt's work (especially with his border to Cepio, *Gesta Mocenici*, 1477), but the style is carried to an extraordinary finesse in technique.

Bolder and even more characteristic Spanish work is the four-piece border first used by NICOLAUS SPINDELER at Valencia in his *Tirant lo Blanch* (by Juan Martorell?), 1490 (K. 252, Haebler 639; fig. 474). The page also includes a narrow fifth panel to divide the columns of text, and two initial letters. The book is only known in three copies, those of the British Museum (the finest of the three), Valencia and the Hispanic Society, New York. The border-pieces were used later (without the fifth panel) by J. Rosenbach, e.g. in his *Constitucións de Cataluña*, 1494 (K. 148 and 149, Haebler 167 and 168), and by Pere Miquel and Diego de Gumiel in their *Usatges de Barcelona e Constitucións de Cataluña*, 1495 (K. 98, Haebler 652). In Spindeler's border the character of the animals is Gothic rather than Islamic. Both of the borders reproduced (figs. 473 and 474) are undoubtedly cut on metal.

Another border of indigenous character, of bold and handsome design, with scroll-work and heraldic animals, and again certainly cut in metal, appeared in Jacob ben Ascher, *Tur Orach Chajim*, printed by ABRAHAM BEN SAMUEL D'ORTAS, at Leiria (Portugal), 1495 (K. 211, Haebler 331, Frankfurt, Valladolid). The animals show more relation to Islamic style than those of *Tirant lo Blanch*.

Initial letters on black ground are used by most of the good Spanish printers, some of the best series belonging to UNGUT and STANISLAUS POLONUS at Seville (fig. 475), SPINDELER at Valencia, ROSENBACH at Barcelona, ARNAO GUILLEN DE BROCAR at Pamplona, and FRIEDRICH BIEL at Burgos.

The Spanish craftsman of the xv century was usually happy in the execution of heraldic designs, and the *Arms of Ferdinand and Isabella*, which so constantly occur, offered a most decorative pattern (fig. 476). The title-designs to the *Flors de Vertuts*, printed by DIEGO DE GUMIEL, Barcelona 1495 (K. 180, Haebler 275), and to Bernardus de Gordonio, *Lilio de Medicina*, printed by UNGUT and STANISLAUS POLONUS, Seville 1495 (K. 64, Haebler 300), are characteristic examples. And the most attractive of the printer's marks is certainly that of Ungut and Stanislaus Polonus (fig. 477).

Fig. 476. The Arms of Ferdinand and Isabella, from Garcia, *Peregrina*, Seville 1498.

I have already referred to the use of metal in certain of the borders and initials, and in white-line work it was fairly common in Spanish book-illustration. Crude metal-cuts occur in the first Spanish illustrated book, the *Fasciculus Temporum* of 1480, already mentioned (see p. 741), i.e. in the *Signs of the Evangelists* used as corner-pieces of the subject of *Christ blessing*. Apart from borders and initials perhaps the most interesting series in this manner occurs in Enrique de Villena, *Trabajos de Hércules*, printed by JUAN DE BURGOS, Burgos 1499 (K. 368, Haebler 689). If, as seems probable, these cuts are in metal, it cannot be said that the method is very aptly used, for though here and there the white-line serves some purpose, in general the style is black-line, with a dull regularity of shading, and the series of short lines laid in parallel series for the ground, as in Netherlandish woodcuts.

Isolated examples on metal will be mentioned in dealing with the work of various printers.

I would now offer a short survey of the chief woodcut illustrations in Spain and Portugal, apart from those already mentioned, to some extent in order of the various printers.

Fig. 477. Mark of the Printers Ungut and Stanislaus Polonus, Seville.

SEVILLE—VALLADOLID—ZAMORA

I have spoken of the *Fasciculus Temporum* printed by PUERTO and SEGURA at Seville in 1480 as the first Spanish illustrated book.

If any woodcut illustration precedes this it is only in the unimportant representations of seals (with little figures of the Man of Sorrows, Saints, etc.) on papal bulls. The earliest of these with certain date is the *Bulla de indulgencias en favor de la iglesia de S. Salvador de Avila*, printed at Valladolid, 1481 (K. 28, Haebler 111 [2], Lyell Collection), but a date as early as about 1477 has been conjectured for another bull in Mr. Lyell's Collection, *Bulla de indulgencias en favor de la christianisación de Guinea*, printed by Puerto and Segura at Seville (K. 13, Haebler 111, 6), though both Haebler and Kurz only venture to date it 'about 1480'.[1]

There are few subject illustrations during the eighties of the xv century, except those based on foreign models. The earliest which may be considered characteristically Spanish are those in Enrique de Villena, *Doze Trabajos de Hércules*, printed by ANTONIO DE CENTENERA at Zamora, 15th January 1483 (K. 367, Haebler 688; see fig. 478). In their free outline and open shading they are comparable with certain of the earliest Lyon woodcut illustrations, but might derive their style equally from a source such as that of the Ulm Boccaccio. Apart from these technical relationships, they show a combination of decorative and bizarre qualities which characterise much Spanish work.

I have already spoken of the decorative work of the printers UNGUT and STANISLAUS POLONUS at Seville, and I would mention one or two of their illustrations. The most excellent is that of a *King enthroned* (fig. 479), the title-cut to Egidio Colonna, *Regimiento de los Principes*, 1494 (K. 94, Haebler 156). The style is to some extent Netherlandish, but the shading

---

[1] See Lyell, pp. 5-7, and figs. 3 and 4.

is somewhat freer and more functional than usual, and the cutting shows individual quality.

Among other books printed by Ungut and Stanislaus Polonus, Gaspar Gorricio de Novaria, *Contemplaciones sobre el Rosario*, 1495 (K. 179, Haebler 301), has two full-page illustrations and various smaller subjects, rendered

Fig. 478. Hercules and Cerberus, from Villena, *Doze Trabajos de Hércules*, Zamora 1483.

more decorative by the variety of their border designs. They are cut more lightly and with a freer hand than most Spanish blocks.

Far poorer in artistic quality than the *King enthroned*, but more typical of the run of Spanish illustration, stiff in its line and regular in shading, is the woodcut of a *Man preaching to Turks* in Ricoldus de Montecrucis, *Improbatio Alcorani*, 1500 (K. 319, Haebler 577). By the same hand is the subject of *Master and Pupils* which occurs in an edition of Juan Infante, *Forma libellandi*, probably printed by Stanislaus Polonus about 1498–1500, which I do not find recorded in Haebler or Kurz (B.M., IA. 52875 [1], fig. 480).

Among other illustrated books printed at Seville, the *Historia di Vespasiano*, printed by PEDRO BRUN, 1499 (K. 360, Haebler 674), has an interesting series of cuts, which shows both French and Netherlandish influence.

VALENCIA

The most important work done at Valencia, the border to *Tirant lo Blanch*, printed by NICOLAUS SPINDELER in 1490, has already been described. Of an

Fig. 479. King enthroned, from Colonna, *Regimiento de los Principes*, Seville 1494.

earlier Valencia printer, in fact one of the first printers in Spain,[1] LAMBERT

[1] He has until recently been regarded as the printer of the earliest book in Spain (1474), but there is now some question of his having worked at first under the direction of Jacob or Philipp Vizlant (see Haebler, *Geschichte der Spanischen Frühdruckes*, p. 21).

PALMART, I would only mention a rough metal-cut in the *criblée* manner, the *Virgin and Child in Glory, with Four Dominican Saints*, which occurs in Jerònim Fuster, *Omelia sobre lo psalm De Profundis*, 1490 (K. 166, Haebler 285). Metal-cuts may also be noted in S. Bernardus, *Epistola de Regimine Domus*, printed by Spindeler about 1498 (K. 61, Haebler 47, Cagliari),

Fig. 480. Master and Pupils, from Juan Infante, *Forma Libellandi*, Seville, about 1498–1500.

and in the *Obra allaors de Sant Cristofol*, printed by PEDRO TRINCHER, 1498 (K. 283, Haebler 487). The latter book also contains a *St. Christopher*, a black-line cut within a border on black ground, which is thoroughly Venetian in inspiration.

Entirely Spanish in its style, stiff in handling but decorative in character, is the frontispiece of *Figures before a Town Gate* in Francisco Ximenez, *Regiment de la Cosa Publica*, printed by CRISTOBAL COFMAN at Valencia, 28th January 1499 (K. 134, Haebler 708).

BARCELONA
AND MISCELLANEOUS WOODCUTS BY, OR RELATED TO, THE MASTER ID

At Barcelona, PEDRO POSA, JOHANN ROSENBACH, PERE MIQUEL and DIEGO DE GUMIEL are all responsible for interesting work, and several decorative pieces have already been mentioned. I would here add some further notes of subject woodcuts in books by Rosenbach and Pere Miquel.

An interesting series of cuts appeared in Diego de San Pedro, *Cárcel de*

Amor, printed by Rosenbach, 1493 (K. 331, Haebler 606; fig. 481).[1] The subject reproduced certainly shows knowledge of the engravings after Botticelli, with its reminiscence of the illustration to Canto I. in Landino's Dante (Florence 1481).

Fig. 481. The Author meets the Wild Man, from Diego de San Pedro, *Cárcel de Amor*, Barcelona 1493.

Remarkable in style is the large title-cut with the *Author and eight women pupils* in Francisco Ximenez, *Libre de les dones*, printed by Rosenbach, 1495 (K. 132, Haebler 706, Madrid; Widener Library, Harvard; Hispanic Society, New York, reprod. Lyell, p. 47). Though cruder in character, it is similar in style to the work of the Master ID, whose signed cuts, about 1489–90, have already been described above in the chapter on France,[2] and I would refer to that place for the general discussion of his artistic personality. Of greater quality and interest, and equally near to the style of ID, is the *King in Council (Jaime I. and the Cortes of Lleida)* which appeared in the *Usatges de Barcelona e Constitucións de Cataluña*, printed by Pere Miquel and Diego de Gumiel, 20th February 1495 (K. 98, Haebler 652, Madrid, Paris, Boston; fig. 482).[3] The block, which is certainly of metal, is probably by the same cutter as the border in the same book, which first appeared in 1490 in Spindeler's *Tirant lo Blanch*.[4] Other cuts not unlike ID in character are the *David kneeling in prayer at the head of his Army*, which appeared in Narcis Vinyoles, *Omelia sobre lo psalm del Miserere*,

---

[1] Good copies were printed by Friedrich Biel, Burgos 1496 (K. 332, Haebler 604).

[2] See pp. 614-616.

[3] Kristeller (*Kupferstich und Holzschnitt*, 1922, p. 124) refers to an edition of 1480, with the cuts, and told me personally that he had noted a copy in the Archivio Municipal, Barcelona, but Haebler does not recognise any edition before 1493 (Haebler 166, Barcelona, Univ. Library), and that one without the illustrations. Cf. Olschki, Bibliofilia, Florence 1903, p. 127.

[4] See p. 746 and fig. 474.

Fig. 482. Jaime I. of Aragon in council, from *Usatges de Barcelona*, Barcelona 1495.

printed by Spindeler at Valencia, 1499 (K. 370, Haebler 692, reprod. Lyell, p. 25), and the *Author writing*, in Livy, *Las Decadas*, printed anonymously at Salamanca, 1497 (K. 231, Haebler 365, Paris, Madrid, reprod. Lyell, p. 71).

Whether the Master ID is responsible for any of these cuts or not, one signed woodcut by him is known in a Spanish book, the large *Christ on the Cross between the Virgin and St. John*, which appeared in Fernandez Perez de Guzman, *La Cronica del Rey don Juan II.*, printed by ARNAO GUILLEN DE BROCAR at Logroño, 1517 (reprod. Lyell, p. 287). Though not known in any earlier book it was probably done between 1490 and 1500. There is also a smaller woodcut, the *Last Judgment*, signed ID (in monogram form) in Gomez Garcia, *Carro de dos Vidas*, printed by JOHANN PEGNITZER and MAGNUS HERBST at Seville, 1500 (K. 174, Haebler 288, Madrid), but I have not seen the print, and the monogram form renders it likely that it is by another hand.

SALAMANCA

At Salamanca a long series of cuts, fairly crude in execution, appeared in Guillermus, *Postilla super Epistolas et Evangelia* (in Spanish), issued by an anonymous press in 1493, of which the only known copy is at Upsala (K. 190, Haebler 250 [3]).[1] An earlier edition is recorded, that of Pablo Hurus, Saragossa, 20th February 1485 (K. 189, Haebler 250), but cannot now be traced, so that the relation of the blocks is uncertain. Probably both editions were based on that issued by Philippi at Lyon about 1483–84 (Cl. iii. 141), which in its turn may have derived from one or another of the numerous German *Plenarien*.[2] Later editions, with similar cuts, were issued by Ungut and Stanislaus Polonus, Seville, 28th February 1497 (K. 191, Haebler 309, Madrid), and by Rodrigo Alvarez at Porto, 25th October 1497 (K. 192, Lisbon). More attractive is the vivacious design on the title to Boccaccio, *La Fiammetta* (in Spanish), printed anonymously, 1497 (K. 68, Haebler 55, Pierpont Morgan, New York; Huntington, San Marino; reprod. Lyell, p. 54). In its open line it is near in character to early Lyon woodcut (e.g. to *L'Abusé en Court*).[3] Interesting also, and not without decorative value, is the series of illustrations of chess in Luis Ramirez de Lucena, *Repetición de Amores y arte de Ajedres*, printed by Leonhard Hutz and Lope Sanz, about 1497 (K. 234, Haebler 371).

---

[1] See Isak Collijn, *Notas sobre un incunable español desconocido*, Madrid 1906.
[2] See pp. 604 and 290.   [3] See p. 600.

SARAGOSSA

The work of PABLO and JEAN HURUS at Saragossa[1] consisted largely of copies of foreign work, which we have already mentioned. German in character, and showing the influence of the school of Wolgemut, is the frontispiece of the *Author* (or *translator*) *presenting his book to a king*, in Aristotle, *Ethica*, in the Latin translation of Leonardo Bruni (Aretino), 1492 (K. 52, Haebler 29). More characteristic of Spanish work, in their stiff outline and regular shading, are the illustrations in the *Expositio Aurea Hymnorum*, printed by Pablo Hurus, 1499 (K. 139, Haebler 254, Stuttgart) and the several versions of Hurus's printer's mark, a design with two heraldic lions, sometimes accompanied by side-pieces of St. James and St. Sebastian (Juchhoff 110-113).

BURGOS

At Burgos also we have found various copies of foreign woodcuts, in the illustrated books printed by FRIEDRICH BIEL and JUAN DE BURGOS. I would mention a few other works issued by these printers.

Well designed and cut is the *Author writing in a Study*, somewhat in the manner of the Lyon *Terence* of 1493, in the *Libro del Anticristo*, printed by Biel, 1497 (K. 42, Haebler 17, Paris, reprod. Lyell, fig. 59), a cut which re-appeared in the same printer's Donatus, *De octo partibus Orationis*, 1498 (K. 126, Haebler 236 (5), present locality unknown, once in Rosenthal's possession). A border which appeared in the latter work has already been described.[2] In David Aubert, *Oliveros de Castilla y Artus dalgarbe*, 1499 (K. 57, Haebler 494, Hispanic Society, New York), Biel issued numerous cuts again showing a blurred reflection of the style of the woodcuts in the Lyon *Terence*.

In the Netherlandish style, but heavier in character, is the subject of a *Knight kneeling before a King* in Alfonso de Cartagena, *Doctrinal de los Caballeros*, printed by Juan de Burgos, 1497 (K. 27, Haebler 126, Madrid, Hispanic Society, New York). And again under Lyon or Netherlandish influence are the numerous column cuts in Voragine, *La Leyenda de los Santos*, printed without date (probably about 1500) by Juan de Burgos (Haebler 698), some in broadly cut lines, others in a finer technique nearer to the quality of metal-cut. The only other illustrated Spanish *Golden Legend* of the xv century to which I can refer is the *Flos sanctorum Romançat*,

---

[1] See J. M. Sánchez, *Bibliografía zaragózana del siglo XV*, Madrid 1908. For P. and J. Hurus, cf. above, p. 602.   [2] See p. 743.

printed by Rosenbach at Barcelona, 1494 (K. 208, Haebler 297, Barcelona, Madrid).

PAMPLONA—TOLEDO

At Pamplona a typical cut of Spanish character is that of the *Preacher* (within a black-ground border of branches, leaves, and flowers), on the title of Gulielmus Peraldus, *Doctrina de los religiosos en romançe*, printed by ARNAO GUILLEN DE BROCAR, 1499 (K. 188, Haebler 533, Oxford, reprod. Lyell, fig. 75). At Toledo appeared, printed by PEDRO HAGENBACH, a Spanish translation of Julius Caesar, *Los Comentarios*, 1498 (K. 82, Haebler 113, Escorial; Hispanic Society, New York) with a good title-page containing the arms of Ferdinand and Isabella, and the handsome *Mozarabic Missal* (*Missale mixtum secundum regulam beati Isidori dictum Mozarabes*), handsomely printed by Pedro Hagenbach, 9th January 1500 (K. 273, Haebler 446), with a *Canon* cut of *Christ on the Cross with the Virgin and St. John*, clearly influenced by, if not based on, French models.

MONTSERRAT

Characteristic metal-cuts are the *Standing Madonna of Montserrat* (in the form of a seal), which appeared in Bonaventura, *Meditationes vitae Christi*, printed by LUSCHNER at Montserrat, 1499 (K. 76, Haebler 69, Madrid; Paris; Hispanic Society, New York; Manchester), and the *Seated Madonna of Montserrat* which Luschner used as his printer's mark (Juchhoff 87), e.g. in Bonaventura, *De Instructione Novitiorum*, 1499 (K. 74, Haebler 63, Madrid, Paris, Huntington).

The number of illustrated books printed in Portugal during the xv century is small, and they are described in detail in the late Don Manuel's fine work on the Portuguese books in his own library. Apart from the Jewish books with borders and initials printed at Lisbon by the Rabbi Eliezer, and at Leiria by Abraham ben Samuel d' Ortas, to which reference has already been made,[1] there only remains the production of VALENTIN FERNANDEZ, of Moravia, who printed at Lisbon between 1493 and 1516.

His most important work, done in collaboration with NICOLAO DE SAXONIA, is an edition of Ludolphus de Saxonia, *Vita Christi*, 1495 (Don

---

[1] See pp. 744 and 746.

Manuel 5, K. 237, Haebler 373, Lisbon, Porto, Evora, Don Manuel Collection).[1]

Beside the handsome border of scroll work, with vine branch and squirrels, which has already been mentioned,[2] there are woodcuts of a *King and Queen at Prayer* (fig. 483), a *Christ on the Cross between the Virgin and*

Fig. 483. King and Queen at Prayer, from Ludolphus, *Vita Christi*, Lisbon 1495.

St. John (copied from the Master E.S., Lehrs 31), some heraldic cuts, and a good series of capital letters (copied from Israhel van Meckenem).

The most elaborate of the woodcut initals, the letter A, is an isolated example from a set of which various other letters appeared in Fernandez's edition of Marco Polo's book of travels, 1502 (Don Manuel 8, Lisbon; Paris; Don Manuel Collection). The border of the first page, which encloses an illustration of the traveller's ship, is partly made up from the Ludolphus border. Pieces of the same border, and initials from the Ludolphus, also reappear in *Os Autos dos Apostolos*, 1505 (Don Manuel 11, Evora; Don Manuel Collection).

The only other woodcut illustration in Fernandez's books during the xv century which might be mentioned is that of the *Author adoring the Virgin and Child* in Kaminto, *Regimento contra ha Pestenença*, n.d., about 1496? (Don Manuel 7, K. 228, Haebler 346, Madrid; Don Manuel collection).

[1] Apart from the copy in the collection of the late Don Manuel, the only other copy known outside Portugal was recently in the possession of Maggs Bros. (Catalogue 416).

[2] See p. 743

CONTEMPORARY SINGLE CUTS

Practically nothing is known to me of xv century single woodcuts produced in Spain or Portugal. The only example to which I would refer is a *St. Anthony of Padua* of about the end of the century (Schreiber 1216 a and 1233 a), once in the Schreiber Collection, and presented to the Ashmolean Museum, Oxford, by Mr. C. W. Dyson Perrins in 1917.[1] A long inscription at the foot begins *O proles hyspanie*, and the cut also contains the arms of Portugal. The heavy outline, the stiff drawing, and regular shading are all in keeping with Spanish and Portuguese work, and the inscription and arms both tell in favour of Iberian origin. The cut shows kinship to certain French woodcuts already described, and was found, like them, in a box-lid, but neither consideration justifies, in my opinion, the attribution of the cut to France or Savoy.[2]

BIBLIOGRAPHY

HAEBLER, Conrad. Early Printers of Spain and Portugal. Bibliographical Society, Illustrated Monographs, iv. London 1897 (for 1896).

HAEBLER, Conrad. Spanische und portuguesische Bücherzeichen. Strassburg 1898.

HAEBLER, Conrad. Bibliografía ibérica del siglo xv. 2 vols. The Hague 1903, 1917.

HAEBLER, Conrad. Geschichte der spanischen Frühdruckes in Stammbäumen. Leipzig 1923 ('in Stammbäumen' refers to the classification of printers in genealogical trees, or groups).

BIBLIOFILIA. Publicat per R. Miguel y Planas. Barcelona 1914, etc. (a periodical containing much material and illustration of early Spanish book-illustration).

BRITISH MUSEUM. Short-title Catalogue of books printed in Spain, and of Spanish books printed elsewhere in Europe before 1601, now in the British Museum. Edited by Henry Thomas. London 1921.

LYELL, J. P. R. Early Book Illustration in Spain. London 1926.

MANUEL II., King of Portugal. Early Portuguese Books 1489–1600 in the Library of H.M. the King of Portugal. I. 1489–1539. London 1929. II. 1540–1569. London 1932. III. 1570–1600, and supplement, 1500–1569. London 1934.

   The late Don Manuel (†1932) left his library to the Portuguese nation.

KURZ, Martin. Handbuch der iberischen Bilddrucke des xv Jahrhunderts. Leipzig 1931.

[1] Schreiber sale, 1909, No. 26 (with reproduction).

[2] Cf. p. 700 and see Schreiber, *Manuel* and *Handbuch*, and Dodgson, *Woodcuts of the xv Century in the Ashmolean Museum, Oxford*. Oxford 1929, No. 42. St. Anthony was actually born at Lisbon.

INDEXES

INDEX I

DESIGNERS AND ENGRAVERS OF WOODCUT

In the above title *engraver* is used for *cutter* or *engraver*. As far as possible indication is given as to whether an artist was designer, cutter (with knife) or engraver (with graver or burin). These categories are abbreviated as wood-d., wood-c., and wood-en. Metal-c. is used to denote both the cutter in white line on metal and the engraver in the dotted manner. The distinction between designer and cutter is often very obscure in xv-century work. A certain number of printers of books have been admitted who seem to have been woodcutters, but a query is added after the description in cases of uncertainty. It also includes names recorded as of *printers* in early documents, before the discovery of movable type, no doubt of craftsmen engaged in the printing and colouring of early woodcuts, even if they were not actually cutters. Their titles as recorded are quoted in italics. Printers of block-books are given in this index, not with printers of books.

Masters known by monograms, initials and descriptive titles are indexed in the alphabet under *Master*.

The first page reference generally indicates the principal passage dealing with the designer or engraver in question.

b. = born; d. = died; w. = worked.

PAGE

INDEX II

PRINTERS AND PUBLISHERS OF BOOKS

This list has been made from many bibliographical sources. Though it cannot claim to be authoritative, it will probably be a useful guide to the student of woodcut illustration.

A certain number of craftsmen known in early documents, before the discovery of movable type as *printers*, i.e. printers and possibly cutters of wood blocks, are given in the Index of Designers and Engravers of Woodcut. Known or presumed printers or producers of block-books are also given in the Index of Designers and Engravers.

The first page reference generally indicates the principal passage dealing with the printer's or publisher's books.

b. = born; d. = died; w. = worked.

INDEX III

BOOKS ILLUSTRATED WITH WOODCUTS

THE books are indexed under author when such is known; otherwise under title.

The first title quoted is usually the original.

The omission of date may generally be assumed to indicate an undated edition, *n.d.* only being added to distinguish an edition from dated issues in the same reference.

The first page quoted generally indicates the principal reference to each book.

The first group, entitled *Horae* with no further qualification, includes for the most part General *Horae* (Roman Use), whether in Latin or French. I add 'for the most part', as the conditions under which the index has been made render it probable that I have not avoided inconsistencies. Arrangement is by town, printer and date.
Then follow (1) *Horae* according to the use of different dioceses and in various languages; (2) Latin editions printed in Italy and Spain, mostly under the title *Officium Beatae Virginis Mariae*; (3) editions in Dutch, German and Spanish under various titles.

INDEX IV

PRINTS MENTIONED OR REPRODUCED

No attempt is made to classify subjects systematically. Thus many events in the Life of the Virgin and of Christ are indexed under the first word of their most familiar title, *e.g. Death of the Virgin.* There may be many inconsistencies, but it is hoped that the sacrifice of a more rigid system in favour of familiar headings will facilitate reference. Occasionally the same subject may be quoted under various titles, *e.g. Virgin and Child* and *Madonna.*

The *Crucifixion* subject is for the most part divided in the index between *Calvary* (i.e. the Three Crosses), and the more symbolic subject *Christ on the Cross* (generally *with the Virgin and St. John*), which is the usual *Canon* cut in Missals. *Crucifixion* may have occasionally been used in the text for either subject. It would be necessary to have three lives to clear up such inconsistencies in description.

INDEX V

SUBJECTS DISCUSSED IN THE TEXT

INCLUDING ARTISTS OTHER THAN DESIGNERS
OR ENGRAVERS OF WOODCUT

THE END